Early Christian Art
and Architecture

1. Votive plaque from the Water Newton treasure.

Early Christian Art
and Architecture

ROBERT MILBURN

Wildwood House

First published in 1988 by
SCOLAR PRESS
This paperback edition published in 1989 by WILDWOOD HOUSE
Gower Publishing Company Limited
Gower House, Croft Road
Aldershot GU11 3HR, England

British Library Cataloguing in Publication Data

Milburn, Robert
   Early Christian art and architecture.
   1. Christian art and symbolism
   I. Title
709'.01'5   N7830

ISBN 0-7045-0597-5

Printed in Hong Kong by South China Printing Co.

Foreword

The forms of Christian art and architecture are at first rudimentary enough: they spring from practical needs and those of no very elaborate a nature. Restricted in their development by the thought that the world might be hastening towards its end or, in any event, that right conduct was of far greater importance than aesthetic sensibility, they yet have the interest that belongs to primitive, uncomplicated artefacts. Soon, however, converts arriving from more refined circles brought with them a clearer awareness of civilised values as ministering to truth. So, when, at the behest of Constantine and his successors, the Christian Church found itself called upon to assume moral and even cultural leadership in a declining Empire, the Church rallied to its cause craftsmen as skilful as any who worked in the secular field. Contemporary fashions of style and construction were adapted to Christian uses just as were the current modes in philosophy and the well-tried arrangements of political organization. Even so, there remained for churchmen a common ground of aspiration and belief which gives to the products of Christian art, however varied their social or geographical backgrounds may be, a certain unity and coherence. Such feeling for a shared heritage persists even as the classic ideals of proportion and elegance take on a new and distinctive emphasis in the stately splendours of Byzantium.

The purpose of this book is to survey the several elements of this Christian heritage from its early beginnings to the middle of the sixth century, when the death of Justinian may be claimed as marking the end of an epoch. The few examples that go slightly beyond this range are included because of their close connection with the earlier period.

The twentieth century has witnessed a remarkable increase in the number of sites examined and objects unearthed which illustrate the growth of the Christian Church and its way of life. Selection of examples therefore is no easy task. While the celebrated achievements of Rome and Ravenna insist on being included, discoveries made in the outposts of Syria or the Balkans or the valley of the Rhine add their lively witness to the picture of an age when, amid menacing signs of collapse, practical good sense and lofty speculation were closely allied in a creative partnership.

The literature on the subject is enormous. In order to keep the bibliography to a manageable size, it has seemed best to offer a selection of general works followed by a list of the more specialized treatises arranged according to locality or subject. Nearly all the works thus included themselves refer fully and in detail to the many articles in periodicals relevant to their particular field. Such articles are therefore mentioned only sparingly in the text.

R.L.P.M.

Contents

List of Illustrations

List of Abbreviations

ACIAC   *Atti del congresso internazionale di archeologia cristiana* (Rome, 1929–).

CSEL   *Corpus scriptorum ecclesiasticorum latinorum*, ed. C. Halm (Vienna, 1866–).

DACL   *Dictionnaire d'archéologie chrétienne et de liturgie*, ed. F. Cabrol and H. Leclercq (Paris, 1907–53).

DOP   *Dumbarton Oaks Papers* (Cambridge, Mass., 1941–).

GCS   *Die griechischen christlichen Schriftsteller der ersten drei Jahrhunderte* (Leipzig, 1897–).

JAC   *Jahrbuch für Antike und Christentum* (Munster, 1958–).

JEH   *Journal of Ecclesiastical History* (London, 1950–).

Loeb   *The Loeb Classical Library* (London, 1913–).

MAMA   *Monumenta Asiae Minoris Antiqua* (New York and London, 1928–).

NPNCF   *A Select Library of the Nicene and Post-Nicene Fathers of the Christian Church*, ed. P. Schaff and H. Wace (New York and London, 1887–1903).

PG   *Patrologiae Cursus Completus, Series Graeca*, ed. J. P. Migne (Paris, 1857–1912).

PL   *Patrologiae Cursus Completus, Series Latina*, ed. J. P. Migne (Paris, 1844–64).

RAC   *Rivista di archeologia cristiana* (Rome, 1924–).

RLAC   *Reallexikon für Antike und Christentum*, ed. T. Klauser (Stuttgart, 1950–).

Studi   *Studí di antichitá cristiana* (Pontificio Istituto di Archeologia Cristiana) (Rome, 1929–). Overlaps with *ACIAC*.

Maps

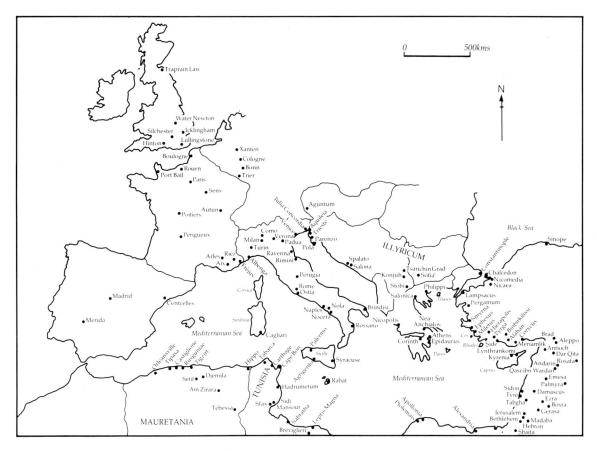

Map I. Christian sites and monuments, 200–600 AD.

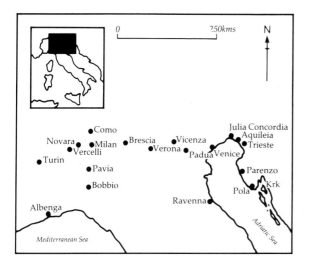

Map II. The main churches of North Italy in the sixth century.

Map III. Sites and monuments of North Africa.

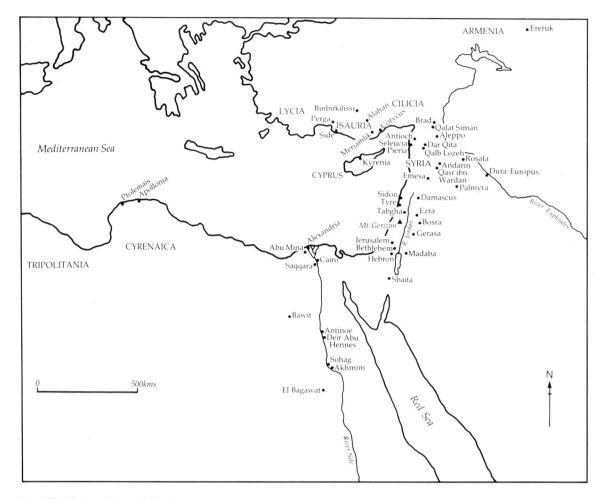

Map IV. Western Asia and Egypt.

1

Signs and Symbols

THE SATOR SQUARE

When St Paul determined to move on his missionary journeys westward along the Mediterranean, he found himself hospitably entertained, on the Italian coast, at Puteoli and, a week later, in Rome. At both places groups of the 'brethren' were established, thus indicating rapid expansion of the Christian Church from its original centre at Jerusalem. Concerning these 'brethren' no records whatever exist, but it is the west Italian coastland which furnishes what may be claimed as the earliest monument of Christian archaeology. This is the inscription found in 1936 on the plaster covering a column in the remains of Pompeii and again, somewhat damaged, in the house of one Paquius Proculus nearby. The city of Pompeii was destroyed by a torrent of molten lava from Mount Vesuvius in the year 79 AD; hence the inscription cannot be of later date than that. It is in the form of a square, with five words arranged in an acrostic which can be read equally well from right, left, top or bottom:

ROTAS

OPERA

TENET

AREPO

SATOR

The meaning is, to a casual glance, not very profound. *Arepo* is an outlandish word from Gaul meaning a plough, so that the inscription amounts to something like 'The sower, with his eye on the plough, holds its wheels with care.' Wild attempts were made at interpreting this banal remark before it was noticed that all the letters are paired off except the central N. Working with this clue, scholars[1] came to recognize that the square can be rewritten as a cross:

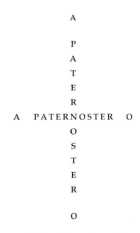

What is concealed, therefore, from the eye of those not initiated into the secret, is a cross, made up of the opening words of the Lord's Prayer and terminated by alpha and omega, the symbols of eternity mentioned in the Book of Revelation. In other words, the Crucifixion occupies the central place in God's everlasting counsels. Moreover, the letter T was 'destined to have grace' and 'indicates the cross', as the author of the second-century Epistle of Barnabas[2] declares, and in this Sator Square the T, repeated four times, stands always between the A and O which denote the eternal Divine Nature. Other significant echoes resound. From a very early time, Christ could be referred to as the Sower or Plough,[3] and it is he, through the sacrifice on the cross, who has the power to check the turning wheel of destiny. Veiled hints of this type lie behind the commonplace inscription which Christians were happy to set up, as a charm, in their houses and which, whether fully understood or not, extended its range by the third century AD from the eastern to the western bounds of the Roman Empire, from Dura on the Euphrates to Manchester.

Not all critics accept the Christian origin of the Sator Square; it has also been interpreted as a Jewish inscription or as Mithraic. Others regard it as little more than an entertaining word-game.[4] But it is difficult to believe that the particular relevance of the Square to Christianity comes about merely by accident, and, whatever its origin, the popularity of the Square was due to the ease with which it could be given a Christian interpretation. The Sator Square demonstrates the touch of symbolism found at every level of early Christian practice. Not merely is it true that the Church grew up at first in a world which, for reasons of prejudice or statecraft, was inclined to view it with disfavour, but an awareness of mystery, a sense of 'something far more deeply interfused' in the rough and tumble of events, led men to express their faith in allusive and symbolic terms.

PALESTINIAN SYMBOLS

It seems, however, that Christian charms and sacred numbers of even earlier date than the Sator Square may have been discovered in Palestine. The bishops of Jerusalem were Jewish until 135 AD when the legions of the emperor Hadrian expelled all Jews from the city, and, even after that event, many Christians of Hebrew stock returned to Jerusalem or lingered nearby, preserving for two or three hundred years their own customs concerning such matters as the way to reckon the date of Easter. Jewish Christianity generally was less concerned with philosophic debate than with signs and symbols possessing an almost sacramental power of crystallizing the Faith and making it an effective passport to the presence of God. A cemetery, recently discovered on the Mount of Olives, contains more than a hundred ossuaries, vessels in which had been placed the bones of the departed. This cemetery, now known as 'Dominus Flevit'—'the Lord weeping over Jerusalem'—appears from the style of the objects found in it to date back to the first century AD. The ossuaries, rectangular with flat or domed tops, often bear emblems roughly scratched both on the outside and within. Comparison of these emblems with those to be seen on ossuaries found elsewhere and preserved for the most part in the Palestine Archaeological Museum at Jerusalem, or with the inscriptions and marks recently found on engraved stones under the mosaic of a fifth-century church at Nazareth, indicates that the Dominus Flevit examples are by no means unique. It shows, moreover, that many of the emblems found their place, justified by the explana-

tions of the Church Fathers, within the normal repertory of Christian art.

Forms and symbols already in existence were cheerfully taken over, so that it is not always clear whether a decorated ossuary is Jewish or whether it was prepared for some Christian in the belief that the conventional signs would help to guide him through the valley of the shadow of death.

Clement of Alexandria, head of what might be termed a School of Advanced Christian Studies from about 190 to 202 AD, gave his pupils some instruction concerning the devices that should be engraved on their signet-rings:[5]

Now our seals ought to be a dove or a fish or a ship running before the breeze or a tuneful harp or a ship's anchor. And if there should happen to be a fisherman, he will call to mind the apostle and the children drawn up from the water. We must not engrave our rings with the countenance of idols, nor indeed is a sword or bow appropriate to those who seek after peace nor wine-cups to those who live a life of sobriety.

Clement is talking about signet-rings but his word for a 'seal' (*sphragis*) had deep significance in early Church circles. It is used for the sign, whether circumcision or baptism, which marked entry into particularly close relationship with God, and it appears in the Book of Revelation as the 'seal of the living God' which the angel was required to impress on the heads of those who should be saved in time of calamity. Another work of roughly the same date, the so-called 'Odes of Solomon',[6] supplies a commentary: 'I turn not my face from those who are mine, for I know them. Even before they were born I knew them: I have set my seal upon their brow.' The sign or seal *par excellence* was of course the cross, which so deeply influenced imaginations that likenesses to it were detected on every side. Justin Martyr went so far as to say that 'nothing in the world can exist or form a whole without this sign of the cross',[7] by which he meant that everything on which the eye rests will be found to offer hints and suggestions of the cross-shape. In various parts of his writings he mentions star, plant, unicorn's horn, serpent, ship, plough, axe, ladder and rod as being particularly significant, and it is such emblems as these which are found on the Jewish–Christian ossuaries of Palestine.

Many symbols of this nature have a long history. The ship, for example, occurs in Egypt, Greece and Rome as an emblem of hope and immortality, and of the journey which the soul makes from this world to the Islands of the Blessed, while Noah's ark naturally offered itself as a sign of salvation. But the first Jewish Christians seem to have placed a rather different emphasis on the sign of the ship, valuing it largely because of the shape of its masts. Deeply scratched on the lid of one of the ossuaries in the Dominus Flevit cemetery is a ship with its two masts depicted as crosses. For, as Justin expresses it: 'the sea cannot be traversed unless this sign of victory, the sail outspread, is firm set in the midst of the ship.'[8]

There were several other ways in which Jewish Christians hinted at the cross without portraying it directly:

The Tree, or Tree of Life. This appears, in the Dominus Flevit cemetery, as a primitive fern-frond (fig. 2a). A similar conventional representation has been found at Bethphage, Gaza and elsewhere in Palestine, the point being sometimes pressed home by converting the top of the fern-frond into a roughly executed cross. Trees recalled such passages as the Psalmist's 'He shall be like a tree planted by the waterside',[9] and early commentators likened both the Word of God and the faithful believer to a tree. But, closely connected with such ideas, the tree stands naturally enough for the cross also: 'not that tree in Paradise which brought death on our first parents, but the tree of Christ's passion, from which our Life hung.'[10]

The Ladder. This is found at Hebron, as well as on a

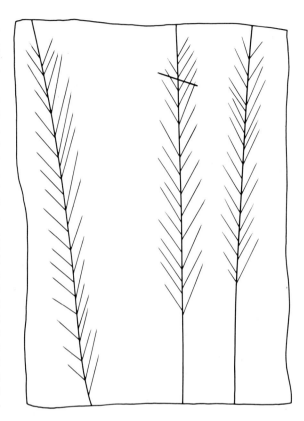

2a. Fern-frond or Tree of Life: an emblem scratched on an ossuary from the Dominus Flevit cemetery at Jerusalem.

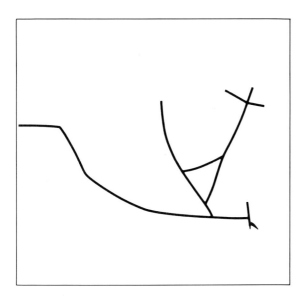

2b. Plough: an emblem scratched on an ossuary from the Dominus Flevit cemetery at Jerusalem.

number of Coptic stelae and in the Catacomb of Priscilla in Rome. An Easter sermon of the third century[11] explains the reason why: 'Now, the Cross is the ladder of Jacob and the angel's path, at the top of which the Lord is truly set.'

The Serpent. In Psalm 91 the man who is under the protection of the Most High is told: 'the young lion and the serpent shalt thou trample underfoot', and snakes and serpents often represent powers of evil. On the other hand, Moses in the wilderness 'made a serpent of brass and set it on a standard';[12] those suffering from snakebite had only to look at the brazen serpent and their lives were spared. A parallel between the uplifted serpent and Christ uplifted on the cross is drawn in St John's Gospel: 'as Moses lifted up the serpent in the wilderness, even so must the Son of Man be lifted up.'[13] And on one of the Dominus Flevit ossuaries[14] a vigorous, horned serpent, coiling round a rudimentary cross, is probably to be seen as an early reminder of the Crucifixion.

The Lintel. Another parallel sometimes drawn is that between the cross and the doorways smeared with blood at Passovertide. A fourth-century commentator explains:

The Jews even now display a 'type' of the cross, when they mark their thresholds with the blood of a lamb. For the snow-white lamb, without spot, was Christ, that is to say the innocent, just and holy one who was sacrificed by those same Jews. He is the Saviour of all who have marked their brow with the sign of blood, that is the sign of the cross. For the brow is the lintel[15] of a man and wood smeared with blood is an indication of the cross.

Along the same line of reasoning, an ossuary from Emmaus shows two columns surmounted by a large lintel-stone, with a Tree of Life growing on either side.

The Star appears much more frequently as an emblem on the Dominus Flevit ossuaries and elsewhere. The 'star which shall come forth out of Jacob',[16] taken in connection with such passages as Isaiah's 'the people that walked in darkness have seen a great light', naturally suggests the Lord's Anointed or the brightness which accompanies his arrival. Some commentators, moreover, saw in its shape a reminder of the cross, while the cross or star set within a circle owes its form to speculations like those in a Coptic apocryphal Gospel: 'Now the star which appeared at Christ's birth was not a star like the others: it was a large star in the form of a wheel, and its shape was like that of a Cross.'[17]

The Plough suggests a cross for three reasons: its shape, the material of which it is constructed, and its work. A fifth-century writer of popular homilies[18] comments fully on the shape of the plough:

When the good ploughman prepares to turn over his land in quest of food to sustain life, he does not attempt to do so by any other means than by the sign of the plough. When he fixes on the ploughshare, secures the mould-boards and attaches the handle, he imitates the form of the cross.

And much earlier, Justin Martyr had declared: 'Without the cross the earth is not tilled.' This idea finds its counterpart on certain Dominus Flevit ossuaries, where ploughs are shown with handles, mould-boards and uptilted share apparently designed to indicate a cross (fig. 2b). Those who cared to reflect on the matter would recall that the plough, like the cross, is made of wood and that its work—clearing the untilled ground of weeds—resembles Christ's work on the cross whereby he uprooted the weeds of sin.

The Axe has certain features in common with the plough. Its handle is of wood, and the whole, composed of wood and iron, acquires great significance, for those with a liking for the mystical interpretation of Scripture, in the story of Elisha causing the axe-head to swim after it had fallen to the bottom of the river Jordan.[19] Justin interpreted this event as foreshadowing the way in which Christ, on the cross, redeems humanity weighed down by sin[20]; while another Church Father asked, 'What is plainer than this figure of wood? The hard-heartedness of this world, sunk in the deep waters of error, is delivered by the wood of Christ.'[21] When, therefore, an axe-head appears on one of the Dominus Flevit ossuaries[22] it may in effect be a cross, symbolized and commented on. Some of these emblems find a regular place in Christian art throughout the centuries, while others drop away. But the recent discoveries in the cemeteries of Palestine, taken in connection with the early writings which discuss the meaning of the symbols, serve to emphasize the importance of Jewish Christianity in setting the patterns of the Church's thought and worship.

The cross itself was thought to be a sign not so much of pathos as of power, and could even be painted on the brow or face of believers as a safeguard against the powers of evil. It is not surprising, therefore, to find it on the Jewish Christian tombs of Palestine, occasionally in the form of a trefoil[23] or with the upper half enclosed in a square.[24] The square represents the length, breadth, depth and height of the world; thus the cross enclosed within a square is a lesson in theology, pointing to the all-powerful sovereignty of the Cross over the whole created order. But when, on the ossuaries, a plain cross or x appears, this is not so much a direct reminiscence of the Crucifixion as a shorthand summary of the Sacred Name.

The valuable and protective name of Jahweh, in virtue of which both Moses and Christ performed their miracles, was indicated in Greek by the letter *omega*, and in Hebrew also by the final letter of the alphabet, the *taw*. The *taw*, as currently written, bears little resemblance to a plain cross, but in ancient Hebrew and related dialects it was so formed. When, therefore, + or x was stamped upon a tomb, it was a sign of life and immortality.[25] But the Name could refer also to Christ, as being the last, decisive Word in God's self-revealing message to mankind. The earliest Christian liturgy contains the prayer 'We give thanks to thee, Holy Father, for thy Holy Name which thou hast made to tabernacle in our hearts',[26] and, to clarify the interpretation, a second-century sermon,[27] strongly tinged with Judaeo-Christian ideas, may be called in evidence: 'Now the Name of the Father,' it explains, 'is the Son.' When, therefore, the churchmen of Palestine used the sign of Jahweh's name, they thought also of Christ and the simple cross served as a particularly appropriate reminder of his saving power.

Just as the word Jahweh could be shortened, in Hebrew, by omitting the vowels, so, in Greek, several abbreviations for the name of God or the name of Christ came into vogue. The shortened version of Christ's name was a compact reminder of the truths declared in Scripture; it could appear by itself or, on tombs, in such forms as *In pace XP*—'in the peace of Christ'. At the beginning of the fourth century the monogram ☧ was set in stylized form on the standards of Constantine's legionaries, but by then it already had a long history. It is found, for instance, marked in charcoal on a Dominus Flevit ossuary,[28] the sign of Christ being on the outside of the burial casket and the name of the deceased, a certain Judas, within.

The earliest type of that concise summary of the name of Jesus, which as IHS gained much popularity in the Middle Ages, is shown simply as three upright bars crossed by a horizontal bar.[29] The I stood as the initial letter of Jesus, while H (the Greek letter *eta*) regularly signified the *Ogdoad*, or eightfold completeness of Creation, of which Christ, 'in whom the fullness of the Father dwells'[30], was cause and counterpart. Hence IH, the beginning of the word Jesus, or, with the horizontal line extended, H—H . The plain + or x indicating the divine name occasionally developed into a cross with six limbs instead of four: ✳ , and this shape may have helped to ease the way for the widespread adoption of the 'saving sign' of the chi-rho, the first two letters of the word Christos.

It is not uncommon to find, on the Palestinian ossuaries, as well as the sacred name or in place of it, the representation of a house with courses of bricks, or a tower, set on steps, beneath which sometimes runs a zig-zag representing water. Such towers, equipped with sturdy columns and perhaps embellished by solar discs or plants having a significant number of leaves (three, six, eight or twelve), represent the Church, and a literary parallel is supplied by the curious second-century apocalypse known as the Shepherd of Hermas. One of the things which the Shepherd, or Angel of Repentance, shows to Hermas in his vision[31] is a 'great tower being built on the water with shining square stones'. The Angel explains that the tower symbolizes the Church, the square white stones being 'the Apostles and bishops and teachers and deacons who walked according to the majesty of God'.

In such obscure and sometimes bizarre figures the Jewish Christians of first- and second-century Palestine displayed in an extreme form the tendency to veil the deep mysteries of the Faith under an allusive and fanciful imagery, understood only by a restricted circle of initiates. The signs themselves, however, spread far beyond Palestine, and became the common property of the Church, though in this process they naturally lost part of their original meaning and were mechanically repeated, without a great deal of comprehension, by persons who saw in them a supernatural value likely to be of use to both living and dead.

Note. The question of Jewish Christian symbols is a controversial one. The view here taken is based on two lines of recent enquiry, one literary and one archaeological. The French scholar J. Daniélou, in the course of his investigations into the earliest shape of Judaic Christianity, was impressed by the fact that Christian doctrine is there conveyed most readily by means of an all-pervading symbolism whereby everyday natural forms are thought to be charged with the power of conveying spiritual truth. In particular, the cross is held to be repeatedly hinted at in a variety of commonplace objects. This mode of interpretation is supported by many of the systematic Christian writers, and, though some of Daniélou's patristic quotations are comparatively late, Justin Martyr, one of the main exponents of this method, was composing his works as early as the period 130–160 AD.

From the archaeological point of view, researches carried out by members of the Franciscan College at Jerusalem have apparently discovered emblems symbolizing the Cross on a number of ossuaries at Hebron, Nazareth, Jerusalem and elsewhere. Many of these emblems are no more than rough scratches, but a few of them are painstakingly worked and appear to be securely datable to the late first or early second century AD. The Judaeo-Christian interpretation has not passed unchallenged, particularly as regards the *taw*-cross itself, which can be explained either as a 'Jewish religious symbol based on Ezekiel 9.4' or as 'an artisan sign intended to indicate points where lid and receptacle match'.[32] Nor may the possibility of faking by unscrupulous dealers be wholly disregarded.

NOTES

1. Particularly Felix Grosser in *Archiv. für Religionswissenschaft* xxix (1926). The inscription is sometimes, perhaps first on an Egyptian papyrus of the fifth century, written the other way up, with SATOR on top.
2. Kirsopp Lake, *The Apostolic Fathers* (Loeb, 1925), i.372.
3. E.g. Acts of John 109, written not later than 150 AD. M. R. James, *The Apocryphal New Testament* (Oxford, 1924), 268.
4. M. W. C. Hassall and R. S. O. Tomlin in *Britannia* x (1979), where a list of references is given. For a fuller treatment see D. Fishwick, 'On the origin of the Rotas–Sator square', *Harvard Theological Review* 57 (1964). The fullest and most exact discussion is by H. Hofmann in Pauly's *Realencyklopädie der klassischen Altertumswissenschaft*, Supplementband xv (1978).
5. *Paedagogus* iii.11, PG 8.633.
6. viii.9, ed. J. R. Harris (Cambridge, 1909).
7. *Apology* i.55.2, ed. G. Rauschen (Bonn, 1911), 92.
8. *Ibid.* i.55.3.
9. Psalm 1.3.
10. Tertullian, *Against the Jews* 13, PL 1.636.
11. Ps. Hippolytus, *Homilia Paschalis* 51.177. The idea is worked out in detail by St Zeno, *De scala Iacob*, PL 11.428.
12. Numbers 21.9.
13. 3.14.
14. Ossuary 11.
15. 'the top of the threshold', i.e. the block (lintel) at the top of a door. Lactantius, *On the True Wisdom* iv.26, PL 6.530.
16. Numbers 24.17.
17. *Coptic Apocryphal Gospels*, ed. Forbes Robinson (Cambridge, 1896), 165.
18. Maximus of Turin, Homily 50, PL 57.342.
19. II Kings 6.
20. *Dialogue* 86.6, PG 6.680.
21. Tertullian, *Against the Jews* 13.19, PL 1.636.
22. Ossuary 43.
23. Dominus Flevit: ossuary 94.
24. In wall-plaster at Nazareth.
25. Cf. Ezekiel 9.4.
26. *Didache* 10, in *The Apostolic Fathers* (Loeb), i.324.
27. *The Gospel of Truth* 38, ed. K. Grobel (London, 1960), 180.
28. Ossuary 21.
29. As in Palestine Archaeological Museum: ossuary 362171. It appears like this also on a second-century stele now in the Lateran Museum.
30. Colossians 1.19.
31. *Shepherd of Hermas*, Vision 3, in *The Apostolic Fathers* (Loeb), ii.30.
32. D. Fishwick, as note 4 above.

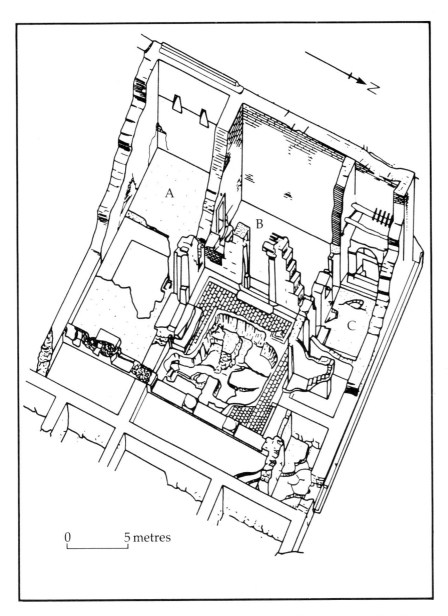

3. The church at Dura-Europus, Syria. Isometric plan: A. Main assembly-hall; B. School-room; C. Baptistery chapel.

2

House-Churches

The first places of worship, after the Church detached itself from temple and synagogue, were rooms in private houses. 'Breaking bread at home, they partook of food in gladness and simplicity of heart,' says the author of the Acts of the Apostles,[1] and it appears that assembly for worship took place daily. Almost at once, however, stress was laid on 'the first day of the week',[2] and when St Paul, in the course of his missionary journeys, arrived at Troas people gathered together to break bread and listen to Paul's address. Whether the meal on such an occasion should be thought of as a Eucharist or as a community supper is not entirely clear. For the dining-room, in accordance with eastern practice, was at the top of the house; when the boy Eutychus, overcome by the heat of the lamps and the length of Paul's discourse, fell out of the window, he tumbled from the second storey to the ground. In the Italian cities, particularly Rome and Ostia, houses of humbler type were built on the tenement system, with shops in front and living quarters arranged as flats behind or above the shops. Any variety of worship could take place in such houses 'with freedom of speech and none to hinder', as St Paul found,[3] unless suspicions of treason caused a particular cult to be regarded as a 'pernicious superstition'—the ground given by the historian Tacitus[4] for the persecution of Christians in the reign of Nero.

DURA-EUROPUS

It was a meeting-place, then, with facilities for the rite of baptism, that was required in an early Christian church, and that is what is found in the oldest church-building extant. This building is at Dura, or Dura-Europus, situated in the Syrian desert close to the river Euphrates. Originally founded at the end of the fourth century BC, the town was occupied by the Romans in 165 AD. It prospered as a frontier garrison, but fell after a siege by the Persians in the year 257 and was then abandoned. The emperor Julian hunted lions in its ruins, which later became completely buried by sand and remained so until they were discovered through some chance trench-digging in the course of a guerrilla campaign in 1921. Detailed excavation, carried out over a number of years, has proved extremely rewarding, and the general layout of the town, with its fortifications, public buildings and considerable number of houses, is now quite clear. More than a dozen shrines co-existed in, it would seem, harmonious tolerance. The Palmyrene gods have their temple, as do Mithras, Adonis, Artemis and other deities of rather more outlandish character. Jewish synagogue and Christian church have their places close by.

The synagogue seems originally to have been one of a row of private houses, bought by the Jews and adapted, by the demolition of internal walls, to form a wide meeting-room, with inner court at the back and a small side-room. Inscriptions show that the synagogue was rebuilt in the year 245 and the meeting-room enlarged. The long side of the room faced west towards Jerusalem, and in the centre of this western wall was set a rather elaborate niche probably used for the occasional display of the books of the Law. The decoration of the synagogue disposes once and for all of the view that the Jews would never tolerate representations of the human form. That may have been true as regards Rabbinic Judaism, characteristic of the stricter circles of Palestine, but liberal, Hellenized Judaism, of which Philo is the most notable exponent, would have nothing of such restrictions. In the Dura synagogue, not only are Biblical incidents depicted with vigour and a wealth of allegory, but symbols have also been introduced from pagan imagery, such as the vine and panthers of Dionysus, and Orpheus playing his lyre. The Jews were perfectly capable of showing themselves to be exclusive and unyielding—'a suspicious and malevolent race', as Cicero[5] called them—but they were prepared, at least outside Palestine, to accept a number of ideas and art-forms having their origin in wider religious circles. The search for security in a dangerous world and influences drawn from the cult-rooms of other faiths weighed more heavily, in the popular practice of Jew and Christian alike, than the austere demands of imageless monotheism.

The Christian church was located in the same street as the temple of Mithras and the synagogue, from which it does not greatly differ in form. It began as a respectable middle-class home built of unbaked brick on rough stone foundations, with carved blocks of gypsum set round the doors. The rooms were arranged, in conventional Asiatic fashion, around a paved court to which a narrow vestibule gave access. Inside, the walls were covered with thick plaster. An inscription, apparently scratched while the plaster was still wet, gives the date 232 AD, though there are some indications that the surface was worked over again about ten years later (fig. 3).

A fourth-century writer[6] records that, when St Peter went to Antioch, the number of baptized rose in a week to ten thousand, and a certain Theophilus gave up part of his house to serve as a meeting-place for the Christians. There Peter set his episcopal chair, and crowds gathered to hear his preaching. Something of the kind seems to have happened at Dura, in the sense that certain alterations were made, simply but care-fully, to the original structure which had the effect of transforming it from house to church. Two rooms on the south side were combined, by the removal of a wall, to form one substantial assembly-room, 13.1 metres in length. Unlike the synagogue's meeting-room, with its elaborate niche as a central feature, the Christian assembly-room is of very plain construction. A low platform on which the bishop could stand or sit is the only piece of liturgical equipment. It is, however, possible that wall-paintings were planned but not completed by the time the Persians arrived.

At right angles to the place of assembly was another room half as large. It is entirely featureless, so that its use is a matter for conjecture; perhaps it served as a school, a place of instruction for the 'catechumens', who were not yet full members of the Church. From this room a doorway led into the baptistery chapel. There is no sign of any receptacle for the bones of a martyr, and both the arrangement and the decoration of the chapel accord with its use solely as a baptistery. It is thus the ancestor of the square baptisteries which were constructed at Dar Qita and other places in Syria during the fifth and sixth centuries. Three inscriptions give a touch of homely devotion. On a doorpost at the entrance to the chapel from the courtyard are inscribed the words 'There is one God in heaven'. The other inscriptions refer to individuals: 'Remind Christ of the humble Siseos.' 'Remind Christ of Proclus in your midst.' This is all in the fashion that later became characteristic of the national, or Jacobite, liturgy of Syria, where the opening intercession runs: 'We commemorate our fathers and our brethren and our masters who taught us the word of truth and all the faithful departed, particularly and by name those that are of our blood and those that had part in the building of this shrine.' Siseos and Proclus may owe their memorial to the fact that they were the pious benefactors who adapted or embellished the chapel.

At the west end of the room is set a niche, arched over and supported by two free-standing columns and two pilasters that back onto the wall. Beneath the canopy thus created lies the font-basin, too small for the immersion of candidates, who were presumably here baptized by the sprinkling of water. The Dura baptistery is decorated with paintings in a manner which resembles the fragmentary remains in the temple of the Palmyrene gods and, more particularly, the Jewish synagogue. Four or five artists seem to have

4. Dura-Europus, wall-painting: the healing of the paralytic.

5. Dura-Europus, wall-painting: the women at the Tomb.

been employed, none of the highest ability and all content to use a rough, impressionistic style. Thus the figures are stiffly posed, face the spectator directly, and, perhaps touched by eastern influences, lack the easy variations of much Hellenistic art; but the subjects are carefully chosen and rich in symbolic value.

Over the font itself, the ceiling is so decorated as to represent a starry sky, the work of a benevolent Creator. Then, on the west wall, two subjects appear. There are the diminutive figures of Adam and Eve, standing one on each side of the fatal tree, while pillars indicate the walls of the earthly Paradise they have forfeited. Above them, painted on a larger scale, stands the Good Shepherd of St Luke's Gospel, bearing a huge ram on his shoulders, in the midst of a flock, untidily sketched, of seventeen sheep. The candidate for baptism might well reflect that Adam's transgression calls for the Saviour's arrival to seek and to save that which was lost.

The north wall displays three examples of the Saviour's power. The first of these is the healing of the paralysed man. Most examples of this theme, in the compressed, almost shorthand style of early Christian art, show the 'sick of the palsy' walking away with his bed on his back, thus indicating his cure, while the Healer himself is either absent from the scene or stands on one side. In the Dura painting, however, the Saviour is to the fore and stretches out his hand in a compassionate gesture over the man still lying on his bed (fig. 4). This is the oldest known representation of Christ, and portrays him as a beardless young man, a second David rather than some august, superhuman figure. The next picture illustrates St Peter's attempt to walk on the water. Bearded, with thick curly hair, and wearing tunic and mantle, Peter, though his feet are visible on top of the brownish water, is so drawn as to give the impression of insecurity and extends his right hand to clutch the outstretched hand of Christ. Meanwhile, the apostles, wearing bright-coloured garments, stand in attitudes of amazement on the deck of the brilliantly painted ship. The remaining scene shows the three women at the Tomb (fig. 5).[7] They advance, each with a torch in one hand and a bowl containing spices in the other, towards a large sarcophagus with gabled top. No other figures are in sight, but two stars—possibly Hope and Salvation— shine overhead.

The south wall displays firstly a scene of

deliverance. The painting is in a poor state of preservation, but the names 'Daouid' and 'Golitha' make it clear that the victory, against all the odds, of David over Goliath is here set forth as an encouragement to any neophyte to remember that the race is not always to the swift nor the battle to the strong. The last picture is the most graceful. It shows the woman of Samaria stooping over the well and preparing to draw water.[8] Christ himself does not appear. Perhaps the artist found himself pinched for room; perhaps he considered that the woman alone, representative of the Church dispensing the water of baptism, was sufficient to convey his message.

The layout of the building at Dura and the interests manifested in its scheme of decoration are no doubt typical of many house-churches at the beginning of the Christian era. Aware that, to Roman officials, they seemed peculiar and unbending individuals not necessarily able to claim the justification of belonging to the peculiar and unbending nation of the Jews, the first churchmen remained exultant in what they regarded as the imperishable hope of future blessedness. Yet they were children of their time to a greater extent than some of their more fanatical apologists were prepared to admit. They had their treasure in earthen vessels, and of these earthen vessels—the art-forms, the conventions and the world view of their time—they made free and unselfconscious use.

THE DEVELOPMENT OF HOUSE-CHURCHES

If Dura, remote on the banks of the Euphrates, provided the typical example of the 'house-church', other buildings of this same simple pattern exist which show arrangements made for religious practice in a domestic setting. Instances of this may be found in Rome, in Spain and in Britain.

The title-churches of Rome are the oldest established churches in the city, and were administered by clergy who regarded a district, more or less fixed, as their parish. But the word 'title' in this context originally referred to a 'name'—the name, that is, of the owner of the property on which the church was situated. This at first indicated merely the private house in which one or more rooms were set apart for religious purposes. The next stage came about when an architect designed a structure which, when viewed from the outside, looked like other buildings in a given street, but which inside was specially adapted to the uses of congregational worship, the chief requirement being a hall of substantial size.

The literary evidence for churches, recognizable as such, corroborates the findings of archaeology. As early as 257 AD the emperor Valerian ordered that 'nowhere shall assemblies be held nor shall any enter the cemeteries'.[9] These assemblies (conciliabula) naturally imply some place in which to assemble. Within fifteen years of Valerian's decree, moreover, Aurelian is to be found making a legal judgement—enthusiastically described, from the Christian point of view, as 'extremely just'—concerning the ownership of a 'church-building' at Antioch.[10] And then, some thirty years later, in 303 AD, Diocletian ordered that all churches should be razed to the ground[11]—confirming their presence while denying their right to exist.

The type of building which aroused the interest of the emperors is that of the earliest Roman 'title-churches': a large hall together with the ancillary rooms required for purposes of administration. The remains of a structure of this kind may be discerned in the Titulus Byzantii, beneath the church of St John and St Paul. Originally there existed on this site a Roman villa of two storeys, containing attractive frescoes: flowers and birds in the dining-room and a more ambitious Marriage of Peleus and Thetis nearby. According to tradition, this villa became the residence of two men, John and Paul, who suffered martyrdom. To commemorate the event a Roman senator, one Byzantius, converted the house into a Christian sanctuary. The historical details of all this are most uncertain, but the present state of the building suggests that it was remodelled early in the fourth century. At a higher level than the frescoes is a small chamber which displays, within panels enclosed by red lines, a series of paintings which seem to be of Christian inspiration. Among the images is a man, with hands extended in prayer, who stands in front of curtains drawn back to indicate the soul's entry into Paradise. This little room may reasonably be claimed as a confessio, or chapel designed to shelter a martyr's relics.

The Titulus Equitii, set far beneath the Baroque church of S. Martino ai Monti, presents its original plan rather more clearly because the ground floor has been subject to little modification beyond some clumsy attempts at buttressing and strengthening pillars and columns, carried out by monks in the Middle Ages. What can still be clearly recognized is a large central hall, built perhaps as early as 250 AD, and expressly designed for regular assemblies, with adjacent service buildings, and a storey above probably intended as a residence for the clergy.

But it is San Clemente, now in the Via di San Giovanni, which most obviously displays traces of crude, early arrangement. The present church of St Clement is a structure of the eleventh century, much restored; underneath this, however, a complex of earlier buildings has been discovered. One first enters a hall, presumably a public building of some kind; close beside this is a house or shop built on the 'island' plan, that is to say, with rooms above in a second storey. The material used here is large blocks of tufa. Whether any part of this original house was used for the purposes of Christian worship cannot now be determined; certainly rooms within it were assigned to the cult of Mithras, the Persian God of Light. The ante-room, with its stone benches, may still be seen, and the alley-way leading from it into the triclinium, or dining-room, where sacrificial meals were held. This, again, has a large, sloping stone bench on each side. There is a recess at one end and, in the middle, a splendidly carved stone altar showing Mithras, all vigour and action, slaying a bull.

The Mithraeum seems to have been constructed about the beginning of the third century but it was not long before the Christians dominated the entire site. Above the tufa walls was erected a substantial structure of brick, of which the main feature was a large rectangular hall with, on the long sides, a range of openings communicating with courts or porticoes. Whether all this was built for the Christians or taken over by them, the hall would have provided a meeting-place for increasing numbers, and may reasonably be claimed as the third-century 'title-church'. It was transformed, a hundred years later, into a regular 'basilica',[12] by the addition of an apse at one end and, at the other, a narthex, or entrance-porch, with five arches leading into the main body of the church. Two rows of columns divided the interior into three aisles; the emphasis now was on length, leading up to the altar. It should be noted, however, that some would postpone the overthrow of Mithras and the construction of the apse to a later period, the reign of Theodosius I (379–395), when the mystery cults were suppressed.

Another example of the transition from house to church as place of worship has been provided by excavations carried out at Mérida, in south-western Spain. Near the Roman theatre in this town archaeologists discovered a building of entirely different character. The walls are constructed with irregular layers of stone varied here and there by sections of brickwork. The chief portion that remains consists of a square courtyard, approached through a vestibule and surrounded by a cloister paved in patterned mosaic. The east side of this courtyard communicates with a large room ending in an apse pierced by three windows. Here are found remains of a mosaic pavement and wall-paintings in 'Pompeian' style, mostly geometric patterns but including a dove, a child riding on a dolphin and, between the windows, four large figures, each standing on a pedestal but now in a fragmentary state and unidentifiable. Adjoining the north side of this apsidal room is another room, of similar shape but less wide; this is equipped not only with the three windows but also with three niches cut into the partition wall and with a rectangular water-tank.

Both the type of construction and the decoration resemble those of the primitive Christian basilicas, and it appears that Mérida was an early home of vigorous Christianity, if one accepts the tradition that Eulalia, martyr-patroness of Spain, met her death in that city.[13] So, although the building offers no clear trace of Christian emblems, it may reasonably enough be accepted as a church building of the early fourth century or, more probably, as a private house transformed to serve as such.

The evidence for places of Christian worship that mark the transition from house to basilica is more abundant in Britain. A little building at the Roman settlement of Calleva Atrebatum (Silchester) can be regarded, without qualification, as a church proper. Here, as at Mérida, no Christian symbols have been discovered within the building itself, but small objects found elsewhere on the site make it clear that

Christianity had its established place in fourth-century Silchester.

The church follows the general plan of temples erected by devotees of Mithraism and other Oriental cults. The entrance is by a porchway or ante-room, perhaps just large enough to accommodate those who were not yet fully initiated into the mysteries and, in this case, containing at its north end a round base on which could be set a reading stand or offertory table. Next is the hall, or nave, terminating in a western apse[14] that is diminutive but allows room for a clergy bench behind the altar. The Silchester building is equipped also with two small wings, or transepts, to be regarded not as side-chapels but as areas for preparing the eucharistic elements and for other ritual needs.

More demonstrably Christian than Silchester, though more primitive in pattern, is the villa discovered in 1949 at Lullingstone, in Kent (fig. 6). Here three intercommunicating rooms on the north side of the house were sealed off some time in the middle of the fourth century. Entrances that led to the rest of the building were blocked up and a new entrance constructed. The series of chambers, as approached from the outside, begins with a small square vestibule, lacking any decoration and apparently converted from earlier uses as a kitchen. A doorway from the vestibule led into a rectangular ante-chamber embellished with a certain amount of painting on plaster, including the alpha and omega symbol for God, 'the beginning and the end'. The large hall, or chapel, beyond was much more richly decorated and by a skilful artist probably not of British origin. The west wall was brilliantly painted to show a portico with seven columns, some blue and some red, and with a human figure set within each opening. Though varying in age and sex, each person, so far as can be judged from the reconstructed fragments of the plaster, wears splendid, ceremonial array and stands gazing straight ahead with hands raised in prayer. But the most striking figure is that of a young man, handsomely attired in tunic and pearl-bordered surcoat (fig. 7). His dark eyes contrast with flaming red hair and his arms are stretched outwards and bent at the elbow in an attitude of supplication. Behind the man a curtain is suspended in token that he has died and 'passed beyond the veil'; it is reasonable to suppose that the other figures are the living members of his family.

Nearby was found a specifically Christian symbol:

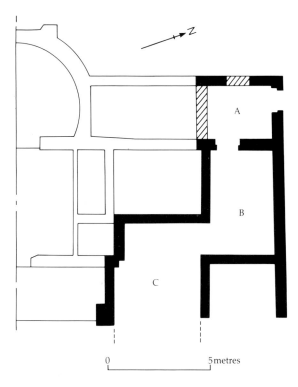

6. Lullingstone, Kent. The Christian apartments shown in their relation to the rest of the villa: A. Vestibule B. Ante-chamber; C. Chapel or hall.

7. Lullingstone, wall-painting: the young man.

set between two columns, a large wreath encloses a blood-red chi-rho emblem. The bottom of the wreath is tied with a ribbon, at each end of which stands a bird pecking at berries. This may be interpreted as a depiction of human souls enjoying the fruits of life growing on the garland of victory which Christ has won. Fragments of a second chi-rho monogram enclosed by a wreath occur on the east wall, while other paintings in the sequence include not only details of a landscape but also a man holding the martyr's palm-branch, and a seated figure, clad in chainmail, who may have been intended as a soldier-saint. The Lullingstone villa can be explained simply as a private house decorated to accord with the aesthetic tastes and religious beliefs of the occupants, but the compact and serviceable unit cut off from the rest of the building seems rather to indicate a house-church used by the local Christians.

The fine mosaic floor uncovered at Hinton St Mary, in Dorset,[15] is thought to have formed part of a Christian chapel inside a fourth-century private house. For the circular panel in the centre of the floor (fig. 8) contains the head and shoulders of a golden-haired young man wearing a toga while behind his head the chi-rho is prominently displayed. This is a portrait of Christ, shown full-face and confronting the worshipper in what comes to be known as the 'Byzantine' manner: here photographic realism is less valued than a motionless, hieratic posture that suggests the rich and mysterious nature of the underlying essence. It is, however, very odd to find this explicit piece of portraiture set in the floor, where presumably it was often trodden on. Even if the composition was originally designed for a domed ceiling and then transferred to decorate the floor-space, it appears that Christian belief, as demonstrated here, was of the same tolerant and adaptable character as is evidenced by a mosaic pavement found at Frampton (Dorset), where the chi-rho symbol for Christ coexists with a representation of Neptune.

8. Hinton St Mary, Dorset. Mosaic panel: head of Christ with chi-rho emblem.

NOTES

1. 2.46.
2. Acts 20.7.
3. Acts 28.31.
4. *Annals* xv.44.
5. *Pro Flacco* xxviii.
6. *Clementine Recognitions* x.71, *PG* 1.1453.
7. St Mark 16.1. The hairstyle of the women confirms a date round about 230 AD.
8. St John 4.7.
9. *Acts of Cyprian*, tr. E. C. E. Owen, in *Some Authentic Acts of Early Martyrs* (Oxford, 1927), 96.
10. Eusebius, *Ecclesiastical History* 7.30 (Loeb), ii.
11. *Ibid*. 8.2.
12. For explanation of this term see p. 86.
13. Prudentius, *Peristephanon* iii, *PL* 60.340.
14. S. S. Frere in *Archaeologia* (1976) sees in the arrangements, which include a place for ablutions, the influence of merchants from Syria or the Mediterranean coastland rather than any connexion with Gaul.
15. Now in the British Museum. See K. S. Painter in *Antiquaries' Journal* (56), and *British Museum Quarterly* 32.

3

The Catacombs I

CONSTRUCTION OF THE CATACOMBS

The settled conditions of comparative security which marked the early years of the Roman Empire greatly favoured the rapid diffusion of the Christian faith. Yet to churchmen of the first and second centuries, faced by opposition from the Jews and regarded by the man in the street as tiresome and fanatical, the world seemed no easy place in which to live, nor were there, generally speaking, either the desire or the resources available for carrying out works of architecture or any other art. The earliest evidences of Christian practice on any large scale are therefore connected with the pious impulse to care for the dead, as shown particularly in the catacombs of Rome.

The word 'catacomb' originally meant no more than 'by the hollow'. It is a description applied to one particular district of Rome, near the Circus of Romulus on the Appian Way, where, in the fourth century, the church of St Sebastian was built. Beneath the church there was a large cemetery in which the bodies of the apostles Peter and Paul were thought to have rested for a time, and the lasting repute of this cemetery caused its name to be applied in a general way to any subterranean burial-place in Rome and indeed elsewhere, as, for instance, at Naples.

The Romans thought it right that their dead should be disposed of beneath the earth, although, for reasons of convenience, this was often done after cremation. The Jews, however, objected to the practice of cremation, and preferred to place the bodies of their dead in recesses cut from the rock in a series of underground galleries. And the Christians, influenced by thoughts of resurrection or at any rate by a keen sense of the fellowship of believers in death as in life, adopted the Jewish custom, constructing large groups of burial-chambers close to the cemeteries which, as the law[1] directed, lay just outside the city boundaries and usually along the main roads. Quite apart from the Jews, pagan practice furnished ample precedents for underground burials in the fashion of the catacombs. A number of Roman households and guilds saw to it that there were excavated 'dove-cotes' (*columbaria*)—so called from the rows of openings like pigeon-holes in which urns, containing the ashes of the deceased, were stored: the *columbarium* assigned to the household of the empress Livia contained as many as three thousand urns. All burial places enjoyed the protection of the law, and disturbance of tombs was, at least in theory, strictly avoided. Thus the emperor Alexander Severus, who was quite prepared to persecute Christians if occasion arose, defended their tenure of one such property against the rival claims of a group of restaurant-proprietors.[2]

It was no very difficult task to excavate the tombs in the soft volcanic tufa of the Roman district, and to be a grave-digger (*fossor*) was a recognized calling. A fourth-century picture in the Catacomb of Domitilla shows one such grave-digger,[3] named Diogenes, clothed in a loose tunic and holding a pickaxe over his shoulder, with a lamp in his other hand. Nearby one can see other tools of his trade—axe, hammer and pair

9. The Roman Catacombs: a typical gallery with burial-niches.

of compasses. The method of constructing catacombs was to start with a piece of ground already designated as a graveyard, whether privately owned or bestowed on the Christian community as a gift. From the surface, steps were cut leading downwards and giving access to a number of horizontal galleries (fig. 9), normally about two metres high and one metre wide, driven at right angles and then continued in a network of gridiron pattern. The burial-niches were ranged in tiers along both sides of the gallery walls, each space being sealed by a slab of marble or terracotta. When the space corresponding to the owner's plot of ground had been fully used, there was no alternative but to strike downwards with another flight of stairs giving access to galleries at a second, lower level. As soon as it was judged that enough interments had taken place on this level, if collapse of the walls was to be avoided, further descent was made to a third level. Thus the older tombs are at the top and the newest at the bottom of the catacomb. The number of levels linked in this way sometimes extends to five or, exceptionally, as in the Cemetery of Callistus, to seven.

The monotony of the rows of niches (*loculi*) may be varied here and there by a sepulchre of more distinctive character. This is the table-tomb, in general form resembling a medieval altar-tomb and either cut in a piece of soft rock or built up with stone or tile, the whole being topped by a slab of marble. A tomb of this nature may be set in a rectangular recess or, as an *arcosolium*, beneath a semicircular arch, but they appear most frequently within the private burial-chambers (*cubicula*) which lead from the galleries in the manner of bedrooms from a hotel corridor. It is in these *cubicula*, corresponding to the tombs of other well-to-do citizens above ground, that decoration, usually painting on plaster, is found. The burial-chambers, which vary considerably in size and shape, resemble the family vaults sometimes constructed in English churchyards during the eighteenth century, in that they were thought large enough to receive several generations of the family which owned them. In later periods, this desire to remain with the family in death no less than in life or, more particularly, to be associated with the bodies of the martyrs, led to some rather casual hacking of the walls in order to create niches for an increased number of corpses, and the grave-diggers, who had by then gained a firm control, found it not unprofitable to sell burial sites '*retro sanc-*

tos'—just behind the saints.

Rome is not the only place where the nature of the soil permitted easy excavation of subterranean burial-grounds, but the Roman catacombs are on an altogether different scale from those found elsewhere, amounting to some thousand kilometres of passages with much still to be explored and mapped. After lying for centuries in almost complete oblivion and neglect, the catacombs aroused some slight interest among dilettanti during the Renaissance, but it was not till the year 1578, when workmen, digging in a vineyard near the Via Salaria, happened to discover the Catacomb of the Jordani, that any popular enthusiasm was aroused. For here it was not just a case of another row of dark and featureless passageways: the complex of rooms, some of them richly decorated, appeared, as a contemporary observer put it, to resemble 'a city underground', demonstrating the antiquity of the Roman Church and powerful to confute all disbelievers and heretics. The Cemetery of the Jordani was soon forgotten once more, but the Catacomb of Priscilla nearby remained in mind and was one of those commented on with scholarly zeal by the antiquary Antonio Bosio in the early years of the seventeenth century.

Thereafter progress was very slow until Giovanni Battista de Rossi (1822–1894), combining historical genius with fanatical industry, initiated the modern, systematic study of the catacombs, Byron's 'choked-up vaults and frescos steep'd / In subterranean damps'.[4] De Rossi was inclined to carry the dating of the oldest catacombs back as far as the first century. He considered, for instance, that the Catacomb of Callistus had belonged to Christian members of the Caecilian house during the reign of Nero, on the strength of an allusion made by the historian Tacitus[5] to a certain member of that family, Pomponia Graecina, who was accused of 'foreign superstition' in the year 58 AD. But it is by no means certain that Pomponia's 'superstition' was in fact Christianity, and a similar doubt affects the Catacomb of Domitilla. De Rossi favoured the suggestion that the ground had once belonged to a certain Flavia Domitilla, exiled by the emperor Domitian about 90 AD, and that a number of her kinsfolk who 'rushed headlong to observe Jewish customs'[6] were in fact Christians who met a martyr's death and were buried in this catacomb. But the view that any of the Flavii embraced Christianity as early as

the first century is conjectural, and the evidence used to support it can no longer stand. For this evidence consists primarily of inscriptions which prove to be of somewhat later date, and which found their way into the catacomb as so much rubbish hurled there from outside. In any case the Catacomb of Domitilla is probably earlier than the oldest Jewish catacombs, of which the most remarkable is that of the Villa Torlonia, on the Via Nomentana.

The Torlonia catacomb resembles Christian examples in that, where decoration occurs, it consists of emblems proclaiming the traditional piety of a particular faith but combined with art-forms of universal appeal. In one semicircular recess, for example, may be noted a pedimented building, drawn in childish fashion, which represents Jerusalem. On each side stands a large, indeed lumpy, seven-branched candlestick, fashioned 'in the likeness of a trident'[7] according to directions laid down in the Book of Exodus[8] for furnishing the Ark of the Covenant. Other cult emblems shown in the picture include the *lulab* and the *ethrog*. The first of these is a palm-branch, denoting victorious immortality, and as such taken over by the Christians[9] and customarily placed, by later artists, in the hand of the martyrs. The *ethrog*, or citron, carried by all in the procession which marked the Feast of Tabernacles, stood for the fruit of the Tree of Life and therefore also hinted at immortality. But this emblematical scene, of singular appropriateness in a Hebrew burial-chamber, is accompanied by a band of classic decoration which might have appeared in any third-century Roman house. And not far away in the same catacomb one sees a dolphin, swimming, perhaps, to the Islands of the Blest, but not particularly characteristic of the Jewish faith.

As some of the Christian catacombs seem to be slightly older than those of the Jews, they may be said to derive their form not so much from Hebrew originals as from the common stock of funeral customs practised by the Etruscans and handed down to such families as the Volumnii, for whose interment, near Perugia, an underground vault with a number of passages was constructed in the second century BC. The development of the catacombs was to some extent conditioned by the needs which they were designed to serve. While the humbler members of the Christian fellowship had to be content with the simplest and least pretentious sepulchres, the general custom was for the interment to be accompanied by prayers,[10] and commemorative meals (*refrigeria*) were regularly held at which family and friends took part. This meant that, in cases where the·money was available, a certain amount of space was asked for and provided.

The second-century Martyrdom of Polycarp records that when, after his execution, Polycarp's body was spitefully burnt, 'we, at last, took up his bones more precious than gold and laid them in a suitable place. There the Lord will permit us to come together in gladness and joy and celebrate the birthday of his martyrdom.'[11] In order that similar practices could take place in the catacombs, some of the more handsome tombs were set in an area which offered ample space in front or at the side, as may be seen, for instance, in the 'Vault of the Flavii' in the Catacomb of Domitilla. Scenes of feasting are quite frequently painted on the plastered walls of catacombs, and in such illustrations realism is not easily separated from symbol. Paintings of this kind could be taken as a graceful allusion to heavenly peace and repose, but they found their everyday counterpart in the *refrigerium*. Occasionally benches, even couches, were provided for those who attended and an inscription from North Africa,[12] in honour of a certain Statulenia Julia, records that a table was set up: 'we made it our business to supply a stone table on which food and cups and dishes could be placed when we were commemorating her many admirable deeds.' The optimism of the Christian faith, in its early years, had taken some of the sting out of death, and the feastings by the tomb could, on occasion, follow the form almost of birthday parties, accompanied by much joviality. Nevertheless these excesses were frowned on, and such austere spirits as Tertullian liked to contrast the charitable, disciplined nature of the Christian celebrations with the gluttonous licence of paganism.

Most of the illumination needed in the catacombs was supplied by lamps hanging from the ceiling or placed on brackets, but airshafts were sometimes driven down from ground level and, in the words of the poet Prudentius,[13] allowed 'those beneath the earth to perceive the brightness of the far-off sun and to enjoy light'. The shafts, which were large enough for the martyr St Candida to be hurled down one to her death, might be ingeniously expanded, as in the Cemetery of Marcellinus and Peter, to serve the needs of two burial chambers on opposite sides of a passage.

The effect on an excitable boy of descending into the catacombs is described by St Jerome in these words:

When I was young and being educated in Rome it was my custom every Sunday, along with other boys of my own age and tastes, to visit the tombs of the apostles and martyrs and enter the crypts excavated in the very bowels of the earth. The walls on both sides as you go in are full of dead bodies and the whole place is so murky that one seems almost to find the fulfilment of those words of the prophet 'Let them go down alone into Hell'. Here and there a little light coming in from above is sufficient to give a momentary relief from the horror of darkness; but when you go forward and find yourself once more enveloped in the utter blackness of night, the words of the poet come spontaneously to mind: 'The very silence fills your soul with dread'.[14]

Between fifty and sixty Christian catacombs in Rome are normally listed as separate units, though a few are so close to one another as to be almost part of the same complex. The most densely packed area is to the south-east of the city, along the Appian and the Ardeatine Ways, near the Catacombs of Praetextatus, Domitilla and Sebastian. Not far off, on the Via Latina, the Cemetery of Trebius Justus marks the centre of an important zone which has only recently come to receive full attention while, rather isolated and a little further north, on the Via Labicana (now Casilina) is to be found the extensive catacomb 'Between the two Bay-trees' which developed around the graves of the martyrs Marcellinus and Peter. The second great family of catacombs lies to the north of Rome, in the district of the Via Salaria, and includes those of Priscilla and the Jordani as well as the so-called *Coemeterium Maius*. Then, on the road towards Ostia, at the east end of the city, occurs another group, of which the Catacomb of Commodilla is the most important. The catacombs in the S. Lorenzo district and on the west side of the Tiber have hitherto offered rather less of interest.

It is possible to draw some distinction between private and public catacombs. The first Christians in Rome, so far as can be discovered, were content with burial in the large cemeteries with persons of any faith, but by the beginning of the third century the Christian community had grown in numbers and confidence, and, as the historian Eusebius puts it,

the word of salvation began to lead many a soul out of every race to the pious worship of the God of the universe, so that now many of those who at Rome were famous for wealth and

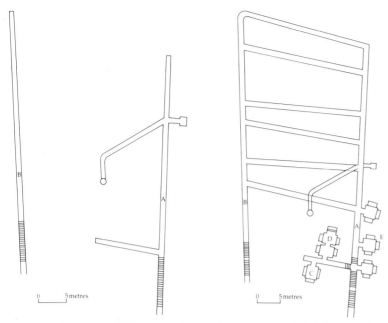

10. Rome, Catacomb of Callistus: as it was about 200 AD, and as it became after enlargement about 220 AD. C. Cubiculum of Orpheus; D. 'Crypt of the Popes'; E. the three Sacrament Chapels. Their number was doubled a few years later in the course of much further development.

family turned to their own salvation along with all their household and all their kinsfolk.[15]

At this point, pious individuals established and endowed catacombs where their entire family might be buried in a fellowship of common hope and expectation, and this privilege was widened, here and there, to include servants of the family and those who had no relationship beyond that of being 'brethren in the faith'. From that beginning two tendencies proceeded. The dominant one was enlargement and ecclesiastical control as catacombs fell, by gift or purchase, under the direct authority of the Church. A succession of vigorous popes emerged eager to encourage popular reverence for martyrs and to draw both the ritual and the art which centred around the martyr-tomb into serving the interests of orthodoxy. But, side by side with the communal cemeteries, a certain number of private burial-places continued in use, sometimes by persons who had no scruple about combining a version of Christianity with ideas and art-forms proper to other religions.

The way in which catacombs developed may be illustrated by the examples of St Callistus on the Via Appia and St Priscilla in the northern quarter of Rome.

Both have been carefully studied[16] and, while points of detail are obscure and likely to remain so, the main outlines seem now to be established. The S. Callisto area divides naturally into two parts, the Crypts of Lucina and the Cemetery of Callistus itself. The Lucina catacomb began with two small burial-grounds, each consisting of a gallery reached by a staircase from ground level. Dating cannot be exact, but to judge from the style of both inscriptions and paintings it seems that gallery A was excavated about 210 AD and enlarged a dozen years later by the construction of a second stairway and another gallery terminating in a double *cubiculum*, or funeral vault. Close by, the second burial-ground was hollowed out in the period 225–30 AD. It consisted of two short galleries set at right angles, with a crypt of substantial size leading off one of them. Into this crypt the body of Pope Cornelius was transferred in 255 AD, an event which led to the transformation of two little burial-grounds into one catacomb of considerable size. The two sets of galleries were connected by a passage driven through the intervening soil, the level of gallery B was lowered and extensions made to it, while another staircase was driven downwards in order that further burials might

11. Rome, Catacomb of Callistus: the 'Crypt of the Popes'.

take place in galleries constructed at a lower level.

The Crypt of Lucina and the adjoining Catacomb of Callistus run beneath an ancient cemetery where burials took place, often in rather magnificent tombs, as early as the fourth century BC. Pagan burials continued until the end of the third or the beginning of the fourth century AD—that is, after the construction of the Crypt of Lucina. Neither pagan hostility on the one hand nor Christian scruple on the other had refused to accept the combination of old-fashioned, pagan practice above ground with Christian ritual below. The cemetery remained in divided ownership until, when the Church became dominant in the reign of Constantine, the Christian community found itself able to take over an area hallowed by the presence of martyr-sanctuaries and to erect churches and ancillary buildings there. Before this, however, the cemetery, or 'resting-place', seems to have been largely under Christian control if the rather obscure notices[17] may be relied on which imply that Pope Zephyrinus (198–217 AD) entrusted its supervision to the priest Callistus, who became the next pope. Whatever may have been happening above ground, the Cemetery of Callistus became the regular burial-place of the popes from the time when the body of Pontianus, who died in exile, and his successor Anteros were interred there in the year 236. Their epitaphs, along with those of succeeding popes, remain as evidence.

The catacomb appears to have been constructed in an orderly fashion within a clearly defined circumference (fig. 10). Firstly, two staircases were excavated and a gallery driven from each, the one nearly parallel with the other. One of these galleries (B) remained for a time merely a straight line, but the second (A) was modified in two respects: a short passage was driven leftwards from the foot of the steps while, twenty-three metres farther on, another gallery was made to run also to the left but inclining backwards in the direction of the steps and ending at a well. All this excavation dates from the period just after 200 AD. The next stage, perhaps carried out by Callistus himself, was a deepening of the galleries A and B, which were then connected by means of three cross-galleries. But the demand for space continued and, about the year 220, further works were carried out. Three more cross-galleries were constructed between A and B, and two sets of crypts formed. The short passage running at a right angle from the staircase now led to the 'Cubiculum of Orpheus' on the left and, almost opposite, to the double chamber known as the 'Crypt of the Popes'. At the same time, three crypts were excavated from the other side of gallery A, just beyond the foot of the staircase; these are the 'Sacrament Chapels'. Their number was doubled a few years later when the level of the galleries was again lowered.

The growth of the catacomb continued throughout the fourth century. Pope Damasus, in particular, was responsible for many of the alterations which sometimes embellished and strengthened, but sometimes also destroyed, the original pattern as eagerness for burial in so renowned a sanctuary strained its capacity to the utmost. The 'Crypt of the Popes' (fig. 11), like the catacomb as a whole, experienced considerable, and fairly rapid, changes. It began as a double *cubiculum*, irregularly shaped, in which some sixteen popes and bishops were deposited within simple, unadorned niches. One of these was set in the wall at the end, but this was soon transformed to become a table-tomb, decorated with marble and strengthened with a low wall. The suggestion, not entirely convincing, has been made that this marks the resting-place of Pope Sixtus II, who, together with four of his deacons, met a martyr's death in 258 AD. A doorway was squeezed in without much refinement at one side and a window cut to admit some light from the adjoining gallery. Later works, however, perhaps those of Damasus, destroyed this primitive but quite effective pattern. A light-shaft, driven down from above, spoilt the painted ceiling, the window was blocked up, and two barley-sugar columns, still in existence, were erected partly as decoration and partly to provide an architrave from which lamps might hang. Through such casual methods the Roman catacombs developed.

The Catacomb of Priscilla, one of the largest of those found in Rome, is rather less easily interpreted than that of Callistus. It received its name from a certain Priscilla whose inscription, with the title of *clarissima*, indicates that she was of senatorial rank. It has often been supposed that, belonging to the distinguished house of the Acilii, she established this burial-ground for use by members of her family and by the poorer members of the Christian community in that quarter of Rome. Recent excavations,[18] however, have shown that the so-called '*hypogeum* of the Acilii' can no longer be claimed as a Christian burial-place of first- or second-century date. The area originally consisted of two galleries set at right angles and approached by a staircase. The galleries were in time subjected to a certain amount of enlargement and a sloping passage took the place of the staircase which was then blocked with a wall of brick and tufa. The longer arm of the gallery ends in a large chamber which apparently served as a water-reservoir before being transformed into a place of burial at the end of the third century; it is to this period that the earliest Christian tombs and inscriptions may be assigned. There was, however, a pagan cemetery above ground from which material fell into the catacomb passages, and the memorials to Priscilla and M. Acilius 'of consular rank' are displaced fragments belonging to the period when members of the Gens Acilia were not yet Christian. The nearby area of the 'Greek Chapel' (fig. 12), so named from inscriptions in the Greek language painted on a wall of the main chamber, seems to have begun as the undercroft of a private house. The layout is complex, but the largest aisle took the form of a chapel ending in three recesses, resembling an apse and two diminutive transepts. The whole is richly decorated by the hands of two skilled artists, one of whom thought it right to exhibit a eucharistic feast of the type celebrated, no doubt, within the Chapel, but not earlier than the end of the third century.

The other main feature of the Catacomb of Priscilla is the 'Sandpit', a maze of intersecting galleries, wider than catacomb galleries usually were, and cut out of the soft stone. This seems to have been a popular burial-ground for persons of little substance; the unpretentious sepulchres are closed with rough brickwork bearing the names of the deceased or the simplest emblems of Christian hope. In the course of time the walls showed signs of collapse and had to be reinforced by crude buttresses. Subsequently the arrangement found in many other catacombs was followed and a second level was constructed, deeply sunk below the first. This consists of a very long, straight gallery, regularly intersected by side passageways containing thousands of tombs.

The Catacomb of Praetextatus follows a similar pattern in that, as is now apparent,[19] a long and comparatively wide gallery serves as a main thoroughfare from which tributaries extend on both sides to form a maze of interrelated passages. Inscriptions point to 291 and 307 AD as relevant dates.

12. Rome, Catacomb of Priscilla: the 'Greek Chapel'.

THE PAINTINGS IN THE CATACOMBS

The catacomb paintings represent the straightforward use by churchmen of the art-forms prevailing in their day. The artists, seldom men of notable creative power, decorated the *cubicula* as they might have decorated the walls of a house, in the manner which they understood and which happened to be 'in the air'. Christianization of the painting simply meant adopting not only a contemporary style but also, often enough, popular subjects, and applying both to a declaration of the Gospel in ways capable of being understood at that particular time. The style used for the earlier catacomb paintings at least is the so-called Late Antique, a sketchy, impressionistic way of suggesting figures in action by means of light brush-strokes of colour on the plaster background. The Greek aim of displaying the human body in a perfection more often imagined than perceived, and the Roman genius for detailed observation of individual character yield to a fashion which, for all its clumsy, provincial air, can be used to suggest rather than to define and thus hint at a supernatural reality lying behind the neat face of everyday existence. It may be that, as the painter Apelles declared, 'works which have charm touch Heaven', but the Christians on the whole preferred to make their approach to Heaven less by the avenue of beauty than by symbolic allusion to the hope that was in themselves. Nor did they often attempt to portray the mysterious character of the Divine as vividly as did the followers of Dionysus who, at Pompeii for example, show the initiate subjected to the most powerful emotions of terror and exhilaration.

The subjects chosen for representation in the catacombs naturally tend to be those appropriate to private tombs, with an emphasis on scenes of deliverance illustrating the power of God to save those who put their trust in Him, but straightforward decoration also appears frequently. Though there is nothing comparable for artistic quality with the graceful scenes of nature, tamed and formalized, which make the walls of the Villa of Livia[20] look like a William Morris wallpaper, paintings do exist to show that the Christian artists, or those whom Christians employed, had an eye for the beauty of the world around them. One such example may be seen in the birds of the Praetextatus Catacomb; even more impressive is the landscape, with its trees and animals, which forms a background to the stylized, classical figure of the Good Shepherd in the Catacomb of Domitilla.

The artists responsible for these paintings employed two methods, fresco and tempera, with a distinct preference for fresco. Both processes required careful preparation in advance, the wall being smoothed and covered with a layer of coarse plaster made of slaked lime, sand and volcanic earth. On top of this was placed the more finished plaster surface, usually composed of lime and marble dust. The technique of fresco requires that the colour should be applied while this plaster coating is still moist. The pigments then penetrate the wet plaster and a film of calcium carbonate forms which fixes the colours. The technique of tempera, by contrast, involves the application of paint to a surface already hardened with the help of some such fixative as milk or white of egg. During the Italian Renaissance, critics used to maintain that fresco is 'the sweetest and subtlest technique that exists', but it was a difficult process to manage partly because the result of the brush-stroke was immediately absorbed into the plaster and mistakes could therefore not be concealed, partly because the work was rather slow. It was desirable also to match the amount of wet plaster prepared every day with the area which the artist might reasonably be expected to cover; hence the measurement lines sometimes to be seen scratched on the walls and the rough, preliminary sketches traced, for instance, in the Catacomb of the Jordani.

The variety of colours is somewhat restricted. Comparatively bright and well-contrasted colours are necessary in underground, dimly-lit vaults, so that delicate shading, particularly with grey or black, is entirely out of place. On the other hand, some of the more brilliant reds and blues are not amenable to the fresco technique. Catacomb painting was therefore usually carried out in broad brush-strokes of yellow, dull red, green and brown, the figure subjects being enclosed, as a rule, within a simple framework of straight or semicircular lines.

While few of the families concerned had either the money or the inclination to search out the best contemporary artists, paintings of outstanding quality occur here and there. Two of the earliest deserve special mention. One ceiling in the Crypt of Lucina

13. Rome, Catacomb of Callistus: a ceiling in the Crypt of Lucina.

(*cubiculum y*) illustrates with exceptional grace a form of decoration derived from the idea of a canopy set up within the house (fig. 13). It is marked out in a scheme of circles, diagonals and crosses which, by their intersections, provide a number of compartments of various sizes, each containing a figure or a flower motif. In the Lucina Crypt ceiling, the figures are elongated and refined, very different from, say, the dumpy cherubs of the Dino Campagni Catacomb. The circle in the centre encloses twenty-one compartments. Four semicircular lunettes contain flowers; then, within a pattern composed of the eight arms of an upright and a diagonal cross, appear four matching heads of youths with wind-swept hair and a number of standard decorative themes with Daniel occupying the place of honour in the middle where he stands, naked and dominant, between two diminutive lions. The divisions between the circle and the enclosing rectangle balance each other precisely, containing four winged angels of classic pattern, two '*Orants*' and two shepherds, each bearing a lamb on his shoulder.

One may assign to the same period, about the middle of the third century, a painting in the Catacomb of Priscilla which, although much damaged, displays both skill and keen perception. It consists of two scenes enclosed within a rectangular frame having a primitive cotton-reel pattern on top and some loosely drawn semicircles below. On one side, beneath a pair of luxuriantly spreading trees, stands the Good Shepherd, with a lamb on his shoulders and a large sheep, looking gratefully up at him, on each side. These figures were originally moulded in stucco —plaster raised above wall level—a technique appearing only rarely in the catacombs. Beside this scene is a small group, painted in a uniform shade of pinkish brown (fig. 14). The figure on the left is crudely sketched and his right arm, with hand pointing upwards to a star, is over-large in relation to his body. While, however, it is commonly assumed that this error of draughtsmanship is due to a lack of competence on the artist's part, it may be that the arm and its gesture have been intentionally emphasized. For the mother and child, who make up the rest of the group, have about them touches of the majesty and mystery which characterize paintings of a much later period, such as the fifth-century Christ in the Catacomb of Marcellinus and Peter. The woman looks directly at the spectator; the child too, though clasped

14. Rome, Catacomb of Priscilla. Wall-painting: Virgin and Child with Prophet.

in his mother's arms, turns his head away from her to direct a steadfast gaze straight ahead. Damaged as it is, and situated in the least distinguished part of the Priscilla Catacomb, this representation of the Virgin and Child, with a prophet indicating that 'there shall come forth a star out of Jacob',[21] offers a hint and early likeness of the art of the Middle Ages.

Painting of a rather more finished type appears in the Catacomb of the Aurelii. Here the figures reveal a classic feeling for arrangement and proportion while a touch of impressionism serves to avoid academic rigidity and impart a sense of vigorous life. One head, that of a bearded man with strong features and the eyes of a prophet who 'sees visions and dreams dreams', is a notable essay in portraiture, made more effective by the contrast it presents with the sketchy lines of the tunic and pallium below.

SUBJECTS OF THE CATACOMB PAINTINGS

The subjects of the catacomb paintings are presented in two different ways. Many scenes are drawn from the Old or New Testament; alternatively, symbolic figures are used to summarize as if in shorthand the essence of Christian hope. The symbols may, in their turn, be divided into those representing Christ and those which stand for mankind—or, rather, for the individual soul rejoicing in the prospect of eternity. Much of the imagery, however, while amenable to a Christian interpretation, is drawn from a common stock of general themes suggesting the bounty of nature and the graceful circumstances of country life.

Of the various symbols, the cross is perhaps the most important. But in the catacombs, as in Palestine, this is really a mark of transition; the *taw*, reminder in Old Testament times of God's saving mercy, is transformed into the cross of Christ, which dominates the New Testament. The cross appears in many forms: the long Latin cross ✝ , the Greek cross with equal arms ✚ , and occasionally, as in the Catacomb of the Jordani, the swastika, adapted for western purposes after long use as a religious emblem in the East. Again, as in Palestine, the cross can be shown in combination with a ₽ , as ₽ or ✖ , when it conveniently summarizes the name of Christ. Or it may be merely hinted at through the forms of anchor or trident.

The fish, with its varied history as a religious symbol in Egypt and other lands, was readily adopted into Christian uses, serving both for Christ and for the believer. By a happy accident the Greek letters *I X Θ Y C*, which spell the word for 'fish', can be interpreted as an acrostic making up the initial letters of the phrase 'Jesus Christ, Son of God, Saviour'. This, when taken in connection with references to fish in the Gospel story of the miraculous feeding of the multitude, made it easy for Christians who partook of the eucharistic bread and wine to think of themselves as receiving through faith the body of Christ, described allusively as the fish.[22] The epitaph of Abercius, bishop of Hieropolis in Phrygia, contains the words 'Faith has provided for us as our food a Fish from the fountain, mighty, pure, one whom a virgin brought forth', and a gravestone from Autun retains this eucharistic reference in the words 'Eat when you are hungry, receiving the Fish in your hands.'[23] Such references find their parallels in catacomb painting. Thus a diminutive wall-painting in the Crypt of Lucina shows a fish swimming along with a basket of loaves on its back (fig. 15). In the middle of the basket and beneath the five loaves is a reddish patch which some explain as a vessel containing wine. No doubt a reference to the Miraculous Feeding is intended and, if the fish is seen as alive and swimming, the thought comes close to that of the Fathers who declared that 'Christ, himself the true bread and fish of the living water, fed the people with five loaves and two fishes.'[24]

Allusion to Christ is also made by the representations of a shepherd boy bearing a sheep on his shoulders (fig. 16), a popular theme found about one hundred and twenty times in the catacombs. This type of the sheep-bearer is extremely ancient, being found in reliefs from Carchemish that date back to 1000 BC. Here the suggestion is of an animal being held by its four legs and carried off for sacrifice, but the Greeks transformed the figure into that of Hermes, god of compassion, or in more abstract terms, an emblem of effective sympathy. The Christians had little hesitation about adapting pagan art-forms to their own uses and, in this particular case, there was an

15. Rome, Crypt of Lucina. Wall-painting: fish and basket of loaves.

16. Rome, Catacomb of Domitilla. Wall-painting: the Good Shepherd.

abundance of Scriptural texts to assist the process. Ezekiel had proclaimed the divine message: 'I will set up one shepherd over them and he shall feed them, even my servant David: he shall feed them and he shall be their shepherd', or, in the words of the second Isaiah, 'He shall feed his flock like a shepherd; he shall gather the lambs with his arm.' Prophecies of this kind found their echo in the parable[25] of the shepherd who searches for the lost sheep, and their fulfilment in the discourse[26] concerning 'the good shepherd who layeth down his life for the sheep'. Tertullian, writing in North Africa around 200 AD, spoke of 'the Shepherd whom you depict on your cup'[27] when referring to engraved glass vessels which illustrated the theme of the shepherd protecting his flock. At roughly the same time catacomb paintings were being produced which showed Christ not simply in realistic terms as a Galilean peasant who lived when Pontius Pilate was procurator, but with the implication that he was indeed a second David, with the power to preserve his sheep from danger and uphold them even in death. Occasionally the shepherd becomes part of an idyllic, pastoral scene, providing milk for his flock or watching over it with a countryman's staff in his hand, no doubt in the Pastures of the Blessed to which the sheep have been conducted.

One of the surprising figures that may occasionally be found in the Christian catacombs is that of the pagan hero Orpheus, who is shown rather more predictably, on an ancient relief at Delphi, aboard the ship *Argo* and clasping a lyre in his hands. Such was the charm of his playing that, according to the Greek poets, wild beasts and even trees and stones were attracted and pacified by him, while his presence in a cemetery is made particularly appropriate by the story that he was allowed to penetrate to the underworld and reclaim his wife Eurydice. In the Catacomb of Domitilla, for example, Orpheus appears painted rather crudely in heavy strokes of pink and brown, with his right hand raised and his left holding the lyre. Around him are gathered a lion, a camel and a varied company of animals and birds whom he has subdued just as Christ pacifies and tames the passions of men.[28] Naturally enough, scruples of conscience prevented the demi-god Orpheus from finding a place in many Christian burial-vaults, but the fact that he occurs at all testifies to the willingness of early churchmen to adapt for their own purposes the best known and most attractive emblems of virtue and hope.

Other symbols of Christ include the vine, for which the Scriptures provided sufficient justification. In Ecclesiasticus[29] the words are put into the mouth of Wisdom: 'As a vine I put forth grace.' This imagery enables Christ to proclaim 'I am the true Vine.'[30] The Lamb was naturally suggested by another Johannine text: 'Behold, the Lamb of God',[31] though the formalized picture of the 'Lamb standing on the Mount Zion',[32] a popular subject in the Middle Ages, appears very seldom and then only in so late a catacomb as that of Marcellinus and Peter.

The human soul is also frequently represented as a lamb, standing in security near the Good Shepherd, or as a dove. This last emblem finds an early commentary in the eye-witness account of the martyrdom of Polycarp, bishop of Smyrna, who met his death about the year 155 AD. When the flames failed to consume the martyr's body 'lawless men ordered the executioner to approach and stab him with a dagger, and when he did this, there came out a dove'[33]—Polycarp's spirit flying away to seek the joys of Heaven. But in the catacombs the more usual manner of representing the human soul is through the *Orans*, a figure with both hands stretched outward and upward in supplication. The *Orans* is usually shown as a woman of mature years, but there are occasional variations and, on a ceiling in the Catacomb of Marcellinus and Peter, scenes from the life of Jonah are flanked by four *Orants* (one destroyed), the conventional female figures alternating with those of young men in tunic and cloak.

The figure of the *Orans* was taken directly from its widespread use in classical imagery, and implied for the Christians much the same thing as it had meant for their pagan precursors. For the *Orans* represents *pietas*—the affectionate respect due to state, to ruler, to family or to God. On coins from the time of Trajan to Maximian Hercules, throughout the second and third centuries AD, the *Orans* appears quite frequently, accompanied by some such motto as *Pietas Publica*; an assertion of, or plea for, the 'righteousness that exalteth a nation'. Piety as a state of mind naturally expresses itself in prayer; thus the *Orans* is shown in a prayerful attitude, looking directly at the beholder in what was considered to be the natural pose of sincere and candid spiritual power. Sometimes, however, the *Orans* represents not piety personified but some individual rejoicing in salvation. The Brooklyn

17. Funeral stele: the *Orans*.

18. Rome, Catacomb of Priscilla. Wall-painting: the 'Woman with a Veil'.

Museum collection includes a funeral stele, probably of the third century AD, on which, by means of pillars and carved gable, a chapel is indicated. Within stands a man, clothed in a tunic, facing solemnly to the front and with hands raised exceptionally high in prayer (fig. 17). His name is given in an inscription as Chaeromon, and that he comes from a Greek-speaking district of Lower Egypt is confirmed by the presence of two jackals, emblems of the god Anubis.

The *Orans* as found in the Christian catacombs may be said to display one or other of the two emphases of pagan art. A striking figure, the so-called 'Woman with a Veil' of the Priscilla Catacomb, follows the classic pattern of pious supplication (fig. 18). Her hands, projecting from the sleeves of her red tunic, are raised, with thumbs pointing heavenwards and fingers extended, to the level of her head. The large and awkward hands may have been so drawn in order to emphasize the idea of prayerful entreaty, for the woman's face, with its touches of high colour and its deep-set, uplifted eyes, shows the artist to have been a man of sensibility and skill. But he used as his *Orans* a recognized type which is repeated almost exactly in the Catacomb of the Jordani. By contrast the *Orans* in

the Catacomb of Domitilla, standing in a graceful and composed attitude between two trees, suggests rather the soul at rest in the enjoyment of paradise.

Many other symbols were drawn into Christian service from the pagan repertory. One of these was the phoenix, of which it could be written:

Let us consider the strange sign which takes place in the East, in the districts near Arabia. There is a bird which is called the phoenix. This is the only one of its kind and it lives for five hundred years; and, when the time of its dissolution in death is at hand, it makes for itself a sepulchre of frankincense and myrrh and other spices, and, when the time is fulfilled, it enters therein and dies.[34]

The belief that the phoenix then came to life again suggested resurrection and immortality, and it is no doubt for this reason that the phoenix sometimes appears painted in the catacombs. The most splendid example is that in the Priscilla Catacomb, with a 'crown of rays fitted all over its head, in lofty likeness to the glory of the Sun-God',[35] and its body enveloped in jutting tongues of flame. More frequently depicted is the peacock. Its flesh was thought to remain incorruptible and thus, together with the brilliance of its

19. Rome, Catacomb of Callistus. Wall-painting: the banquet.

new plumage in springtime, again to suggest the glory of resurrection. Peacocks were often set face to face, as in the Cemetery of Dino Compagni, with a vase, representing the water of life or the eucharistic cup, between them.[36]

The various banqueting scenes that appear in the catacombs may be seen as the link between compact symbol and the fuller pictures of Biblical incidents. On a wall in one of the 'Sacrament Chapels' of the Callistus Catacomb seven young men recline at the *sigma*, or semicircular couch, in order to share a meal (fig. 19). In front of them are set two dishes, each containing a fish, and seven baskets of bread. The artist may well have been thinking of the meal by the Sea of Tiberias which is recorded in the final, supplementary chapter of St John's Gospel. In fact, there is no mention in this passage of baskets, which are more naturally connected with the Feeding of the Four Thousand,[37] when 'they took up, of broken pieces that remained over, seven basketfuls.' Moreover the number seven was regarded, in the days of the Roman Empire, as the proper number of diners to take their place at one *sigma*.[38] The artist of the Callistus Catacomb may therefore have been working merely from a general

reminiscence of Christ's miraculous acts. However, a commentary by St Augustine, though later than the catacomb paintings, indicates the line of thought which connects such meals with life in the world beyond. Referring to the Tiberias incident, Augustine writes:

Now the Lord made a feast for his seven disciples, that is to say, from the fish which they saw laid on the fire of coals, to which He added some of the fish which they had caught, as well as the bread which they are said to have seen. Just as the fish was consumed in the flames, so Christ suffered: He himself is the bread which came down from Heaven; and to Him is joined the Church in order that it may have a share in everlasting blessedness.[39]

Nearby, in the same chapel of the Callistus Catacomb, is another scene which may be no more than a shorthand version of the larger picture. A man, clothed in the long mantle of the philosopher but with right arm and shoulder bare, extends both hands towards a three-legged table on which are set a fish and a loaf of bread. At the other side of the table, a woman raises her hands to heaven in the typical posture of the *Orans*. This woman is probably

20. Rome, Catacomb of Priscilla. Wall-painting: the banqueting scene in the Greek Chapel.

'Thanksgiving', or, in St Paul's language,[40] 'Blessing', who acclaims the action of Christ, purveyor of the divine wisdom, as he hallows the food which satisfied the apostles by the Sea of Tiberias. In the continuing life of the Church, this historical meal represents the Eucharist, which, as 'the medicine of immortality',[41] sustains the believer and guarantees eternal life. The picture therefore accords with a wall-painting found in one of the Christian catacombs of Alexandria. Here Christ is shown seated on a throne with someone on either side approaching hastily. One of the figures, named Andrew, brings two fish on a plate; the other man, now much defaced, was presumably Philip bearing the bread. At Christ's feet stand two baskets containing loaves. On either side of this scene is a group of people partaking of a meal. To the left, the marriage-feast at Cana can just be made out; on the right three people are reposing beneath the shade of trees while an inscription offers a motto for the whole rather elaborate composition: 'eating the blessings of Christ'.[42]

When it came to the choice of subjects drawn for illustration from the Scriptures, the primary theme which painters naturally desired to emphasize was that of deliverance from peril by the power of God. As early as the beginning of the second century, the author of the First Epistle of Clement from Rome to the Corinthians alludes to grave troubles afflicting the Roman church. He instances Daniel in the lions' den and the three men, Ananias, Azarias and Misael, cast into the fiery furnace as persons who were oppressed 'by hateful men, full of iniquity, who did not realise that the Most High is the defender and protector of those who serve his excellent name with a pure conscience'.[43] Thereafter Daniel, and the three companions in the fiery furnace, regularly find their place in the litanies which invoke God's aid for a Christian in the hour of his death.

The pictures in the catacombs often deserve to be examined not merely as individual compositions but as parts of a series of connected themes, and the 'Greek Chapel' of the Priscilla Catacomb provides a good example of the varied scenes that go to make up an essay on the subject of salvation. On the left wall of the entrance chamber appear first the three young men standing unharmed in the fiery furnace; opposite them the deceased man stands in the posture of an *Orans* as, with arms uplifted, he too invokes divine succour. On the inner surface of the arch above, the lone figure of Moses, rod in hand, strikes the rock to make water flow for the thirsty Israelites,[44] and thus prefigures baptism as a requirement for Christian 'pilgrims in a barren land'. On the ceiling of the chapel, the man sick of the palsy is shown cured and carrying his bed away. The Four Seasons, typifying God's bounty in the world of nature, appear on the ceiling also, together with what is perhaps another baptismal scene, while the further archway is decorated with a picture of the Three Wise Men adoring the infant Christ. The two side walls display episodes from the story of Susanna and the elders: first, Susanna surprised by the elders, then the accusation laid against her and, finally, her acquittal. This gay little story from the Apocrypha was another of the examples frequently used to illustrate God's power to save in time of need.[45]

Proceeding onward from the nave into the first of the small chapels, the devout Christian of the third century would be heartened by a remarkable scheme of decoration. On the ceiling are four *Orants*, then, to the right, Daniel in the lions' den followed by Abraham's sacrifice of Isaac, another instance of God's timely and effective intervention. The next picture, the raising of Lazarus, is clearly appropriate to a place of burial,[46] while Noah in the Ark, who follows after, may be said to indicate the soul of the departed whom God is ready to protect from destruction just as he saved Noah from the flood. The series ends with an illustration of a banqueting scene, similar to that of the Callistus Catacomb but executed with greater delicacy and charm (fig. 20). Here, too, seven people recline at the couch. There is nothing stiff about the figures; with their varied gestures, they are knit together in a vividly portrayed group. The food before them consists of bread and fish, together with a jar of wine. Seven baskets containing loaves, four on one side and three on the other, continue the line of the banquet. It would be unwarranted to maintain that this scene literally and directly portrays the Christian liturgy, but its eucharistic overtones would remind the faithful that the sacraments are appointed means to bring about divine assistance.

INSCRIPTIONS IN THE CATACOMBS

A commentary on the ideas of those who constructed and decorated the catacombs is provided by the frequent inscriptions found within them. These inscriptions are carved or painted on tiles, stone slabs or walls, and range from a few simple, illiterate words to elaborate versifying in the later period. The language used may be Latin, Greek—which was current as a common tongue all round the Mediterranean—or a combination of both.

More than twenty thousand of these inscriptions are known, and many of the early ones may be distinguished from contemporary pagan epitaphs only by some reference to 'peace'. By contrast with the wistful farewells of third-century paganism, Christian burial-places displayed mottoes indicating the hope of happiness in a sphere where the painful irregularities of earthly life might be exchanged for peace and justice. Typical inscriptions therefore run: 'Zosimus, peace be with you',[47] 'Dear Faustina, mayest thou live in God',[48] 'Mayest thou sleep in the peace of the Lord.'[49] The dove, the palm and the anchor are emblems traditionally linked with inscriptions of this nature. Thus, in the Catacomb of Priscilla, two anchors and a palm emphasize the message 'Peace be with thee, Filumena', while the tomb of Felicissima in the Praetextatus Catacomb bears the name alone, written in bold Greek characters and surmounted by an *Orans* figure, two doves and two palm trees (fig. 21a, b). The same kind of hopeful prayer is sometimes put rather differently: 'Mayest thou live in the Holy Spirit' or 'Live to eternity'. A memorial in the Domitilla Catacomb to the 'dear and well-loved Siricia' concludes with the entreaty 'Lord Jesus, remember our daughter'. This epitaph, too, receives the addition of anchor and dove together with the monogram for Christ. The chi-rho monogram, along with the letters alpha and omega, served to suggest, or perhaps to ensure, that the departed was living, as other inscriptions declare, 'In Christ' or 'Among the Saints'. But the close connection between living and dead was not thought of as a purely one-sided matter. The living might indeed be required to pray for the dead, as in a verse inscription from the Priscilla Catacomb which commemorates a certain Agape: 'I beg you to pray

21. Rome, catacomb epitaphs: a. Filumena, b. Felicissima.

when you come here and to entreat Father and Son in all your prayers. Do not fail to remember dear Agape so that God Almighty may keep Agape safe for ever.'[50] But the dead were also asked to pray for the living: 'Atticus, sleep in peace, carefree in your security, and pray earnestly for our sinful selves.'[51] Moreover the intercession of the saints is valued. Peter and Paul are frequently asked to concern themselves with particular individuals. 'Paul and Peter, pray for Victor' is one of a number of such inscriptions found in the 'Memoria Apostolorum' of the Sebastian Catacomb, just as, at a point near the Crypt of the Popes in the Callistus Catacomb, the plea was inscribed: 'Holy Xystus, have Aurelius Repentinus in mind during your prayers.' By the fourth century, the inscriptions were tending to become longer, and compact symbols, such as the fish, gave place to statements of belief in

Christ, in the Holy Spirit and even in so fully developed a doctrine as the Trinity. Other inscriptions were concerned with the tomb itself, as a valued possession purchased and prepared during the owner's lifetime. A stone now in the Vatican Museum records: 'Fortunatus made this (tomb) for himself while he was still alive so that he might have a place in Christ all ready for the time when he should rest in peace.'[52]

Those who had no claim to a suitable property might, through legal process, acquire a tomb in a public burial-ground, and this led to homely declarations concerning the vendor and even the purchase price handed over in the presence of witnesses: 'This double tomb was bought by Artemisius, at the price of 1500 *folles* paid to the grave-digger Hilarus in the presence of the grave-diggers Severus and Laurentius.'[53]

THE VATICAN

The Vatican area presents problems rather different from those of the other catacombs, while its importance is enhanced, and in some respects clouded, by the arguments concerning St Peter and the primacy of the Pope as Peter's successor. Two distinct questions emerge: first, did Peter live for a time and finally suffer a martyr's death in Rome; second, does the Vatican mark the place of his execution and burial? The tradition which connects Peter with Rome is ancient and impressive, even though, as with most matters concerning the early Church, no clear pattern appears before the beginning of the second century. The First Epistle of Peter, in the New Testament, may perhaps be his; as it was composed in Greek, however, and both thought and language fly somewhat higher than might be expected of a Palestinian fisherman, it is safer to say that the Epistle was probably written at Rome, by someone who knew Peter or claimed to follow his life and teachings, to the Christians of Asia Minor. As early as the beginning of the second century, literary allusions connect Peter closely with Paul. The letter of exhortation sent from Rome to Corinth 'through Clement'[54] belongs to this period. It has much to say about the evils of jealousy and discord, by reason of which 'the greatest and most righteous pillars of the Church were persecuted and contended unto death'. The writer continues:

Let us set before our eyes the good apostles: Peter who because of unrighteous jealousy endured not one or two but many trials and having thus borne his witness went to the place of glory which was his due. Amid jealousy and strife Paul showed how to obtain the prize of endurance.

By 170 AD, when Dionysius, bishop of Corinth, sent a 'written communication'[55] to the Romans, the tradition was firmly crystallized.

You [Dionysius says] have united the planting that came from Peter and Paul, of both the Romans and the Corinthians. For indeed both planted also in our Corinth, and likewise taught us: similarly they taught together also in Italy, and were martyred on the same occasion.

This is usually taken to indicate that Peter and Paul suffered death in the distressful times of the emperor Nero, who did not hesitate to select the Christians when, in the year 64 AD, he felt obliged, for political reasons, to find and persecute unpopular scapegoats.[56] By the time of Bishop Dionysius it was evidently accepted that Peter, like Paul, had been active at Rome and met his death there.

The further stage is reached about 200 AD, when Gaius, a Roman priest, alludes, in the course of a doctrinal argument, to the 'trophies', that is to say the shrines or tombs, 'of the apostles'. 'For', Gaius explains, 'if it is your will to proceed to the Vatican or

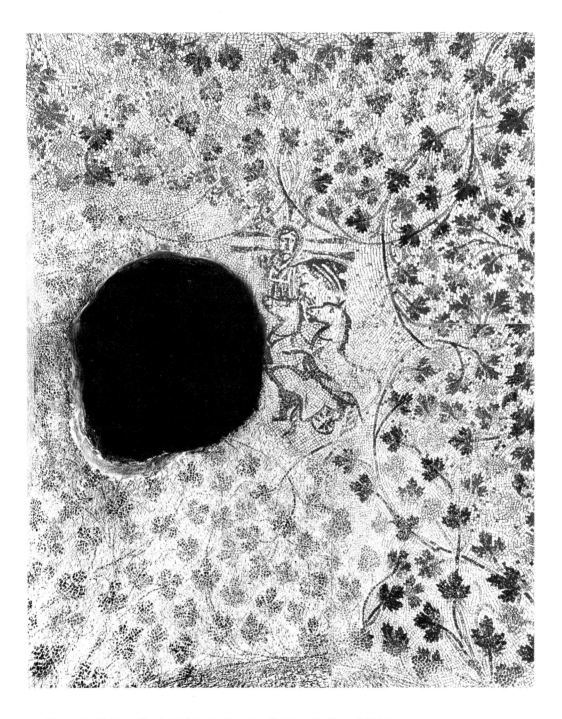

22. Rome, the Vatican, Tomb M. Mosaic showing Christ as the Sun of Righteousness.

23. Rome, Catacomb of Sebastian. Inscription: 'Paul and Peter, pray for Victor'.

to the Ostian Way, you will find the trophies of those who founded this church.'[57] And from the days of Gaius onwards to the present the opinion has been widely held that Peter was executed in the Circus of Nero below the Vatican Hill and buried nearby.

It remains to consider how far such beliefs have been confirmed by the excavations systematically carried out in recent years. At the time of Nero, the Vatican had a cemetery on the north-east side of the hill, together with a number of other tombs scattered in and around the area. No trace of the Circus, the traditional scene of Peter's martyrdom, has been found underneath the church, and it appears that this probably lay on the level ground rather further south. Precisely below the present St Peter's, running from west to east, is a double line of tombs flanking each side of a street. Their form has been modified to some extent by the works found necessary in the course of building Constantine's church; in general, however, they constitute a sequence of well-preserved sepulchres belonging to prosperous middle-class citizens of the second century AD. The layout resembles that of cemeteries recently excavated at Ostia and on the Isola Sacra, near the harbour which Trajan constructed

some sixteen miles from Rome. The date of the tombs can be determined partly by the style of brickwork and decoration, and partly by the names of the people buried there, some being freedmen of the second-century emperors Trajan, Antoninus Pius and Marcus Aurelius. The tombs take the form of single chambers, occasionally with a small forecourt in front; they resemble a row of little houses with vaulted roofs, and often display rather splendid decoration inside. They were conscientiously maintained until Constantine's day, and into this dignified burial-place Christianity made its way during the third century, sometimes combined, in tolerant fashion, with other beliefs.

An example of this coexistence can be seen in the Mausoleum of the Caetennii, where, amid a noble series of pagan inscriptions, there suddenly occurs the burial-place of a Christian woman, Gorgonia, 'remarkable for beauty and chastity', who is shown in the act of drawing water, no doubt the 'water that springs up into life eternal',[58] from a square-headed well. Even more remarkable for the combination of various religions is the so-called Tomb of the Egyptians, one of the few that still remain accessible on the south side of the street. This mausoleum acquires its name from a painting of the Egyptian god Horus, who clasps in his left hand the *ankh*, or symbol of life, with its rounded handle, crossbar and prong—in this case prongs —projecting below. Apparently the tomb was built for a well-to-do Egyptian family and, in keeping with the fact that the Egyptians never burned the bodies of their dead, there is no sign here of the cremations to which several of the other tombs bear witness. But near the picture of the Egyptian god appear two handsome sarcophagi of different inspiration, connected with the cult of the Greek god Dionysus. The first displays, amid scenes of frenzied revelry, the discovery by Dionysus of the sleeping Ariadne, who represents, in type and symbol, the soul awakened by the touch of divine power to enjoy eternal felicity. The other sarcophagus, later in date and somewhat more restrained, also shows Dionysus and his retinue, but here sea-monsters are depicted, flanking the central panel, as if ready to conduct the soul across turbulent waters to the Islands of the Blessed.

Four other sarcophagi are contained within the Tomb of the Egyptians. One is a plain and humble affair made of terracotta. Painted inside the recess where this coffin lies are the figure of a woman and a fragmentary inscription including the word *deposita* ('laid to rest'), a Christian formula confirmed by the Christian symbols of palm-branch and dove. In this tomb, then, the three emblems of Horus, Dionysus and Christ declare a common message of undying hope.

The burial-place, however, which provides the classic example of a transition from pagan to Christian uses is the diminutive Tomb M, approached by a short passageway from the north side of the street. This tomb was constructed during the second century for the family of the Julii. In addition to the evidence of cremation, the epitaph, now lost, of a child named Julius Tarpeianus bears witness by its form to pagan beliefs. But either the Julian family became Christian or they rendered up their mausoleum to another family, which held that faith and saw fit to decorate the ceiling and top portions of north, east and west walls with pictures made up from the little cubes of opaque glass known as 'mosaic'. Some of the cubes have fallen from their place and disappeared; they have, however, left impressions in the plaster which held them and on which the designs had been painted in fresco for the mosaicist to follow.

The subjects shown on these walls are typical of the funerary art of the third century: Jonah falling into the whale's mouth, the Good Shepherd, and the Angler fishing for souls in the waters of baptism. But on the ceiling, where fortunately the mosaic is in large part preserved, occurs a more striking figure that owes its form to pagan models. Within a framework of vine-leaves—some light, some dark, but all brilliant green—Helios, the Sun God, ascends heavenwards in his chariot drawn by two prancing white horses (fig. 22). Behind his head is a halo, from which rays of light shoot forth, but their arrangement powerfully suggests a cross, and, in this Christian context, it proves that the figure is in fact not Helios but Christ,[59] the Sun of Righteousness, arising, as the hymn says, to 'triumph o'er the shades of night'.

A little further west the row of dignified sepulchres gives place to a confused scattering of humble tombs, and it is here that the 'Shrine of St Peter' is to be found. The tradition which held this to be Peter's burial-place was sufficiently strong, early in the fourth century, to present the emperor Constantine with great practical difficulties in constructing his majestic church on a hilly and inconvenient site from which, moreover, at the risk of causing considerable offence, he had to remove a number of existing tombs. But the excavations which have in recent years been carried out beneath this venerated spot have failed to discover any obvious tomb of St Peter, still less his body lying in a large coffin of solid bronze to which reference is made in the earliest official biography of the Roman bishops.[60] What has been found, at the central point now marked by Bernini's great canopy, could be described as a shrine, but it is one which leaves many questions unanswered. Set amidst a cluster of tombs, one or two certainly pagan, others possibly Christian, runs the so-called Red Wall, which can be dated with very fair assurance to the period 160–70 AD. Built into this wall, and contemporary with it, are the remains of a structure consisting of three niches, one on top of the other and resembling, in general architectural style, the inscribed monuments which were sometimes added to the front of grandiose tombs. In this case the two upper sections, slightly over two metres in height, seem to have looked like a diminutive altar, with a marble slab, supported on two small detached columns, separating the niches. The columns, in their turn, rested on another slab of marble, below which is a rectangular recess which may be seen as the third niche, usually held to be later than the rest of the structure, and cut into the Red Wall when this had already been built. The recess when discovered contained nothing but rubble; but nearby, under and at the back of the Red Wall, human bones were found—no very surprising discovery to make in a cemetery area. The suggestion has been put forward, reasonably but not with complete assurance, that this niched structure is the 'trophy' of Peter on the Vatican Hill mentioned by the presbyter Gaius.[61]

The little shrine which Constantine made the focal point of his basilica may or may not have been Peter's 'trophy'. That it was regarded, at least by the end of the third century, as a place of pilgrimage is witnessed by the large number of graffiti scratched on the walls nearby. These inscriptions are, however, simple prayers on behalf of relatives—'Nicasius, mayest thou live in Christ', and so forth—without any reference to Peter, except one short appeal, written in Greek, which alludes to a Peter who is by no means certainly the apostle.[62] This is in marked contrast to the numerous invocations of both Peter and Paul found in the Catacomb of Sebastian: 'Peter and Paul, remember us', 'Paul and Peter, pray for Victor' (fig. 23) and many more of similar type. That the apostles were here called upon for aid in a shrine frequented by simple pilgrims has led to the fanciful theory that the bodies of Peter and Paul were moved to a crypt in San Sebastiano during a persecution carried out by the emperor Valerian in 258 AD and subsequently returned, in the time of Constantine, to their proper resting-places on the Vatican and on the Ostian Way. It may indeed be noted that the Calendar of Filocalus

(354 AD)[63] records festivals of Peter on the Vatican, Paul on the Ostian Way and both 'in the catacombs', that is, in the Catacomb of Sebastian. Of this particular cemetery Pope Damasus I stated, in an inscription now known only from medieval copies: 'Anyone who is enquiring about the history of Peter and of Paul likewise must understand that the saints dwelt here once upon a time.' By 'dwelt' Damasus meant 'were buried', but this evidence comes from the latter part of the fourth century, and a crabbed reference in the Filocalian Calendar to events in 'the consulship of Tuscus and Bassus' (258 AD) is far from clear. It may mean only that, in the distressful times of Valerian, celebrations in honour of Peter and Paul were initiated and the aid of the apostles invoked.

The evidence of archaeology concerning St Peter may therefore be summed up concisely, though in a manner which leaves much detail uncertain. Peter was honoured, together with St Paul, in the Catacomb of Sebastian, and it appears that some may have supposed that this was his place of burial. On the other hand, his name is closely connected with the Vatican, where a monument to him was pointed out as early as 200 AD. The precise nature of this 'trophy' can hardly be determined, but it may very plausibly be identified with the niched structure, now rather fragmentary, which Constantine made the focal point of his great church and which remains so today. Of Peter's grave, as such, no trace remains, nor did Constantine leave any record to say whether he interpreted the shrine as marking the site of Peter's tomb. Nevertheless, as in Palestine, so in Rome the emperor clearly went out of his way to mark by a building of much splendour one of the sites hallowed by local tradition.

NOTES

1. Especially the Lex Julia municipalis of 44 BC.
2. *The Augustan History*, ed. D. Magie (Loeb), ii.49.6. Severus was emperor 222–35 AD.
3. Several other paintings of a fossor have been discovered recently. See *Studi* 33 (1979).
4. *Childe Harold* iv.107.
5. *Annals* xiii.32.
6. Dio Cassius, *Roman History* 67.14 (Loeb), viii.
7. Josephus, *Jewish War* 7.5 (Loeb), iii.
8. Exodus 25.31.
9. Revelation 7.9.
10. Tertullian, *On the Soul* 51, PL 2.758. *Martyrdom of St Cyprian*, ed. E. C. E. Owen (Oxford, 1927).
11. Ch. 18. *The Apostolic Fathers*, (Loeb), ii.
12. The date is 299 AD. Diehl, *Inscriptiones latinae christianae*, 1570.
13. *Peristephanon* xi.161, PL 60.
14. *Commentary on Ezekiel* 60. Jerome was writing in the latter part of the fourth century, but his description would apply as well to the earlier period.
15. *Ecclesiastical History* 5.21 (Loeb), i.
16. Especially by de Rossi and Wilpert, whose conclusions

were much modified by P. Styger (1937) and later, at least as regards St Callistus, by L. Reekmans (1964). Styger is by no means superseded, but more recent work, by F. Tolotti and others, is noted and discussed in *ACIAC* IX (1975).

17. See *Liber Pontificalis*, ed. L. Duchesne (*note 60*); Hippolytus, *Refutation of all Heresies* ii.12 (ed. P. Wendland) in *GCS* 26 (1916); Hippolytus, *Apostolic Tradition* 40, *PG* 10, critical edition by G. Dix (1937).
18. F. Tolotti, *Il cimitero di Priscilla* (Rome, 1970).
19. Tolotti in *ACIAC* IX, 160–87.
20. Now at the Museo delle Terme, Rome.
21. Numbers 24.17.
22. Cf. St Mark 8.1–21.
23. The 'Inscription of Pectorius', in Autun Museum. For this and other passages see M. Vloberg, *L'Eucharistie dans l'Art* (Paris, 1946).
24. Paulinus of Nola, *Epistle* 13, *PL* 61. This, however, is a later expression of the idea.
25. St Luke 15.4.
26. St John 10.11.
27. *De Pudicitia* 10, *PL* 2.1000.
28. Clement of Alexandria, *Protrepticus* i.44, *PG* 8.56.
29. 24.17.
30. St John 15.1.
31. *Ibid.* 1.29.
32. Revelation 14.1.
33. *Martyrdom of Polycarp* 16, in *The Apostolic Fathers* (Loeb), ii.
34. *First Epistle of Clement* 25, in *The Apostolic Fathers* (Loeb), i.
35. As Lactantius expresses it in his poem 'Phoenix', *PL* 7.280.
36. The vase is characteristic of a period rather later than the catacomb paintings, but occurs on a stone of the third century found in the Cemetery of Praetextatus.
37. St Mark 8.8.
38. Martial x.48.6.
39. *Tractate 123 on St John's Gospel*, *PL* 35.1966.
40. I Corinthians 10.16: 'the cup of blessing which we bless'.
41. Ignatius, *Letter to the Ephesians* 20.2, in *The Apostolic Fathers* (Loeb), i.
42. This painting is late, as compared with many of the Roman examples, probably fourth century, retouched in the sixth.
43. I Clement 45, in *The Apostolic Fathers* (Loeb), i.
44. Exodus 17.
45. In the Catacomb of Praetextatus the story of Susanna is given in symbolic fashion. A lamb, with the name 'Susanna' over its head, stands between two wolves designated as '*Seniores*', 'the Elders'.
46. *Apostolic Constitutions* v.7, *PG* 1.844.
47. Diehl, *Inscriptiones latinae christianae* i.2251.
48. *Faustina dulcis, vivas in Deo*, Diehl, i.2196 A.
49. *In pace Domini dormias*, Diehl, i.2288.
50. *Vos precor o fratres orare huc quando venitis*
    Et precibus totis Patrem Natumque rogatis,
    Sit vestrae mentis Agapes carae meminisse,
    Ut Deus omnipotens Agapen in saecula servet. Diehl, i.2392.
51. *Attice dormi in pace de tua incolumitate securus et pro nostris peccatis pete sollicitus. Inscriptiones christianae urbis Romae* i.1283.
52. *Fortunatus se vivo sibi fecit ut cum quieverit in pacem in locum paratum ha(beat).* (*ICUR* iii.8910.)
53. *ICUR* i.1282. The follis is a bronze coin, but of variable value. In the middle of the fourth century, a pound of pork could be bought for six *folles*.
54. I Clement 5, *The Apostolic Fathers* (Loeb), i.
55. Eusebius, *Ecclesiastical History* 2.25 (Loeb), i.182.
56. Tacitus, *Annals* xv.44.
57. Eusebius, op. cit. 2.25.
58. St John 4.14.
59. Some commentators, e.g. W. Oakeshott, *The Mosaics of Rome* (London, 1967), 51, describe Christ as 'heavily bearded', and thus with a countenance unlike that of Helios. But the beard, though suggested by some of the photographs, cannot be clearly deduced from the mosaic itself.
60. *Liber Pontificalis* i.23, ed. L. Duchesne, second edition (Paris, 1952). This is in the main a sixth-century compilation but based on chronologies written two or three hundred years earlier.
61. Eusebius, *Ecclesiastical History* 2.25. 'Trophy', in the language of the early Church, usually means a 'sign of victory', in particular the Cross, or the memorial of some victorious action, such as a 'house of prayer' which takes its name from the Resurrection.
62. The form is variously recorded; it seems to read 'Peter, in peace'.
63. As amended in the *Martyrology of Jerome, PL* 30. The best observations on Filocalus occur in H. Stern, *Le Calendrier de 354* (Institut français d'archéologie de Beyrouth, 1953). For the Damasus inscription see Toynbee and Ward-Perkins, *The Shrine of St Peter* (London, 1956), 168 (note 45).

4

The Catacombs II

CATACOMB PAINTINGS: ADVANCES IN STYLE AND SUBJECT

The painting of Christian catacombs persisted throughout the vigorous military dictatorship of Diocletian and the surprising reversal of fortune whereby the Church, under Constantine's patronage, became the chief religious and cultural force in the Empire. For another century or more, thereafter, the painter's art continued in the service of the Church, yielding only gradually to the rich splendour of mosaic. As in the earlier period, the principal examples of Christian paintings occur in Rome, in catacombs which, however, were coming to be somewhat less highly regarded. In general, the style in which the paintings were executed followed contemporary fashion, though certain contrasts exist between the work of artists who favoured careful, realistic technique and those who preferred an impressionistic, more 'primitive', approach which suggests rather than portrays. These two tendencies, between which most visual arts oscillate perpetually, jostle together in the paintings of the Roman Empire.

It is customary to detect, at the end of the third century, a coarsening of taste linked with Diocletian's dependence on the support of a 'brutal and licentious soldiery' and his transfer of the capital from Rome eastwards to Nicomedia. A squat and expressionless manner of representing human beings is thought to give place, in the time of Constantine and his successors, to more exact and refined techniques, to a sensitive and softened version of the Hellenistic baroque. But, where Christian art is concerned, such stylistic evolution cannot be traced very precisely. Much depends on the abilities of individual artists, which vary from the roughest sketches to delicate portraiture with a timeless air. Nor is the question made any easier by the fact that few of the paintings can be dated with absolute assurance. Yet it is not difficult to discern the changing spirit of the time in its artistic productions. There is first of all the feeling that the crabbed, shorthand symbolism beloved of the earliest churchmen has been outgrown and that the characters depicted should be real people rather than abstractions. Thus the figures in the Chapel of the Five Saints in S. Callisto, dating from about 320 AD, are shown not just as representative intercessors but as Italian women, lively yet devout, with dark curly hair and finely marked features. When painting their portraits, the artist recognized the value of contrasting highlight and softer flesh colour, and set his *Orans* under a graceful canopy of bluish leaves and russet flowers. Beauty of colour and form, even a certain splendour of costume, are thought to further what Origen called 'the comeliness of spiritual understanding'. Such tendencies may, however, be carried a little too far in the direction of magnificence: in the Catacomb of Thraso, about 340 AD, one woman combines a gaze of rapt devotion with somewhat imperious lines about the nose and mouth as well as a highly ornate robe and much jewellery.

As the art of Christian painting developed, influenced by and apparently in turn influencing con-

24. Rome, Catacomb of Domitilla. Wall-painting: Veneranda ushered into Paradise.

temporary pagan style, signs of a greater opulence appear, together with emphasis on authoritative power and majesty. Nor is this surprising as the reflection of an age when Constantine and his successors held a vast and diverse empire together by means of an efficient bureaucratic system allied to a mysterious sense of the emperor's superhuman dignity and power, and when fourth-century bishops eagerly set themselves up as ecclesiastical counterparts of the provincial governors. Nevertheless most of the old themes of Christian art continue in the new order of the Church triumphant. They are augmented, however, by two new elements: one an increased respect paid to the virtues and influence of the saints, the other a widening of the range of subjects depicted and a keen interest in the historical details of the Biblical record. Emblems of a distinctly pagan character continue to appear beside Christian symbols, sometimes to an extent which makes it hard to decide whether the burial-place has been prepared for Christians, for adherents of another cult, or for persons of varied faith.

The classic example of a developed doctrine of the saints as effective helpers is provided by one of the chapels of the Domitilla Catacomb. A small panel in this *arcosolium* shows two full-length female figures standing side by side. The one on the left wears a red and yellow garment reaching to the ground; her hair, touched with the highlight of the picture, is drawn up under a veil and she faces the spectator with eyes downcast in contemplation (fig. 24). This, as the lettering indicates, is Veneranda, the dead woman. Her companion, described as 'Petronilla the martyr', looks toward her with gestures that express a kindly solicitude. For St Petronilla—'Peter's little daughter', as tradition had it—is conducting Veneranda safely into Paradise. It must, however, be added that the idea of the soul of the departed as ushered into Paradise by a friendly guide of higher spiritual stature is found as frequently in pagan as in Christian wall-painting of the early fourth century, as the tomb of a certain Vibia[1] clearly demonstrates. Here the scene, painted in red-brown and blue on a pale background, is supplied with short inscriptions which remove any possible ground for misinterpretation. Vibia enters through an archway, her whole demeanour expressing timidity and wonder. The Good Angel (so labelled) clasps her hand reassuringly and draws her towards a banquet-

25. Rome, Catacomb of Commodilla. Wall-painting: Christ as Ruler of the Universe.

ing-couch where guests recline, raising their right hands in greeting to Vibia as she comes forward to join them. The whole composition closely resembles some earlier pictures of a Christian *agape* held in the world beyond, for the various faiths drew readily enough from a common stock of images and the craftsmen employed were ready to put their techniques at the disposal of patrons of any creed.

Preoccupation with the authority of the emperor naturally led to emphasis on the majesty of Christ. No longer the youthful hero of David's line, he sits, bearded and dignified, in austere contemplation. This, at least, is how he is shown in the Catacomb of Marcellinus and Peter, his red robe contrasting with the white apparel of Peter and Paul. Below, the saints—Gorgonius, Marcellinus, Tibertius and another Peter—raise their hands in adoration of the Lamb, whose destiny of innocent, sacrificial death is the reverse of the grandeur depicted above. This impressive painting, with its lively sense of religious truth, is thus arranged, after the fashion of certain sarcophagi of the period, in two tiers, the one being an explanatory comment on the other.

The idea of Christ as Ruler of the Universe finds clear expression in the Catacomb of Commodilla where, within a frame coloured red and brown, the Master's head and shoulders are set in a manner expressing authority, almost the remote authority of unyielding cause and effect which marks the medieval pictures of Doomsday (fig. 25). Christ's brown hair falls in ordered waves to meet his long beard as he gazes into eternity with eyes firm-set under the splodgy curves which represent his brow. A halo surrounds his head and, to press home the lesson, the letters alpha and omega, placed at each side, declare him to be the Beginning and End of Creation. And since Christ's authority is mediated through the Church, 'One, Holy and Catholic', to show him seated among a council of apostles is to proclaim him at his most majestic and, incidentally, to emphasize the value of orthodox faith as opposed to heretical speculations. A fourth-century painting in the Catacomb of the Jordani, for instance, shows Christ as the central figure between two groups of six men rhythmically balanced in a double row, all wearing white togas with black shoulder-stripes but each displaying individuality of pose and expression. Here, however, Christ is still the youthful hero-figure among companions in a high enterprise, and that is also how he appears in a semicircular lunette of the Domitilla Catacomb: a striking, prophetic figure enthroned in the midst of nine roughly painted and wooden-looking apostles.

By the middle of the fourth century the medieval pattern is relatively well established—Christ is the source of life and power, which operates within the context of the Church and is especially manifested by the victories and influence of the saints. Something of this spirit seems to appear in a series of small-scale pictures, painted on plaster covering a background of brick, that may be seen in a shrine beneath the church of St John and St Paul in Rome. The various scenes are neatly arranged in panels enclosed by red lines. Placed centrally and within half-raised curtains denoting the close interplay between this world and the hereafter stands the *Orans*, clothed in a white robe with two vertical stripes of black ending in a bold leaf-pattern on each shoulder. The lines of his face suggest dignified contemplation rather than entreaty, and two persons crouching at his feet are an additional reason for supposing that this *Orans* is a saint rather than a suppliant. The upper panel on the left contains five figures, all women, the central one being clearly the leader of the group and regarded with respectful awe by the others; meanwhile a stag drinks at the waters of life. The lower panel is much damaged, but enough remains to show a woman bearing a vase. On the right side three martyrs, with hands tied behind their backs, are about to be executed while, below, a female figure stretches out her hand in greeting to another who stands doubtful and irresolute. While not all the details are clear, the paintings of this diminutive shrine seem clearly designed as a homily on the virtues and spiritual power of the saints.

Other steps made in the fourth century towards the viewpoint of medieval art include a lively interest in the Labours of the Farmer's Year,[2] so that reapers and olive-pickers appear together with the more obviously symbolic shepherds. Pictures of the professional grave-diggers continue, but they are joined by other bands of craftsmen, quite in the manner of the guilds shown in the thirteenth-century glass of Bourges, including bakers and the coopers who, in the Catacomb of Priscilla, stand in a huddled group confronting two enormous casks. Even more striking is the extension of subjects represented. Here again, the Scriptural scenes of deliverance—Daniel among the lions or Lazarus raised from the tomb—remain a frequent choice, but to them is added a considerable number of incidents drawn mostly from the Old Testament: Noah drunken, Absalom hanging from the oak tree, Elijah in his fiery chariot, Job seated on the dung-heap and so forth. It may be that some of these representations owe their form to Jewish originals, but the doctrine was inherent in the Church from very early times that Old Testament happenings, apart from their own particular interest, hint at and prefigure New Testament fulfilments. As early as the third century, philosophers of the Platonist school complained that their Christian counterparts 'boast that things said plainly by Moses are riddles and treat them as divine oracles full of hidden mysteries',[3] while St Augustine laid it down as a principle for the interpretation of Scripture that 'In the Old Testament the New lies hid; in the New Testament the Old becomes clear.'[4]

Some of these Old Testament stories make their first appearance as subjects of Christian art in tombs which can hardly be thought to represent orthodox faith but rather indicate a wide variety of bizarre speculations for which the vague term 'Gnostic' may conveniently be used. For two opposing tendencies were at work during the fourth century. There was on the one hand a desire, shown by Christian philosophers and ecclesiastical statesmen alike, for precise definitions of dogma which might be upheld and made obligatory as the standard of religious truth. But there was also, within the wide embrace of the Roman Empire, a multitude of cults; some of these could be said to exist on the fringe of Christianity, others were pagan but willing to accept many of the stories and symbols of the Christian tradition.

A tomb which invites comparison with Christian examples is that of Trebius Justus, a young man who died at the age of twenty-one. Trebius is depicted twice; the bolder of the two portraits shows him standing on a stool between his father and mother, who spread before him a richly ornamented cloth on which are laid plates and a wine-cup, suggesting the festival to be enjoyed in Paradise. Most of the descriptive painting nearby is drawn not from literature but from the everyday life of home and farm, with reapers, bricklayers and other workers going about their business in a grave and dignified manner. Though the boy and his parents have about them a solemn and watch-ful air, the rest of the decoration recalls the keen practical Roman interest in agriculture and building and in the careful guardianship of possessions rather than spiritual yearnings. There is nothing distinctively Christian in the tomb of Trebius Justus, but it is more difficult to interpret those tombs where straight-forward Biblical pictures mingle with scenes drawn from a classical mythology which the Fathers of the Church were at pains to discredit. It may be that such burial-places were prepared for members of heretical or sub-Christian sects, though a casual and wide-ranging choice of subjects is sometimes found in apparently orthodox surroundings.

Concerning the half-dozen catacombs which display a complete mingling of Christian and pagan themes, it is difficult to know whether the work reflects the patronage of Christians admitting stock types which the artists had forced upon them from the classical repertory, or of pagans who were attracted to Christian art-forms because they provided an agreeable supplement, with a certain spiritual vitality, to the standard scenes of Roman mythology. Comparison is sometimes made with the emperor Severus Alexander (222–35 AD), who 'set up in his private chapel a statue of Christ along with those of Abraham, Orpheus, the philosopher Apollonius and his own deified ancestors'. But this report[5] is now recognized as a fourth-century hoax.

The Catacomb of the Aurelii, on the Via Labicana, provides an example of mixed religious ideas. Some of the paintings, from the end of the third century, display the conventional Christian scenes; within one small panel, a human figure, now nearly obliterated, raises his hand to point to a cross. Elsewhere within the catacomb a bearded man, seated and wearing tunic and pallium, clasps the open scroll of philosophic knowledge while, below, rams wander in a pastoral landscape. This might be a unique variant on the theme of Christ, the Lord of truth, guarding his flock. But it could equally well represent a philosopher of quite different type. The same doubt exists in the case of another splendidly painted head of a bearded man whose eyes are fixed, in rapt contemplation, on wonders invisible to the spectator. Whether he is a Christian apostle or some thinker trained in the discipline of the Muses remains undecided, but the decoration of the vestibule in this catacomb is of clearly non-Christian character. Within a graceful pattern of late

Pompeian style four solitary figures, each standing on a pedestal, clasp the scroll and the wand which seem to be the marks of one qualified to teach rites and mysteries. This interpretation is confirmed by the large central medallion, which shows two grave philosophers, in tunic and pallium, standing at either side of a less clearly drawn figure over whose head one of the philosophers raises a long wand; the whole scene suggests a solemn initiation into secret arts.

The combination of pagan and Christian themes is found at its most striking in the attractive little burial-place lately re-discovered on the Latin Way and usually known as the Catacomb of the Via Dino Compagni. This has none of the higgledy-piggledy character shown by many catacombs. The three shafts of which it is composed have the look, on plan, of an engineer's drawing, while much less space is taken up with galleries than with a well co-ordinated series of chapels. Both the elaborate nature of these tomb-chambers and the quality of the painting indicate wealthy patrons, and emphasize the change which had come over Christian art by the middle of the fourth century. This change shows itself here in three ways. First, there is a wide variety of styles, corresponding to the ability and background of at least four groups of artists. Secondly, a richness and amplitude about the whole place mark the establishment of the Christian faith in sophisticated circles, so that burial-vaults beneath the ground are built with elaborate cornices and all the architectural features which characterize the best type of mausoleum above ground. Thirdly, the conventional scenes drawn from the Old and New Testaments are handled with freedom and many new subjects are introduced; about a dozen appear here for the first time in the development of Christian art.

Most of the figures in the Biblical scenes are drawn with a marked economy of action and facial expression. Balaam, mounted on his ass, and the angel, looking like the typical philosopher, who bars his way with a dagger raised in the air, do not gaze at each other but are shown full face, confronting the spectator with round, dilated eyes. The disciples listening to the Sermon on the Mount are shown rather more realistically in that, although their rounded heads and garments falling in vertical folds present a common pattern, they look intently towards the figure of Christ who, raised on the rock above them, dominates the scene.

The Samaritan woman at the well, though painted in a style resembling that of the Balaam episode, is more lively. The youthful Christ stands in an attitude of elegant mastery while the woman is so impressed that she ceases to draw her pitcher from the well and gazes at Christ in amazement from under her strongly-marked brows and neatly-dressed mop of black hair.

The lunette which shows Samson routing the Philistines with the jawbone of an ass is a still more vigorous composition (fig. 26). Here Samson stands in front of a house or shrine which occupies a third of the picture though it has no place in the story as given by the Book of Judges. He raises the jawbone in an attitude of poised, philosophic triumph while the Philistines flee in a rhythmically moving mass, their faces expressing with much individuality the emotions of fear and dismay.

Two crowd scenes, resembling one another in that they are similarly arranged over two panels set at right angles, present a contrast in method. The raising of Lazarus, no longer a matter restricted to Christ, the sister of Lazarus and one or two friends, has developed into a theme of world-wide application. Christ, shown as a young man barely distinguishable, except in size, from his companions, extends his rod towards the gabled tomb in which, however, Lazarus is not to be seen. Behind Christ is ranged a multitude of men, close-packed and attentive. They narrowly resemble each other in clothing and posture; emotion is concentrated in their faces which, furrowed with dark, emphatic lines, show enough variety of movement to avoid the woodenness which might easily have marred so compact and stylized a company. But the other crowd scene, the crossing of the Red Sea, displays a more developed artistry. The little band of Israelites, painted in that pinkish purple which is the dominant colour in the picture, huddles to one side while the waters over which Moses stretches his magic wand form a central zone of unencumbered space before the jumbled but intensely dramatic onrush of the Egyptian cavalry with their blue helmets and long faces expressing horror at their impending doom.

A clearly differentiated group of paintings includes such Old Testament themes as Jacob's dream and Abraham entertaining the three angels by the oaks of Mamre. Here the prevailing colour tends to be yellowish brown against a green background. The eyes,

26. Rome, Catacomb of the Via Dino Compagni. Wall-painting: Samson and the Philistines.

noses and mouths of the figures are robustly marked by thick lines of paint, while the rest of the face receives no emphasis; the hair falls, in a characteristic manner, amply and in a curving sweep from the crown of the head to the neck. The Mamre picture is notable for an elementary attempt to render perspective which causes the seated figure of Abraham to lean backwards and the three angels, wingless like those on Jacob's ladder, to incline forwards from what appears to be higher ground.

The Via Latina burial-place thus presents paintings of a quality unknown anywhere else in the catacombs for skilful technique, variety of subject and a richness of decoration which now and again comes near the sophisticated exuberance of baroque. The occurrence of the pagan themes confers an added interest. The winged genii are no more out of place than when they appear on a Christopher Wren screen, but the goddess Tellus (Earth), reclining on the ground amidst her flowers, with hand raised and a halo round her head, occupies the whole of the lunette above one of the tombs, which must be pagan, even though the peacocks above, birds of immortality drinking from the cup which holds the water of life, are found in

Christian art also.[6]

Another example of a mingling of pagan with Christian themes in the Via Latina burial-place is found in the chambers attached to the octagonal Room I. In one of the recesses Christ is shown, august and bearded, enthroned in majesty between Peter and Paul, who hold their scroll of apostolic authority. Nearby another niche contains a remarkable picture, of well-ordered and realistic classical style, which shows eleven men wearing the philosopher's customary garb and seated together in a row (fig. 27). One member of this group stretches out his long wand to touch a small, naked figure lying on the ground in front of them all. This has been interpreted as depicting Aristotle's achievement in withdrawing the soul from a boy's body and then restoring it with the help of a wand. If this explanation is correct, the pagan philosopher would in some measure correspond to the enthroned Christ in a mixed faith which takes something from both worlds. But the leader of this group sits in the centre; he is appreciably larger than the rest and he alone wears his pallium thrown back from the right shoulder in the manner of a Cynic philosopher but also typical of Christ as he is represented on some

27. Rome, Catacomb of the Via Dino Compagni. Wall-painting: the philosophers and the dead boy.

of the earliest sarcophagi.[7] The man with the wand is one of the disciples rather than the master, and the identification with Aristotle must therefore remain extremely doubtful.

Nothing, however, could be plainer than the events taken from the life of Hercules which are the sole theme of the paintings in the two niches of Room N. Hercules was the divine hero whose exploits were most particularly concerned with the conquest of Death. One of the most admired of his twelve Labours was the rescue of Alcestis, who had generously offered to die in place of her husband Admetus. Forcing his way past the monstrous dog Cerberus, who guarded the entrance to the lower world, Hercules raided Hell and brought Alcestis safely back to Admetus, a scene which the artist appropriately chose to illustrate in the catacomb. Nor is this surprising. For, although the emperor Constantius ordered the closing of all pagan temples in the year 356, he was so overawed by the majesty of Rome when he visited it that he did little to enforce the principles which he had proclaimed[8] and when, a little while later, Julian vainly attempted to substitute a revived paganism for Christianity, Hercules was put forward for imitation

as a model of courage and wisdom. Thus people of conservative and patriotic temper, even if members of predominantly Christian families, might well choose to retain Hercules, an emblem of Rome's greatness as well as of immortality, beside the colourful incidents of the Bible story.

By the latter part of the fourth century interest in the catacombs was yielding to concern for churches above ground, though a few paintings of high quality exist here and there which reflect changes of taste observable in the mosaics and ivories. The Crypt of the Lambs in the Cemetery of Callistus presents a remarkable variation on the Moses story (fig. 28). This painting, which dates from about 380, shows Moses in two scenes. On the left he is removing his shoes in obedience to the command given from the midst of the burning bush; here he appears as a young man with long face and rounded head. But just alongside occurs another figure of Moses, striking the rock and drawing from it a copious stream of water towards which a soldier hastens with flying cloak. In this second portrait he is shown bearded and with a mass of long, curly hair. The highlight on his nose is emphasized by the dark vertical line at each side and his eyes, brilliant

28. Rome, Cemetery of Callistus. Wall-painting: Moses.

but deep-set, express awe and foreboding at a miracle which he feels obliged to perform but at the cost of incurring God's anger.

The chapel constructed in the Catacomb of Commodilla to the honour of the martyrs shows the final stage alike of thought and style. Eyes are no longer round but almond-shaped, faces are elongated and thin, hair is so tightly drawn down over the head as to look almost like a helmet and haloes[9] are a regular embellishment of all saintly persons. Realistic portraiture entirely disappears and the solemn, timeless atmosphere of Byzantine art prevails. One notable example of this transition is the painting which commemorates a certain Turtura (fig. 29). This woman is being presented by two saints, Felix and Adauctus, to the Virgin and Child, but the mood is one of abstract dignity. The martyrs, one young, the other old, stand at either side of the Virgin's richly jewelled throne and, like all the figures, look straight ahead. Both are motionless except that Felix places one hand on Turtura's shoulder while Adauctus raises his hand in passionless assent. The Virgin, in her long, purple robe, has become an empress, calm and unmoved save for the protective gesture of her right hand with

which she holds the Child seated in priestly costume on her lap. The art of the catacombs has advanced a very long way, in three or four centuries, from the primitive sketches of shepherd, anchor or fish.

Motives of ease and economy gradually caused catacombs to become unpopular for burials except near the shrines of martyrs, and, in the commotion caused by the onslaught of Goths, Vandals and finally Lombards, it was judged expedient to transfer the bones of martyrs to churches above ground, a move which led to complete oblivion and neglect for the subterranean tombs. But before these events, about the year 370, the zealous and turbulent Pope Damasus had, with his habitual energy, carried out many works of restoration and improvement to those burial-places where the martyrs rested. He widened passages, constructed new staircases and inserted light-shafts to make access and devotion easier for pilgrims, as well as beautifying certain sanctuaries with marble. But his greatest achievement was to compose a set of versified inscriptions in honour of the martyrs and to employ a craftsman of the highest skill, Furius Dionysius Filocalus, to carve these inscriptions on marble slabs. The lettering, subsequently copied by such artists as Eric

29. Rome, Catacomb of Commodilla. Wall-painting: Virgin and Child with Turtura.

Gill, is of exceptional grace and clarity, which is more than can be said of Damasus' poetry itself. The pope showed much perseverance in tracing the stories of the martyrs' lives, even if he sometimes allowed his enthusiasm to outrun his critical judgement, but he was inclined to summarize his researches in language so vague and verbose as to obscure his meaning.

Pilgrims to the shrines diligently copied Damasus' pedantic hexameters and thus it is often possible to complete fragmentary remains of the originals. One set of verses, found on the Vatican, runs thus:

The waters surrounded the hill and in their slow wandering soaked the bodies, the ashes and bones, of many. Damasus could not allow that those who had been buried, in the destiny that falls to all, should in their repose be obliged to suffer a second time so sad a fate. Straightway he set about undertaking a heavy task: he threw down the towering peaks of the vast hillside and examined with anxious care the inmost entrails of the earth. He dried all that the water had drenched and discovered the fountain which offers the grace of salvation.[10]

A rather less fulsome instance of the same style of composition is provided by an inscription derived, with the help of a later copy, from fragments found in the Crypt of Hippolytus on the Tiburtine Way:

It is said that, although the tyrant's commands were oppressing us, the priest Hippolytus continued in the schism of Novatus. But at the time when the sword rent the very heart of our Mother the Church, then in his devotion to Christ he sought the kingdom of the just and when the people asked which way to turn he bade them all follow the catholic faith. Having thus borne witness to the truth he deserves to be called our martyr. It is Damasus who records this tradition but Christ who brings all to the test.[11]

The Spanish hymn-writer Prudentius speaks of this particular crypt in words which would serve to describe many catacombs and the emotions of those who descended into them:

Not far from the city rampart, in the open farmland, the mouth of the crypt gives entry to its murky pits. Into its secret recesses a steep path with curving stairs guides the way, while its winding course bars out the light. The brightness of day comes in, however, through the opening at the top and illumines the threshold of the entrance-hall. Then as, by gradual advance, you feel that the darkness of night is closing in everywhere through the mazes of the cavern, there occur openings pierced through the roof which cast bright rays about the cave. Although the passages cut at random weave a pattern of narrow chambers and murky galleries, yet, where the rock has been cut away and a vault hollowed out and pierced through, light makes its way in abundantly. To such secret recesses the body of Hippolytus is entrusted hard by the place where an altar is dedicated to God and set up. The same altar-table bestows the sacrament and faithfully guards the martyr's bones. Now the shrine which encloses the relics of that brave soul gleams with solid silver. Wealthy hands have set in place a smooth surface of glistening panels, bright as a mirror and, not content to overlay the entrances with Parian marble, have added lavish gifts for adorning the whole place.[12]

CATACOMBS OUTSIDE ROME

Burial-vaults and underground chapels occur at a number of places other than Rome, those at Naples, Syracuse and Malta being especially notable. The catacombs of Naples and Syracuse resemble each other and to some extent depart from the Roman pattern because of the nature of the ground in which they are constructed. The soil is a great deal firmer and more compact than the Roman *pozzolana*, so that it was possible to design boldly and to avoid the excessive intricacy of many Roman catacombs. The general plan was then to drive a wide corridor straight ahead and provide it with *arcosolia*, the arched tomb-recesses occupied by the wealthier citizens. Across this principal corridor small galleries were cut and then lined, more often than not, with simple *loculi* just large enough to hold corpse or coffin.

Of the half-dozen catacombs at Naples, that of St Januarius is the most extensive and the best preserved. It remained in use until the tenth century and was enlarged at various times, but consists essentially of two catacombs, independent and set at different levels, but of similar form. The first of these is approached by way of a large entrance hall, converted into a baptistery about the year 760. To the right is an oratory, containing an altar hewn from the rock; this altar has a shallow niche, designed as the bishop's seat, hollowed out behind it and a recess large enough to hold an ample supply of relics. Fragments of marble decoration and of a protecting screen have come to light and there is no reason to doubt the tradition that this is the oratory of St Januarius,[13] even though it seems to have been constructed, perhaps in the fifth century, by amalgamating three earlier burial-chambers. On the left of the entrance hall there still exists a comparable arrangement of burial-chambers, while the back wall of the vestibule is pierced by three large corridors, the middle one being somewhat broader and higher than the other two. This central corridor is the spine of the catacomb, providing space for a large number of graves, as does the subsidiary passage running parallel with it on the right. The left corridor is blocked by the stairway leading to the second catacomb. Here again there is a vestibule, which in this case is no more than a very large burial-chamber, equipped on each side with *arcosolia* ranged in two rows. Robust columns of tufa divide the back of the vestibule to provide the entrance, up several steps, into the principal gallery, which is flanked by two more *cubicula*.

At Naples as in the Roman catacombs a certain amount of the decoration remains but varies considerably in date. In one of the side rooms leading off the vestibule of the first catacomb, a painted ceiling displays a geometric pattern embellished with birds, animals and flowers but having no specifically Christian emblems. The ceiling of the vestibule itself is similar in general pattern, with a preference for rectangles outlined in red. A winged Victory occupies the central position; around her are dancing cherubs, antelopes and seahorses as well as masks, grapes and bowls of flowers. But Scriptural scenes also find their place in this composition, presented as panels set within a semicircular garland at each of the four sides. One of these panels has been broken away; in another, the identification of David casting a stone at Goliath is by no means certain; but in a third picture Adam and Eve stand beside the apple tree, and a fourth scene, unique in the history of Christian art, shows three women wearing blue tunics and engaged in building a tower. This apparently refers to a passage in the second-century apocalypse known as the *Shepherd of Hermas* where a company of maidens carry stones with which to build up the Tower of the Church.[14] Evidently at Naples the *Shepherd* won, at least for a time, its struggle to be received among the canonical books of the New Testament. Elsewhere within the

Naples catacombs the stock figures of Noah, Moses, Jonah and Daniel occur, as well as a group of portrait busts different in type from anything found in the catacombs of Rome. 'Here rests Proculus' is the inscription round the bust of a young man wearing a red mantle over a yellow tunic and shown as an *Orans* with a lighted candle at each side of his outstretched arms. Another circular medallion shows a man and wife with four children crowded together between them. These paintings are, however, not earlier than the fifth century, to which period also belong two realistic and well differentiated portraits of the apostles Peter and Paul. Both are set within rectangular frames on a background decorated with large chi-rho emblems: Peter, with his hair in a fringe, looks austerely downwards, while Paul, nearly bald, stares straight ahead in wide-eyed contemplation.

The largest of the numerous catacombs at Syracuse[15] is that of S. Giovanni, constructed in the fourth century according to what was, anyhow at first, a carefully conceived plan. A principal gallery, almost a main road, 90 metres long and about 3 metres wide, was driven in an east–west direction and crossed by half a dozen passages of fair size, each with its complement of graves and leading to circular burial-chambers remarkable for enormous tombs hewn out of the rock. Special privileges are here awarded to sanctity as well as to social distinction. The saints have ampler space and more elaborate ornament assigned to their tombs, while an area near the centre of the catacomb seems to have been reserved for influential citizens just as certain ranges of *loculi* were restricted to the interment of children. Among the group of inscriptions found in S. Giovanni is a rare reference to the three persons of the Trinity: 'May God and Christ and the Holy Spirit remember you.'

Catacombs occur at a number of places along the North African coast. Those at Alexandria have the interest of showing that underground burial-places of the 'gridiron' type were being constructed during the period of the Ptolemies,[16] three or four centuries earlier than the typical Roman examples. But such Alexandrian catacombs as can be considered specifically Christian have been desecrated to such an extent that neither the details of their construction nor the eucharistic wall-paintings which formerly adorned them can now be readily appreciated.

Further westwards at Cyrene appear several groups

of burial-grottoes hollowed out of the cliffs. In one of the grottoes,[17] two stumpy columns with rudely carved Ionic capitals uphold a frieze worked with a pattern of floral and geometric motifs but including three crosses, one with a serpent entwined about it and thus suggesting the serpent of bronze which Moses lifted up in the wilderness.

There is, however, more to see at Hadrumetum (Sousse), 150 kilometres from Tunis. This area experienced a vigorous upsurge of Christianity in the latter part of the third century, and several catacombs were constructed by driving a shaft through the intensely hard but thin layer of travertine stone that lies just under the soil, to reach the friable tufa beneath. Through this tufa parallel passages could easily be cut with rows of *loculi* set in the walls. The usual custom was to place the body on a layer of moist plaster and cover it entirely with a plaster sheath, so that, when the tiles are removed from the mouth of a *loculus*, it is still possible to trace the form of the body modelled in its chalky covering. The Catacomb of the Good Shepherd and the Catacomb of Hermes, with its mosaics of fishing scenes, were adapted from earlier pagan uses, but the Catacomb of Severus appears to have been designed solely for Christian families. The chi-rho symbol is found several times in these catacombs, and an anchor, turned upside down, serves to suggest the cross. One epitaph deserves remembrance for its combination of hopeful assurance with the belief that the departed can influence for good the life of those members of their family left behind on earth:

Parthenope, you left Smyrna and came to Libya. Then you entrusted the end of your life to God. But, even now, remember your child and your father. For you are alive in God, enjoying everlasting glory.

The island of Malta is extremely rich in underground shrines and burial-places of varied type, dating from 2000 BC onwards. Most of the catacombs constructed or adapted in Christian times occur at Rabat. Of these, the Catacomb of St Paul is by far the largest. Here the principal staircase leads to a room which may have been a chapel and thence to another, larger hall, from which passages lead off in an ill-arranged manner to the tombs. *Loculi* are few and those mostly the graves of children, the greater number of burials having taken place in substantial table-tombs, flat-topped or saddle-backed, that are enclosed under canopies. As a variant of this type, some tombs were cut into the side walls, and then the square niche through which the body was inserted is preceded by an *arcosolium*. Occasionally, and notably in the case of three splendidly carved table-tombs at Salina, further north on the island, the burial-place is designed to receive two bodies lying side by side. In the main hall of St Paul's Catacomb, as also at Salina, a circular table is to be seen, carved from the rock and surrounded by a stone bench recessed at one point to give easy access to the table. The purpose of this table is presumably to allow for the celebration of an *agape*, or commemorative Eucharist, on behalf of the departed. But the Maltese catacombs are poorly equipped with symbols or decoration of early Christian character; with the exception of a few crosses, the present frescoes point to a comparatively recent re-painting.

NOTES

1. The Tomb of Vibia is on the Via Appia not far from the Catacomb of Callistus. Another elaborate painting shows Vibia standing before the judgement-throne on which sit Pluto and Persephone.
2. Early examples include Norman fonts like that at Burnham Deepdale, Norfolk.
3. Porphyry quoted in Eusebius, *Ecclesiastical History* 6, 19.
4. Commentary on Exodus 73, *PL* 34, 625.
5. *Historia Augusta*, 'Severus Alexander' 29 (Loeb), ii; R. Syme, *Studies in the Historia Augusta* (1971).
6. Eusebius, *ad Sanctum Coetum* 15, *PG* 20.1276, supplies a text: 'Remember that the Son of God calls all to virtue and reveals himself to all men's understanding as the Teacher of the Father's commandments.'
7. See for example the polychrome sarcophagus in the Museo Nazionale at Rome, no. 67606.
8. Ammianus Marcellinus, *Life of Constantius* 16.10, ed. S. C. Rolfe, i.248.
9. The halo, or nimbus, is derived from the 'misty radiance', or crown of rays, sometimes shown as a circular plate of metal, which, in Hellenistic as in Roman art, bedecked the heads of gods and heroes. At first no more than a symbol of honour and dignity, it comes to represent the effulgence of supernatural brightness.
10. *DACL* iv.i.167.
11. *Ibid.*, 183. Novatus supported a rival of Pope Cornelius, but the account as given by Damasus seems to have little substance in history.
12. *Peristephanon* ii, ed. H. J. Thomson (Loeb), ii.316.
13. Januarius, a shadowy figure, is thought to have met a martyr's death in 305 AD.
14. *Shepherd of Hermas*, Similitudes ix.4, in *The Apostolic Fathers* (Loeb), ii.225.
15. Extensive catacombs are found elsewhere in Sicily: at Agrigentum, Lilybaeum (Marsala) and Palermo. Cf. G. Agnello in *Studi* 26 (1965).
16. In particular, the necropolis of Anfouchi.
17. Discovered by J. R. Pacho in 1827. See his *Relation d'un voyage dans . . . la Cyrénaïque* (Paris, 1827).

5

Stone Carving

THE SARCOPHAGI

As with painting, so with sculpture. The Christian church unselfconsciously adopted the classical fashion of carving stone surfaces with figures in relief. The noblest and earliest example of this technique in Rome is the Ara Pacis Augustae, a monument dedicated by the Senate, about 10 BC, to commemorate the safe return of the emperor Augustus from military operations in Gaul and Spain. The building consists of an altar enclosed within walls that are decorated on two sides with a procession of men advancing in pairs. The whole composition, sometimes described as a Romanized version of the Parthenon frieze, breathes a spirit of controlled grandeur, while the variety of the figures and the sense of perspective gained by alternating high with low relief bestow a liveliness not always found in the columns and triumphal arches set up a little later by the emperors. The east and west sides of the Ara Pacis show figures, not in procession but in static groups, celebrating the rites of sacrifice or enacting scenes drawn from classical myth; the frieze below luxuriates with foliage.

What is here demonstrated is the complexity of Roman artistic taste. A liking for clear, realistic portraiture joins with religious or allegorical scenes as if to show that human life, however down-to-earth, is touched with mystery and aspiration, just as the frieze pattern of leaves and tendrils bears witness to keen, Wordsworthian delight in the varied charm of Nature's works. Not all Roman carving in relief matches the quality of the Ara Pacis; it can easily become lumpy and overcrowded or degenerate into the lifeless repetition of standard themes, as may be observed in certain of the sarcophagi.

Sarcophagi are large but moveable coffins originally, it would seem, developed from the sculptured tombs of Asia Minor. The Etruscans made use of stone sarcophagi with figured lids showing people recumbent at a banqueting-couch and in Rome, as the practice of cremation gradually declined, sarcophagi made to contain the bodies of distinguished personages came into fashion. Many of these coffins were produced in Asia Minor for export. Some, particularly those made of marble from Proconnesus, are decorated on all four sides with wreaths of flowers or leaves and bunches of grapes. The stone sarcophagi, by contrast, usually show human figures, carved in high relief, standing or sitting within niches marked off, one from the other, by the roofs and columns of Greek architecture. On occasion Apollo and the Muses[1] are introduced as a theme suggesting the harmonies of heaven or, with no less acceptance, the Labours of Hercules, as a reminder that perseverance in arduous and honourable tasks brings its eventual reward. Another type of sarcophagus, perhaps a more purely Roman product, was carved on three sides only, the back being left plain in order to fit against a wall: the ends, whether squared or rounded, often had a mask or lion's head as decoration.

The front of the sarcophagus was treated in various ways, and three principal types may be distinguished.

The first consisted of panels, plain or fluted, with a portrait bust of the deceased in the centre. Another type was characterized by heavy, stiffly carved garlands of fruit and flowers, upheld by cupids, nymphs or Victories. The garlands resembled those presented to the dead at the time of burial or on their anniversaries, while the cupids and other allegorical figures conferred a vague aura of other-worldliness, touched here and there with terror when ghastly masks stood out, in harsh contrast, against the rich abundance of natural life. On the third type of sarcophagus, however, there could be clearer and more definite representations, with human figures standing immobile like statues on the west front of a Gothic cathedral or, more often, jostling together in a mélée which only great artistic skill could preserve from confusion. These scenes sometimes displayed the works of husbandry appropriate to the various seasons. More often, however, well-known incidents from ancient story were set forth—Bacchus, perhaps, revelling in triumph over evil, or Dionysus, in all the charm of youthful beauty, rescuing Ariadne, asleep on the Naxian shore, from the envious grasp of Death. Such was the heritage of forms and ideas readily taken over ·by the Church when the first Christian sarcophagi came to be made in the late third century AD—a period in which the wealthier Christians found themselves able to emulate pagan neighbours in the splendour of their funeral arrangements.

The best and most frequent examples of Christian sarcophagi are, naturally enough, to be found in Rome; many of them are now gathered in the great collections of the Vatican and the Museo Nazionale. But Spain and North Africa have supplied quite a number, while the agreeable and civilized Province of Southern Gaul (later Provence) has yielded sarcophagi of high quality that deserve to be seen as products of a distinctive local school, with Arles as its centre.

Most of the early sarcophagi were made of marble, commonly white Carrara, though coarse-grained marbles from the Ionian Islands and veined marble from Asia Minor were regularly imported. Porphyry, by reason of its rarity and the magnificence of its purple colour, seems to have been reserved for members of the imperial house. The sculptors preferred to work on a single block but might be obliged, if their patrons tightened the purse-strings, to piece together coffins from several chunks of marble, not always suitably

30. Rome, Vatican Museum: the inscription of Beratius.

matched, or to carve in one of the softer, and cheaper, limestones.

The sculptor worked with two tools, the chisel and the drill, this last being used for boring holes to indicate eyes or other features and for channelling out the lines of drapery. One such Christian craftsman is known by name, Eutropus, and his grave-slab, discovered in the Cemetery of SS. Marcellinus and Peter in Rome, has on it, beneath the elegant lettering of the inscription, a rough engraving of Eutropus at work. He is seated in a chair opposite a raised sarcophagus on which wavy lines and lions' heads have already been carved, and, assisted by an apprentice, he operates the drill by means of a cord; near his feet lie chisel and mallet.

Occasionally the marble was tinted with yellow, red, gold, or blue, and became a 'polychrome'. The colours could be lavishly applied, in the way the Etruscans had liked to treat marble, but more often the figures were delicately touched so as to soften the portraiture and give it a supernatural reference. By contrast with such graceful artistry some of the carving was extremely crude. One example of this rough but undeniably sincere workmanship is the inscription of a certain Beratius, now in the Vatican Museum (fig. 30). This, a grave-slab rather than a sarcophagus proper, exhibits three figures: on the left a ravenous monster of indeterminate type is swallowing a man; on the right a roaring lion raises a paw to strike; in the centre stands the Good Shepherd. The drawing may be childishly incompetent, but fear of death could hardly be more vividly displayed than by the man, nor firmer hope represented than by the shepherd with the lamb straddled over his shoulders and the symbolic anchor at his feet.

While the Christian sarcophagi cannot be precisely dated, the general course of their development is reasonably clear. The turbulent conditions experienced in the early part of the third century, when emperor succeeded emperor with bewildering rapidity, gave a certain topical appropriateness to the vast battle sarcophagi with which victorious generals were honoured. But expressions of pride and triumph gave place to the agonized grimaces of suffering just as, on the companion-pieces which illustrated lion-hunts, courage and vigour came to be less emphasized than the ferocious torments which beset mankind. The Christian version of this theme, following the

pattern of the Beratius inscription, is illustrated by a large tub-shaped sarcophagus found at Rome but now preserved in the Louvre (Number 2982). On this coffin a juvenile Good Shepherd is shown, standing between two trees. He bears an enormous ram on his back, while a smaller sheep at his feet looks confidently upward. On either side, near the two ends of the sarcophagus, appears a very large lion's head, with elaborate mane and mouth savagely opened to gobble up those who have no protector.

Just as, in the most distressful times, Roman emperors put 'Peace' or 'Concord' on their coins, so wistful glances were cast at the gracious round of country pursuits and these, rather than scenes of tribulation, became in time a favourite choice for the decoration of sarcophagi. The work of plucking or treading grapes, with its Bacchic overtones, was especially popular. The usual formula runs, with slight variations, along these lines: in the foreground husbandmen, or naked genii, cheerfully trample grapes in a tub ornamented with a lion's head, as though in sombre reminder that, even amid the happiest occupations, danger lurks. The owner of the vineyard, standing beneath the roof of a farm building, surveys the lively prospect; to the left someone on a ladder is picking grapes while, opposite, two men carry away a basket of grapes under the guidance of a third. This vine-treading motif gained ready acceptance in Christian circles where passages such as 'I am the true Vine' were well known. A splendid, if close-packed, sarcophagus,[2] now shown in the Vatican, combines it with no less than three representations of the Good Shepherd, one bearded and two without a beard.

The god Dionysus can also appear, in Greek tradition, either as a mature, bearded man or as a graceful youth, and it seems that Christians happily absorbed into their art traces of his imagery. The entire front surface of the Three Shepherds sarcophagus (fig. 31), carved in marble of the finest quality and excellently preserved, is packed with the typically Bacchic figures of gay little winged cupids picking the grapes, carrying bunches away in baskets and trampling them vigorously in a tub. At one corner, however, the emblem of exuberant life, in this world and the next, is not wine but milk, the natural drink-offering of a pastoral people. In Aeschylus' tragedy *The Persians*, sweet white milk is one of the propitiatory gifts made

31. Rome, Vatican Museum. Sarcophagus 191A: the Three Shepherds.

to the departed, and, in Christian symbolism, milk, taken in connection with the Good Shepherd as the life-giving sustenance of lambs, implies the sacrament of the Eucharist. It was therefore not surprising that St Perpetua, shortly before her martyrdom at Carthage, had a vision in which 'a man with white hair and a shepherd's tunic engaged in milking his sheep' offered her a morsel of curdled milk which she received with hands clasped together and ate rejoicing to find in her mouth a taste of great sweetness.[3] On the Three Shepherds sarcophagus, then, the symbols of milk and wine combine in a scene of lush growth and vital energy. No wonder that a spectator, seated under one of the vines, raises his right hand in thankfulness while, with his left, he clasps the bowl into which an attendant is about to pour his share of the produce.

Another theme taken over without the slightest scruple was that of the contemplative philosopher, and here again the Christians adapted current practice to their needs. For the figure of the philosopher, representing education in its highest and purest form, seems to have derived originally from the influence of the Neoplatonists, whose leader Plotinus was teaching in Rome between 244 and 270 AD, though in Christian hands the philosopher is, of course, the teacher who finds his answer to the mystery of life in the scroll of the Gospels. Christ may indeed be shown as the typical Cynic philosopher with long beard and dishevelled hair, a broad, almost naked, torso, and highly-strung, expectant gaze—the whole portrait is closer to fanaticism than to anything like sophistication.[4] Usually, however, the Christian philosopher is more confident and composed because he knows the answer to the really important questions, and one attractive group of early Christian sarcophagi readily combines the symbolic types of philosopher, Good Shepherd and *Orans*.

The best example of this combined theme is a sarcophagus found near the Via Salaria and now exhibited in the Vatican collection (181: fig. 32). Within a frame bounded by two vast rams' heads, the figures are arranged with a classic, harmonious sense of form. On the left sits the grave and bearded philosopher, clasping his book which contains, as his expression indicates, 'all we know and all we need to know'. Two companions press close to the philosopher in an attempt to learn his secrets. At the other end of the sarcophagus, another group of three persons precisely

32. Rome, Vatican Museum. Sarcophagus 181: Philosopher, *Orans* and Good Shepherd.

33. Rome: Sarcophagus of S. Maria Antiqua.

34. Rome, Vatican Museum. Sarcophagus 119: Jonah.

balances the philosopher and his friends. Here it is a woman, also seated between two attendants, who clasps the scroll of divine learning with one hand while the other is raised in a gesture of prayer. The attendant maidens are not, however, looking at her: one is turning away, with hands outstretched, in the typical posture of the *Orans*, and both have their gaze riveted on the central figure of the composition, a young, curly-haired shepherd, standing between two rams and holding a third over his shoulders as he turns to face the suppliant women. The whole composition, dignified and well-spaced, is a concise sermon to the effect that true wisdom consists in turning to Christ as the guarantee of safety.

Philosopher, *Orans* and Good Shepherd continue for many years as symbols of true wisdom, faith and salvation, although, by the end of the third century, they tend to be overwhelmed by a riot of detail drawn from incidents in Biblical history. The carving is, however, still disciplined and orderly on the celebrated sarcophagus in the church of S. Maria Antiqua, in the Roman Forum (fig. 33). This sarcophagus is of an elongated tub-shape, with the narrative sculpture continued round the two ends but not at the back. The first scene is an elaborate version of the story of Jonah: Neptune seated, then the boat with two men in it, and finally Jonah lying in an attitude of graceful repose under his gourd tree, with the horrific monster, looking singularly unlike a whale, extended in all its menace nearby. The top of the tree is flattened to form a second register of carving, in which three horned rams appear. After the Jonah scene comes the *Orans*, standing between two trees and having a bird with upturned head near her feet: the whole composition is thus rich in allusions to Paradise. The philosopher is shown next, seated on a cross-legged stool and holding an open scroll. He is followed by a Good Shepherd of the 'young countryman' type and, immediately afterwards, by a Baptism scene. Here the Baptist, large and bearded, with his garment hanging loosely from his left shoulder, contrasts with the diminutive, boyish figure of Christ, who links this scene with the Good Shepherd motif by stretching out his right hand to touch one of the sheep. Finally two fruitpickers are shown, one sitting, one standing, beneath the trees from which they are filling their basket. The subjects of the Maria Antiqua sarcophagus may be conventional, but they are rendered in a manner which indicates

high artistic imagination as well as technical skill.

As a theme chosen to illustrate the benevolent and effective power of God, the story of Jonah became a firm favourite, even though the manner of showing his escape from peril is odd. It might be expected that the casting up of Jonah onto the seashore[5] would be the incident most commonly shown, particularly as this is understood by St Matthew[6] as a sign of the Resurrection; but in fact this part of the story is far less often depicted than Jonah beneath his gourd tree. And even here the Bible account is not followed very closely. So far from appearing as a prophet angrily awaiting the destruction of Nineveh, Jonah is represented as lying, naked and carefree, in complete repose. Two influences may be at work here. Jewish legend recorded that Jonah's clothes were burnt inside the whale which threw him up on the shore weak as a newborn baby, whereat God graciously allowed a tree to grow up and shade him from the elements.[7] Perhaps more important as an influence on Christian art is the Greek story of Endymion, the beautiful youth beloved of the Moon, to whom Zeus granted the blessing of long-lasting slumber in perfect contentment. A pagan sarcophagus in the Museo Nazionale at Naples shows Endymion lying asleep in graceful felicity, and there are other parallels to the Christian artform, such as an Italian terracotta, now in the Louvre, on which Dionysus appears naked and sleeping beneath a vine. Jonah is in fact a symbol less of the final resurrection than of that sojourn of the departed in regions where, under the divine protection, they peacefully await the last trump. *In pace*, therefore, 'in peace', is the epitaph attached to the Jonah scene which forms the frieze on a Vatican sarcophagus[8] commemorating 'Exuperantia, a very dear daughter'.

During the confusions and failures of nerve which marked the latter part of the third century, pagan sarcophagi reverted to a chaste simplicity of classical forms. A typical example, from the church of S. Sebastiano, has slim pilasters at the end, followed by a series of seventeen vertical channels on each side of a circular frame containing realistic portraits of a husband and wife. But the expression on the faces shows a melancholy characteristic of this period when Roman culture seemed to be breaking down: the eyes stare upwards into nothingness, the lips are tight set in despairing resolution.

By contrast the Christians, while not blind to contemporary disasters, were inclined to view them as signs that the world was drawing to its end. A crisis of this nature provoked not pessimism but a confident trust in the God who controlled the end of things no less than their beginning, and the ground for that trust was provided by the incidents, demonstrating the divine power, which were recorded in Holy Scripture. The decoration of the sarcophagi therefore marks a certain change from hints and symbols to the open, literal proclamation of Biblical scenes. In the excitement at all this, some of the earlier restraint and dignity is lost, and the surface of the coffins frequently becomes over-crowded.

This change is illustrated by the most famous of the 'Jonah sarcophagi', Vatican 119 (fig. 34). The entire surface of the front, considerably restored, is covered with sculpture, but vigour and a sense of rhythm prevent the detail from becoming tedious. The middle of the scene is occupied by two enormous whales, of almost identical size and shape. While their bodies coil in parallel curves, their heads are turned in opposite directions. The creature on the left opens its mouth to receive Jonah, who is hurled from a sailing-ship into the sea by three members of the crew. His hands are stretched out in what appears an attitude of supplication, and his gesture is precisely the same when he is vomited forth, by the whale in the right of the picture, onto the shore. Here are reeds and bushes, rendered in a somewhat impressionistic manner by deep use of the drill, as well as a heron, a crab, two snails and a lizard. An angler, with his basket on his arm and assisted by a small boy, is in the act of drawing a fish out of the water; above, a shepherd tends his beasts in front of a sheepfold of elaborate workmanship. Nearby, Jonah appears for the third time, under a gourd tree depicted with accuracy and much artistic skill. Sleeping in his conventional attitude of perfect composure, he is, perhaps, the little fish hooked by the Angler as he swims in the waters of baptism, in any case one of the sheep whom the Good Shepherd guards in his heavenly mansion. He is, moreover, contained in the ark of salvation, typified by Noah floating in a tiny chest by the side of the whale.

Here the story of Jonah has been worked out with an assured delicacy and invention along the lines of a recognized formula. But the artist was not content merely with his cycle of Jonah scenes. The upper part of the sarcophagus is marked off by a horizontal boundary-line which supports three Biblical illustrations, though the predominance of the Jonah motif is such that it intrudes into the space assigned to this top register. The first of the events is difficult to interpret: three men are rushing hastily away to the right and, in doing so, trample on two others who have fallen down. The meaning is obscure, but among the guesses which have been made at it are Lot's flight from Sodom and the arrest of St Peter. In the centre stands the dignified figure of Moses, who, with his wand, strikes the rock from which the thirsty Israelites eagerly drink the water assuring them of life. Some maintain that the figure is really that of St Peter, the counterpart of Moses in the New Covenant, who refreshes the Gentiles with the waters of true and saving doctrine. Whether the figure be Moses or Peter, his action illustrates the principle laid down by Hermas, the second-century prophet, in one of his visions: 'Your life was saved and shall be saved through water.'[9] At the left-hand side, amid a group of astonished onlookers, Christ stands in a similar attitude of benevolent power as, with hand outstretched, he summons Lazarus to 'leave his charnel-cave'.[10]

The raising of Lazarus, which provided a secure Biblical foundation for the doctrine of the resurrection of the flesh, became, from the end of the third century, a subject frequently presented on the sarcophagi in a classic pattern. An early example, carved before restrained formality had given place to an exuberant medley of small, jostling figures, is provided by a child's sarcophagus now preserved in the Capitoline Museum at Rome. The front surface of the coffin is divided by vertical lines into five panels of unequal size. The two end-panels show the father in philosopher's costume and the mother as an *Orans*. The central panel contains the boy's portrait within a circle having two birds above and a pastoral scene, with tree, shepherd, and sheep below, while the two large intermediate panels offer their message of hope. That on the right side shows the philosopher seated and clasping his copy of the Gospels, from which he reads to an attentive, eager group of two men and two women. This philosopher has about him no air of the frenzied prophet or half-naked Cynic: the pallium with which he is clothed hangs in dignified fashion and there are sandals on his feet. He is in fact the type and exemplar of one who teaches meaningful truth.

With almost exactly the same appearance and clothing Christ appears, on the left side, standing with two companions before a little shrine that has two columns supporting a triangular pediment. At the top of four steps within the entrance of this formalized tomb is set the figure of Lazarus swathed from head to foot in burial garments. Christ, retaining the roll of the Gospels in his left hand, stretches out his right hand which clasps the miracle-worker's wand. The word of philosophic wisdom is thus ratified by an act of majesty and power which serves for the bereaved as a heartening precedent.

Another comforting episode that frequently recurs is the Multiplication of the Loaves, where the Feeding of the Five Thousand, reduced to a convenient short-hand summary with no more than two or three persons present, hints at the Eucharist. Thus emphasis is given not only to the idea of the true philosophy bringing light, but also to the concept of sacraments as unfailing spiritual nourishment.

SARCOPHAGI AFTER CONSTANTINE

The battle of the Milvian Bridge in 312 AD may justifiably be seen as one of the turning-points of history. Thereafter,

Constantine, the most mighty victor, resplendent with every virtue that godliness bestows, formed the Roman Empire into a single united whole. So then there was taken away from men all fear of those who formerly oppressed them; they celebrated brilliant festivals; all things were filled with light and men, formerly downcast, looked at each other with smiling countenances and beaming eyes.[11]

In other words, the emperor Constantine brought the persecution of Christians to an end and set about using them as the cement of what he hoped would be a unified and purposeful Empire.[12]

Christian art-forms during this period not unnaturally acquired a touch of triumph and exhilaration; buildings suddenly became large and their decoration magnificent. But the fortunes of life and death, as they affected individuals, remained uncertain, and the sarcophagi continued to proclaim that security could be found only through faith in a God whose mighty works were the guarantee of his benevolent power.

The sarcophagi of the early fourth century exhibit two principal characteristics. One group, of which the sarcophagus of the Villa Doria Pamphili may serve as an example, shows a pastoral scene set amidst all the exuberance of nature. The Good Shepherd, stocky and bearded, stands in the centre. A large tree, occupying each end, stretches out horizontal branches which, in effect, divide the entire front into three registers crammed with men, birds and beasts jostling each other in guileless companionship. The composition as a whole reflects that spirit of idyllic harmony which breathes through the Georgics of Virgil, the authoritative poet and seer of imperial Rome. But for Christians, the meaning is even more profound, recalling the untroubled delights set by God's command in the Garden of Eden and destined to be restored when the time of deliverance arrives:

They shall come and sing in the height of Zion, and shall flow together unto the goodness of the Lord, to the corn and to the wine and to the oil and to the young of the flock and of the herd; and their soul shall be as a watered garden.[13]

But the most typical characteristic of these sarcophagi is a tight-packed row, or double row, of figures displaying a set of Biblical scenes not always to be easily disentangled from one another. The dominant personality is Christ, displaying his acts of power and thus proving himself worthy to receive honour and glory. As in the case of the catacomb paintings, new subjects are introduced at this time but usually with a clear bearing on the central theme. Thus incidents drawn from the Old Testament, such as the sacrifice of Isaac, look ahead to the Christian dispensation, while episodes which illustrate the life of St Peter proclaim, or at least hint strongly at, the continuing miracle of Christ's power operative within the Church and spreading far and wide among the nations of the earth.

The Jairus sarcophagus in the museum at Arles (fig. 35) reveals something of this new mode of interpreting Christ's majesty. For here the middle is occupied by the figure of Christ, seated rather formally in a chair set on a plinth, as though he were another Diocletian or Constantine. Meanwhile the apostles offer their homage in the conventional manner, veiling their hands and inclining their bodies. During this period, however, such a display of obsequious reverence was rare: more typical are the Vatican sarcophagi 191 and 161, which show a similar frieze effect but in two distinct forms. Number 191 represents the group of Abraham–Christ sarcophagi in which Old Testament scenes are eagerly introduced as a commentary on Christ's achievement. The usual practice is to show, at the left corner of the tomb's face, Abraham preparing to slay his son Isaac—an event which was held to forecast the Crucifixion. As a symmetrical counterpart of this incident, Christ arouses Lazarus from the tomb and the churchman is thereby reminded that Christ by his death awakes mankind from death. The obvious symbol of this conquest of mortality is the life-conferring Eucharist indicated, in the middle of the frieze, by Christ multiplying the loaves of bread for those who otherwise would have starved to death.

On this particular sarcophagus the Lazarus scene is not shown in accordance with the usual convention of the mummified figure standing at the entrance of his tomb. For here Christ, attended by two apostles, stretches out his magician's wand to touch the head of a dead man—whether Lazarus or another—lying at his feet, while nearby the corpse's counterpart stands, diminutive but very much alive. What the artist has done is to compress not only the spatial extent of the picture but also its time-sequence: the 'before and after' of Christ's action are shown as simultaneous parts of one miracle of deliverance.

The standard themes found in this type of frieze sarcophagus were often filled in, more or less according to taste, with shorthand versions of Gospel events or their prefigurations in the Old Testament. Vatican sarcophagus 191 illustrates Christ healing the man born blind, the paralytic and the woman with the issue of blood. Accompanying these scenes is another, marking the cause of the distresses which require Christ's intervention, namely Adam and Eve standing coyly beside the Tree of Knowledge and clasping their figleaves to their bodies. One end of the sarcophagus is decorated with Moses striking the rock, the other with Daniel and with the three men in the fiery furnace. Thus the artist, ranging his figures in a stiff, rather monotonous manner, has found himself able to include a great deal that, to the understanding eye, would make for edification and comfort.

Sarcophagus 161 belongs to the other contemporary group, which omits Old Testament subjects and chooses instead events from the life of St Peter. The three most commonly shown are the denial of Christ, who gazes reproachfully at Peter as the cock crows, the arrest, when two soldiers in flat helmets and military boots grasp the Apostle from either side, and the scene where Peter is likened to Moses, as the inspired wonder-worker capable of causing water to flow even from the stony rock (fig. 36). This last illustration was deemed to be of especial significance and it therefore occupies one corner of this and other sarcophagi, balancing the miracle of Lazarus at the opposite end. In one of the many apocryphal stories which circulated in Rome concerning Peter, it was recorded that the stream of water from the rock so astonished the Roman soldiers who benefited from it that they embraced Christianity. But the point stressed on the sarcophagi is not conversion but the flow of the water of life dispensed by the chief of the apostles. In the third century the idea that the salvation of God may be readily symbolized by the refreshing power of water receives artistic expression in pictures of the Baptism of Christ, Moses striking the rock or the Samaritan woman at the well. Thereafter St Cyprian's view prevailed, that the Church alone has power to dispense this saving grace. With the increasingly firm belief in the authority of Peter and his successors, this gift is displayed as mediated by Peter representing the Church.

The two corners of sarcophagus 161, and others in the same group, are thus closely connected as depicting two parts of one process. Peter, as he causes the saving water to flow, indicates the starting-point of a Christian life—reception through baptism within the bosom of the Church—while Christ, raising Lazarus from the tomb, shows concretely that the end of a Christian's course on earth is advancement to eternal life. Peter and Christ complement one another as Pupil to Master, Church to Eternity, Prophecy to Fulfilment. Appropriately enough on sarcophagi of this type, the central position is taken by an *Orans*, the faithful soul who is the subject of this stupendous process, and the water pots of Cana no less than the baskets containing bread enough to feed five thousand hint at the sacramental means whereby the life of the faithful is maintained within this divine economy of redemption.

35. Arles, Musée Lapidaire d'Art Chrétien. Sarcophagus: Christ seated among the Apostles and the raising of Jairus's daughter.

36. Rome, Vatican Museum. Sarcophagus 161: miraculous events. Peter drawing water from the rock balances the raising of Lazarus.

37. Rome, Vatican Museum. Sarcophagus 104: the Trinity Sarcophagus.

Sarcophagus 161 is one of those richer in symbolic content than in artistic achievement. Participants in the action, together with the onlookers, are lined up in two rigid rows, facing more or less straight ahead in stiff formality. Other examples of the same period are less crowded and rather more flexible in the arrangement of the figures. Thus the Monograms Sarcophagus, found during excavation under the Vatican, displays vigour of movement as well as a somewhat more adventurous rendering of the scenes. At the left corner, the soldier drinking from the stream of water is no diminutive puppet but stands, stern and strong-featured, as tall as St Peter. The Apostle, in his turn, performs two functions. With his right hand he clasps the wonder-working rod, but his face is sharply turned away from the thirsty soldiers to confront the youthful Christ, shown with long, curly hair, right hand raised in blessing, or reproof, and left hand clutching a scroll marked with the sign of victory. Meanwhile the cock, looking more like a fanciful bird from some medieval bestiary, crows vociferously. The deep-channelled lines which mark the folds of the garments run in contrasting directions and the whole scene conveys liveliness and spiritual tension.

The crowded appearance of the frieze sarcophagi is avoided in the variety which alternates carved scenes at the ends and in the centre with two panels of wavy 'strigillations' cut in the stone. There is less condensed instruction to be had, but the eye is rested by the curving lines and can concentrate more readily on the subjects illustrated. These are usually of the conventional type. One sarcophagus from the Catacomb of Praetextatus shows an *Orans*, in the centre, being escorted to Paradise by two venerable companions who are no doubt the apostles Peter and Paul, while at each end an identical Good Shepherd, with a bulky ram on his back, turns a benevolent gaze in the direction of the *Orans*. Occasionally a more surprising combination of themes is offered, as on a sarcophagus from the monastery of St Catherine at Rome.[14] Here the central scene displays Christ as teacher, between two disciples, while at each end a winged, naked male figure clasps a half-clothed female form. The classical emblems of Amor, the divine Love, embracing Psyche, the individual human soul, here replace the Biblical sign of the Good Shepherd.

Another means whereby some feeling of repose may be obtained amid the confused activity of a frieze is when a circular 'tondo', containing a portrait of the deceased, interrupts the narrative. From the viewpoint of artistry this device of the tondo becomes particularly effective when, in the full development of style during the reign of Constantine, the lessons of Christian history are deployed in a double row, separated merely by a straight horizontal line. An important example is supplied by the Trinity Sarcophagus (Vatican 104) where the workmanship seems, though more elegant, akin to that found on Constantine's great triumphal arch. On this sarcophagus (fig. 37) the story of Fall and Redemption is given a pleasantly personal twist. The upper register begins with the creation of Eve, who receives a blessing from the three Persons of the Godhead,[15] shown as dignified, bearded men, while Adam lies supine on the ground. Closely attached to this scene is another, in which God, appearing this time as a young man with curly hair, stands between the naked Adam and Eve while the Serpent, unabashed, coils its way up the Tree of Knowledge. As if to show that there are grounds for hope, a lamb stands on its hind legs in front of Eve, reaching up towards her. The tondo follows, upheld by two little angels. It contains a realistic portrait of husband and wife, their faith indicated by the scroll of Christian learning which the man clasps in his left hand. The other half of the top register contains the two sacramental scenes of the water at Cana being turned into wine and the Multiplication of the Loaves. Finally comes the conventional Lazarus scene which includes Mary, the sister of Lazarus, or perhaps the woman with the issue of blood, crouching at the feet of Christ. Immediately below the portraits of the deceased man and wife, and thus in the centre of the composition, appears the sturdy figure of Daniel standing on a plinth which represents the lions' den. The two lions, one at each side, have the air of heraldic animals rather than of ravenous beasts and over their head Habakkuk is allowed quietly to pass the basket of loaves which sustained Daniel in prison.[16] This whole scene, set at the focal point of a funeral monument, suggests the safe emergence of human souls from the midst of trials and danger.

The left side of the lower register is taken up almost entirely with an extended illustration of the visit of the Magi. Joseph stands in amazement behind the throne on which the Virgin sits as the Three Wise Men, wearing their pointed Phrygian caps, approach

38. Rome, Vatican Museum. Sarcophagus 183B: the Two Brothers.

39. Rome, S. Sebastiano: the Sarcophagus of Lot.

40. Rome, Vatican Museum. Sarcophagus 171: a Passion-Sarcophagus.

expectantly with their gifts for the Christ child. This intimation of the Redeemer's advent is designed to balance precisely the Creation and the Fall, shown by the figures above; thus there is space only for a very compressed version of the healing of the blind man before Daniel appears. Then, on the other side, the mission of the Church is suggested by the three customary incidents from the life of St Peter—the denial, with Peter clutching his beard in dismay, the arrest, and the water drawn from the barren rock to help the thirsty soldiers.[17] Recessed behind the protagonists, a number of heads imply that the drama is of universal importance.

As the fourth century advanced, the sculptors came to realize that a jumbled frieze, however rich in symbolic value, might become obscure and tedious to look at. They therefore emphasized the central tondo, now often enriched with channelled decoration, to such an extent that the busts of the departed, much larger in scale than the other figures, dominate the whole. Probably the noblest example of this style and period is the Two Brothers sarcophagus in the Vatican Collection (fig. 38).[18] Here the central medallion, in classic scallop-shell form, contains the busts not of husband and wife but of two grave and bearded men so alike that they may well have been twin brothers. The figures which compose the various scenes are no longer sketched in low relief; they stand out to a depth of about 15 centimetres, like so many statuettes, delicately modelled, with deep-set eyes directed on far, eternal realities. There is a certain novelty in both choice and treatment of the subjects illustrated. At the left corner of the upper register the gabled columns of Lazarus' tomb are shown in conventional fashion, but no corpse fast tied in burial bands can be seen at the open door. Instead, Mary, the sister of Lazarus, bows forward to kiss the hand of Christ. This touch of indirect suggestion and human pathos is matched by the appearance of Christ himself, a graceful youth who expresses the keenest sympathy as he inclines his head gently towards the woman whose grief has been turned to sudden joy. This natural mode of portraiture and concern for historical event is borne out at the other end of the frieze, where there occurs a rather elaborate representation of Pilate preparing to wash his hands in token that he is 'innocent of the blood of this just person'. This scene can hardly be regarded as a compact symbol; rather it bears witness to a vivid

interest in the details of the Passion story and those who participated in it. Pilate is shown not as a stylized figure but as an individual Roman, authoritative yet gripped by doubt and apprehension. The space immediately below the scallop-shell medallion once more displays the confident figure of Daniel between his upward-gazing lions. But beside Daniel, and still beneath the medallion, another subject is illustrated: an elderly scholar sits contemplating the tablets on which his philosophy is inscribed while two soldiers stand nearby, one clutching at the precious tablets, the other spying through a tree. This scene, which might be the equivalent of Peter's arrest, is of artistic importance by reason of the two trees, one stunted, one with clumps of deeply-drilled foliage, which frame it. For the trees serve to check the monotony of figures in sequence, and thus lead up to the system of dividing a frieze into panels by means of columns.

An early essay in this style (about 340 AD) is provided by the Sarcophagus of Lot, recently discovered near the church of S. Sebastiano in Rome (fig. 39). The workmanship of this sarcophagus rivals the finest pagan examples; indeed the rhythmical symmetry of the well-spaced figures and their imaginative poses have about them an air of Renaissance culture. This impression is confirmed by the traces of colour still evident and by the ready alliance of pagan with Christian themes. The upper row of subjects, flanking the husband and wife in their scallop-shell medallion, closely resembles the arrangement of the Two Brothers sarcophagus, but the lower register is entirely different. Two robust columns, with capitals and the suggestion of an arch springing from them, enclose the dramatic spectacle of Lot's flight from Sodom. The other side is similar in pattern though here, for whatever reason, the figures have been left incomplete. But immediately below the medallion with its portraits of the departed, five naked little boys trample out the vineyard grapes in a Bacchic ecstasy of abundant vitality; the lid of the sarcophagus with its cherubs and hunting-scenes repeats the theme of life and vigour.

The use of columns, suggested by the Sarcophagus of Lot, led to the adoption in the Roman workshops of a dignified, formal style which, in the middle of the fourth century, transformed the muddled lively frieze into a range of separated scenes, each within its own frame. Yet the message of the sarcophagi retains its

41. Rome, Vatican Grottoes. Sarcophagus of Junius Bassus, central panel of lower row: the Triumphal Entry.

unified character by reason of the closest connection between one subject and another, nowhere more clearly shown than on the various 'Passion-sarcophagi' which compose, at this period, a clearly-marked group. The interest has shifted momentarily from Christ as wonder-worker to Christ victorious through suffering. The suffering is real enough, but it is understood in terms of triumph rather than pathos, of hope for all rather than despair.

The sarcophagi are, in fact, an artistic expression of doctrines which were being pronounced at the time by such Fathers of the Church as Athanasius:

For the Word, knowing that the corruption of men could not be undone unless there was a death, and it was not possible for the Word to die, being immortal and the Son of the Father; for this reason he takes to himself a body that can die, so that this body, sharing in the Word who is above all, may become liable to death on behalf of all, and on account of the indwelling Word may remain immortal, and in future the corruption may cease in all by the grace of the resurrection.[19]

Following this line of argument, scenes from the Passion of Christ become valuable emblems of hope and confidence. The earliest Passion-sarcophagus is a splendidly designed example, worked in pinkish marble, now in the Vatican collection (fig. 40).[20] The front is divided by an elaborate architectural arrangement of columns and entablature into five panels. On the right side a helmeted soldier leads the youthful Christ along as prisoner, while Pilate, supported by his legal assessor, sits in front of his city prepared to wash his hands in token of guiltlessness. To the left, a soldier crowns Christ with a laurel wreath while another soldier forces Simon of Cyrene to bear the cross uphill to Golgotha. These realistic scenes are summed up, or commented on, in the symbolic language of the centre panel, surmounted by little faces representing sun and moon as if to emphasize that the matter is of world-wide and lasting importance. Within the panel stands a simple cross; beneath its arms two soldiers crouch, one fast asleep, the other numbed and bemused, as though in the presence of a miraculous resurrection. This much might be viewed as a continuation of the plain narrative, but over the summit of the cross a laurel crown, enclosing the chi-rho monogram, hangs from the beak of an eagle while two doves peck at the berries. Just as the victorious general on the field of battle received the unfading crown of laurel as a sign of

his triumphant prowess, so here the theme of the unconquerable cross works itself firmly into the midst of the Passion scenes. In accordance with this, Christ is shown not in terms of the agonized realism that became fashionable in the Middle Ages, but as the youthful hero, attractive and composed in face of inevitable destiny.

A few years later, in the middle of the fourth century, the idea that the Passion of Christ was an earth-shaking triumph receives its proper development as a teaching and a trust handed over to the Church. On a vast sarcophagus in the Vatican Grottoes (174) scenes from the Passion are repeated within a regular framework of columns decorated with a wealth of abundant detail which suggests that the craftsmen were of Asiatic origin. To the left, the sacrifice of Isaac serves as Old Testament commentary, while the arrest of St Peter hints that those who continue the life of the Church may not hope to escape their share of redemptive suffering. In this respect they present a contrast with Pilate who, on the right side of the sarcophagus, looks not at the graceful figure standing before him but straight ahead as he dips his fingers into the bowl of water which might be hoped to relieve him of responsibility. Meanwhile, at the centre of the drama, there is no veiled symbol of cross and laurel crown but Christ himself enthroned in gracious majesty above the submissive, obedient figure of Earth. Two apostles reverently attend him as, with right hand upheld in blessing, he extends with the other hand his scroll of authority towards the crouching, half-bowed form of Peter.

The fashion of decorating tombs with the figure of Christ in triumph developed along several distinct lines, but a common factor is a frame or background of architectural motifs and the presence of apostles, both themes having some connection with the political propaganda of the civil power, as illustrated on the Arch of Constantine.

Following this style of presentation, Christ is portrayed as dominant before the columns and arches of a heavenly city and flanked by the company chosen to bear his words to the ends of the earth. While this Christ is usually shown as the pattern of youthful comeliness, he may also appear in the form of a venerable, bearded figure, resembling the Zeus or Asclepius of pagan mythology, and dispensing to his eager yet awed apostles the scroll of the Law which, as the Ancient of Days, he promulgates for all time. A scene of this kind is clear enough in itself and additional commentary, however edifying, is hardly necessary. It is nevertheless sometimes provided, as when, on a fragmentary sarcophagus in the church of St Sebastian, the lambs of sacrifice, one bearing a cross on its head, crowd around the Master's feet.

The architectural theme, developed in such a way that it displays a line of recesses in the wall of a fortified city, is characteristic of a group known as the City-gate sarcophagi. One example, now in the Louvre, shows this particular background with, before it, the Ascension of Elijah, as this event is recounted in the Second Book of Kings.[21] Below the hooves of the four prancing horses that bear Elijah aloft is shown a river-god, presumably Jordan, holding a long reed and portrayed in the conventional manner found in first-century wall-painting from Pompeii.[22] This river-god seems to be acclaiming Elijah while, nearby, Moses appears receiving the Law from the hand of God, on Mount Sinai.

Almost exactly the same type of city-gate background, with its arches, windows and battlements, is used on a large sarcophagus of Asiatic type and distinctly 'ecclesiastical' tone, found in the Vatican area but later transferred to the Louvre.[23] The whole of the front surface is devoted to a single scene, that of Christ delivering his Law to the apostles. Christ stands bearded and majestic on a rock, his unique power emphasized by the elaborate patterning of capitals and pediment which frame his head and shoulders. On each side are ranged six apostles, uniformly clothed in their ample robes but so grouped—one, two, three on the left side; one, three, two on the right—as to avoid dullness or excessive rigidity. At Christ's feet two diminutive attendants crouch as, from his position head and shoulders above the apostles, he dispenses the scroll of his teaching to Peter, who advances bearing a jewelled cross on his shoulder. It would scarcely be possible to demonstrate more clearly the idea of celestial authority, standing over against the transitory might of the civil power.

A variant on the victory theme, and one that adheres more closely to that earlier style which emphasized the miracles of healing, is provided by those sarcophagi which make a particular feature of Christ's triumphal entry into Jerusalem. This scene is found, on one of the Vatican examples,[24] with Adam and Eve at one end of the composition and Lazarus raised from the tomb at the other end, while a more crowded and elaborate manner of stressing the same lesson is provided by the sarcophagi of the so-called Bethesda group. A typical example, again in the Vatican collection,[25] shows a rather mixed architectural background of gateways and pedimented columns before which occur the healings of the two blind men and the woman with the issue of blood. In the middle comes a double register with two scenes divided by a horizontal bar. Below lies the paralysed man, whether of Bethesda[26] or Capernaum;[27] above, he bears his bed away on his back at Christ's command, while the bystanders raise their hands in amazement. Then, on the right, Christ is shown, like some victorious emperor, riding into Jerusalem triumphantly, on the donkey. The artist has been concerned to bring out as many details of the Biblical narrative as possible in the confined space. One man solemnly raises his hand as if to say, 'Blessed is he that cometh in the name of the Lord'; others clasp branches which they have 'cut from the trees' while others again 'spread their garments in the way'. At the end an apostle holds the conqueror's garland in readiness. This type of Bethesda sarcophagus, with its crowded and confused middle section, was quite widely copied and is found as far away as Spain.

The noblest of all the sarcophagi, one that combines bold and attractive design with singular grace of craftsmanship, fortunately bears inscribed on its lid the date, 359 AD, and the name of Junius Bassus, who was prefect of Rome and received baptism on his death-bed. The front of this sarcophagus is divided by means of ornate columns into ten niches each containing a complete scene, but with never more than three figures shown, so that jostling and overcrowding are successfully avoided. The five scenes of the upper register have a sober, elegant framework of rectangular lines, while the lower five are topped by flattish semicircles alternating with triangles, the resultant spaces being occupied by figures of lambs, delicate and charming enough but hinting at the idea of sacrifice. The profuse ornament of the carving as a whole and the gracefully posed forms suggest Hellenistic models, but the deep relief in which the figures are cut and the dignified Roman look on some of the faces point to a local artist of wide and generous sympathies. The panels are paired in a series illustrating doctrinal themes. The sacrifice of Isaac occurs at the top left while below, having lost all, Job is seated, disconsolate but faithful, on his dunghill. Next, Adam and Eve stand in shamefaced dismay; above them, the arrest of Peter suggests that the original sin and failure of mankind is countered by the atoning reconciliation to be found within the Church. The lower panel of the central pair (fig. 41) shows Christ, graceful and half-smiling, upon the donkey that bears him to Jerusalem and to his doom; above, still the youthful counterpart of David but now calm and dignified as befits a heavenly Judge, he sits enthroned between the two princes of the apostles while the sky-god crouches beneath. The arrest of Jesus, shown once more as the prince of David's line clasping his scroll of office but with head bowed to accept the destiny of 'a man of sorrows and acquainted with grief', fittingly caps the type and example of Old Testament endurance, Daniel in the lions' den.[28] Lastly, Pilate, staring irresolute into space as he prepares to wash his hands of Jesus' arrest, proclaims a worldly incapacity to perceive truth; he is contrasted with St Paul, the martyr-figure below him, who, determined but submissive in defence of the faith, inclines his head as he awaits the executioner's sword. The decoration of the ends of this sarcophagus, though conventional enough, completes the picture. The gathering of grapes, the reaping of corn and other figures which suggest the recurring seasons serve to indicate the blessedness of the eternal kingdom which the just would peacefully and thankfully enjoy.

The sarcophagus of Junius Bassus marks the high point though not the end of this particular branch of funerary art, for, under the emperors Theodosius and Honorius, many such sepulchres were still being produced. Some of the movement and vitality is lost in later examples, however, and the figures are lined up, rigid and statuesque, with Christ, as lawgiver or conqueror, dominant in the centre. These figures often show a characteristic helmet-like hairstyle, bunched up on the nape of the neck and marked rather mechanically with holes made by the drill. Eyes are narrowed to an almond shape with the pupil regularly set in the middle; drapery is arranged in stiff and formal folds. An example of this style is furnished by the sarcophagus of Probus, contained in the Vatican grottoes. The front is divided, by semicircular arches rising from barley-sugar columns, into five niches.

The central niche, larger than the rest, contains the figure of Christ, youthful but august, standing on the mount of authority and flanked by Peter and Paul. With his right hand Christ holds a jewelled cross, while in his left he clasps the scroll of his law. Each of the other niches contains a pair of apostles who, in courtier-like fashion, turn to acclaim Christ as the risen and divine Law-giver, a theme which is continued on the narrow ends of the sarcophagus. In order to avoid any interruption of this majestic frieze the full-length figures of husband and wife clasping hands have necessarily been relegated to the back of the sarcophagus, where they occupy the central position flanked by two rectangular frames containing wavy strigillations. This 'all-over' decoration of the sarcophagus is thought to imply eastern influence, mediated perhaps through Milan. Certainly Milan and North Italy provided a number of sarcophagi which date from the end of the fourth century and stress the theme of Christ, the victorious lawgiver, and his council of apostles. The most famous example is the so-called 'Sarcophagus of Stilicho' in S. Ambrogio, Milan (fig. 42). This great chest of marble, carved in high relief on all four sides, finishes in a triangular pediment at both ends. The well-tried Christian emblems find their place on the richly decorated surface together with a conventional choice of Old Testament themes. But the essential message is conveyed by Christ, who stands raised on his mountain pedestal with a lamb below his feet and a small figure crouching in reverence at either side. The apostles are ranged, in stiff and timeless fashion, facing their Master and backed by the towers and ramparts of the Eternal City which is theirs to guard. The whole statuesque panorama, with its anticipations of the Middle Ages, seems designed to answer the questions 'Where shall wisdom be found?' and 'By what authority doest thou these things?'

At St John's, Verona, there is another sarcophagus of the late fourth century, on which the action is played out before a framework of rounded arches alternating with rectangular doorways supported by columns. Christ is shown four times as a curly-haired young man whose gestures, in a tableau which ranges from the conversation with the Samaritan woman at the well to the betrayal by Judas, are nevertheless those of power. Then, as though set on a different plane of historical truth from the lively realistic scenes of his ministry, Christ stands, bearded and august, on

42. Milan, S, Ambrogio. Sarcophagus of Stilicho: Old Testament patriarchs ranged beneath the chi-rho sign.

43. Rome. The sarcophagus of Constantina: cherub gathering grapes.

a lofty pedestal and raises his hand in declaration of his sovereignty.

An even clearer essay on the subject of Christian authority can be found on certain sarcophagi named, after a town in Lydia, the Sidamara group. These sarcophagi, carved by Asiatic workmen but coming from a number of workshops, reveal a characteristic pattern. They are large, and the surface of all four sides is divided into an arcade of niches by means of columns, channelled in spirals throughout and ending in Corinthian capitals. The capitals in their turn are surmounted by an impost, or second order of carving, usually worked in a special manner with an egg-shaped device in the top half and an inverted trident below. Within the niches, ornamented in a rich lace-like pattern by means of the drill, stand full-length figures, facing front and, by contrast with their exuberant background, rather stiffly posed.

The earliest examples of this type are pagan in character, but the style also answered well to Christian requirements, as shown on a fragmentary sarcophagus brought to Berlin from Constantinople. Here a beardless Christ, with curly hair and a nimbus round his head, holds himself firmly in the conventional

attitude of an orator, with right arm clasped across his chest and the ample folds of his toga. The apostles are distinguished from Christ by their short, cropped hair and the absence of a nimbus. Framed in somewhat narrower niches, they turn towards him as to the source from which they draw their power.

The Sidamara sarcophagi are a group clearly marked off by regional characteristics, and the same may be said concerning those of Aquitaine, which have a look all their own with rounded base and a top made up of two, sometimes four, steep slopes. Christ may appear in the centre with apostles, stylized and isolated, at each end, but most of the surface is covered with vines, ivy and a varied assortment of plants and geometric patterns. Perhaps Syrian influences may be traced here rather than those of Italy and southern Gaul.

The sarcophagi made from porphyry, the blood-red marble quarried in the Egyptian desert, stand somewhat apart from the others. There is, first, a series made at Constantinople for members of the imperial house. These sarcophagi take the form of rectangular chests with high-pitched lids having acro-teria, or plain wing-like additions, raised up at the

44. Ravenna, S. Francesco: marble sarcophagus.

corners. Usually nothing is carved on the surface beyond a monogram, and dignity is secured through plain, regular line and quality of material rather than by any attempt at decoration.

Very different are the sarcophagi of Helena and Constantina, mother and daughter of the emperor Constantine. These vast and majestic tombs testify more to imperial pride than to any new-found piety and indeed it may be questioned whether Helena's sarcophagus, which bears no emblem of religious character at all, ever did contain her body. The account given by Eusebius[29] indicates that Helena set out on a pilgrimage to the holy places of Palestine towards the end of her life and that her funeral took place with great pomp at Constantinople, but western traditions connect her death and burial with Rome and it is in the Vatican that her sarcophagus is now installed. This is a rectangular chest with an elaborate lid, also rectangular at first but changing half-way up into the base of a pyramid. Along the sides of the chest are carved figures of Romans and barbarians in conflict. Horsemen gallop bravely, as on some monumental column, while barbarians fall headlong or walk away, captive and bound, in an attitude of melancholy detachment.

But the whole frieze gives the impression of a series of studies rather than of any particular battle scene. The lid is decorated with garlands held in place by cherubs; near the top corner, four other winged figures recline with garlands and animals at rest between them.

The sarcophagus of Constantina (fig. 43) retains the motif of garlands at the base of the lid, but the resemblance in decoration ends there. For the surface is dominated by an intricate pattern of stylized vine-stems into which are fitted cherubs actively engaged in gathering the grapes or trampling an enormous pile of them in a press. With this scene of Dionysiac exuberance, and the hope of future blessedness which it implies, two peacocks, birds of immortality, are completely in accord. Other birds in the vine-branches and a rather lumpy sheep complete the picture while from above, on the lid, four graceful portrait heads, one apparently that of Constantina, look calmly out over this assurance that the best is yet to be. The body of Constantina was brought to Rome from Asia Minor after her death in 354 AD and a circular mausoleum, the church of S. Costanza, was built to enclose her tomb.[30]

By the beginning of the fifth century, the art of the carved sarcophagus was dying out in Milan as well as

45. Ravenna, S. Apollinare in Classe: sarcophagus of Archbishop Theodore.

in Rome, but Ravenna continued to produce examples, made probably by Asiatic craftsmen of considerable skill even if well content to repeat conventional formulae rather than seek for novelty. Some of the picturesque Biblical subjects which dominate the earlier period at Rome were retained but seem gradually to lose their vigour. The theme of the Magi demonstrates this process. The panel of a fifth-century relic chest, now in the Museum of the Archiepiscopal Palace in Ravenna, shows the three kings wearing their Phrygian caps and pressing eagerly forward in perfect symmetry, while the Virgin, seated on a throne resembling a wickerwork chair with high back, can scarcely restrain Jesus as he bounces forward to receive his gifts. When the same scene occurs on the sarcophagus of the governor Isaac in S. Vitale, admittedly a late example, the cloaks still flow gracefully backwards in the wind but the figures have become rigid and lifeless.

A more abundant group of sarcophagi at Ravenna repeats the theme of Christ dispensing authority. One of these, which, having lost its lid, now serves as the altar in San Francesco, is decorated with an arcade of round-head arches, supported by barley-sugar col-umns and deeply-drilled Corinthian capitals. Each arched recess contains only one figure. Christ, seated within the central arch on the west side, is shown as remarkably youthful and eager, in the true manner of a second David 'withal of a beautiful countenance and goodly to look upon'.[31] Some of the apostles likewise seem to embody the vigour and enthusiasm of young men while others, by contrast, are represented as bearded and grave.

The same church contains another sarcophagus, made in grey marble of high quality, which interprets Christ as a pattern of youthful beauty (fig. 44). Some of the accompanying apostles clasp their scrolls of authority while one of their number approaches, his hands veiled by the folds of his pallium in token of reverence, to receive the scroll which Christ himself is offering. The lid of this sarcophagus takes the form of a high-pitched roof, with large acroteria at the corners, and a bold decoration of lion-head masks. At each end, birds face one another with a cross between them. This particular type of symbolic ornament became increasingly common in the sixth century; like much symbolism it does not invite exact analysis but suggests powers of the spirit, or perhaps the souls of mankind,

46. Ravenna, S. Apollinare in Classe. Sarcophagus: Christ receiving the homage of the Apostles.

finding full realization in the light of Christ's redemptive activity. In that sense the lid repeats, with a rather different emphasis, the motive of the frieze below.

Sometimes the artist is quite content with these emblems and the associations which have accumulated around them. Thus, the sarcophagus of Archbishop Theodore in the church of S. Apollinare in Classe (fig. 45) is decorated with the chi-rho monogram, appearing six times on the lid as well as in the centre of the front face, where it is set between two peacocks; a partridge and another bird nearby peck at bunches of grapes hanging from a carefully cultivated vine. The ends, both of the chest and of the lid, which has the form of a high-pitched coffer, continue, in a rich but somewhat stylized pattern, the theme of a bounteous and meaningful universe, with flowers, crosses and a dove as well as further pairs of birds solemnly confronting one another. Ravening lions' heads also retain their place, this time as projecting handles.

The collection of sarcophagi in S. Apollinare includes several which follow this same design of long chest topped with a high rounded lid. The marble sarcophagus standing next to that of Theodore resembles its companion in that both sides of the lid display three large wheel-like crosses. The back shows peacocks facing a cross and the ends are elaborately carved with the customary birds, to which, however, three human figures are added—perhaps in order to complete the scene portrayed on the front. This is another variation on the theme of Christ in majesty, worked out in a restrained and orderly fashion (fig. 46). Within a frame bounded by channelled columns six apostles, exactly balanced one against the other, move rhythmically towards the centre, where Christ, looking straight before him, sits on a plain rectangular throne. He is here represented as the august, impassive ruler though long, curly hair adds a softening touch of juvenile grace. On the right side of Christ St Paul advances, with hands veiled, to receive the scroll of the Law; on the left, Peter clasps the long cross and the key which betokens his authority. Two other apostles raise their hand in acclamation, and at the ends of the panel, two more hasten forward, supporting the laurel crown of triumph on a cloth which covers their hands as a sign of reverence. Considered in the light of the crowded vitality of many earlier sarcophagi, this sixth-century chest exhibits a sense of spacing and control which, though the figures may be rather stiffly posed, recalls the classic period of Greek art, and it is with these dignified examples from Ravenna that the carving of sarcophagi draws to an end and yields to other interests.

STATUARY

By contrast with the abundance of sarcophagi, examples of statues carved in the round during the early centuries of the Christian Church are very rare. Both the Mosaic condemnation of graven images and a general desire to separate themselves from pagan associations led such third-century Fathers as Origen to blame those who 'fix their gaze on the evil handiwork of sculptors'.[32] Even when peace was restored to the Church and Constantine, an impassioned collector of statues, presented fine examples not only to his new capital city but also to the various churches which enjoyed his patronage, the growing desire for splendour was, in general, satisfied rather by painting and mosaic than by statuary.

Writing in about the year 310, Eusebius notes[33] that in his day one might see at Caesarea Philippi two bronze figures carved in relief, of the woman with the issue of blood crouching before Jesus 'clothed in comely fashion in a double cloak'. Whether Eusebius was correct in his interpretation cannot now be determined; it was not unknown, in later periods, for pagan statues to be Christianized and to be stamped, in confirmation, with the sign of the cross.

The marble statue of a philosopher, seated in an attitude of calm authority, was found at Rome in 1551 and is now in the Museo Pio Cristiano. Head and hands are missing but the pose of the figure and the manner in which the draperies are executed point to a skilled craftsman. One side of the philosopher's chair is engraved with a list of writings attributed to Hippolytus, a scholarly controversialist exiled from Rome in 235, while the other side offers tables for calculating the date of Easter such as were contained in Hippolytus' treatise 'On the Pascha'. The excellence of the carving has led some observers to doubt whether the statue could have been produced in Christian circles in the first half of the third century, and to suggest that it may have been the product of a pagan workshop and adapted in commemoration of Hippolytus.

An attractive marble figure, of unknown provenance but now in the Museo Nazionale at Rome, has commonly been described as 'Christ teaching his followers' (fig. 47). The young man, enveloped in drapery and seated with one knee raised, holds a scroll in his left hand; but the soft, effeminate lines and luxuriant coiffure explain the title by which the statue was originally known: 'seated poetess'. The touches of romantic idealism would accord with a second-century date and thus make identification with Christ extremely doubtful. But, although the third century, with its frequent upheavals, set a fashion for artefacts of a rougher and harsher nature, the old ideals and art-forms maintained their hold in aristocratic as well as in religious circles.[34] The boy-Christ shown on the sarcophagus of Junius Bassus and the curly-haired Christ of the Passion-sarcophagus (174) display an easy grace amply charged with sentiment, and one may assign to the same period of manufacture, roughly 360 AD, the 'seated poetess', accepted as Christ teaching his disciples.[35] Similar in feeling is the marble statue of a youthful shepherd, also of unknown origin but now in the Vatican Museum (fig. 48). Clad in the rustic *exomis*, a sleeveless tunic, and with purse slung over his right shoulder, he clasps with both hands the sheep which he bears across his back. In the treatment of the eye, with the pupil slightly off centre in order to emphasize the reflective upward glance, may be recognized, with reference to the sarcophagi, a device typical of the middle of the fourth century. Statuettes of the Good Shepherd may have been thought useful in protecting houses from misfortune, for several other examples have come to light. A rough and homely specimen, unearthed at Corinth, is now in the Byzantine Museum at Athens, while another diminutive example, skilfully carved in bone, has found its way to the Louvre. The Cleveland Museum of Art also contains just such a statuette (fig. 49).

Another sign of prayer or thanksgiving for deliverance from peril seems to have been provided by marble statuettes, of eastern Mediterranean origin, showing Jonah's escape from the whale. One set of these, now in the Cleveland Museum of Art, is associ-

47. Rome, Museo Nazionale. Statuette 61565: Christ teaching.

48. Rome, Vatican Museum: sculpture of the youthful Good Shepherd.

49. Cleveland, Museum of Art: sculpture of the mature Good Shepherd.

50. Cleveland, Museum of Art. Marble statuette: Jonah escaping from the whale.

ated with a group of male and female portrait-busts which, by reason of clothing and hairstyle, point to a date near 285 AD. The Jonah figures represent a type of garden ornament favoured by wealthy pagan families, and it seems strange that themes of Christian interest should be incorporated, in defiance of official policy, into a form of luxurious decoration more commonly exemplified by Orpheus.[36] The statuettes, though considered by some not to be genuine early Christian artefacts, may nevertheless be seen as refined essays in the tradition of Hellenistic baroque. Jonah is shown as a mature man with full beard and mop of hair. The most dramatic of the figures presents a rhythmical, circular shape with the tail of an exceptionally sinuous whale curving over almost to touch Jonah's head as he emerges from its mouth (fig. 50).

The bronze statue of St Peter, majestically enthroned with the key of authority in his hand, which is one of the attractions of St Peter's in Rome, is now firmly ascribed to the thirteenth century rather than the fourth, though its posture was probably suggested by a seated figure, carved from polychrome marble but extensively restored, in the Vatican Grottoes.

NOTES

1. An attractive example of this theme is furnished by sarcophagus 874 in the Museo Nazionale Romano.
2. 191 A.
3. *Martyrdom of S. Perpetua* iv, tr. E. C. E. Owen, 81.
4. Fragments of a polychrome sarcophagus in the Museo Nazionale at Rome, no. 67607
5. Jonah 2.10.
6. St Matthew 12.40.
7. Strack-Billerbeck, *Kommentar* (Munich, 1922–8) i.642.
8. Museo Pio Cristiano (Vatican), no. 11.
9. *Shepherd of Hermas*, Vision iii. 3.5, in *The Apostolic Fathers* (Loeb), ii.
10. Tennyson, *In Memoriam* xxi.
11. Eusebius, *Ecclesiastical History* 10.9.6.
12. N. H. Baynes, *Constantine the Great and the Christian Church* (1929).
13. Jeremiah 31.12.
14. Museo Nazionale no. 52264.
15. This interpretation was confirmed by the recent discovery of another sarcophagus apparently from the same workshop. Here Adam stands with Eve before the throne of God. The figure of the Logos, young and beardless, places his hand on Eve's head. Of the other two Persons, grave and bearded, one is majestically seated and the other clutches the side of the throne. An additional figure, with his hand on Adam's shoulder, can be seen as an angelic assistant or, more probably, as a repeated illustration of one of the three Persons. Since 1974 this sarcophagus has been in the Museum of Christian Art at Arles.
16. *Bel and the Dragon* 34.
17. This portion of the sarcophagus is damaged.
18. 183 A.
19. Athanasius, *On the Incarnation* 9.1, ed. F. L. Cross (London, 1939).
20. No. 171.
21. II Kings 2.1–14.
22. Also now in the Louvre.
23. No. 2980. Formerly Borghese Collection, No. 1808.
24. No. 186.
25. No. 125.
26. St John 5.
27. St Mark 2.
28. This figure is a modern restoration.
29. *Life of Constantine* iii.42.
30. The tomb now in Santa Costanza is a copy of the original, which has been transferred to the Vatican. For the mausoleum, see p. 98.
31. I Samuel 16.12.
32. *Against Celsus* vi.66.
33. *Ecclesiastical History* 7.18.
34. For Constantine's gifts to the church of St John Lateran see p. 88.
35. F. Gerke, *Christus in der spätantiken Plastik* (Mainz, 1948), 38. W. N. Schumacher, in *Studi* 37, maintains that the statue is part of a sculptural relief.
36. E. Kitzinger in *ACIAC* ix.

6

Church Buildings

The remains of synagogues at places other than Dura, excavated for the most part during the last fifty years, reveal two facts of importance in the history of Christian art and architecture. They indicate first of all that the pagan basilica was, by the second or third century AD, being readily adapted to the religious uses of the Hebrews and, secondly, they show that the themes of pagan mythology, far from being resolutely shunned, were drawn with relative ease into the service of a liberalized Judaism.

The synagogues of Capernaum and Gerasa, more or less contemporary with Dura, may be cited, but still more striking are the ample remains of the somewhat later synagogue of Beit Alpha, situated in a valley just south of Mount Tabor. The building here divides into three sections. First comes the courtyard with, almost at the centre, the pool of water to be used in ceremonial ablutions. Going eastwards the worshipper arrived at the narrow rectangle of the narthex, its wall pierced by three doorways leading into the synagogue proper. Measuring some 10 metres in length by 12 in width, this basilica–hall bears an extremely close resemblance to a Christian church, as it is divided into a nave and aisles by two rows of three squat pillars with a pilaster attached to the wall at each end. A platform, set up against one of the columns towards the south end of the building, provided the ambo[1] or pulpit, from which the rabbi gave readings of the Law, though more commonly this pulpit was approached by a double staircase. No trace remains of the 'presbytery' where the elders sat in a semicircle, facing the people, but some of the small columns remain which supported the ceiling over the women's gallery running above the side aisles. The likeness to a Christian church continued even at the south end which, facing towards Jerusalem, corresponded in sanctity to the east in a normal Christian orientation. Here a semicircular apse extended from the wall to accommodate not an altar but an ark containing the scroll of the Law and the seven-branched candlestick 'in the likeness of a trident',[2] as ordered by the Book of Exodus.[3] The synagogue may be said to have cleansed the basilica of its pagan associations and helped to prepare for the free use of the basilican style in Christian churches, but the influences ran both ways and synagogues of the late fourth to early sixth century, such as Beit Alpha (c.520 AD), seem to have been indebted, on points of detail, to Christian buildings.

The floor throughout the synagogue of Beit Alpha was originally decorated with a colourful mosaic, and large parts of this remain. Not only do geometric patterns occur but in the nave three large rectangles, set within a variegated border, show clearly that the horror of representing human and animal forms which stemmed from the rigid ideas of the first century was not maintained even in Palestine. The mosaic immediately in front of the apse reproduces objects used in contemporary Hebrew worship. At the central point is shown the richly patterned front of the cupboard in which the sacred writings were kept; the

51. Beit Alpha synagogue. Central panel of mosaic: the Sun in his chariot.

cupboard itself is surmounted by a stepped gable up which, on either side, a large bird climbs. Two candlesticks, each with its seven lights, occupy much of the field and two lions, roughly designed in a ferocious attitude, guard the sacred cupboard. Other religious objects are dotted casually about: trumpets and cases for the scroll of the Law as well as the *lulab* and the *ethrog*, two types of leafy wand waved during the Feast of Tabernacles.

The central panel of the nave mosaic consists of a wheel within a square. Between the spokes of the wheel are ranged the twelve signs of the Zodiac, each marked with its name in Hebrew, and the spokes converge on a round medallion which, in a curiously slapdash manner, represents the Sun riding in his chariot (fig. 51). Helios is shown as a beardless youth with a halo encircling his head, while his body is hidden by a shield-like object intended for the front of the chariot. At either side appear two grotesque masks, that is to say the horses' heads viewed from the front and bearing little relationship to the legs which are shown, rather vaguely, in profile. At each corner of the square is a female head, with curly hair and long neck. These are the four seasons, each accompanied by appropriate emblems. Another synagogue, that of Na'aran near Jericho, likewise provides a mosaic showing the sun god, the seasons and the signs of the Zodiac.

The third panel of the nave mosaic at Beit Alpha is remarkable as illustrating Abraham's sacrifice of Isaac. In Hebrew theory, Abraham was preeminent among the patriarchs and the so-called Binding of Isaac took its place among the intercessory prayers of the synagogue[4] as a valued means of securing the divine favour:

Remember unto us, O Lord our God, the covenant and the loving-kindness and the oath that thou swarest unto Abraham our father on Mount Moriah; and may the binding with which Abraham our father bound Isaac his son on the altar be before thine eyes.

The event was eagerly grasped by Christian teachers, from the second century onwards,[5] as a type of the sacrifice of Christ, and representations of it occur often enough in the wall-paintings of the catacombs, as in the Sacrament Chapel A3 of the Callistus Cemetery and in the Capella Graeca. But since the theme is found also in the synagogue at Dura, it can hardly be claimed as directly borrowed from Christian sources. The design in the Beit Alpha mosaic is childishly crude to the point of caricature. Abraham himself is shown wearing a vast, lopsided turban and a tunic which clings closely to his body. With his left hand he clutches the babyish figure of Isaac, who is about to be slaughtered with a long cutlass and then cast into the flames which rise from the altar. The two servants mentioned in the Genesis account stand at their ease, looking after the ass. In the centre of the composition, there appears an extraordinary creature identifiable by its horns and the Hebrew inscription as a ram. But a desire to make more space for the human figures has triumphed over artistry, so that the ram is made to squat on its tail and to look as if it were climbing vertically up a tree.

THE BASILICA—EARLY ESSAYS

The earliest church-buildings, as found at Dura, are nothing more than rooms in a house, yet they were built, or adapted, according to a pattern which met the needs of the Christian community. Grouped around a central courtyard, and thus avoiding any undue public attention, they generally consisted of a fair-sized room for meetings, a smaller room equipped with a font for baptisms, and a third chamber in which to hold the eucharistic meal. To these might be annexed an office or store-room and a place for the instruction of converts. In affluent centres and during periods of prosperity a building of some size might be required, and benefactors came forward such as one Theophilus of Antioch, 'who was a man of more distinction than all the influential people in the city and consecrated the large hall of his house on behalf of the church'.[6] The historian Eusebius, writing of events immediately before the last great outburst of persecution in 303 AD, comments on the greater luxury which grew up in Christian circles along with the rapid increase of numbers:

How could one describe those crowded assemblies and the multitudes gathered together in every city and the remarkable concourses in the places of prayer? The result was that people were no longer satisfied with the buildings of olden time and began to erect from the foundations wide and spacious churches throughout all the cities.[7]

This is a somewhat vague and rhetorical flourish on Eusebius's part, but it may be that, even before Constantine's victory, Christians here and there were emboldened by tolerance or driven by necessity to try their hand at rather more pretentious church-building than the adaptation of a middle-class house.

The copying of pagan temples was ruled out, not so much through fear of the corruptions of heathenism as because the temple was essentially designed to attract crowds of worshippers around it, while the form of a Christian church was intended to draw a congregation for devotion and fellowship within. Porphyry, a vigorous opponent of the Christians, charged them about the year 300 AD with putting up 'great buildings in imitation of the structure of temples',[8] and this, if the words can be taken in any literal sense, seems to imply something of a more distinctive and public character than the house-church. The walls which have been discovered far below the church of S. Crisogono in the Trastevere district of Rome have been interpreted as one such building. A simple, aisleless hall is indicated, 28 metres by 15.5 metres, with a covered portico running along its flank and some attempt at a façade with a large central opening and a smaller one at each side. The brickwork is thought to date from the very beginning of the fourth century, but whether the building was in fact a church rather than some form of covered market is uncertain. In any case, exceptions are few and dubious: the general rule is that churches were parts of houses, or buildings which resembled very ordinary houses, until 313 when Constantine, by the Edict[9] of Milan, granted to Christians the right for local churches to retain and enjoy the use of their places of assembly as 'the lawful property of their corporation'.[10] A year earlier Constantine had written to Anullinus, governor in Africa, ordering him to restore to the churches all that they had possessed before the last outburst of persecution, 'whether gardens or buildings or whatsoever belonged to these same churches by right', while Caecilianus, bishop of Carthage, was informed that money from the imperial treasury had been made available to meet the expenses of 'certain ministers of the lawful and most holy catholic religion'.

These clear signs of the emperor's favour caused the Church to prosper both in numbers and in the social standing of its adherents and the process was rapidly hastened whereby the organization of the Church in dioceses ruled by bishops was modelled in detail on the dignified arrangements made for civil government in the provinces. The liturgy also continued its process of development; from being a simple matter of scripture reading and a fellowship supper, it became a solemn ceremonial which borrowed and adapted certain features of court procedure. A new type of church was therefore required to meet the desire for size and splendour, and one such building, consecrated at Tyre about the year 318, is described by Eusebius, who was called upon by his friend, Bishop Paulinus, to deliver the inaugural speech. He speaks of a large outer enclosure, bounded by a wall, and of an entrance-porch. Within came a colonnaded court 'having pillars raised on every side and the spaces filled with wooden barriers of lattice-work rising to a convenient height'.[11] In front of the church itself fountains played, and entry to it was gained by one of three porches, the central doorway being larger and more richly decorated than those at each side. Paved in marble and roofed with cedar, the church, in Eusebius's opinion, presented an appearance of 'brilliant beauty and dazzling workmanship', while the seating was conveniently arranged 'with thrones, very lofty, to do honour to the presidents'. The altar was apparently no longer a moveable wooden table but fixed 'in the midst of the holy of holies' and protected by a screen of lattice-work, 'delicately wrought with the craftsman's utmost skill'. Eusebius refers to this handsome church at Tyre as a 'royal house', and it was in fact an early example of the basilica, the type of building which served as a church, at least in the West, for several centuries.

The word basilica means 'king's hall' and may have been first applied to the throne-room in Egypt or another of the Hellenistic monarchies of the Near East. But the expression need not amount to anything more technical than 'lordly' or 'splendid', and the basilica is a common enough type of building used for a variety of purposes in Rome, as elsewhere, from the second century BC. The architect Vitruvius, who erected a basilica at Fano, on the Adriatic coast, discusses[12] the method of basilica construction. He stipulates as essential a lofty, rectangular hall, the breadth being not more than half nor less than a third of the length. Vitruvius's basilica had columns placed all round the inside of the building to form an aisle or portico with a gallery on top and clerestory windows. The main entrance was set in one of the long sides, exactly opposite the apse, within which the presiding magistrate occupied his elevated seat and the shrine, which in the imperial age sheltered the emperor's effigy, conferred an air of religious solemnity. The same architectural design served for a market or for a covered hall in which to take exercise during cold weather. The general plan could be modified according to the requirements of the site and it was just as easy to construct the entrance in the short side as in the long, when it was felt desirable to emphasize the sacred character of the east end.

Private houses of the ampler type were sometimes equipped with a basilica used for receptions, and, during the second and third centuries AD, members of religious cults took to holding their assemblies in specially constructed basilicas. One such building, the Basilica Crepereia, came to light in the seventeenth century and gained its name from the inscription recording that the chapel had been founded by Lucius Crepereius Rogatus, 'priest of the Sun-God and devotee of Pan'. It is described as a fair-sized shrine consisting of three aisles, the central aisle being wider than the other two. There was an altar, raised on a number of steps, and a decoration of mosaic, the wolf suckling Romulus and Remus as well as a figure which resembled Mars, brandishing a spear.

The best example of such cult basilicas is the one discovered in 1916 lying some 13 metres below the level of the railway-line from Rome to Naples, near the Porta Maggiore (fig. 52). This underground basilica, in a very good state of preservation, is now protected by a casing of concrete. An entrance-porch gives access to a rectangular room divided into three aisles by a double row of three columns and ending in a semicircular apse. It is richly embellished with unusual plasterwork representing Greek myths which have a bearing on the after-life.

The basilica, the aisled hall suitably adapted, might be said to represent what, according to the tastes and fashions of the time, seemed the most fitting architectural form for churches as for other public buildings. So when the emperor Constantine, whose reforming vigour was tempered with respect for established

52. Rome: underground basilica near the Porta Maggiore.

custom, decided on an energetic programme of church-building, he naturally adhered to the basilican style, which was both practically convenient and generally acceptable. In Joseph Bingham's words: 'The Basilicae which heretofore were wont to be filled with Men of Business were now thronged with Votaries praying for the Emperor's safety.'[13]

The first church established by Constantine in Rome was that of St John Lateran. A palace in that district, belonging to a senator named Plautius Lateranus, had been seized by Nero and added to the imperial property. The area duly came into Constantine's control on his marriage to Fausta, daughter of the emperor Maximian, and in 313 AD a Church council assembled 'in the house of Fausta of the Lateran'. When Fausta died, Constantine presented the palace to Pope Silvester, and it remained the official residence of the popes until their departure from Rome to Avignon nearly a thousand years later. The basilica, 'Mother and Head of all the churches of Rome and the whole world', was established nearby on a site levelled and prepared when the barracks of the Horse Guards were demolished. Overthrown by Vandals and subsequently shattered by an earthquake, the church was rebuilt by Pope Sergius about 905–910 AD, at which time it acquired its dedication to John the Baptist. During the seventeenth century the interior was completely transformed by Borromini and rather later a new façade on classical lines was designed by Alessandro Galilei. The long chancel represents a nineteenth-century addition, and until recently it was assumed that no traces of Constantine's original foundation were left; moreover the transepts seemed at variance with the conventional plan of a basilica. Recent excavations, however, continuing the scanty evidence of old drawings, have revealed the nature of Constantine's building. It consisted of a large hall, 76 metres in length and divided by columns into a central nave with two aisles north and south. The columns of the nave were massive and topped, in all probability, with an architrave and clerestory windows. The inner aisles, much lower than the nave, were supported by columns of green marble set on substantial bases and continued for the whole length of the nave; thus the transepts are clearly an addition made in the course of the tenth-century overhaul. The outer aisles on each side may have been curtained off as places to which the catechumens might withdraw during those parts of the service in which they were not permitted to share. What is more certain is that these outer aisles were equipped with large windows and that they were cut short by the transverse walls of rectangular vestries or rooms used for administrative purposes. At the western end of the basilica projected a semicircular apse, its wall sturdily built of masonry with a brick facing. The bishop and clergy had their seats within the apse, and across the space that separated them from the congregation in the nave ran a silver gable, supported by columns. Statues of silver, representing Christ enthroned among his Apostles and Christ triumphant after the Resurrection, were attached to this screen. They lent an air of magnificence to an interior which, by contrast with the plain external walls, seems to have been brilliantly decorated with mosaic, golden altars and an array of candlesticks fashioned in gold or silver.[14] The Lateran basilica is thereby shown to have been typical of what was thought appropriate in the fourth century—a plain, unambitious structure, eminently serviceable and very soundly built along traditional lines with a wealth of light, colour and atmosphere within.

Not all the basilicas were set up directly under the emperor's patronage, but his example and the mood of optimism which his policy encouraged were an inducement to vigorous church-building.[15] This unity of inspiration could however be moulded by the influence of local customs in architecture and liturgy alike. While Rome continued to favour the basilica, Milan showed a preference for variety which included several cross-shaped churches. Istria, around the head of the Adriatic, inclined towards an aisleless nave and at such places as Trier and Aquileia experiments were made with the double basilica.

MEMORIALS AND MARTYR-SHRINES

The strange notion of placing two churches side by side, which is what a double basilica amounts to, may perhaps be explained in terms of a difference of function. For, in addition to the churches required for straightforward congregational worship, another type of building found favour as a place where commemoration might be made of the departed and, in particular, of the martyrs. Here also Christian practice had been influenced by the customs of the pagan world. In Rome offerings and banquets in honour of the departed, particularly on the ninth day after a death, were a part of pious family practice, while the festival of Parentalia, in February, served as a kind of All Souls' tide when such celebrations were the general rule. During that week the temples were closed and magistrates appeared without their badges of office; it was a time of solemn commemoration when living and dead might seem to feast together in clannish solidarity. Sometimes a tube was forced down into the vessel containing the ashes of the dead in order that these might literally have their share of the wine which the rest of the family were enjoying above.

In Christian circles the commemorative rites were of two kinds: the offering of the Eucharist, 'medicine of immortality',[16] and the gathering together of family and friends for a community supper. But the two are not always clearly distinguished in the accounts and sometimes Eucharist and supper were combined, the one following the other. It was laid down, certainly by the fourth century,[17] that the third, ninth and thirtieth days after a death in the family were fitting times for ceremonial observance, though the funeral suppers on occasion diverged from being the 'perfectly sober feasts' which Constantine approved into occasions of luxury and even licence which bishops felt obliged to curtail.

The desire therefore arose for buildings other than the churches designed for everyday use, where proper respect might be paid to the departed[18] and, in particular, where the martyrs could be honoured. The Greek poet Hesiod had described the men of the Golden Age as 'kindly, deliverers from harm and guardians of mortal men',[19] and similar virtues and powers were assigned, in Christian practice, to the martyrs. Theodoret, a scholarly Syrian bishop, explains the tradition of the Church by adopting Hesiod's lines and commenting on them in this way:

Now we, in similar fashion, acclaim as 'deliverers from harm and healers' those who were distinguished for devotion and met their death on that account. We do not call them 'divine'—may such mad folly be ever far from us!—but we speak of them as friends and servants of God who use their free access to him for the kindly purpose of securing for us an abundance of good things.[20]

The value thus attached to the effective virtue of the martyrs led to a keen desire for burial as close as possible to a martyr's tomb, and funeral inscriptions bear witness to the belief that, when the day of Resurrection arrived, the martyrs, as they rose to life eternal, would draw along with them those whose bodies lay nearby. The earliest shrines, usually discovered only by excavation beneath two or three stages of later building, lack adornment or distinction of any kind but are tight packed with a disorderly lumber of coffins. This clustering of tombs continued, at least in the West, when, in spite of Roman law, which declared that tombs should be inviolate, relics of the martyrs were transported from place to place and set in or close to the altars. St John, in his Revelation,[21] 'saw underneath the altar the souls of them that had been slain for the word of God', and the original fixture, around which the martyr-shrine and, later, the martyr-church developed was the altar-slab adapted for funeral feasts.

Sometimes the first thing necessary was to clear space around the tomb in order to allow free access for the faithful. The Via Tiburtina in Rome, for example, was flanked with mausolea and tombs of every sort to which the Christian catacombs below ground provided a counterpart. One of these complex networks acquired high renown as containing the body of the martyred St Laurence. When peace was restored to the Church, the number of pilgrims increased greatly and Constantine, in an attempt to prevent ungracious jostling, isolated the tomb from its surroundings and hollowed out in the tufa a precinct[22] of ample size, equipped with silver railings and much other decoration. It became customary for the pilgrims to assemble here, gaze at the tomb through a grating and let down strips of cloth which were then valued as bearing some touch of the martyr's healing power. A few years later Constantine constructed another church close to and parallel with the original structure.[23] This, the so-called *basilica maior*, eventually fell out of fashion and was allowed to collapse. Even its whereabouts were forgotten until excavation during the period 1950–7 disclosed the foundations. It proves to have been a large building, 95 metres in length, consisting of nave and two substantial aisles sweeping round and enclosing the apse. This style of building, which became a standard type in the fourth century, had two advantages in addition to its dignified appearance. Firstly, the break in the roof surface allowed the craftsmen to work with timbers of moderate size; secondly, as the aisles were lower than the nave, it was possible to insert clerestory windows all round and thus improve the lighting.

Even before the Peace of the Church some attempt had been made to ensure that the faithful might share in the liturgy celebrated on a martyr's anniversary. The underground chapel of St Alexander, on the Via Nomentana, shows the nature of these efforts (fig. 53). At first the bodies of Alexander and his companion Eventius lay in tombs that were difficult of access and the need therefore arose to construct nearby a *triclia*—the word originally means a bower or summer-house—where a modest number of people might congregate for the services. This *triclia* was still separated from the tombs by a partition-wall, so that the next stage was to excavate further and include the tombs within a more ample cult room which was enlarged a second time by breaking through some of the adjacent corridors. An altar-slab was set directly over the double tomb and enclosed by marble-lined panels with a grating (*fenestella*) in front which gave access to the relics below, while small columns rose from the four corners to support a canopy of honour. As Zeno, bishop of Verona, put it, the Sacrifice took place within 'sepulchres turned into temples' on 'tombs converted into altars'.[24]

Development of a similar type occurred when the martyr's body lay not in a catacomb but in an open-air cemetery. Examples are provided by two cities that were military outposts of Empire in Lower Germany, Bonn and Xanten. At Bonn, excavations indicate arrangements of the simplest nature. The original shape of the cemetery was an informal, walled enclosure, pagan in character and containing two stone cubes which served as small tables for funeral banquets. One of the cubes still retains an earthenware vessel, let into its upper surface, designed to receive offerings of food and wine. The cemetery appears to have passed into Christian hands about the year 300 and to have been enlarged at that time to provide space for numerous burials clustered around four sarcophagi which contained the bones of the soldier-martyrs Cassius, Florentius and their companions. The higgledy-piggledy layout was naturally felt inappropriate after a few years, and a paved meeting hall was built. Pagan tombstones were freely incorporated in the structure but crosses and the chi-rho emblem on the pavement marked it as a holy place where ever more imposing edifices might arise with the passing of the years.

Comparable arrangements have been noted at Xanten. Here too excavations carried out quite recently under successive layers of St Victor's church revealed a rectangular cavity enclosing two skeletons of men about forty years of age who had died as the result of repeated blows on head and chest. The skeletons have been identified, not unreasonably, with the local martyrs Victor and Mallosus. Whether that be so or not, there is certainly a funeral-table, roughly carved to receive offerings or to serve as an altar when the Eucharist came to be celebrated. Other tombs jostle one another on all sides, and, as at Bonn, an enclosure for Christian burials seems to have taken the place of an even more haphazard series of pagan interments. At a number of other places, in eastern France as well as in the Rhineland, clear evidence has been found of venerated burial-places, such as those of St Severinus at Cologne, Irenaeus at Lyon or the local saints of Metz and Mainz, lying beneath churches often of much later construction.

The precinct, open to the sky, transformed by stages into a martyr-church of great magnificence: such seems to have been the usual course of development. A modest example may be traced at Tipasa, on the coast of Algeria. The site seems to have been at first a simple burial-ground, enclosed by a wall and connected with a subterranean grotto. In about the year 400 Bishop Alexander converted the precinct into a chapel, its pillars irregularly ranged within a building that is five-sided rather than rectangular because one wall is awkwardly re-aligned to include the entrance to the grotto. Many tombs and at least one semicircular table for use at funeral feasts were dotted about the floor, while two parts of the chapel were set aside for special purposes. An apse at the west end contained a single tomb, perhaps that of the founder bishop, while a group of revered tombs was gathered together and packed closely one against the other to form the floor of a sanctuary beneath and just behind the raised altar. The men thus honoured are described in an inscrip-

53. Rome: underground chapel of St Alexander.

tion as 'the righteous of an earlier time', an expression which may mean that they were martyrs but might also refer simply to Alexander's predecessors as bishops of Tipasa. In either case this church illustrates the fashion whereby the tombs of saintly persons, grouped in the open air during a period of persecution, were subsequently protected by a shrine both from the elements and from undue pressure by less worthy persons.

Something of the same kind occurred at Nola, near Naples. Here the wealthy bishop Paulinus modified and in large measure rebuilt the church at the beginning of the fifth century. His particular interest was the tomb of St Felix, which he enclosed in a courtyard skirted by low walls pierced with arches on supporting columns. This courtyard formed a graceful portico set in front of the new church, a rather splendid basilica with trefoil choir.[25] Walls, columns and paved floor were of marble while the roofs of mosaic shone in the light of numerous lamps suspended from the ceiling. But attached to the church was a complex of rooms, some of which, modest in dimension and with no claim whatever to artistic excellence, were no more than rectangular halls set up at an earlier period to protect such martyr-relics as had been gathered together for the edification of the faithful. Not only were these first halls of an unpretentious type, but the tombs made no claim to distinction and were quietly covered, without any feeling that their virtue was thus extinguished, by the flooring of stone slabs and mosaic which Paulinus provided. The curious effect of the constructions at Nola is that, although the great St Felix lay in an honoured tomb, this tomb remained outside in a shrine of its own. At Nola, as at Bonn and Xanten, martyrs might be revered piously yet with an entire absence of display.

Antioch, in Syria, provides several examples of collective martyr-shrines. There is, in the first place, the Cemetery, a precinct within which lay the bodies of numerous martyrs who had met their deaths in a series of persecutions. Some enjoyed the dignity of a chapel assigned to their own particular cult, but many were packed closely together with the tombs of the faithful crowding about them. There is the 'Martyr-shrine of the Romanesian Gate', where the bodies of a number of saints were deposited, with what might seem a certain lack of ceremony, in a low crypt underneath the pavement of the sanctuary. The coffins lay

54. Salona, Manastirine cemetery: coffins jostling the tomb of Domnio.

on the ground and could be moved about in any emergency, so that, when the crypt became a place of interment for Arian heretics during the latter years of the fourth century, the coffins of the orthodox were transferred to an uncontaminated resting-place in the upper part of the church.[26]

The development of the martyr-shrine is illustrated best of all by the excavations which have been carried out at Salona, a military base on the Dalmatian coast where the emperor Diocletian, a native of the place, built himself a vast palace rather on the lines of an elaborate army camp. Naturally there was no lack of buildings appropriated to the various cults of the Empire, and these served to suggest the form taken by the shrines dedicated to the Christian martyrs. Pagan chapels could indeed be taken over with little adaptation for Christian uses. One instance of this is offered by the chapels sacred to Nemesis, the goddess of Fate, which were part of the equipment of the amphitheatre at Salona. These chapels were situated close by the passage along which the gladiators passed into the arena and along which, in the time of Diocletian's persecution, the company of Christian martyrs advanced to meet their death. After the vic-

tory of the Church, oratories where the gladiators had made their vows to Fate became memorial chapels to the martyrs who were commemorated, before the end of the fifth century, by inscribed pictures which adorned the walls.

Salona fell completely into decay after its sack by the Avars in the year 614. The pattern of Christian life has therefore to be reconstructed from fragmentary remains, but three principal cemeteries may be distinguished where churches took their form under the influence of martyrs' tombs and the holiness attributed to them.

At one of these cemeteries, Kapljuc, the church, constructed by Bishop Leontius about 360 AD, is shaped as a basilica. The plan is commonplace enough, composed of a nave from which aisles are marked off on each side by a row of columns, an apse, and, at the opposite end of the building, an area largely taken up by tombs and memorials. But it looks as though the basilica of Leontius represents the final stage in a process of development extending over half a century. Originally the apse was set up against a piece of wall to shelter the body of the martyred priest Asterius, in accordance with an earlier practice, illustrated by frescoes at Pompeii, whereby semi-circular walls, occasionally amplified into the form of a vaulted apse, served to protect a votive column or funeral monument. The saint's devotees gathered in the open air, but there was not a great deal of room and only a little way off stood another celebrated martyr-tomb which took a rather different form. This was the sepulchre of four military saints who, like Asterius, had met their deaths in Diocletian's persecution, and the upper surface of the tomb, with holes for the pouring of libations, provided a convenient table at which the faithful might celebrate their feasts of commemoration; for this purpose a bench also was supplied. These two rather primitive martyr-shrines were subsequently linked together, in that they were enclosed by a rectangular precinct isolating them from more ordinary graves. The third stage was reached when Bishop Leontius, regarding as inadequate an arrangement which left the worshippers standing in the open air, constructed his basilica which, without disturbing the precinct that contained honoured tombs, should simply include it within the space of an ample chancel. Around this a miscellaneous array of tombs and mausolea sprang up, clustering as close as possible to the shrines of the 'holy martyrs whose ashes drive far away the wicked demons'.[27]

The Manastirine cemetery at Salona had a history not unlike that of Kapljuc. The nucleus seems to have been a martyr-tomb, probably that of Bishop Domnio, attached to the wall of a villa and sheltered by an apsidal canopy. Around this the faithful thought it fitting to construct a precinct shaped with a fairly wide cross piece and a rather narrow approach section: in other words it resembled a church lacking aisles but with the rough equivalent of a transept. The picture is complicated by the large number of competing shrines which jostled up against that of Bishop Domnio, and when the church was extended lengthways to form a basilica of more regular shape, the whole area near the martyr's grave was cluttered with the chaotic jumble of tombs discovered when excavations were carried out at the end of the nineteenth century (fig. 54).

The Marusinac cemetery, also at Salona, tells a similar story (fig. 55), though here the area was apparently in private hands and development followed a somewhat more leisurely course. Here again the focal point was a tomb, that of the martyr St Anastasius, a fuller who was thrown into the sea by

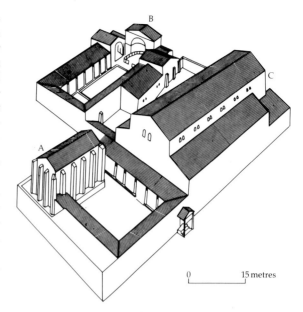

55. Salona: reconstruction of Marusinac cemetery.
A. Original shrine; B. Second shrine;
C. Roofed basilica.

order of Diocletian. Apparently the body of Anastasius was first laid in a chapel constructed by a wealthy woman named Asclepia. This chapel, a buttressed rectangle with small, internal apse, was arranged on two floors. The altar of remembrance was perhaps set on the upper floor immediately above the martyr's grave while, more certainly, places were reserved at the lower level for the tombs of Asclepia and her husband. This somewhat restricted arrangement did not last very long, and the body of Anastasius was removed to a vaulted apse, easier of access, nearby. Two matching rectangular rooms were built north and south, making a transept in rudimentary form. The central space was left open to the sky so that when, as at Manastirine, the funeral complex was enlarged, the appearance inside was that of a

courtyard set in front of a sanctuary and flanked by covered enclosures. The general shape, again, is that of a basilica but one with a roofless nave. The colonnaded portico of this church extended to meet another church of St Anastasius, a roofed basilica of conventional pattern built with considerable splendour as indicated by the well-preserved mosaic of geometrical patterns which adorns the floor. The shrine of Marusinac therefore came to possess two churches set very close together and nearly parallel.

Though now in a sadly ruined state, the cemeteries at Salona serve to demonstrate how the cult of the martyrs, adopting some of the practices and architectural forms of pagan hero-worship, influenced, at any rate in detail, the development of Christian churches.

THE BASILICA—THE ACHIEVEMENT OF CONSTANTINE

To the impulses of Christian piety were added the solid encouragements of imperial favour. Constantine cast himself in the role of reconciling a divided world through the two instruments of an enlightened public policy and the unifying force of a common faith. His triumphal arch in Rome showed him crushing the forces of Maxentius in the fashion of Moses delivered from his adversaries at the Red Sea, while the motto inscribed on the arch declared him to be acting 'through divine inspiration and with the greatest breadth of sympathy'. While refusing to alienate paganism he sought to ensure the support of Christians by furthering the spread of their doctrines so that, as Eusebius enthusiastically put it:

We saw every place which, but a little while ago, had been laid in ruins by the evil deeds of the tyrants reviving as though from a long and deadly destruction, and temples once more rising from their foundations to a vast height and receiving a magnificence far greater than that of the buildings which had formerly been demolished.[28]

Constantine extended his patronage widely, but the principal scenes of his activity were Rome, Constantinople and the holy places of Palestine. Unlike the medieval builders, with their desire to demonstrate

their faith by vaults, windows and towers soaring heavenwards, Constantine remained content with the unobtrusive though effective forms of basilica-hall and martyr-shrine. The choice of materials might vary according to local custom, but lavish expenditure on decoration was expected in order to convey a sense of unearthly splendour and, incidentally, to demonstrate the emperor's 'generosity and piety'. One class of Constantine's churches, however, seems to have lacked any great elaboration because the buildings were closely packed with tombs and funeral monuments of every type: such were the large basilicas constructed over a martyr's underground grave. Like the *basilica maior* of St Laurence, the church recently mapped out beneath the Baroque trappings of S. Sebastiano at Rome[29] seems to have consisted of a large nave with clerestory windows looking out over much lower aisles, the apse being enclosed by an ambulatory, or passageway, large enough to permit orderly movement of the devout sightseers.

The church of S. Sebastiano is not attributed to Constantine in the *Liber Pontificalis*. This, the official chronicle of the Roman bishops, assigns to his enterprise seven churches, three outside the walls and four

56. Pola, the Museum: ivory casket showing St Peter's, Rome.

within, which, though serving adequately as general meeting-places for worship, owed their form and individual character to the presence of a revered tomb. Just as, in Palestine, the exact points traditionally linked with the Nativity and the Holy Sepulchre dictated the shape of Constantine's structures, so, in Rome, convenience was sacrificed in order to make the martyr's grave a readily accessible focus of honour. Nowhere is this zeal to derive the utmost benefit from a sacred spot more amply demonstrated than in the case of St Peter's.

There it was not a matter of using an obvious and ready site but of removing a number of tombs and then constructing an enormous platform cut into the hillside at one end and, at the other, raised on massive foundations to a height of nine or ten metres. The whole affair represents a notable feat of engineering, and indeed Constantine's church lasted more or less unchanged throughout the Middle Ages. It was then judged insecure and replaced during the sixteenth century by the vast building set up to the designs of Bramante and the other Renaissance architects who succeeded him. Fairly extensive traces of Constantine's church have, however, been revealed by excava-

tions which confirm three other types of evidence. In the first place there are several written accounts, beginning with a notice in the *Liber Pontificalis*.[30] This begins by making the rhetorical and not very exact claim that Constantine, urged on by Bishop Silvester, built the basilica of St Peter and enclosed the Apostle's coffin within layers of solid bronze. More valuable is the information which follows: 'Above the grave Constantine set columns of porphyry as an adornment together with other spiral columns which he had brought from Greece.' The barley-sugar columns, carved in spiral channels with alternating bands of vine ornament, exist to this day though moved from their original site. Their curious shape, and a medieval tradition that they had once formed part of Solomon's Temple, appealed to Raphael and, perhaps through the influence of his cartoons, they were widely copied in such unlikely places as the University Church, Oxford.

Another piece of historical evidence is furnished by the fifth-century ivory casket found near Pola, in Dalmatia, and now in the museum there (fig. 56). One side of the casket is carved with a stiffly formal representation of the shrine at St Peter's. The barley-

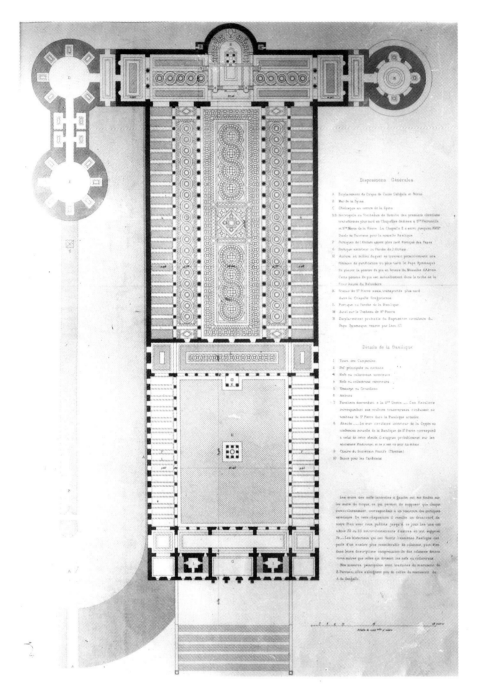

57. Rome, Old St Peter's: Ground-plan, c. 1820, based on the work of Tiberio Alfarano,
De Basilicae Vaticanae structura.

sugar columns support a rather elaborate cornice beneath which stand male and female worshippers with raised hands or, since there are curtains drawn back behind them, figures of the faithful departed. The cornice is recessed on each side of the shrine itself and supports the four ribs of a canopy from which hangs a circular lamp such as, in the *Liber Pontificalis*, receives mention as one of the gifts bestowed by the emperor. The shrine itself, protected by a low screen, is made to resemble a large cupboard with doors and surmounted by a cross, while two devotees crouch beside it.

The third piece of evidence is the drawings made by sixteenth-century artists shortly before Constantine's church was destroyed; attractive in themselves, they appear from the evidence of recent excavations to be accurate also.[31] The church faced westwards and it was that end which Constantine finished during his lifetime, as a dedicatory inscription on the triumphal arch indicated, while the rest of the building seems to have been completed slowly, over a period of about thirty years, but in accordance with the original design. The visitor approached it from the east by means of a flight of steps leading into a large, enclosed courtyard with an elaborate fountain in the shape of a bronze pine-cone. He then saw, ahead of him, a plain portico set in front of the five doorways leading into the church itself. This, following the precedent of St John Lateran, consisted, for the greater part of its length,[32] of a high nave with double aisle on each side (fig. 57). The large hall, colourful but bare, impressed the spectator with its forest of lofty columns dividing nave from aisles, as Gregory of Tours records:

St Peter the Apostle is buried in the temple which in ancient times used to be called Vaticanum: it has four rows of columns, marvellous to see and ninety-six in number. There are four more around the altar, making a hundred in all, besides those which support the canopy over the tomb.[33]

The basilican part of the church seems to have served, like the nave of a medieval cathedral, as a meeting-place for all and sundry, beggars and pilgrims, the curious as well as the devout. It was used also as a place of burial.

While the nave resembled that of St John Lateran, the west end was markedly different: it was not so much a congregational meeting-place as the precinct of a martyr-shrine. The transept, taking the form of a small nave set at right angles to the main nave, was something of a novelty. It came to be a convenient and familiar element in Gothic architecture but in the fourth century it was provided as an exceptional feature to meet the special purpose of accommodating a throng of worshippers. It could, however, be claimed as a Hellenistic form derived from the cult room set in front of pagan hero-shrines.[34] As regards the form of the sanctuary at St Peter's, Gregory of Tours is again informative:

The tomb is placed under the altar and is kept entirely on its own. But, if anyone desires to pray, the screens which surround the place are unbolted and he has access to the point just above the tomb. A small window may be opened there, so he puts his head inside and asks for whatever his need requires.

The site of the altar is not exactly known; it may indeed have been movable until Gregory the Great arranged for Mass to be celebrated 'over St Peter's body'.[35] In that case, the altar would be set somewhere in front of the shrine at the time of services while the clergy, emerging from the apse, ranged themselves on either side with the people behind them.

Constantine's churches at Rome, combining classic simplicity of design with richness of internal decoration, set the pattern for later builders. But all, whether large basilican meeting halls or compact, centralized martyr-shrines, survive only as fragments beneath later reconstructions. They are, however, sufficiently preserved to indicate the ways in which Constantine faced the problem of connecting a large hall, adapted for congregational worship, to the relics of the martyr whose presence was a focus for devotion. The general pattern of S. Lorenzo and S. Sebastiano was followed in the church of St Marcellinus and St Peter, adjoining the tomb of Helena, mother of Constantine, on the Via Labicana, and, again, in the case of St Agnes on the Via Nomentana. Nothing is known concerning the details of St Agnes' martyrdom: it may be supposed that she was a victim of the final persecution in the time of Diocletian. At any rate she found her resting-place in a tiny shrine contained within a catacomb taken over by Christians from its previous use as a pagan burial-place. A church was constructed over the top layer of this catacomb, apparently a fair-sized hall with galleries projecting above ground. But the site was transformed when Constantine, or perhaps his son Constantine II, set up a large basilica,[36] with the customary aisles and clerestory, alongside. Pope Honorius I, about 630 AD, again modified the whole arrangement by building a new church in place of, rather than incorporating, Constantine's basilica. The precise location of St Agnes' shrine was obscured, but presumably she lies directly beneath the massive altar which, as though by substitution, took on the appearance of a sarcophagus and bears, carved on its front face, the figure of a female saint with hands outstretched in prayer. It is possible to compare the great basilica of SS. Nereus, Achilles and Petronilla, constructed at the end of the fourth century and partially sunk into the earth in order to include a range of tombs immediately below the paving of the floor.

Another type of Constantinian building was the mausoleum, a name applied by the Romans to exceptionally elaborate tombs constructed for imperial personages. The sepulchre still partially preserved in the Castel Sant' Angelo was built about the year 135 AD for the emperor Hadrian and served as the resting-place of the emperors and their relatives for seventy or eighty years. A circular tower some 68 metres in diameter sprang from a vast square base, the whole structure being elaborately decorated with colonnades, statues and a glistening surface of Parian marble. At the top rose a pyramid, surmounted by a large bronze cone still preserved within the area of the Vatican. Constantine, in his turn, saw nothing inconsistent with the Christian faith in the practice of commemorating members of the imperial house with awe-inspiring splendour, though he naturally chose to link such sepulchres with a church. His own mausoleum, a rotunda placed alongside the Church of the Holy Apostles at Constantinople, has disappeared, but the circular mausoleum assigned to his mother Helena still exists, somewhat decayed, under the name of Tor Pignattara in the eastern suburbs of Rome.

A better idea of such buildings is, however, conveyed by the round church of S. Costanza in the northern outskirts of the city (fig. 58). This was in fact erected as a mausoleum for Constantina, the emperor's daughter, some twenty years after Constantine's death, but it reflects the style and pattern of earlier structures. S. Costanza adjoins the basilica of S. Agnese, but, whereas S. Agnese was to a large extent rebuilt in the seventh century, S. Costanza remains

substantially in its original form. The outside is a circle of unadorned masonry, varied only by an entrance hall, 18 metres in breadth and flanked by two apses. Splendour alike of design and colour was reserved for the circle of the mausoleum itself. The entrance gives onto an ambulatory which leads all round the building. This passageway, topped with a barrel vault,[37] has on one side the main external wall, into which have been recessed several niches of varying shape; on the inner side, it is divided from the high drum of the cupola by twelve pairs of granite columns (fig. 59). The columns are all of identical pattern, being topped by richly-carved 'composite' capitals, in which the scrolls of the Ionic are added to the acanthus leaves of the Corinthian style. The capitals, in their turn, are surmounted by lofty imposts of stone which directly support the brickwork of the arcade. At the four cardinal points the arches are bigger than the rest, one of these enlarged arches marking the entrance while, directly opposite, another encloses Constantina's vast sarcophagus.[38] Windows pierced in the drum of the cupola give a certain amount of light which would have been enhanced by the glow of lamps playing upon the brilliant decoration of mosaic.

Constantine, when carrying out his ambitious programme of church-building, was at least as vigorous in Palestine as at Rome, though in the Holy Land his martyria were designed to shelter a venerated place rather than a venerated relic. His mother Helena had visited Palestine as a pilgrim and established several shrines, including one over the grotto of the Nativity. In the words of Eusebius,

the holy Empress, wishing to preserve with diligence the memory of Christ's infancy, took care to give to the holy grotto a rich and varied decoration. Soon afterwards the Emperor himself, surpassing the splendour bestowed by his mother, embellished the same spot in a truly royal manner with the use of gold, silver and rich tapestry.[39]

St Luke, in his Gospel, merely records that, after the birth of Jesus, they 'laid him in a manger' but, from the second century, the Cave of the Nativity was pointed out[40] and there Constantine built his church, as a pilgrim from Bordeaux, who came to Bethlehem in the year 333, bears witness.[41]

In spite of much rebuilding by Justinian, who enclosed the whole of the east end with a trefoil sheath, the present structure still bears the impress of

58. Rome, S. Costanza: the outside, as shown in an engraving attributed to S. J. Neele, 1796.

59. Rome, S. Costanza: interior.

Constantine's handiwork (fig. 60). The church consisted of three main parts: the atrium or forecourt, the basilica and an octagonal chapel set up over the Cave itself, thus providing an early example of a church for congregational worship being combined with a martyr-shrine or its equivalent. The atrium, some 27 metres wide, was enclosed by a covered colonnade which developed, on the east side, into a portico marking the entrance doors. The basilica, conventional in design, was divided by rows of columns into five aisles, the central aisle being about double the width of the others. The original foundation of large limestone blocks has been discovered beneath the floor of the present church, as have considerable portions of the mosaic floor, its richly patterned borders contrasting with the simple white mosaic of the atrium. Argument persists concerning the style and age of the columns. They have been claimed as part of Constantine's church but assigned by other archaeologists to the sixth-century restoration: possibly the answer is that they are original columns used a second time and increased in number by copies. From the centre of the nave, at its eastern end, a flight of steps led up to the octagonal shrine, where again the scene was brightened by a carpet of mosaic on the floor. And, since devout pilgrims would wish to look into the Cave, a circular shaft, about twelve feet across, was driven down from the level of the floor and surrounded by a plain stone kerb with steps arranged on an octagonal plan.[42] A metal screen seems to have been provided together with colourful hangings while, above, a hole was pierced in the roof to admit rays of light illuminating the birthplace of the Son of Righteousness.

Tinged as it may have been with political prudence and a streak of vanity, Constantine's fervent piety drove him restlessly on, at the end of his reign, to mark three other sacred places of Palestine with appropriate shrines.

One of these was the ancient sanctuary of Mamre, where the angels met Abraham with the encouraging message that 'Abraham shall surely become a great and mighty nation'.[43] A yearly fair was held at Mamre when Jews, Arabs and Christians carried out an elaborate ritual which included the lighting of lamps and the offering of libations. Constantine was shocked by such irregular superstition and suppressed it,

establishing instead a church 'worthy of the antiquity and holiness of the place'.[44] This church, so far as it can be traced now, was quite small, having only three columns on each side of the nave with an apse at the end, enclosed within the rectangle of the building. At the west side, a long porch (narthex) was continued to form additional rooms on both sides, while another set of side chambers, apparently used as sacristies or for administrative purposes, projected at the east end. The whole was enclosed within a precinct containing the oak tree near which Abraham was sitting when he received the divine message.

With this sanctuary at Mamre may be compared the Church of the Loaves and Fishes discovered at El Tabgha by the shores of Lake Gennesareth in 1932. This was a squat basilica of standard type, with courtyard and narthex. A mosaic of high quality, found within the curve of the apse, shows a basket flanked by two fishes and containing some loaves marked with crosses, thus linking the miracle with the Eucharist, while in front, at the centre of the apse, lies the stone referred to by the pilgrim Aetheria: 'the stone upon which the Lord laid the bread has been turned into an altar. Visitors take away chips of this stone, since it heals all ills.' Aetheria[45] wrote in 385 AD while church and mosaic belong to a period some fifty years later, but underneath remains have been found of a diminutive, earlier church, just under 17 metres long, which must have been the one which Aetheria knew and goes back to a time not much after Constantine's death, even if it is not to be numbered among his foundations.

Constantine's Church of the Holy Sepulchre, including both the tomb of Christ and the rock of Calvary, was a larger and more ambitious structure than that at Mamre, but gained its distinction less from its size than as the result of a stately sequence of courts and buildings leading from one to the other. Everything has been so completely remodelled in the course of time that the description given by Eusebius in his *Life of Constantine* offers a clearer picture than is yielded by any results of excavation. Standing close to the centre of Jerusalem, it supplanted a temple of Aphrodite which the emperor caused to be demolished, revealing the cave and the rock which the church was then built to enshrine. The impressive entrance (fig. 61)—'very attractively designed', as Eusebius remarks—led from the main shopping street

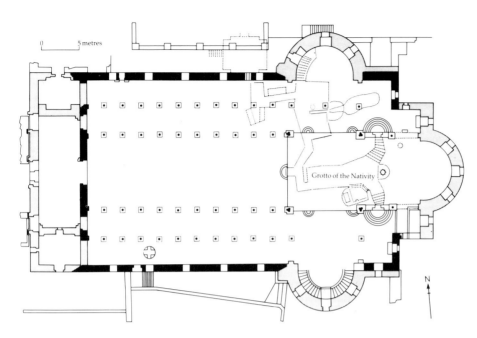

60. Bethlehem, Church of the Nativity: ground-plan.

of Jerusalem into an open courtyard. The courtyard, with its rectangle of columns and fountain in the middle, gave access to the façade of the church where, to borrow Eusebius's words again, 'three doorways, well arranged, admitted the crowd of those who came in from outside.' No measurements are recorded but the church was clearly a wide building, and distinctly stumpy. What amazed all beholders was the brilliance of the decoration. Constantine, in a letter to the bishop of Jerusalem, had instructed him to ensure that this building should be 'better and more beautiful than any in the world', and insisted that there should be no lack of marble or precious metals. And so it worked out. The two rows of columns on each side separating nave from aisles, and the galleries set above the aisles, may have presented an unremarkable design but

the inner surface of the building was hidden beneath layers of polychrome marble: the ceiling was decorated with carved panels which, resembling a great sea, surged continuously over the whole basilica and the glistening gold with which the ceiling was covered made the whole shrine sparkle with a thousand reflected lights.

Such was the impression of Eusebius, who added that the exterior had by no means been neglected:

The outer aspect of the walls, bright with polished stone admirably laid presented an unusual beauty in no way inferior to that of marble. As regards the roof, its outer surface was covered over with lead, a sure protection against the winter rains.

At its west end, the basilica was completed with what Eusebius calls the 'hemisphere', decorated with twelve columns corresponding to the number of the apostles. Large silver bowls, presented by Constantine, capped the columns, which were enclosed at roof height by some kind of dome. This seems an elaborate structure if it was designed merely as an apse in which to seat the bishop and other clergy. Its use can only be guessed at; but a possible explanation is that it enshrined a relic of the True Cross. Another opinion is that Eusebius failed to get his facts right, and that the curving range of twelve columns extended from the basilica into the inner court to honour the relic of the Cross which the pilgrim Aetheria described as being in the open air. Still other critics interpret the 'hemisphere' as an early form of the rotunda encircling the Sepulchre.

Calvary, the traditional scene of the Crucifixion, was in the uncovered courtyard immediately to the

61. Jerusalem: the Church of the Holy Sepulchre in its relation to the city today.

west of the basilica. The rock itself, some four metres in height, had been chopped in forthright fashion to give it a more regular shape and to render it serviceable as a pedestal for the jewelled cross erected on top of it. The stately complex of buildings, well adapted for solemn, liturgical processions, extended still further west to include the circular, domed structure which sheltered the Sepulchre. Some of the lower courses of masonry here belong apparently to Constantine's own period, while the dome is illustrated by a little painting on the top of a seventh-century Palestinian reliquary now in the Vatican: it was made of stone, or just possibly wood, and had a range of semicircular windows round the base. The edifice as a whole contained a wide passageway running all round the inside of the main wall. Next came a circular colonnade, leading up to the smaller columns of the gallery above, which served as a support for the dome. And last, exactly in the centre of the rotunda, was the rock cave which bore witness to Christ's victory over death. With a certain lack of historical sense this monument again had been modified from its original shape, in order to suit Constantine's architectural arrangement. The tomb was cut out in isolation from

the surrounding rock and the approaches levelled in order to provide a smooth surface for the pavement of the rotunda. Columns, with metalwork grilles between them, were set round the grotto to protect it and to support a pointed canopy, while 'embellishment of every possible kind'[46] conferred the splendour required by the fashion of the time. Veneration was paid not only to the tomb itself but also to the stone which, as St Matthew records, served as a seal and was rolled away by the angel. This stone was held to offer a 'witness to the Resurrection';[47] at some point it seems to have been broken in two, and one piece, enclosed within a metal sheath, used as an altar. The majestic combination of holy places on Golgotha so impressed the historians that they likened it to the New Jerusalem foretold by the Prophets and appearing in the visions of the Apocalypse where the Throne of God and of the Lamb is seen to supplant the Temple of the Ancient Law.[48]

Less than three hundred years after its construction this great shrine of the Anastasis, devised by the emperor and attributed by tradition to an architect named Zenobius, had been destroyed by the Persians.

62. Madaba: the mosaic map of Jerusalem.

Subsequent rebuildings transformed the coherence of the earlier plan but some idea of what it looked like may be drawn not only from the rhetorical language of Eusebius but from two ancient illustrations. One is the fourth-century mosaic in the church of S. Pudenziana in Rome, where the Church of the Nativity appearing on the left side of the triumphant Christ is balanced by a second church, suggesting the rotunda and adjacent buildings of the Anastasis. The other is a mosaic of very different character, a map found on the site of a Christian church at Madaba, in Moabite territory east of the Dead Sea. This map, now much damaged,[49] dates from the middle of the sixth century and shows the land of Palestine in such fashion as to provide a commentary on events of the Old and New Testament. Various combinations of line and colour are used to indicate sea, mountain and plain, while a whimsical touch is given by the fish in the rivers, a lion chasing a gazelle and two enormous ships, entirely out of scale, afloat on the Dead Sea. The smaller towns are marked conventionally, by a wall with two or three towers and the name inscribed above, sometimes with the addition at one side of a Scriptural text. The larger towns, however, are represented in an individual

manner which could lay claim to realism. Thus Jericho is set in its circle of palm trees, while Lydda is shown with a colonnade surrounding a wide market-place with a splendid church at one end.

But the treatment of Jerusalem is on an altogether grander scale (fig. 62). The entrance by the northern, or Damascus, gateway stands out clearly on the plan, together with Hadrian's column in the open space nearby. Thereafter the central High Street with its arcaded shops strikes firmly through Cheese Market to the fortified Gate of Benjamin. Various buildings may be identified with reasonable assurance, but little attempt is made to maintain proportion. The chief emphasis is laid on the Church of the Anastasis, which, with only a slight deviation from exact geography, is placed precisely at the mid-point of the picture. A strain of symbolism is at work here. Some commentators[50] held, with reference to the Psalmist's words 'God is in the midst of her', that Jerusalem was the centre of the Universe and that the central fact of history, the death and resurrection of Christ, would naturally have occurred at the mid-point of Jerusalem. Such a place was, in any event, particularly appropriate for the tomb sanctuary of the Founder-Prince in his capital city of the New Israel.[51] Something like a bird's-eye view is given of the church, and its various parts are clearly distinguished. The large courtyard leads from the market-place towards the three entrance doorways of the basilica, whose golden pediment and high-pitched red roof contrast, as architectural features, with the large golden apse representing the dome over the sacred spot.

The rotunda of the Anastasis, like that of S. Costanza in Rome, showed how the classic form of an imperial mausoleum could be drawn into the service of the Christian Church. Once the pattern had been laid down with such authority it was widely followed, and circular, or sometimes polygonal, buildings of this general type, which conveniently sheltered sacred remains or marked a hallowed site, became fairly widespread in Palestine and elsewhere. The church of St Carpus and St Papylus in Constantinople, which may date from as early as 400 AD, is sometimes instanced as a direct copy of the Anastasis. Certainly its ground-plan reproduces that of a domed hall surrounded by an ambulatory. But the vaulting is of brick rather than stone, and the ambulatory at one end finishes in a secondary apse which makes the building lop-sided.

Another set of Constantine's grandiose structures marking the holy places of Palestine was situated on the Mount of Olives and linked with the record of Christ's Ascension. But the remains that still exist are scanty and identification by no means easy amid the numerous churches and chapels of ancient foundation built on the mountain; a pilgrim named Theodosius calculated that there were twenty-four by the end of the fifth century.[52] According to the contemporary evidence of Eusebius,[53] the emperor's mother, St Helena, founded two churches there. One was set over the cave in which Christ gave final instructions to his followers: 'Go forth and make all nations my disciples', the other marked the spot which still bore the impress made by Christ's feet at the moment of the Ascension.

The Carmelites of Jerusalem, in the course of their recent excavations, have discovered traces of a large basilica very near to the highest point of the Mount of Olives. The masonry of this church, consisting of rough local stone cemented with lime mortar, points to the fourth century insofar as it indicates any clear date. Beneath the apse lies a grotto which was apparently connected by stairways with the aisles. It is therefore a reasonable, if not an entirely certain, conjecture that this is the Church of the Final Instruction where Christ 'initiated his disciples into secret mysteries'.[54] Some sixty metres away, exactly at the top of the mountain, fragments of walling have been disclosed which seem to fit accounts[55] of the Chapel of the Ascension, founded by Helena.[56] The structure follows, in general, a classical type of domed mausoleum, where the thick outer walls of an octagon, pierced by at least two entrance doorways, enclose a broad ambulatory flanked on the inside by a circle of columns.[57] At the central point within the circle lay the venerated spot, a patch of earth left untouched by the surrounding pavement, which was here raised up sufficiently to allow pilgrims to see without causing damage.

In the year 324 AD Constantine chose Byzantium, on the Bosphorus, as the capital of his Empire. Extensive rebuilding and development continued for six years, and in May 330 the city was officially refounded as New Rome, or Constantinople. Public buildings of the most splendid character were erected, apparently in the balanced classical style adopted also by successive emperors in the fourth and fifth centuries. But little of Constantine's own work survives, except perhaps parts of the Hippodrome, and even the great walls protecting the city were superseded by those, still in part remaining, that Theodosius II constructed about 412 AD.

A similar fate has befallen Constantine's churches. His New Rome was designed to be essentially a Christian community and 'since the city became the capital of Empire during a period of sound religion', in the words of Sozomen, an historian of the fourth century, 'it was not polluted by altars, Grecian temples or sacrifices, while Constantine adorned it with numerous and magnificent houses of prayer'.[58]

The most celebrated of all these buildings was the Church of the Divine Wisdom, 'Santa Sophia', set beside the imperial palace. This may have been started by Constantine, though Socrates,[59] another historian of the period, attributes it to Constantine's son, Constantius, and in any event it was not completed until 356 AD. Fragments of foundation walls found beneath Justinian's noble rebuilding (536 AD) have been held to suggest that the original was constructed on a straight-forward basilican plan with aisles and galleries, the whole enclosed within a precinct and having a fore-court in front of the entrance doorways. Nearby, within the same precinct, stood the church of St Irene, 'Peace'. This was an older sanctuary 'of small dimensions' which Constantine 'considerably enlarged and adorned',[60] re-dedicating it in honour of the peace which his reign had brought to the world. The edifice was burned down, however, and then so completely restored by Justinian that its original form can only be guessed at. Constantine's great Church of the Holy Apostles, built to contain his coffin of gold, has disappeared also but a description of it, offered incidentally by Eusebius[61] when he tells of the emperor's funeral, gives some impression of what it looked like. From Eusebius's account, it appears that the church was placed within a large rectangular precinct, with a portico at each side as well as several meeting halls, baths and lodgings for the staff. The shrine itself was notable for its height and for the brilliance of its decoration. Marble of every variety lined the walls; the panelled ceiling was overlaid with gold. The roof had a covering of gilded bronze so that the central dome appeared from a distance to glow with a bright-

ness like that of the sun. A carved balustrade, also of gilded bronze, ran round the inside of the building, which appears to have taken the form of a circle inscribed within the arms of a cross. The emperor's tomb occupied the central place of honour, protected by twelve columns representing the Apostles and with the altar set nearby. Constantine's position here seems in fact to surpass the prestige which he claimed for himself as 'bishop of those outside the Church' and to reach that attributed to him in a later hymn: 'Thou didst not receive thy call from men but, like Saint Paul, thou hadst it, glorious one, from on high—Constantine, the equal of the Apostles'.[62] Twenty years later, the emperor's coffin was transferred to a nearby mausoleum, resembling that of S. Costanza at Rome, but the Church of the Holy Apostles, though losing thereby something of majesty, gained in return an added lustre from relics of the Apostles themselves. Justinian completely rebuilt the church, but the influence of its pattern, the cross with central tower and dome, spread far and wide and persisted for centuries, as did the versatility and technical skill fostered by the demands of imperial patronage.

DEVELOPMENTS IN THE WEST—ROME: MILAN: GERMANY: AQUILEIA

By the middle of the fourth century, as the vitality of paganism waned, the Christian Church had become the inheritor of both classical thought and classical art-forms, charged with a new significance. Just as the terms of Greek and Roman philosophy were used for the construction of an ever more detailed system of Christian theology, so the church-builders took over and developed the well-tried forms of an earlier architecture. The two principal types of church, the centralized compact martyr-shrine and the elongated basilica hall with nave and aisles well adapted for congregational worship, appear throughout the Empire. Practical needs, no less than precedent, dictated a certain sameness of design, but, as in the Middle Ages, the vigorous impress of local character clearly distinguishes the churches of one region from those found elsewhere.

A standard form of basilica church served to express the artistic ideas and meet the day-to-day require-

ments of the West during the fourth and fifth centuries, and the pattern of architecture varies little from Milan to North Africa. Balanced, austere and dignified, it reflects the old Roman ideal of *gravitas*, 'composure and authority', deceptive only in that it served as a frame containing a rich embellishment of light and colour. By the fourth century, churches were usually designed to run from west to east. The west end was sometimes approached by way of an atrium, or enclosed forecourt, but, more frequently, the architects contented themselves with providing a porch (narthex). This was not, as often in Gothic churches, a small protuberance, but rather a slim, rectangular room running the whole width of the building, either inside or outside the nave. This nave, or general meeting-place, was either a single hall or could be divided by two rows of piers or columns to make three compartments, often of nearly equal size.

Sometimes practical needs dictated that these aisles

should be furnished with galleries, a pattern which may be seen repeated in certain of the Waterloo Churches, buildings set up in a vaguely classical style to accommodate large congregations in the rapidly expanding urban areas of early nineteenth-century England. The columns might be symmetrical and made to match or else, particularly in Rome itself, taken over as spoils from some earlier building, while, above every arch, it was usual to set a clerestory window filled with some such material as a thin layer of alabaster, through which light would filter and strike the decoration of paint or mosaic which covered the wall space. Floors, whether made of polished stone or mosaic, similarly reflected the light, as did the ceilings, panelled or made up of open timber-work but in either case often touched with gold or bronze. The nave led towards the central altar, placed in front of the apse with its formal benches for the clergy, but in the larger churches the aisles might be cut short by a transept, which sometimes projected hardly at all beyond the line of the exterior wall, designed less as an architectural refinement than to serve the down-to-earth purposes of providing vestries or convenient space for liturgical manoeuvre. Nothing in the nature of medieval rood-screens obstructed access from nave to chancel, but low barricades, usually made of pierced stone, and themselves known as 'chancels', protected the area reserved for the clergy from any undue pressure of the devout or the curious alike.

The earliest churches built at Rome along this general plan have without exception been destroyed or overwhelmed in later reconstruction. San Clemente offers the standard example. Here the present structure, with its arcaded nave, aisles and semicircular apse, is built on top of a fourth-century church, similar in general design but larger. The top parts of the arcade dividing the earlier nave from its aisle appear built into the right aisle of the existing church and, in the vault below, sections of masonry outline the older structure amidst the walls and buttresses designed at various times to support the upper church. The fourth-century S. Clemente, itself perched above the remains of houses where religious rites first of Mithraism and then of the Christians were carried out, is shown to have been a broad, low basilica, lacking transepts—a large hall, in fact, with the aisles and arcaded portico forming a graceful ambulatory around it.[63] Such columns as have been uncovered from the foundation walls of the upper church differ from one another both in style and in material, being drawn haphazardly from older monuments.

The basilica of St Paul 'outside the walls' belongs, like the original S. Clemente, to the time of Siricius, who was pope from 384 to 398 and, according to an epitaph written of him, 'built up anew the temples of the saints'. This basilica (fig. 63) superseded the small church which Constantine had erected over the shrine marking the apostle's reputed burial-place on the Ostian Way. Despite pillage by the Saracens, it remained in more or less its original state until 1823, when almost the entire building, apart from the 'triumphal arch' separating nave from transept, was destroyed by fire. The work of reconstruction began almost at once and was carried through vigorously by a group of architects headed by Luigi Poletti. The result is usually criticized as cold and spiritless, since the early nineteenth century was perhaps not the ideal period in which to reproduce the last enchantment of the classical age; nevertheless a determined effort was made to bring the original back to life and its vast dimensions were scrupulously followed, so that, particularly with the help of early illustrations, a clear notion of the fourth-century basilica may be obtained. The nave, approached by way of a grandiose courtyard with columns around it, extended to a length of 97 metres, and was flanked on each side by a double arcade of fluted columns with Corinthian capitals. The aisles thus constructed seem to have been low and dark, in contrast to the nave which was lofty and furnished with a range of clerestory windows.[64] Nave and aisles led to a vast stumpy transept, affording ample space in which the faithful might throng about the shrine while beyond that again was set the semicircular apse. Amply decorated with marble, plaster and mosaic 'in the manner of meadows that blossom when spring comes with her flowers'[65] the whole arrangement was one of classic order adapted to the vitality of a revived and triumphant faith.

The closing years of the fourth century in Rome were marked by the greatest enthusiasm for building or rebuilding churches and, among those attributed to Pope Siricius, the church of S. Pudenziana, on the Esquiline Hill, is the most celebrated. This is a brick basilica, standing below street level, and, though drastically altered, still displays the original marble

63. Rome: the church of 'St Paul outside the walls' as it was before the fire of 1823. From a water-colour by G. P. Panini, 1741. Cambridge, Fitzwilliam Museum.

columns, with small circular channelled capitals, recessed into newer work. The apse, with its splendid mosaic, may claim a similar antiquity despite frequent remodellings.

For classic grace and symmetry, however, nothing[66] of the period can equal the church of Santa Sabina, which occupies a site at the top of the Aventine Hill where the cliff falls precipitously down to the valley of the Tiber. Repairs and alterations carried out during the last century were designed to remove medieval additions and restore the church to its early form as a simple but perfect example of the basilican plan (fig. 64). An uninterrupted line of a dozen fluted columns, ranged opposite one another, divides the nave from each of the narrow aisles and leads directly from the entrance-porch to the apse. The columns, set on their square bases, may be an earlier set reused, but they match one another flawlessly. They support deeply-carved Corinthian capitals from which spring high-pitched, round-headed arches, the whole combining disciplined regularity of form with a feeling of lightness and vigour. Immediately above the nave arcade on both sides runs a decoration of coloured marble, this ornamental scheme, no less than the architecture,

displaying a happy union of dignity and grace. Above the arches the marble imitates brick laid in courses while over the columns are set panels displaying a chalice, paten and cross in the form of military insignia which betoken the victory of Christ. Tall round-headed windows repeat the rhythm of the nave arcade below, and flood the building with light. Formerly this was reflected by the shimmer of mosaic, but all that now remains of this is a large panel occupying the wall space above the doorway. An inscription in letters of gold on a pale blue background records the foundation of the church during the reign of Pope Celestine I (422–32 AD) and is flanked by two large female figures, Roman matrons clad in full-length purple draperies that stand out clearly against a golden background. Each holds an open book in her left hand while the right hand is raised in blessing. Bold lettering beneath their feet indicates that one woman represents the Hebrew Church and one the Church of the Gentiles. In the fifth century these were thought of as the two elements from which the whole united Church is composed, but they also point to a contrast between Jew and Gentile and develop, in medieval imagery, to become the figures of the Christian Church, crowned

64. Rome, S. Sabina: interior.

and victorious, standing in opposition to the blindfold Jewish Church, who clasps a broken standard.

Another medieval idea, that of the 'Agreement between the Old and the New Testament', is foreshadowed by the famous doors of cypress-wood at the principal entrance of S. Sabina. Eighteen out of twenty-eight carved panels survive, well preserved and contained within elegant borders of decoration in which stylized bunches of grapes and vine-leaves predominate. The panels display incidents from the life of Christ roughly paralleled by events in which heroes of the Old Testament, and Moses in particular, play the chief part. The manner of the carving varies; some panels are skilfully composed in the graceful balanced fashion of late Greek art while others proclaim their message in the lumpy uncompromising terms of a rough popular style.

Among the refined examples must be numbered the panel depicting the Ascension of Elijah (fig. 65).[67] At the top the winged angel in his long wind-swept garment stretches out his right hand to touch Elijah as he ascends in the upward-slanting chariot. Below, Elisha clutches at Elijah's prophetic mantle while the onlookers crouch in dismay against a pile of rocks on which crawl a lizard and a snail. Another panel notable for its graceful and vigorous rhythm combined with a certain sophistication is that illustrating the Triumph of Christ and the Church. This is made up of two parts. In the upper half a circular laurel-wreath encloses the figure of Christ, who stands the embodiment of eternal youth as also of untroubled majesty. At each side of Christ is inscribed a large capital letter, the alpha and omega which show him to be the beginning and the end, while outside the wreath are carved the heads of eagle, lion, angel and ox, symbolizing the Four Gospels. The lower part of the panel begins with the vault of Heaven, in which are suspended the sun, moon and stars—as if to indicate that what is being transacted is of universal import. Below stands the figure of the Church, veiled and clothed in flowing drapery. Her hands are raised in ecstatic adoration while the apostles Peter and Paul hold above her head a cross enclosed within the wreath of triumph, to mark her destiny of suffering and glory.

Some of the other panels, however, make no pretence of finesse and present their clear, direct teaching with an artless simplicity. The most

celebrated of these is a tiny panel at the top left corner
of the doors (fig. 66). This is the earliest known
illustration, in clear-cut terms, of Christ crucified.
Even after the triumph of Constantine had made the
cross an emblem of victory, motives of reverence or
conservatism ensured that the death of Jesus was
hinted at, in representations of the sacrifice of Isaac or
the Lamb bearing a cross, rather than openly displayed. The *Orans*, in particular, standing with arms
outstretched more or less horizontally, became
accepted as a veiled indication of the Cross, and, on
the S. Sabina door, the figures of Christ and the two
robbers appear at first glance to be just such men of
prayer extending their hands in confident supplication. Naked except for a loincloth, they stand stiffly,
gazing straight ahead, in front of a brick wall marked
off into three parts by triangular-headed pediments.
Christ's majesty is declared by his size; he is almost as
tall as the panel itself, and the heads of his puny
companions reach no higher than his hands. It is only
when the hands are examined with some care that the
nails driven through them become obvious and the
transverse ends of each cross are seen. Even so, Christ
and the robbers alike stand with feet freely and firmly
on the ground and there is no suggestion of suffering,
so that the crucifixion scene, for all its crude realism,
proves to partake of the timeless symbolic character
which marks the most primitive Christian art.

The slender elegance of S. Sabina admits of no rival
in Rome for beauty of form, but the same style,
harmonious and rhythmical yet perfectly adapted to
the purposes of congregational worship, is used to
excellent effect in the majestic church of S. Maria
Maggiore (fig. 67). Here, however, the fifth-century
simplicity is much modified by a variety of later additions. It seems that there had been an earlier church on
the site, adapted from a civil basilica, but this was
completely destroyed by Pope Sixtus III[68] and replaced
by a more ambitious structure in the neo-classical
fashion of the times. Besides being an enthusiastic
patron of the arts, Sixtus was active in his opposition
to the Nestorians, who stressed the humanity of
Christ at the expense of his divinity, and a desire to
emphasize the newly-propounded doctrine of 'Mary,
the Mother of God' was no doubt one of the influences
which drove him on to erect so grandiose a building in
honour of the Virgin. The nave, 88 metres long and 33
metres high, is separated from the aisles by forty

65. Rome, S. Sabina. Panel of wooden door: the
Ascension of Elijah.

66. Rome, S. Sabina. Panel of wooden door: the Crucifixion.

marble columns, topped by Ionic capitals, that were originally made for a temple of Juno Lucina. The capitals have superimposed upon them not the high-flung arches of S. Sabina but the firm horizontal line of an architrave, a stately and somewhat heavier design which allows ample space for framed panels of mosaic. Twenty-seven of these panels out of the original forty-four remain more or less intact and display a lively interest in the historical details of the Old Testament, from Abraham to Joshua, without much attempt to derive symbolic meaning or doctrinal lessons from them. As early drawings of the church indicate, the mosaic panels were formerly contained within plaster frames with barley-sugar columns at each side and a low pediment above, while the tall round-headed windows of the clerestory were set higher still. There were, however, irregularities and variations in this pattern, and the whole arrangement was simplified in the interests of an ordered uniformity during the eighteenth century. Precious as these nave mosaics are, they must always have played, as they do now, a relatively small part in the decorative scheme of the vast church. The compositions tend to be crowded and, as in the case of medieval stained

glass, it is often difficult from ground level to make out the events represented. A general effect of brilliance would, however, have been secured by the mosaics as the light from the windows on the opposite side of the nave fell upon them.

A similar respect for tradition and balanced good taste appears in a building of very different type, somewhat later in date but archaic in feeling: the church of S. Stefano Rotondo (fig. 68). As its name implies, this is a circular structure, formed more on the pattern of a martyr-shrine than of a congregational meeting hall, and perhaps intended by its founder, Pope Simplicius (468–83 AD), to house relics of St Stephen. The building consists of a large drum set upon a ring of twenty-two granite columns with Ionic capitals of white marble. The columns support an architrave on which rests the dome pierced by twenty-two windows, all but eight now blocked up. This round nave is encircled by the ring of the broad aisle, the outer side of which is marked out by a second series of columns, smaller than those of the nave and topped by arches instead of an architrave. The arches formerly opened onto yet another ring, now destroyed, which consisted of a perimeter wall joining

67. Rome, S. Maria Maggiore: interior.

the ends of four[69] rectangular chapels. These, projecting from the main part of the building, suggest a cross superimposed on the circle and witness to the influence of the Church of the Holy Sepulchre at Jerusalem. Between the chapels there once ran little gardens open to the sky, affording clear light in effective contrast with the comparative darkness of the chapels.

In the Western Empire there were few imitations of this type of building where the tradition of the mausoleum is boldly taken over as the form of a commemorative church. The best example is S. Angelo at Perugia (fig. 69), half a century later than S. Stefano. Here a wide ambulatory with an inner circle of sixteen columns supports the central drum, while four chapels, three square and one shaped as a horseshoe, extend outwards from the ambulatory along the lines of a cross. As at S. Stefano, Asiatic influences have been adapted to the Latin idiom.

The most important city in Italy after Rome itself was Milan, which became the centre of government in the West when, at the end of the third century AD, Maximian divided the imperial power with Diocletian.

Maximian, and others after him, saw to it that Milan was handsomely equipped with public buildings of every description including a theatre, baths, a Circus—'the people's joy'—and a number of temples. Milan had its honoured list of martyrs, Valeria, Victor and the rest, and after the year 313, when the Edict of Milan 'granted both to the Christians and to all the free choice of following whatever form of worship they pleased',[70] numerous shrines were set up throughout the city. In 374 Ambrose became bishop, and his combination of spiritual authority and political shrewdness made Milan for a time the most obvious source of ecclesiastical power in the West; thus the fourth century, for the Christians of Milan, was a period of enthusiastic vigour and enterprise.

Five churches still exist which date from this epoch and, though much altered or even fragmentary, they show, amid considerable variety, characteristic features in common. The buildings are notable externally for a stern solid grandeur. This is evident in the best known of them, the church of S. Lorenzo (fig. 70), more easily visible now that a huddle of miscellaneous buildings has been cleared away from the Piazza Vetra. Four squared and lofty towers rise at the

68. Rome, S. Stefano Rotondo: interior.

corners of the church, flanking what is now a six-teenth-century cupola but which seems originally to have been a dome constructed in stone or timber. Beneath this, the square hall was modified at each side by a shallow apse, its shape repeated in the lines of the ambulatory which surrounded it (fig 71). This attractive design, commonly known as the 'double shell', was copied from baths or other palace buildings and, like so much else, christianized and used experimentally for church purposes in the fourth century. At S. Lorenzo it is modified, apart from a cluster of later additions to the south-east, by three ancient chapels. The largest of these, dedicated to St Aquilinus, is known also as the Queen's Chapel because of a tradition that the empress Galla Placidia wished to be buried there. It is shaped as an octagon with niches in the walls, and retains decoration in marble and mosaic such as originally characterized the whole structure, sombre outside but bright and lively within. The church was approached from the west by way of a large courtyard in front of which stand sixteen marble columns originally used in a pagan temple. S. Lorenzo is sometimes described as the Arian cathedral, but perhaps the most that can be said is that it may well

have been founded by Auxentius, an astute native of Asia Minor who preceded Ambrose as bishop of Milan. Lying rather apart from the main part of the city it could then have preserved Eastern and Arian rituals at a time when the rest of Milan was becoming predominantly Catholic.

Two other fourth-century churches exist at Milan in the sense that large sections of the original walling have been incorporated in a structure which, though modified by later developments, is substantially of the Romanesque or Lombardic period. St Ambrose established his Church of the Apostles in 382 AD on a site hallowed by the presence of an early Christian burial-ground, but it was renamed S. Nazaro when Ambrose placed there the bodies of the local saints Nazarius and Celsus. The form of the building, probably suggested by Constantine's Church of the Holy Apostles at Constantinople, is that of a tall cross. The nave, some 60 metres long, ran without interruption to the apse at the east end; the transepts, forming the side arms of the cross, were connected to the nave by an arcade of three arches, so that those who crowded into the transepts on occasions of high festival could have a good view of the altar, set as it was at the central

69. Perugia, S. Angelo: interior.

point of the cross with the sacred relics deposited beneath it.

The church of S. Simpliciano has a somewhat similar history. Here again the site is that of a primitive Christian cemetery where an unpretentious meeting-house was transformed by the vigour of St Ambrose into a noble cross-shaped building. Originally entitled St Mary and all the Virgins, the church later took the name of Ambrose's successor as bishop of Milan, St Simplicianus, who acquired a number of martyr relics for it. The nave, ending in a spacious apse, was roughly the same length as S. Nazaro but appreciably wider, 22 metres as compared with 14.5. Of this first building some lofty external walls, made of well-laid brickwork, still remain.

Milan Cathedral, the construction of which began in 1386 AD, is well known as a particularly ornate example of the late Gothic style but the construction of air-raid shelters during the last war led to the discovery beneath the Piazza del Duomo of the original cathedral, built towards the end of the fourth century and remodelled about a hundred years later. The indications are that the building was shaped as a rectangle ending in a shallow apse. The nave was

separated from the aisles by columns, a double row on each side running as far as the chancel and then continuing rather irregularly across the two chancel wings which extend to the springing of the apse. These wings may have been no more than sacristies or storerooms but they suggest the tripartite transept of S. Pietro in Vincoli at Rome and similar types of transept which established themselves in favour throughout the Aegean region during the fifth century. Another feature, more characteristic of the Aegean than of the West, which the remnants of Milan's first cathedral indicate, is the arrangement of the chancel. The usual practice was for the clergy to occupy seats around the walls of the bema or 'tribunal' —that is to say the apse alone or the apse together with part of the transepts. In order to provide added dignity for the bema and for the altar which was often placed there, the floor might be raised and, whether raised or not, was equipped with screen partitions 'delicately wrought with the craftsman's utmost skill', so that 'the multitude might not tread in the midst of the holy of holies'.[71] With a view to bringing the clergy more closely into relationship with the populace for purposes of either Communion or sermon-preaching,

70. Milan, S. Lorenzo: view from the south-east, showing the chapel of S. Aquilino.

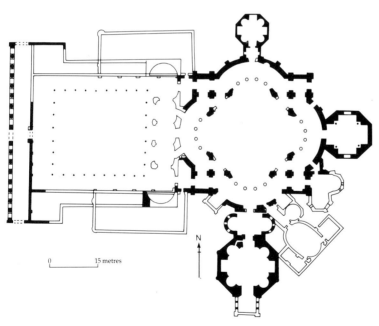

0   15 metres

71. Milan, S. Lorenzo: ground-plan.

72. Trier: the basilica today.

a raised pathway, known as the *solea*, was sometimes extended from the chancel screen into the nave. This Eastern device is repeated at Milan, where portions of the *solea* jut out into the nave for a distance of 12.5 metres.

What may therefore be said in summary is that recent discoveries show the citizens of Milan, in the time of St Ambrose, to have displayed both energy and skill in church-building, receiving and adapting ideas which had developed in Constantinople and possibly initiating certain elements of architectural style which others saw fit to copy later on.

The church of the martyrs Gervasius and Protasius, built by St Ambrose above the cemetery where the two saints were buried, and later named S. Ambrogio, is rightly described by the guidebooks as 'fount and symbol of the religious impulses of Milan', but, though restored with accuracy and good taste after damage suffered during the Second World War, has little to show dating back further than the ninth century. Excavation has served merely to indicate an original building with long nave and aisles terminating in a semicircular apse, a straightforward basilican plan that was widely copied elsewhere in northern

Italy. The attached chapel of St Victor is, however, of very early date and shows the characteristics of fourth-century workmanship—simple, severe lines with a rhythmical arrangement of round-headed windows designed to provide ample light subtly changing with the time of day. The roof of the central portion is a cupola made up of pottery tubes arranged in rings and perhaps originally contained within a protective drum, while the lower surface of the cupola shone with such a splendour of golden mosaic[72] that the chapel was nicknamed St Victor of the Golden Heaven.

The remarkable vigour and ingenuity which the emperor Diocletian passed on as an inheritance to his Christian successors is to be noted further north than Milan, in one or two of the great border towns of Germany. These, though serving from time to time as imperial residences, were in the first place military strongholds, with precise town plans and robust fortifications. But the arts of civilization, and architecture in particular, were not neglected. At Trier the imperial baths were constructed in the liveliest fashion with a number of projecting apses which make up a 'sym-

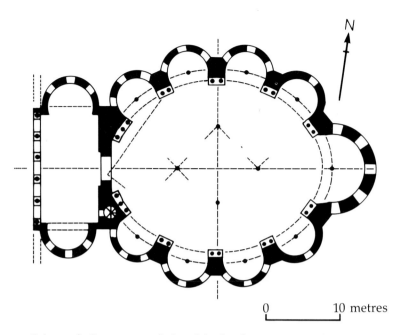

N

0   10 metres

73. Cologne, St Gereon: ground-plan of the fourth-century martyrium.

phony of cross-vaults, domes and half domes'.[73] Nearby, in a contrasting style, plain, rectangular and flat-roofed, rose the basilica (fig. 72)—the town hall which served as law court and market.[74] Moreover the cathedral, though devastated by the Franks and largely rebuilt in the Romanesque style, incorporates a substantial amount of the fourth-century structure. It seems that Constantine handed over the remains of an imperial palace, from which fragments of a richly decorated ceiling still survive, as part of the site on which to build a double church. Both naves are long and narrow, the northern being appreciably the larger, while between the two ran a substantial passageway containing a baptistery. The southern building is completely superseded by the present Liebfrauenkirche, but portions of the earliest walling in the cathedral indicate a structure of red sandstone with binding courses of brick or tile and a plain, plastered exterior. The east end, as remodelled fifty years later by the emperor Gratian, formed a tall, square block. Four vast granite pillars, connected by arches, upheld the central tower, while other compartments were ranged around with complete exactness. At each side of the square in the middle was set a

rectangle, furnished with two rows of large round-headed windows and a sloping roof lower than the height of the square turrets which marked the four corners. The external appearance, severe but in no way lumpy, must have resembled that of S. Lorenzo at Milan, and hints at a close connection, in styles of building and architecture, between the two cities. But the bold design, whatever its artistic merit, was chosen for practical ends. If the discovery of an arcaded recess sunk into the floor beneath the tower is anything to go by, this part of the building served the purpose of a martyr-shrine or perhaps a relic-shrine containing a portion of the True Cross discovered by the empress Helena.

Another outpost city in which such emperors as Constantine and Valentinian I took a keen interest was Cologne. It is claimed on behalf of several of the churches here that they stand on fourth-century sites, but the only one which retains any part of its original form is St Gereon. This structure, now sandwiched between a long Romanesque choir and a square vestibule, is oval in shape, marked out by ten heavy piers supporting clerestory and roof. Between the piers the wall is recessed to form a series of vaulted semicircular niches (fig. 73). The larger ones, which used to mark the entrances respectively to a western narthex and the eastern apse, have been much modified, but the other sides match each other precisely with their four niches of identical size. The church presumably derived its unusual shape from the pattern of a pagan temple or imperial audience hall; it has been compared with the building known as the Temple of Minerva Medica in the Esquiline district of Rome.

The city of Aquileia, seven miles from the head of the Adriatic, grew up to become so powerful a military and commercial centre that it was known as a second Rome; and to Aquileia's rich store of civic halls and private houses Bishop Theodore added a group of ecclesiastical buildings designed with great splendour. The raids of Attila in 452, followed by the Lombard invasions, so devastated the city that it could be referred to as 'a beggar's hovel'. And, though in the Middle Ages life returned to Aquileia, which once again became a bishop's see, the works of the early Christian period have only lately been recovered, in a very fragmentary state, as the result of excavations.

The present cathedral (fig. 74), consecrated in 1031, preserves the basilican form but with sanctuary and apse raised to an unusual height. A large area of the floor is covered by a pattern of mosaic which, as an inscription[75] shows, originally formed part of Theodore's church and is therefore to be dated about 315 AD. The cathedral seems to have grown up in clearly marked stages. The first building on the site was a Roman villa, datable to about 20 AD, from which there remain some portions of tessellated pavement and two walls of enclosure. In the precincts of this villa a fair-sized rectangular building was constructed towards the end of the third century as a hall of assembly for the local Christians. Not long afterwards Bishop Theodore amplified the original structure. The bishop's throne, together with the clergy bench, was placed at the east end, while a substantial screen separated altar and clergy from the pressures of the populace. Theodore then connected this building, by means of a covered vestibule, with another hall further south. The two halls were of the same length, 36 metres, and divided by six columns into nave and aisles. The south hall appears to have been designed as a school of instruction for catechumens but, if so,

the arrangement did not last very long; the indications of an altar, clergy seats and so forth, together with the splendid decoration, point to its use as one of a pair of twin churches.

The richness and variety of the mosaic floor in the southern hall reveal it as a wholly exceptional work for its period. Swirling bands of acanthus leaves divide the mosaic into three zones, each again separated into three compartments; the scheme is completed with a wide band of decoration that once stretched across the entire width of the hall at the east end. In this mosaic, animals, birds and fishes of many kinds are shown with the affectionate realism which allowed even the most austere of the early Fathers to value 'a single tiny flower from the hedgerow, a single shellfish from the sea, a single fluttering wing of the moorfowl'.[76] Sometimes the creatures are intended to point moral lessons. The cock, bird of the dawn, fighting the grotesque tortoise,[77] recalls the struggle between Christian enlightenment and heathen, or perhaps heretical, perversity, while the fish trapped in a vast net worked from a boat by graceful cupids call to mind the task laid upon all heavenly influences to gather the elect into the Church's net through the waters of baptism. Elsewhere round frames enclose portrait-busts of donors, more of them women than men, with whose generous support Theodore was enabled to build. Some of the roundels contain not a human portrait but a fish, while the space nearby is taken up by octagons, each displaying a bird—a peacock, perhaps, or a pheasant—perched on a flowering branch in Paradise. Similar birds, on a somewhat larger scale, are interposed between scenes referring to the Eucharist, the 'medicine of immortality'. Here youths and maidens hold a basket of loaves or grapes or flowers, while, in a large square panel which dominates the whole composition, a dark-robed angel, clasping the wreath and palm-branch which denote victorious perseverance, stands behind the heaped-up loaves and the wine-jar.[78] In entire harmony with such emblematic pictures, the Biblical motifs chosen for illustration are the Good Shepherd and three episodes from the life of Jonah,[79] who is also shown as an *Orans* clothed in the deacon's dalmatic. Framed in the mosaic just at this point is a dedicatory inscription in honour of Theodore who 'built and dedicated the church with splendour'.

Aquileia was the scene of the great Church Council

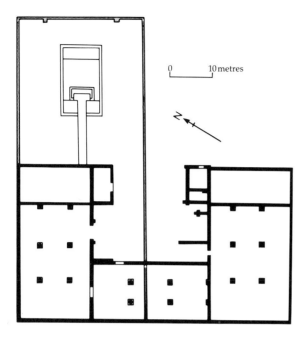

0   10 metres

74. Aquileia: plan of the cathedral about 400 AD, showing the two parallel halls. A few subsidiary buildings have been omitted.

of 381 AD, assembled in a vain attempt to repress the Arian heresy, and it appears that, shortly afterwards, Theodore's northern church was overhauled and enlarged with the addition of new columns, to become a wide nave with narrow aisles though retaining the earlier fashion of a plain, squared-off sanctuary. The outbuildings were extended at this time and the baptistery, with its marble-lined hexagonal font, set at a point where the water supply of the ancient villa could be utilized. The reasons for constructing double churches, a fashion favoured in the North Adriatic region as examples at Parenzo and Trieste show, need not always be precisely the same. A desire for grandeur, the manifold requirements of worship, and administrative convenience could all exert their influence in varying degree.[80]

The Roman colony of Julia Concordia, 49 kilometres west of Aquileia, presents a cluster of Christian buildings designed to protect the city's burial-places and to ensure that the rites of commemoration were suitably observed. The most substantial of these structures began as a trefoil chapel, similar in style to those of St Sixtus and St Soter in the Cemetery of Callistus in Rome or the example at Damous el Karita, near Carthage. Originally this fourth-century 'trichora' consisted of three apses, circular within and roughly polygonal outside, with an open courtyard on the fourth side where the faithful might gather for services. The courtyard was then turned into a rectangular room, giving greater privacy and protection, by prolonging the side walls a little way and closing the gap. After about a century this trefoil shrine was extended to become the cemetery church, enough of which remains to indicate its dimensions. It was a small basilica, 17 metres long by 10 wide, and divided by columns into a nave 4.5 metres across and two aisles rather more than half that width. The trefoil was incorporated to form the sanctuary and the eastern apse was therefore equipped with a bench for the clergy and, in the centre, a block of masonry to support the bishop's throne. At the opposite end of the building came the narthex, of the customary rectangular pattern and containing a handsome sarcophagus set in the place of honour beneath a canopy supported by columns. The inscription runs: 'The holy priest Maurentius lies in his own burial-place at the threshold of the Church of the Apostles'. Beyond the narthex was a cloister, with fountain of the type which Paulinus of Nola described as 'washing with a serviceable stream the hands of those who enter'.[81] There were also sockets, apparently for screens to prevent undue jostling at the entrance, while, at the side, rows of sarcophagi were neatly arranged in parallel lines.

Close to the original shrine at Concordia, and approached by a doorway from it, are two burial precincts of a type hitherto found nowhere else. Each consists of a line of three little rectangular cells, open in front and bounded by a wall on the other sides. On the inmost wall of the cells three niches are hollowed out, as for the reception of three coffins, but almost the whole of the middle cell of the eastern oratory is taken up with one splendid sarcophagus, carved on the front and right side with palms, vines and crosses, and inserted into the wall. An inscription tells the story: 'Faustiniana, nobly born and servant of Christ, in her lifetime entrusted herself and her burial-place to the tabernacle of Christ and shrine of the saints.'[82] Here 'tabernacle' means the chapel where the eucharistic

liturgy could be celebrated, while the reference to the saints is explained by two recesses, intended to contain relics, at the foot of the altar which, as the post-holes show, was placed in front of Faustiniana's tomb.

Generally comparable to Aquileia is a group of churches recently disclosed by excavation in the Austrian Tyrol. These date from the fourth or early fifth century and reflect an uncomplicated 'basilican' style. At Lorch the structure takes the form of a simple rectangular hall, divided in two by a cross-wall. Towards the east end, behind the altar and its associated recess for the storage of martyr-relics, there is a free-standing semicircular bench, a *synthronon*, for the clergy; attached to the north side of this chancel lay a sacristy. The church at Aguntum, though larger and slimmer, offers a closely similar pattern, but more imposing are the remains of the hillside fortress-church of Lavant.[83] Here, behind the clergy bench, occurs a large rectangular compartment, also containing a horseshoe bench and explained either as a private chapel for the clergy or as a baptistery.

NOTES

1. Mentioned in Nehemiah 8.3.
2. Josephus, *Jewish War* vii.5.5.
3. Exodus 25.31.
4. G. F. Moore, *Judaism* (Cambridge, 1946) i.546.
5. *Epistle of Barnabas* 7, in *The Apostolic Fathers* (Loeb), i.364.
6. Ps. Clement, *Recognitions* 10.71, *PG* 1.1453. Revised text by B. Rehm in *GCS*.
7. *Ecclesiastical History* 8.1.
8. *Against the Christians*, fragment 76. See J. Bidez, *Vie de Porphyre* (Gand, 1913).
9. The term 'edict' is normally used; in fact it was a 'rescript' sent to an individual governor.
10. Eusebius, *Ecclesiastical History* 10.5.
11. Eusebius, *Ecclesiastical History* 10.39.
12. *De Architectura* v. 1.6, ed. F. Granger (Loeb), i.258.
13. *The Antiquities of the Christian Church*, viii.1 (London, 1726).
14. *Liber Pontificalis*, ed. Duchesne, i.153.
15. Full discussion by J. B. Ward-Perkins, 'Constantine and the Christian basilica', *Papers of the British School at Rome* XXII (1954).
16. Ignatius, *To the Ephesians* 20.
17. *Apostolic Constitutions* 8.42, *PG* 1. Later edition by F. X. Funk (Paderborn, 1905). English translation by J. Donaldson (London, 1870).
18. 'The sensible Rhetorick of the dead to exemplarity of good life first admitted the bones of pious men and Martyrs within Church walls; which in succeeding ages crept into promiscuous practice'. Sir Thomas Browne, *Urne Burial* (1658).
19. *Works and Days* 122, ed. H. G. Evelyn White (Loeb, 1920), 10.
20. *A Cure for Pagan Ills* 8.915, *PG* 83. 1024. Written about 440 AD.
21. 6.9.
22. Complete reconstruction was carried out by Pope Pelagius II at the end of the sixth century and Pope Honorius III in the thirteenth century.
23. *Liber Pontificalis* i.181.
24. Book I, *Tractatus* iv.ii, *PL* 11.296.
25. Paulinus' description (*Epistle* 32) is to some extent borne out by excavations undertaken in 1936. Reported by G. Chierici: *Studi* 16 (1938).
26. St John Chrysostom, *De coemeterio et cruce* i, *PG* 49.393.
27. St John Chrysostom, *De statuis*, *PG* 49.99.
28. Eusebius, *Ecclesiastical History* 10. 2.
29. S. Sebastiano, however, made no claim to be set up over the original resting-place of a martyr but rather to have housed martyrs' relics for a time at a somewhat later stage.

30. L. Duchesne, second edition (1955), i.176.

31. H. Egger, *Römische Veduten* i (1932).

32. 84 metres out of a total of 111 metres.

33. *Concerning the honour of the Martyrs* 28, *PL* 71.850.

34. An example, given by Grabar in *Martyrium* i.128, is Calydon, in Aetolia.

35. *Liber Pontificalis* i.66.

36. Not identified until 1946. The work of F. W. Deichmann, U. M. Fasola and others is surveyed by L. Reekmans in *ACIAC* ix, 282.

37. It is sometimes argued that the barrel vault points to a subterranean origin for the Roman tomb corridor of this type.

38. For the sarcophagus, see p. 77, for the mosaics, p. 217.

39. *Life of Constantine* 3.43, *PG* 20.1104.

40. Justin Martyr, *Dialogue* 78, *PG* 6.657.

41. *Itinerarium*, tr. A. Stewart (London, 1887), 27.

42. Interpretations of the archaeological evidence vary here. Some prefer to explain the domed shrine as circular rather than octagonal.

43. Genesis 18.18.

44. Sozomen, *Church History* 2.4, ed. J. Bidez (Berlin, 1960), 56.

45. P. Geyer, *Itinera Hierosolymitana* (*CSEL*, 1898), 113. Aetheria's date is, however, disputed. She may be identical with a Spanish nun who lived in the seventh century.

46. Eusebius, *Life of Constantine* 3.34. On points of detail the picture given by W. Harvey in *Church of the Holy Sepulchre* (1935) must be modified to meet the results of more recent excavations. V. Corbo, *La Basilica di S. Sepolcro* (Jerusalem, 1969).

47. Cyril of Jerusalem, *Catecheses* 14.22, *PG* 33.553.

48. Eusebius, *Life of Constantine* 3.33.

49. The map remains *in situ*.

50. The words of several pilgrim-commentators were gathered together by Leo Allatius in a work called *Symmicta* or *Miscellanies* (Amsterdam, 1653).

51. Following the example of early heroes like Alexander, interred by Ptolemy I at the centre of Alexandria.

52. Geyer, *Itinera Hierosolymitana*, 140.

53. The rather obscure wording of Eusebius has to be amplified by the testimony of the pilgrim Aetheria (*Peregrinatio* 83) and such Latin commentators as Paulinus of Nola (31.4) and Sulpicius Severus (*History* ii. 33). See Geyer, *op. cit.*

54. Eusebius, *Life of Constantine* 3.43.

55. Such as that written in the ninth century by Arculf (Geyer, *op. cit.* 250).

56. Or, as another version of the story has it, by a certain Poemenia, fifty years later.

57. There may also have been a covered walk leading round the outside of the octagon.

58. Sozomen, *Church History* 2.3.

59. Socrates, *Church History* 2.16.

60. Socrates, *op. cit.*

61. Eusebius, *Life of Constantine* 4.58.

62. The germ of this somewhat extravagant praise is to be found in Eusebius's *Life of Constantine* 4.71.

63. See p. 14.

64. The number of windows was halved at the time of the reconstruction.

65. Prudentius, *Peristephanon* xii.54.

66. The structure and proportions of S. Sabina are closely paralleled by those of the fifth-century church recently discovered beneath the floor of the Cathedral at Florence. See F. Toker in *ACIAC* ix, 545.

67. II Kings 2.

68. 432–41 AD.

69. Only one of these chapels now remains.

70. Eusebius, *Ecclesiastical History* 10.5.4.

71. Eusebius, *Ecclesiastical History* 10.4.

72. The mosaics may be assigned to the end of the fifth century.

73. Rodenwaldt in *Cambridge Ancient History* xii.568.

74. Since 1856 it has been used as a Protestant church.

75. *Theodore felix hic crevisti hic felix.*

76. Tertullian, *Against Marcion* i.15, *PL* 2.261.

77. Jerome, in his *Commentary on Hosea* iii.12, connects heretics with the tortoise, 'slow-moving and overwhelmed by its own weight, which does not walk so much as shuffle around' (*PL* 25.929).

78. This panel is damaged, and only the foot of the vessel containing wine, or grapes, can be seen.

79. This subject has been claimed as unique among floor mosaics, but another floor mosaic, showing several episodes from the life of Jonah, was recently uncovered in a church at Beit Govrin (Israel). See G. Foerster in *ACIAC* ix, 289.

80. The precise course of development at Aquileia is still open to some doubt, but the general lines have been clearly established by H. Kaehler (see Bibliography) and S. Corbett in *RAC* xxxii (1956).

81. Paulinus, *Epistle* 32.

82. *Faustiniana CF tamula Christi se suamque sepulturam vivens Christi tabernaculo ac sanctorum memoriae commendavit.*

83. R. Egger in *Frühmittelalterliche Kunst in den Alpenländern* (Lausanne, 1954).

7

Church Buildings in Asia

IMPERIAL INFLUENCES AND PRACTICAL NEEDS

Early Christian architecture is an imitation, and little evidence exists of any particular desire to hammer out a novel and distinctive style. The forms adopted had the advantage of being traditional and familiar, in addition to being well tested for usefulness and aesthetic appeal. Moreover, they were enriched by overtones of symbolism and mystical meaning which the Roman emperors, both pagan and Christian, turned to advantage in the design of official buildings and which, by an easy transference of association, gave a touch of supernatural dignity to churches. Thus the palace, particularly the palace-fortress of the kind built by Diocletian at Salona, came to typify a dominion which reproduced on earth the government of the Universe exercised by the Almighty. As it is not easy to take in a whole palace-fortress at a glance, however, and still more difficult to draw a neat likeness of it, the palace gateway is used, as part for the whole, to represent power and authority.

At the very beginning of the Christian era, a coin struck for the emperor Augustus at Mérida in Spain shows a fortified portal with battlements, two large entrance doors and a square tower at each side. This might be no more than a hint of military strength expressed in terms of a contemporary fortress, but later on, particularly in the more barbarous outposts of Empire, figures representing Plenty or Good Fortune were added to recall that the triumphant arrival of the emperor at the city-gate was accompanied by a godlike bounty of peace and prosperity.[1]

Rather more frequently the arcade over the main entrance was stressed as being the gallery from which the emperor looked down to receive the crowd's applause. Whatever the precise steps in the argument may have been, the arcade came to suggest the eternal abode of a divine being. One illustration of this is the Ravenna mosaic which shows Theodoric's palace equipped with an elegant arcaded gallery in imitation of the pattern laid down at Salona where a formal arcade over the ceremonial entrance contained statues of the gods. Christian opinion found it easy enough to connect the formalized gateway with ideas of kingship, human or divine, by reason of passages in the Bible where the relationship is clear. In the Old Testament history kings regularly sit, where their subjects can see them, in the entrance court before the palace, as when

the king of Israel and Jehoshaphat the king of Judah sat each on his throne, arrayed in their robes, in an open place at the entrance of the gate of Samaria[2]

while mysterious hints, suggesting not merely the victorious warrior but the universal Sovereign, echoed in the Psalmist's words: 'Lift up your heads, O ye gates, and be ye lift up, ye everlasting doors, and the King of glory shall come in.'[3] It is therefore not surprising that entrance portals are commonly displayed on the coins of Constantine and his sons (fig. 75) together with such emblems as the 'bright morning star' and slogans, of which *Providentia* was the most popular,

75. City-gate coins: a. Constantine: Arles mint;
b. Gordian II: Marcianopolis mint.

which implied that members of the imperial house kept watch over the welfare of the far-flung Empire.

The significance, on coins, of the royal house with towers at the corners was enhanced when the towers were capped with little domes or when, as on a series of coins struck for Diocletian and Constantine,[4] the façade was decorated with a row of turrets bearing little domes. For dome and cupola had their emblematic value as indicating the vaulted canopy of Heaven, the 'blue dome of air'[5] as poets instinctively describe it. Under the influence, perhaps, of the great Temple of Bel at Palmyra, the dome was adopted not merely as a convenient architectural device but as signifying the universal sway of the Almighty Creator and of the emperor who acted as his visible embodiment. Here again a touch of symbolism joined with custom and the practical needs of the worshipping community to produce the forms of Christian architecture.

The pattern of church-building in Asia Minor was to a large extent shaped by the creative vigour and restless enthusiasm of Constantine and other members of the imperial house. Not only were the sacred sites of Palestine furnished with magnificent shrines but, as Eusebius records, other cities also benefited. Among them was Antioch, where Constantine constructed a church 'unsurpassed for size and beauty'. This has now disappeared, but in the fourth century it was

surrounded by an enclosure of considerable size, within which the church itself rose to a great height. It was octagonal in shape and surrounded on every side by a number of halls, courts and two-storeyed apartments: everywhere there was lavish adornment of gold, brass and other materials of the most costly kind.[6]

This was not the cathedral of Antioch but rather the palace-church, testifying by its splendour not only to the glory of God but to the emperor's magnificence.

Further south, at Baalbek, a city renowned for the vigour of its pagan cults, the emperor constructed a church of 'great size and splendour' and arranged for the clergy to be housed nearby. The two particularly powerful influences were the Church of the Holy Apostles at Constantinople and the rotunda of the Holy Sepulchre, and it was apparently a model of the former that the empress Eudoxia brought, together with a present of marble columns, for the men of Gaza to copy in 401 AD.[7]

Along with the influences exerted from the capital over much of Asia went a preference for classic forms of architecture carried down as a legacy from the Hellenistic age, while the long coastline with its many harbours favoured the free import of both craftsmen and materials. Inland, however, and particularly in the remote mountainous districts, a down-to-earth rustic style prevailed. The early churches, in Asia Minor as elsewhere, fall into two distinct types, adapted for different purposes. There is the basilica, the ample rectangular hall suitable for the celebration of the liturgy in the presence of relatively large numbers of people, and there is the martyr-shrine, circular or octagonal, built around a sacred spot. Similar needs require similar forms, and the basilica throughout Asia differed little in essentials from, indeed closely resembled, the basilican structures of the West. Two special features are, however, characteristic of the basilicas of Asia Minor in the fourth and fifth centuries. The first of these is the ambo which not seldom obstructed the nave. The term 'ambo' is derived from the Greek word for a 'raised-up place' or reading desk, resembling the 'pulpit of wood' from which Esdras, the 'priest and reader of the Law', declaimed the Old Testament Scriptures to the multitude assembled in the 'broad place before the porch of the temple'.[8]

In the West, as for example in sixth-century Ravenna, the ambo is an attractively carved box with steps leading up to it—rather like an English pulpit —but in the East it often became an altogether more elaborate affair. In Justinian's rebuilding of S. Sophia at Constantinople the ambo was mounted by two flights of stairs, running from opposite sides. Constructed of the rarest marbles and decorated with gold, it was upheld by marble columns and had at the top of the stairs sufficient space to allow for an emperor's coronation while there was room for a close-packed choir beneath. The ambo at S. Sophia was exceptional, like the vast building itself, but in earlier and less pretentious churches, particularly in Syria, a stone ambo of horseshoe shape occupied a substantial part of the central nave. Set upon a platform and sometimes approached from the east by a raised pathway, it was used for readings, sermons, announcements and hymn-singing, with the deacon standing before it to ensure liaison with the people clustered in the aisles.

Secondly, the apse, or semicircle reserved for the

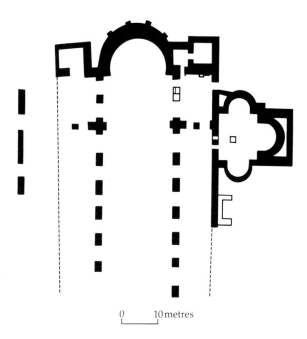

76. Corinth: ground-plan of church with trefoil martyr-shrine annexed.

clergy, was developed in a variety of ways. It might project eastwards and be roofed with a half dome; but far more often, at first, it was enclosed within the rectangle of the church and flanked by two chambers known as *pastophoria*, or sacristies. It was customary to refer to these as prothesis[9] and diaconicon,[10] that is to say the place for making ready the eucharistic offering on the north side and, to the south, the vestry, where the deacons kept offerings, books and church treasure. But, at least from the beginning of the fifth century, the two chambers came to be contrasted with one another. The north side continued to serve as a sacristy, but the southern room, distinguished by a more elaborate doorway, was clearly used on occasion as a chapel containing the honoured relics of martyrs. The later and more elaborate churches of Asia Minor show considerable freedom of design, and sometimes there are three apses projecting eastwards, the central apse flanked by semicircles which terminate the side chambers.

Writing of Palestine about 330 AD, the historian Eusebius, using vague and perhaps exaggerated terms, notes that the remains of martyrs,

placed in splendid church buildings and in sacred places of prayer, were given to the people of God that they might honour them in unceasing remembrance.[11]

This might imply no more than an early form of medieval practice whereby a particular area within a church was reserved for the cult of a local martyr. More frequently the shrines were separate, standing alone or perhaps forming part of a group of buildings. The shrine of St Euphemia at Chalcedon,[12] for instance, was a rotunda with galleries looking down onto a central hall. Although an independent structure, it was attached to the north side of a basilica and entered through that church. The same is true of the martyrium of St Leonidas at Ilissos, near Athens, where the shrine, rectangular in outline, occupies the corner between nave and transept of the basilica, while a church at Corinth (fig. 76) has, attached to its south wall, a large martyrium of trefoil shape.

The independent martyr-shrines, anyhow in fourth-century Asia Minor, were constructed according to the principles and forms of classical sepulchres, as freely adapted by Constantine to mark the holy places of Jerusalem. Such shrines, whether round, octagonal or cross-shaped, displayed a solemn, monumental character. They were places of pilgrimage where, often enough, the relics were kept in tombs of sarcophagus shape, equipped with funnels and an internal basin, so that oil could be poured over the bones and collected in small flasks for use by the pious as medicine. As the numbers of churchmen and the repute of the martyrs grew, the size of the buildings had to be increased also. During the fifth century, when relics came to be freely bandied about from place to place, shrines to contain them were established in towns and began to serve more or less the same needs as the basilicas. The architectural form of the martyrium was therefore modified to enable the liturgy to be celebrated there 'decently and in order'. While, therefore, the basilica was tending to acquire a chapel for relics, the martyr-shrine changed into something closely resembling a parish church, and the distinction between the two quite different types of structure became blurred.

SYRIA AND ARMENIA

It is in the province of Syria that these developments can most easily be observed, particularly in areas where the remote and hilly nature of the country has acted as a guarantee against subsequent rebuilding. Antioch, the capital, has little to show and the churches discovered nearby display a classical sophistication of the kind that varies little around the coasts of the Aegean. Further inland a robust, practical style of building gradually yields to the charm of Greek refinement while maintaining its characteristic sturdiness and a certain discipline in applying ornament only to those parts of a church where it was deemed appropriate. The type of material lying to hand dictated the local characteristics; buildings of the chalky heights of northern Syria differ markedly from those in the Hauran district in the south, where slabs of basalt form the roofs of thin elongated churches built on a framework of arches thrown across the nave. But for all the local differences, churches in Syria bear a strong family resemblance to one another. Made from large blocks of stone, admirably cut and laid, they merge easily with their surroundings and rely for their effect upon sensible proportion rather than upon architectural novelties. Unlike pagan temples standing apart in lordly isolation, most Syrian churches combine with the houses around them to make up a community of dwellings. It is an unsafe generalization to maintain that the simpler buildings are necessarily the oldest, but the first primitive type of church, consisting of a single nave, is barely to be distinguished from an ordinary private house or from the andron, the village meeting hall which served the purposes of a covered market. And the church is often but one of a group of related structures including a baptistery, a residence for the clergy and a storeroom.

Private houses in Syria were customarily built as cubes with one or two rooms on the ground floor and a portico fronting them; this pattern was repeated, if necessary, in a second or third storey. The little church of Qirk Bizze, in the mountains about forty miles east of Antioch, is of precisely the same general type and, reasonably enough, archaeologists at first interpreted it as a villa parallel with a second house separated from it by a narrow lane. Built almost certainly in the middle of the fourth century, it is typical of the next stage in church development that follows on the primitive adaptation at Dura, even though some of the interior furnishings may have been added rather later. Qirk Bizze church, set within a walled courtyard, consists of a rectangle forming a single room, 13 metres long by 5.5 metres wide. In common with many other Syrian churches, it has no western entrance, but there are two doorways on the south side, the eastern being the more ornate. The interior shows signs of well-developed ecclesiastical usage. There is an ambo of horseshoe form, equipped with a bench and, at the middle point, a simple throne for bishop or reader, the whole structure occupying what must have been an inconveniently large part of the floorspace. The entry to the square-ended sanctuary was marked by two steps and by a triumphal arch, later modified to include a screen with columns and doorways. An opening to the south of the sanctuary led into a small rectangular martyr-shrine, while a few receptacles for relics, of indeterminate date, were found in the sanctuary itself.

Unpretentious churches of the Qirk Bizze type, looking from the outside like so many private houses but lavishly arranged for liturgical uses within, are the natural product of Syria as of other countrified districts, but the increasing wealth and ambition of the Christian communities, together with a certain inventiveness and taste, caused churches to acquire marked variation in size and complexity while still following one general pattern. Development can be traced the more easily since a number of Syrian churches bear an inscription which records the date of their foundation and occasionally the name of the architect who was the leading craftsman in a guild of itinerant stonemasons. A certain Julianus, for example, was responsible for the great church at Brad in the period 395–402 AD. This establishment is on a very different scale from Qirk Bizze. The overall length, omitting the western portico, is 39 metres and the width of 27 metres is divided by rows of eight columns into nave and two side aisles. A horseshoe ambo occupies a large part of the central nave while the sanctuary assumes what came to be the standard Syrian form—a wide but shallow semi-circular apse flanked by rectangular sacristies on either side. The attractiveness of the church lies in the precision of its proportions rather than in any elaborate treatment of the squared ashlar blocks of which it is composed. It has an exceptionally large number of entrances—four on the south, two on the north and three at the west end—but only the central doorway on the west side has anything like a formal frame. The decoration within is limited to the triumphal arch in front of the apse and to the capitals on top of the columns. To the south of the church extends a huge courtyard, irregular in form and marked off by columns while at each end of this enclosure there arises a cluster of such buildings as a clergy residence and a hostel for visitors. A martyr-shrine was attached to the north-east corner of the church perhaps a century after the original construction, and the whole site was clearly designed with some magnificence for a varied round of vigorous activity.

A greater refinement distinguishes the work of Marcianus Cyris, who produced a group of churches along the mountain route eastwards from Antioch to Aleppo during the period 390–420 AD. Marcianus retains the prevailing style of Syrian architecture: a robust structure composed of large stone blocks, a threefold nave divided on each side by half a dozen columns with lofty arches, a sanctuary apse kept within the squared end of the building and entered by way of a decorated triumphal arch. But windows tend to become more frequent and greater richness is shown in the bands of decoration which frame the doorways. These may include a string of pearls, intertwining ribbons, a sort of dog-tooth moulding, flourishes of laurel-leaves—all surviving examples of the late Greek spirit translated into the sturdier and more sombre idiom of the Middle East.

Marcianus and his contemporaries experimented with a variety of capitals. There is a plain Doric form with a cube of stone set on top to give greater height to the arch; another is a capital scalloped on its under surface; a third is a type of Ionic capital with the corner spirals tamed and flattened; more particularly, still another shows a variant of the Corinthian style, with the two rows of acanthus leaves tightly drawn together under a cap of spreading foliage. Features such as these, noticeable at Dar Qita and other villages nearby, mark a stage in artistic development when the church is no longer intended to look like an ordinary house or covered market but is separated from other buildings and given its own distinctive form.

A rather different type of construction, within the same neighbourhood, is displayed by the church of Qalb Louzeh, which, still in a good state of preservation, seems to have been built about 490 AD (fig. 77). Here the nave is a vast room framed not by rows of columns but by broad, squat pillars strong enough to sustain wide, low-slung arches; a double row of stone corbels, projecting from the wall above, supported the timbers of the roof. The south aisle, if not both aisles, was covered with stone slabs to form a gallery, with clerestory windows affording a view into the nave. The building at Qalb Louzeh has none of the comfortable domestic air of the earlier Syrian churches. It is set not among a cluster of houses but, dignified and impressive, within its own ample precinct. Sturdy towers enclose a west front with entrance of ambitious pattern: a large square-headed doorway with well-marked jambs and lintel stands beneath a band of decoration drawn up in the centre to form a bold semicircular opening. The east end is of even more elaborate design; here the triumphal arch, corresponding to the chancel-arch of some Norman churches, springs in four carved mouldings from the Corinthian capitals of massive channelled piers, while

the apse, no longer concealed within flanking sacristies, juts out in an ample curve lit by three matching windows. When viewed from outside these round-headed windows are seen to be framed by Corinthian columns placed against the wall with, above, two courses of enormous stones leading upward to a chunky cornice and double band of carved decoration. The south front of the building adheres to the convention that this side should display the fullest external ornament, and a row of windows overtops three formal entrances placed at irregular intervals along the wall. The moulded string-course around all the windows takes the form which was to become characteristic of Syrian architecture, avoiding sharp rectangles and sliding from the vertical to the horizontal with the help of gentle curves.

The Syrian type of basilica reaches its final stage of majestic authority in the cathedral[13] of Rosafa, set in the midst of the desert eighteen miles south of the river Euphrates. This remote place acquired great renown, and the alternative name Sergiopolis, from the tomb of Sergius, a soldier-saint who had been executed during Diocletian's persecution. Rosafa thus became a goal of pilgrimage and gradually equipped to receive a large number of visitors. The cathedral, replacing an earlier structure, was built early in the sixth century to an elegant and sophisticated design. This consists primarily of a rectangle, 59 metres by 27 metres, subdivided into nave and aisles by means of cross-shaped pillars carrying arches with a span of some 10 metres. The pillars are massive enough but doubt apparently arose regarding the stability of the church, with the result that huge chunks of masonry were applied as buttresses to the walls outside and, within, columns were inserted as supports for the great arches of the nave. This latter arrangement had the effect of separating nave from aisles more resolutely than had been at first intended, though smaller arches, less than half the size of the original span, rose from the capitals of the columns and allowed easy movement between the various parts of the building. Entry from the street, at the west end with its flanking towers, was by way of three large doors, one into each aisle and a central one into the nave enclosure, which served as a porch. The south side of the cathedral remained featureless and plain while the north was pierced by three ornamented doorways and a number of windows arranged in

77. Qalb Louzeh: view from the south-east.

pairs, the reason for this breach of normal Syrian practice being that a vast courtyard, surrounded by ancillary buildings, lay to the north. The sanctuary consisted of a broad simple apse, set within the rectangle of the church and having a triplet of modest windows looking out eastwards. The two side chambers, connected not with the sanctuary but, by means of arches upheld by pilasters and columns, with the aisles, boasted an upper storey with stubby columns acting as supports to an ornamental dome. Here again the centre of the nave was obstructed by the reader's platform, a large rectangle with semicircle at the west end and ministering to usefulness rather than to the beauty which the gracefully proportioned church even in its ruins still suggests. Another basilica nearby (Basilica B) reproduces the general style and many detailed features of the cathedral.

The type of Syrian church that is described, in distinction from the basilica, as 'centralized' may take various forms. Perhaps the oldest is the martyr-shrine of St Babylas, twelfth bishop of Antioch, that was uncovered by excavation in 1934 at Kaoussie, a suburb of Antioch. The building forms a precisely regular cross: four rectangular naves, each 25 metres long and

marking one of the points of the compass, meet in a central square formed by massive pillars supporting wide arches, above which apparently rose a roof in the shape of a pyramid. This remarkable monument, to which a number of subsidiary buildings, such as a baptistery, were later annexed, dates from about 380 AD 'in the time of Bishop Flavian', and contains well-preserved geometric mosaics set in place, as inscriptions show, a few years later. There is no sign of a special sanctuary in the eastern arm of the cross or anywhere else, and even the tomb of Babylas was placed not in the middle of the square but in a sarcophagus[14] over against the north-western corner. The central feature, oddly enough, was nothing more than a raised bema of compressed horseshoe form, as found in the nave of the basilicas. From here, presumably, hymns were sung and addresses given in the saint's honour. This would imply that a form originally evolved to help meet the needs of the Eucharist was later adapted to serve a rather different purpose.

The same cross form, though without the mathematical regularity shown at Kaoussie, distinguishes the vast sanctuary built at Qalat Siman in honour of St

78. Qalat Siman: the sanctuary viewed from the north-east.

79. Qalat Siman, basilica.

Simeon Stylites (fig. 78). Simeon's body was transferred to Antioch, but the column on which the saint dwelt for more than thirty years remained as a venerated place of pilgrimage and the focal point of the church. Pious pressures exerted on the emperors Leo I and Zeno seem to have been the reason for a ready supply of men and money from official sources, as was indeed required not only for the whole elaborate structure but also for levelling and preparing the rocky and difficult site. Yet, however powerful imperial patronage may have been, the style of native Syrian structures is retained. The walls are composed of large stone blocks ranged without mortar in horizontal courses while pillars, arches and doorways follow the precedent set by local forms of decoration as applied to both secular and religious buildings (fig. 79). But there is a touch of Byzantine magnificence about the sharply-cut acanthus capitals and the rhythmical course of moulding which runs over the top of arches and unusually ample windows. The design of the church is marked by great originality, since the plain cross shape, emphasizing the august holiness of the saint's pillar, is modified in several ways. The square sanctuary in which the four equal arms meet at Kaoussie is widened at Qalat Siman with four corner recesses which go to make up an octagon, along the lines of the Church of the Ascension on the Mount of Olives. Then each arm, instead of being a plain rectangle, is subdivided to form a Syrian basilica with nave and two aisles. Thus the structure as a whole seemed, at least to one traveller who recorded his impressions, to 'resemble a cross adorned with colonnades on all four sides and having an open courtyard in the midst'.[15] This implies that the central octagon was not roofed over but left Simeon's column exposed to the sky. Finally the eastern arm, rather than being squared off like the others, ends in a sanctuary with three apses. In this way the huge building combined the uses of a basilica with those of a martyr-shrine: a church of conventional pattern in which the liturgy may be celebrated forms part of a sanctuary centred on the sacred relic. In testimony to St Simeon's prestige, the church is allied with a great monastery and other buildings, which include a baptistery, hostels and triumphal entrance gateways. Below, at the foot of the hill, lay Deir Siman, with three monasteries, several hostels for the reception of pilgrims and, no doubt, an atmosphere compounded of devotion and curiosity

such as may today be sensed at Lourdes or Carcassonne.

The martyr-shrine, as it developed through the centuries, took on a variety of forms showing keen inventive powers exercised within the formula set by pagan tombs. The square, the circle and the octagon, alone or in combination, served as the basis for most of them, but the 'tetraconch' also was favoured, its four apses projecting each from one side of a square that was usually indicated only by four robust corner-pillars.

A rather ambitious example of the more advanced type of martyr-shrine is provided by the sanctuary of the saints Sergius, Bacchus and Leontius at Bosra, which served also as the cathedral of the local bishop. This building, which an inscription conveniently dates to 512 AD, is essentially a square from which three apses project. The large central apse, of octagonal shape outside but a flattened semicircle within, is flanked by the two smaller ones, square-ended but semicircular inside the thick walls. Whether these should properly be thought of as relic-chapels or as sacristies, two lesser rooms are squeezed between them and the central apse, thus making the east end of the church a fivefold arrangement of interlocking members connected by substantial doorways. The square nave of the cathedral is converted internally, with the aid of four niches rounding off the corners, into a circle. Windows abound, and the circle itself acts as an aisle flowing around a quatrefoil composed of piers and columns. This central part of the building seems to have been covered in wood while the aisle was roofed, in Syrian fashion, with large slabs of stone.

A variant on this complex but balanced pattern is evident in the shrine of 'the triumphant, holy martyr George' at Ezra, also in the Hauran district of Syria, and bearing the date 515 AD (fig. 80). Here the east end consists of a semicircular chancel with a solitary window piercing exceptionally thick straightened walls. In front of the semicircle lies a rectangular space, well adapted for celebrations of the liturgy, with a subsidiary room at each side. The square nave, once more enriched with semicircular recesses in the massive walling of the corners, is shaped internally as an octagonal aisle enclosing not a quatrefoil, as at Bosra, but another octagon. This internal octagon extends upwards to serve as the drum of the cupola.

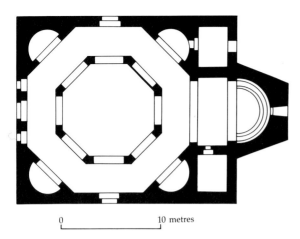

0   10 metres

80. Ezra, the shrine of St George, 515 AD: ground-plan.

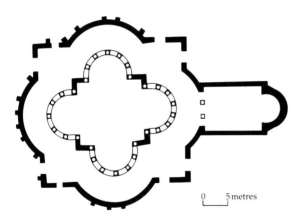

0   5 metres

81. Seleucia Pieria, near Antioch: a recently discovered martyr-shrine of the late fifth century.

Greater stability is secured by arranging the top two courses of stone in the drum so that the eight sides are doubled to form sixteen and then doubled again to make up thirty-two, thus easing the transition from octagonal to circular form. The cupola itself is egg-shaped, perhaps under the influence of precedents drawn from Central Asia, while the small round-headed windows at the base of the cupola are an early essay in the type of clerestory adopted with such impressive effect at Santa Sophia. St George's, Ezra seems to have been a dark building with few windows but with doorways to north and south as well as the bolder feature of a triple entrance marking the west end. The general pattern suggests the influence of early baptisteries, which often consisted of an octagon surmounted by a dome.

One other example of bold design, having much in common with S. Lorenzo in Milan, is the martyr-shrine recently unearthed at Seleucia Pieria, just outside Antioch (fig. 81). Constructed partly of lime-stone, partly of rubble, it has a chancel floor of marble slabs and much gaily-patterned mosaic elsewhere. The basic form of this buiding is that of two quatre-foils, one inside the other. The inner quatrefoil has well-marked rectangular corners suggesting a square from which, in perfect regularity, columns arranged as a semicircle protrude on all four sides. The external walls also are squared off, on three sides, with rather flattened semicircles. These give the building a diameter of some 37 metres. On the east side, and extending for over 15 metres, is an addition shaped like a little basilica, with rectangular hall and a shallow apse contained within thick walling. Along lines such as these the Syrians developed their national style of church architecture, making use of materials to hand, with sensitive regard to practical needs and artistic harmony.

The remote country eastward, the mountainous region of the Tur Abdin and the neighbouring ter-ritories of northern Mesopotamia,[16] formed a deba-table land both politically and ecclesiastically. The emperor Jovian ceded Nisibis to Persia in 363 AD but the redrawn frontier was an unstable one. Generally speaking, the Persians to the east came to provide a refuge for the Nestorians, while the Melkites, the 'King's men' of the Byzantine Orthodox church, prevailed in the west. These divisions, however, were without effect on the style of church architecture, which may be divided into two groups: the parochial and the monastic. The parochial, village churches are unpretentious buildings, longitudinal in form with an entrance on the south side and sometimes a small oratory free-standing nearby. A brick barrel vault covers the whole area of the church, gaining stability from arcades built close up against the side walls. Dating is uncertain and many of these churches are nowadays referred to the period shortly after the Arab conquest in 640 AD.

Examples of the second or monastic type of church are less frequent but distinctive in character. Nearly square in plan, they customarily have three separate chambers, or sanctuaries, attached to the east and a narthex to the west. Low, heavy arcades line the walls, forming the basis of the barrel vault. The only one of these churches securely anchored to a relatively early date is that in the monastic complex of Mar Gabriel at Qartamin. This appears to owe its prestige, as well as its now fragmentary mosaics, to the patronage of the emperor Anastasius round about 512 AD.[17] The church lies broadways on, in what is sometimes described as the Babylonian fashion. Squat and ill-lit beneath its vast tiled roof, it nevertheless gives a firm impression of Syrian stateliness and power.

Armenia, where, under the influence of Gregory the Illuminator, Christianity was recognized as the official religion by King Tiridates III not later than 295 AD, might be expected to offer a distinctive style of Christian architecture.[18] This is indeed the case, though existing churches all display evidence of renovation dating from the seventh century or later. Beneath the alterations, however, a structure such as Etchmiadzin still retains primitive features. It seems that here the fourth-century church was originally built as a square, covered by a cupola based on four pillars and enclosing an eastern apse. This form, practical yet impressive, may owe something to the royal Hall of Audience transformed into a shrine appropriate to the victorious Christ. A hundred years or so later the rectangular lines were modified by semicircular extensions on all four sides. The church at Ereruk, which may be as early as the beginning of the sixth century, shows that the Armenians were also perfectly capable of constructing a basilica on the Syrian model, with barrel vaults to nave and aisles, a tower at each end of the façade, and round-headed windows moulded in flowing lines.

PALESTINE

In Palestine itself the ancient churches surviving, other than those at the sacred sites, are rather less abundant and less striking than in Syria, but show a similar evolution. Large blocks of stone laid in regular courses made up the walls, and the country churches, as represented at Kherbet Kufin near Bethlehem, remain for the most part simple basilica halls having an eastern apse concealed within massive walls and flanked by the two chambers necessary for general administrative purposes. But more sophisticated structures grew up alongside, particularly when the interest of the imperial court had been aroused. The church of the Theotokos, on Mount Gerizim, closely resembles in outline the pattern found at Ezra and is some thirty years older (fig. 82). Erected in 484 AD by the emperor Zeno out of gratitude for his success in quelling a revolt of the Samaritans, it bears the stamp of elegance in its carefully worked walls and in capitals which, Corinthian in general pattern, have the fuzzy

complexity, which sometimes develops in this style, softened by Ionic scrolls. An octagonal nave forms an ambulatory around the central arrangement of angle piers separated by matching pairs of columns which probably supported a wooden dome. The unusual and striking feature here is that the octagon is a double one. The area between the two walls is used to enclose a formal portico on the west and two rather less imposing entrances to north and south, with four small chapels, shaped like tiny basilicas, occupying the rest of the space. The east end is occupied by a shallow apse with a well-defined rectangle in front of it, and the conventional sacristies, approached only through an external door, at each side. Here too, it appears, eucharistic worship found its place at the centre of things while the reverential awe due to particular saints was fostered in the side chapels.

The sanctuary on Mount Gerizim was clearly a place of

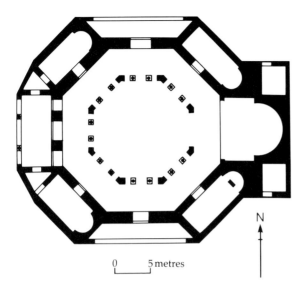

82. Mount Gerizim, Church of the Theotokos, 484 AD: ground-plan.

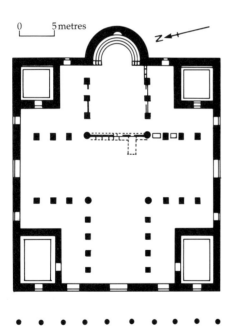

83. Gerasa, Church of the Prophets, Apostles and Martyrs, 465 AD: ground-plan.

much splendour contrasting in every way with the simple churches appropriate to remote villages, but the most remarkable collection of churches in Palestine seems to have been concentrated at Gerasa (Jerash), very near the Arabian border, 'a great city, strongly protected by mighty walls', set in a countryside 'well supplied with fortresses and castles and producing the richest variety of merchandise'.[19] After a period of great prosperity, Gerasa was ravaged by both Arab tribesmen and earthquakes, and during the eighth century fell into decay. Its treasures aroused no interest until the excavations of the last fifty years. The city had possessed many shrines before the Christian epoch—the great temple of Artemis still dominates the ruins—but from about 350 AD Gerasa rapidly developed into a Christian metropolis hallowed by the presence of a fountain which, so men[20] said, gushed with wine instead of water during the Epiphany festival when Christ's miracle at Cana was celebrated. The remains of at least a dozen churches have come to light, all but two being of basilican type, divided by columns or piers into a nave and two aisles. Much of the nave is occupied, as in the case of many Syrian churches, by a screened area where the liturgy was celebrated. At Gerasa this chancel takes the form of a rectangle of varying proportions immediately in front of the apse and continued into the body of the nave by a raised passage to the reader's pulpit.

Gerasa was one of the cities of the Decapolis, a league of communities welded together by Greek colonists, and, as its numerous inscriptions testify, largely Greek-speaking. The architectural style of its churches therefore combines a certain Aegean lightness with the chunky Syrian method of building in courses of vast ashlar blocks. That, at any rate, is the case with the oldest of the churches, the Cathedral set up at the beginning of the fifth century.[21] Here the stairway of thirty-six steps and the colonnaded entrance were taken over from a disused pagan shrine, as were perhaps the Corinthian capitals of the nave and the masonry, finely cut and joined, of the whole building. The apse is shallow, surrounded by a heavy wall and enclosed within a squared east end which provides space also for the small rectangular 'prothesis' and 'diaconicon'. These last are unusual in that they have an entrance leading directly westwards into the aisles. The cathedral extended to a length of 43 metres, the west end being furnished with three port-als which faced towards the courtyard surrounding the miraculous fountain.

The dominant building here, however, is another church abutting on the opposite side of the court and raised above it by a triple flight of steps. This church, as an inscription makes plain, was erected in honour of the soldier-martyr Theodore in the year 496 by Aeneas, 'a bishop infinitely wise and steeped in piety'. It resembles the cathedral in both design and propor-tions, although the masonry is more roughly worked, the nave is narrower in relation to the aisles and the columns, more widely spaced, are topped by arches instead of the straight line of an architrave. Consider-able amounts of gilded glass and marble indicate that here, as in other churches of Gerasa, a lavish decora-tion was employed of glass mosaic in the apse, stone mosaic on the floors and polished slabs of marble on the walls. The rectangular chancel, smaller than many, is attached to the walls of the apse, between which holes have been driven into the pavement to receive the shafts fixing the altar and its canopy. No trace of seating has been discovered in the apse, but the reader's pulpit projects, in characteristic fashion, westwards down the nave.

Roughly a hundred metres from St Theodore's church the outlines of a later[22] and rather more compli-cated structure bear witness alike to the piety and to the inventiveness of the Gerasenes. This building consists of three churches, lying parallel and joined together within the rectangle of a thick external wall. This wall is unbroken except on the west side where a slim, colonnaded portico runs the whole length, in front of the entrance doorways. The churches of SS. Cosmas and Damian and of St George, at the sides, resemble each other very closely, being basilicas of the customary pattern and having, between nave and aisles, sturdy pillars designed to carry arches of wide span. The church of St John the Baptist, however, constructed on the plan of a martyr-shrine, is entirely different. Its basic design is a circle, with rounded apse projecting at the east end. Four horseshoe-like reces-ses interrupt the line of the circle, which, on the inside, forms an ambulatory flowing round a square nave with its four corner-pillars set to uphold a dome. The combination of square with circle is emphasized in that the whole of the rotunda, together with its horse-shoe appendages, is enclosed within a massive square of masonry. The straightforward mathematical balance of this composite church must have contrasted with great richness within, to judge from the quantity of mosaic which still survives. Cupids, the Seasons, animals and birds play their colourful part, enclosed by flowing borders of acanthus or ribbon pattern, while especial interest centres on the sketchy representation of cities, Alexandria with its lighthouse in particular.

The Church of the Prophets, Apostles and Martyrs at Gerasa, erected in 465 AD, differs from all the others but again demonstrates the principle of enclosing a carefully articulated pattern within a square (fig. 83).[23] As in the case of St John the Baptist's church, the whole of the west front, with its five entrances, is preceded by a long narrow porch. The interior of the building is marked out by columns to form the shape of a cross; the eastern limb represents the chancel with reader's pulpit attached. The four rectangular spaces left between the arms of the cross and the side walls are each taken up with an L-shaped aisle set against an enclosed chamber serving either as a separate sanctu-ary or to meet administrative needs, while a shallow semicircular apse, equipped with clergy seats, projects from the east end. This rich and complex design is typical of the artistic power displayed at Gerasa in the fifth and sixth centuries.

ASIA MINOR

Influences from Constantinople and Antioch spread throughout Asia Minor, so that the vigour of religious enthusiasm, acting upon a common culture, led to the building of churches in basilican form all along the eastern coast of the Mediterranean and often far inland. Differences of style and sophistication naturally occurred from place to place, dictated to some extent by local conventions of worship. The basilica, even when hallowed by the presence of martyr-relics, was primarily the place where people gathered for the celebration of the Eucharist, and this, by the fourth century, had developed from a rite resembling a community supper to a majestic drama: it is a 'spiritual sacrifice',[24] a 'mystery which we celebrate behind locked doors after excluding those who are not initiates'.[25] Even so, different views were held about the use of the nave, and these led to certain modifications of architectural form. Some teachers held that the nave was essentially the 'four-square oratory of the people' by contrast with the apsidal sanctuary reserved for the clergy—though naturally anyone as eloquent as St Chrysostom would wish to preach in the nave 'for the sake of being completely heard'. A church might be held to represent the Heavenly Jerusalem or to be a kind of ark of salvation: 'first let the house be oblong, turned towards the east, with the sacristies on either side towards the east, seeing it resembles a ship'.[26] These words were written by a fourth-century Syrian, but it was just at that time and in that part of the world that the clergy were assigning to themselves, as they celebrated the holy mysteries, a large part of the nave, enclosed within chancel screens and colourful hangings. In places where this happened the layfolk were driven to occupy the aisles and the west end of the nave, which was sometimes marked off with an inner portico (esonarthex). When galleries were provided, the aisles, instead of being lightened by large clerestory windows, remained dark except insofar as they were lit from the centre or by lamps reflecting the brilliance of marble decoration. By contrast with the fairly ample remains of early churches in Syria, those still surviving in Asia Minor tend to be fragmentary and rather more widely dispersed. At Constantinople itself the only remaining monument of the period between Constantine's foundations and the great burst of energy which marked Justinian's reign is the church—now roofless —called St John Studios after the name of the senator Studios, who founded it in 463 AD.[27] This, as befits a building in the capital city, wears a classical, conservative air but was evidently decorated in that oriental richness of varied colours which distinguishes a Persian carpet. The layout is that of a standard if stubby basilica. Entered from its portico, the nave was divided from the two aisles by columns of green marble set on bases and topped by elongated capitals supporting the straight line of a moulded architrave (fig. 84). The aisles had large circular-headed windows but apparently the nave was shut in by galleries. The apse, once again, takes the form of a semicircle inside

converted by thick walls into the semblance of an octagon when viewed from without. Brick prevails in the facing of the church but variety is given by bands of stone, three courses in depth.

The portico of St John's church provides admirable examples of the type of capital known as the 'Theodosian'. This is a variant of the 'composite' capital, in which the acanthus leaves characteristic of the Corinthian style combine with the scrolls of the Ionic. Constantinople had borrowed the Corinthian pattern and treated it, with some sophistication, in its own particular way. For the smooth-leaved acanthus was substituted a prickly acanthus, with leaves often twisted sideways as though by the wind. This is the basic theme of the Theodosian capital, usually carved with two rows, one above the other, of eight acanthus and often a further band of acanthus decoration running between the four corner-scrolls. It was not until the end of the fifth century that another characteristic development took place and each capital was topped by an impost, a rather bulky cushion of stone, which provided the springing for the arches. This impost could be plain or it could be enriched over its whole surface with a lace-like pattern of deeply-cut acanthus leaves.

The coastlands of Asia Minor, and the great harbour city of Ephesus in particular, served as the meeting-point for Greek and Eastern ideas as for Greek and Eastern merchandise. But the sentiment in architecture is prevailingly Greek, with an instinct for elegance rather than mass. Remains are, however, not very plentiful. At Ephesus itself, the cross-church set up over the traditional tomb of John the Apostle was largely reconstructed by Justinian, but the stages by which the sanctuary developed are clear enough (fig. 85). At first the entrance to the grotto containing St John's tomb was protected by a square structure resembling a mausoleum. During the fifth century the square was rebuilt with four thick pillars to support a dome, and a covered hall was added at each side, forming a cross-shaped church. An elaborate narthex was set against the west end, while a system of narrow aisles and corridors running round the building enabled the devout to pass from the main entrance to any part of the church without disturbing the central square, which was probably enclosed by metal grilles.[28] St John's was essentially a pilgrim church, in which the revered tomb occupied the central point and

84. Constantinople, St John Studios: capitals.

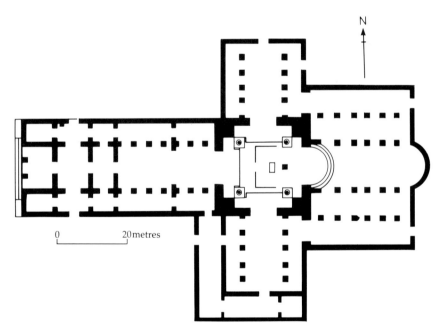

85. Ephesus, St John: plan of the church as it was about 440 AD. A century later the building was much altered and enlarged.

86. Ephesus: the fragmentary remains of the Cathedral of St Mary, scene of the Council of 431 AD.

the eucharistic services were relegated to the east end. This idea of a relic-shrine formed as a free-standing cross spread westwards, and a smaller, simpler version of St John's shrine at Ephesus has been found at Klise-Kjoj in Bulgaria.

Scarcely less renowned than the sanctuary of St John at Ephesus was that of the 'Seven Sleepers' nearby. The essential feature here was a cave developed and extended as an enormous mortuary shrine, with a close-knit series of chapels and a multitude of coffins dispersed over the floor or enclosed in the walls.

At the foot of the hill and near the old harbour of Ephesus, considerable portions remain of the Cathedral of St Mary, where the Council met in 431 AD to consider the speculations of Nestorius concerning the nature of Christ. This church (fig. 86), entirely different from St John's, is a basilica of conventional shape, preceded by a large courtyard with baptistery attached and by a colonnaded portico. Aligned on the walls of an earlier building of basilica type, the nave, separated by a row of columns from each of the slender aisles, runs to a length of 85 metres, and ends with a semicircular apse, flanked by two sacristies and

enclosed in a massive rectangular wall. The church seems to have been unencumbered by galleries or by any substantial chancel advancing into the nave, while small portions of mosaic and marble panelling attest a rich decoration. Pillars and columns combined near the middle of the nave point to the existence of a dome; another dome is known to have crowned the octagonal baptistery.

A dome might be formed as the continuation of a circular drum but was more frequently found raised on a square base. In such cases it maintained its circular form with the assistance of squinches or pendentives (fig. 87, 88). Squinches, usually claimed as a Persian discovery, are small arches fitting into the four corners of the square and thus converting it into the circle or shallow octagon on which the dome can rest. Pendentives, on the other hand, are triangles that prolong the surface of the dome by sliding down in decreasing width to the points, between the supporting arches, where the corners of the square are met. The vaults and domes of Asia Minor, by contrast with those of Roman type, are often high pitched and boldly constructed in rubble, brick or tile.

The pattern of the cathedral at Ephesus is repeated

not only at Miletus[29] and on such Aegean islands as
Cos but also further away, in Isauria and the other
countries bordering the south coast of Asia Minor,
where, however, rubble and brick yield to powerful
courses of stone. But there is no rigid adherence to one
precise design and the architects give play to their
imaginations within the general form which custom
and convenience dictated. A rectangular transept, for
instance, striking across the church immediately in
front of the apse, could be so elaborated as to make up
two broad arms of a cross, with the nave corresponding to the shaft of the cross and the apse representing
the head.

A complex instance of this design is provided by a
church recently excavated at Perga. Here a large rectangular courtyard in front of the triple entrance-
doorways is balanced, at the further end of the church,
by a broad transept having its chancel area marked out
by clustered piers with screens in between. The transept has an oblong aisle to the north and south, while
on each side of the semicircular apse, separated from it
by a massive wall, are matching double chambers
approached through openings from the transept. The
colonnaded nave is slender, by comparison, and the
emphasis rests with the wide arms and intricate head-
piece. Several churches in Lycia,[30] such as those of
Karabel and Alacahisar, offer a somewhat different
pattern on a small scale. Here the head-piece, attached
to a short nave and aisles, consists of a trefoil arrangement of apses, rectangular outside but circular within
and linked together by pendentives which uphold the
dome. The base of this trefoil is spanned by the main
archway which also helps to support the thrust of the
dome.

Further east along the coast, in Cilicia, a local variant
appears several times, in particular at Corycus and in
the vast church built over the tomb of St Thecla at
Meriamlik (Seleucia) (fig. 89). Each church was
entered through a grandiose portico leading to the
nave—rather stumpy at Corycus, but immensely
elongated, to nearly 55 metres, at Meriamlik. The
distinctive feature is the arrangement of the east end,
where the apse is flanked on each side by a chapel, or
sacristy, shaped like a small basilica with semicircular
apse protruding beyond the rectangle. These chapels
are extended some distance beyond the main apse to
the limit set by a straight north–south wall which
therefore marks off an area, put perhaps to no more

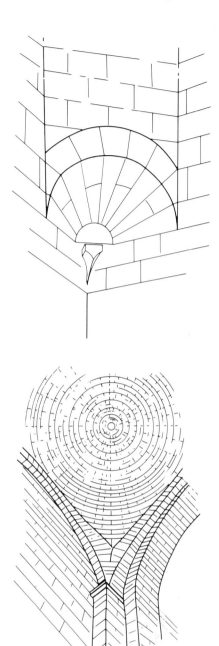

87 and 88. Squinch and pendentive: two methods of
fixing a circle or dome to a square. The squinch is a small
arch set across the corners of a rectangle; the pendentive
is an inverted triangle with curving sides.

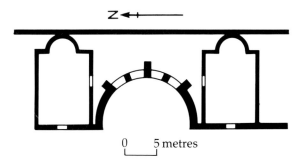

89. Meriamlik, St Thecla: plan of the east end, showing the apse flanked by large side-chapels.

90. Dǎg Pazari: massive pillars supporting the construction of apse and tower.

august use than general storage, between the two side-chapels.

Another church at Meriamlik, to be dated at about 480 AD, took the form of a curiously squat basilica where four massive pillars just westward of the apse supported either a dome or, more probably, a tower as at Dǎg Pazari nearby (fig. 90). This type of building is, however, best illustrated by the well-preserved monastic church of Alahan (Kodja Kalessi) lying in remote country further north in Isauria (fig. 91, 92). Here two bays of the nave, nearly half its length, are covered by a rectangular tower. The additional height thus created enables the windows to be set in a top storey with, below them, a repeated arrangement of triple arches springing from columns set one on top of the other and leading respectively into the aisles and into galleries placed above the aisles. The building material consists of large stones carefully cut and seen to particular advantage in the horseshoe arches which straddle the nave. The general air of elegance may perhaps be due to the personal interest of the emperor Zeno, himself an Isaurian, whose calamitous reign was sweetened by a profound concern for doctrinal subtleties and a lively patronage of the arts.

The high lands of the interior of what is now Turkey contain a number of small churches which date from the fifth or early sixth century and exhibit a common pattern of chunky walls and vaulted naves. Hierapolis, as the result of recent excavation, has rather more to show. It was a substantial town on an east–west trade route and enjoyed the prestige of claiming the tomb of Philip the Apostle, so that greater variety and sophistication might well be expected.

The oldest church seems to be an adaptation, made about 400 AD, of a vast hall previously used for some such secular purpose as a bath or a market. Each side of this hall, now the nave, is furnished with three arches leading into vaulted chambers which presumably served as chapels. The construction of the whole is carried out in the Syrian fashion of piling large blocks of stone one above the other on the assumption that they would hold firmly together by their weight alone, while three domes, succeeding each other along the line of the nave, provided both dignity and space for windows.

Another church dating from about the same period is unusual in general design and unique in its detail. Essentially the building consists of a square, a cross

91. Alahan, the monastic church: a carved capital.

92. Alahan, the monastic church.

and an octagon. The outer part of the square, more precisely a rectangular figure measuring 60 by 61.5 metres, is taken up with an unbroken series of little rooms which may have been private burial-places or lodgings for pilgrims. Four of these chambers, however, one in the middle of each wall, are arranged rather more elaborately, with corner-columns, and are furnished with doorways leading into larger rooms of equal size; these latter rooms thus make up four arms of a cross cut off at the middle by the central octagon. The eight faces of the octagon are symmetrical: in the space between the four arms of the cross are set rectangular, vaulted chambers corresponding in size to those which compose the cross. The intervening triangles which extend behind the massive piers are filled with little trilobe rooms which, again, look as if they were originally lodgings or burial-places. A system of passageways connects the various members of the complicated but regular pattern. The structure as a whole thus composes an intricate martyr-shrine (fig. 93), and the suggestion, unsupported by any direct evidence, has been made that the octagon marked the traditional site of Philip's tomb, around which those of the faithful who could afford it sought

to be buried. The architectural style of this church remains a compromise, however, for the squat piers made up of massive stone blocks contrast markedly with bands of brick and stone in the walling which, together with a lavish use of marble panelling, are characteristic of the Aegean coastland.

A similar combination of materials is found in another of these majestic tomb-shrines, at Side, in Pamphylia, where, however, the layout is simpler and takes the form of a domed rectangle with a wide, shallow apse projecting from each flank.

The most remarkable collection of churches in the hill country of Asia Minor occurs at the place nicknamed Binbir-Kilisse, 'Thousand and One Churches', in the province of Lycaonia, where the remote and barren nature of the countryside has given little encouragement to improve on the original structures. About twenty of these remain, varying in size from moderate to tiny and nearly all conforming to a standard 'Syrian' pattern of the late fifth century (fig. 94).[31] Externally the buildings are plain and sturdy, the massive blocks of stone relieved only by string-courses running round windows and doorways. Naves have taken the form of dark barrel vaults, with

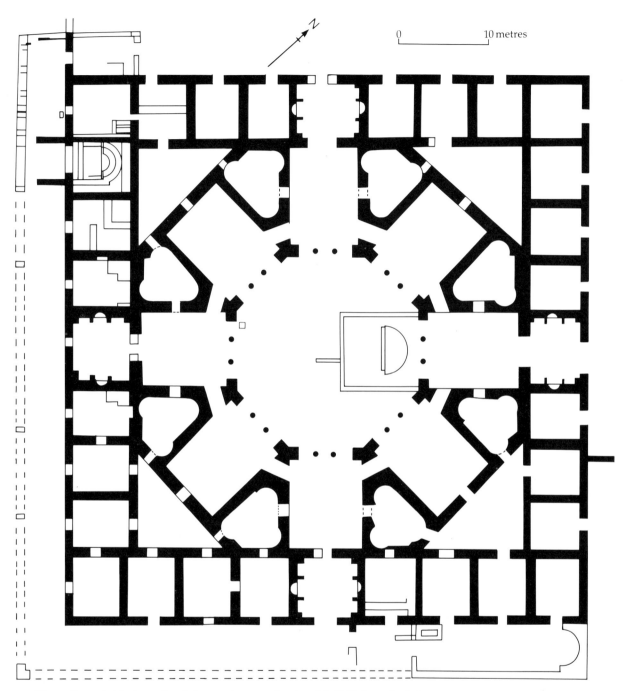

93. Hierapolis: an intricate martyr-shrine, perhaps on the site of St Philip's tomb. A few portions of wall that are missing have been reconstructed in the plan.

94. Binbir-Kilisse (Lycaonia): a typical church of the district, with barrel-vault and domed apse, seen from the south-east.

few windows and these set rather high in the wall. Usually there are aisles, separated from the nave by a row of plain horseshoe-arches on dumpy piers; this arrangement is repeated in the larger arch leading to the apse. The apse, in its turn, projects as a semicircle, covered with a half dome and lit by means of a pair or triplet of windows which once more reproduce, at times rather crudely, the design of the nave arcade. Under grey skies such an accepted pattern of building would be harsh and sombre, but, in brilliant sunshine reflected from rocky hillsides, the group of unpretentious, stocky churches sprang fittingly from their native soil, reserving all they possessed of light and colour to glow around the mysteries enacted within.

NOTES

1. Coins of Septimius Severus, about 195 AD, from Isauria, in Asia Minor, and Anchialus, in Thrace. E. Baldwin Smith, *Architectural Symbolism* (Princeton, 1956), 12.18.21.
2. I Kings 22.10.
3. Psalm 24.7.
4. Baldwin Smith, *op. cit.*, numbers 31–46.
5. P. B. Shelley, 'The Cloud'.
6. Eusebius, *Life of Constantine*, 4.58, PG 20.1209.
7. Mark the Deacon, *Life of Porphyry of Gaza*, 75.84 (PG 65).
8. I Esdras 9, 42.
9. John IV, Patriarch of Constantinople in the sixth century, maintained that the prothesis typified Golgotha, while

Sophronius, Patriarch of Jerusalem, held the prothesis to be of greater sanctity than the Holy of Holies since it represented Bethlehem and the Upper Room.

10. Canon 21 of the Council of Laodicea (368 AD) laid it down that no subordinate was to enter the diaconicon and handle vessels sacred to the Lord. See Lauchert, *Die Kanones* (Leipzig, 1896), 74.
11. *Martyrs of Palestine*, 11.29. Lawlor and Oulton, *Eusebius* (London, 1927), i.393.
12. Evagrius, *Historia Ecclesiastica* ii.3. PG 86.2194. For the three shrines referred to here cf. Grabar, *Martyrium* i.336.
13. Also known as the Basilica of St Sergius or Basilica A.
14. The sarcophagus is a monolith, remarkable in that half-

way down there is a ridge with notches as for little beams. According to St Chrysostom, Babylas 'was not destined, when he went there, to remain alone, but he soon received a neighbour and fellow-lodger', in the person of Bishop Meletius whose body was placed either within the sarcophagus or in a smaller receptacle outside.

15. Evagrius I.14, *PG* 86.2459.

16. M. Mango in the revised edition of Gertrude Bell's *Churches and Monasteries of the Tur Abdin* (London, 1982).

17. F. Nau in *Actes du XIV Congrès des Orientalistes* (Paris, 1906). The nearby church of Salah, closely similar in design, may perhaps be almost as ancient.

18. A. Khatchatrian, *L'architecture arménienne du iv au vi siècles* (Paris, 1971).

19. Ammianus Marcellinus, xiv. 8.13, ed. J. C. Rolfe (Loeb), i. 76.

20. Epiphanius, *Haereses* 51.30.1, *PG* 41.941.

21. Unlike many of the churches of Gerasa, it bears no inscription recording its exact date.

22. Inscriptions here point to 529–33 AD as the date of construction.

23. Not quite a perfect square: the length from east to west is roughly one metre longer than the breadth.

24. Cyril of Jerusalem, *Catechesis Mystagogica* v.8, *PG* 33.1116.

25. John Chrysostom, *Homilia in Matthaeum* xxiii.3, *PG* 57.311.

26. *Apostolic Constitutions* ii.57, *PG* 1.723.

27. Fragments remain also of St Mary in the Chalkopratiae, a church of similar design.

28. The whole building was extensively remodelled by Justinian between 548 and 565 AD. See p. 190.

29. At Miletus the aisles are, in very unusual fashion, extended to form a semicircle behind the apse.

30. The Lycian churches are usually assigned to a date at the beginning of the sixth century. See R. M. Harrison, *Anatolian Studies* xiii (1963).

31. Dates of individual buildings are not easy to establish. They seem to vary from about 470 AD to 700 AD or even later.

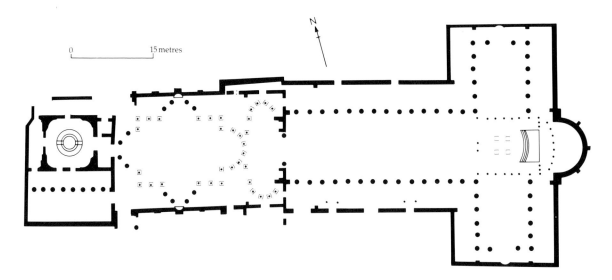

95. Abu Mina: the shrine of St Menas as it was at the end of the fifth century. The crypt and shrine of St Menas lie to the west of the basilica and the baptistery some thirty metres beyond. Excavations carried out since 1950 have disclosed the footings of a tetraconch building, of uncertain purpose, between.

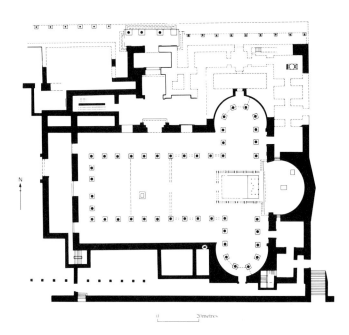

96. Hermopolis: the cathedral church set within its outbuildings.

8

Egypt: Nubia and Ethiopia: The Churches of North Africa

EGYPT: THE CHURCHES AND THEIR DECORATION

Close connections of both trade and culture linked the seaports of Asia Minor with northern Egypt. By long tradition the emperors interested themselves personally in Alexandria as being a granary of vital importance to their empire, and it is therefore not surprising to find near Alexandria a building which preserved the elegant form of a 'Hellenistic' basilica under the inspiration of imperial patronage. This is the shrine of Menas, a local saint held in high regard as a martyr and wonder-worker. So popular did Abu Mina become as a place of pilgrimage that the surroundings of a small tomb chamber were developed to become a complex of buildings rivalling the splendours of the Syrian national shrine of St Simeon Stylites.

Excavation, combined with literary references[1] to St Menas, shows fairly clearly how the growth at Abu Mina took place. An early catacomb provided simple earth-cut rooms round which the burial-places were ranged like the spokes of a wheel. Here pagan emblems jostled against the Christian monogram. The tomb of St Menas, who died about 300 AD, was subsequently protected by a square building of brick, covered by a dome anchored to the square by means of long pendentives. Later, during the times of religious fervour which marked the episcopate of St Athanasius, Menas's body was transferred to an ample crypt, and a memorial church on a cross-shaped plan was erected. Even then 'people suffered distress because the church could not hold the multitudes but they were standing outside in the desert' so more

spacious and elaborate buildings were constructed at the beginning of the fifth century under the patronage of the emperor Arcadius. The crypt was at that time enlarged and approached by a vaulted stairway with marble steps. To the west of the tomb chamber itself lay a small underground chapel, richly decorated with mosaic; confronting the tomb was set a marble image of St Menas, standing with one foot on each of two crouching camels.[2] The position of the crypt, however, partially blocks the west side of the church; formal entrances had therefore to be made in the south wall, which, like the remainder of the church, is built of ashlar blocks, neatly cut and of a modest size.

The form of the church, modified towards the end of the century at the emperor Zeno's instigation, is that of a cross with wide arms and a shallow projecting apse, reinforced by buttresses on the outer face (fig. 95). The nave is just over 55 metres in length, with a range of fifteen columns, set on bases, to mark off the narrow aisles and support the galleries which accommodated the women. This effect of an ambulatory is continued along the sides of the transepts, though here the columns are more widely spaced. The apse seems to have been used principally as a burial-place, and the curved line of raised seats for the clergy, with bishop's throne in the centre, is therefore built well to the west, confronting the high altar and enclosed within the rectangular chancel which occupies the central position between the two transepts. From here a narrow passageway leads down the nave to the reader's desk.

The baptistery is not included in the church but stands on its own with a colonnaded portico in front. This rather grand arrangement is emphasized, here again, by a lavish use of marble. Indeed the monastery as a whole, with its agglomeration of baths, cemeteries, pilgrim-hostels and other buildings, shows an instinct for luxury, always characteristic of Alexandria.

The church of St Menas may thus be classed as a version of Constantine's Church of the Holy Apostles or Church of the Holy Sepulchre, transferred to Egyptian soil. The transepts here take the place of such vestries or side-chapels as often frame the apse in basilican churches, and they provide ample space from which large crowds of worshippers may concentrate their attention on a central feature. When the cross-shape which thus results is found in commemorative churches, it usually serves to glorify the martyr's tomb or to mark some hallowed site, whereas at Abu Mina the shrine lay elsewhere and the high altar, in true medieval fashion, became the focal point.

The influence of Alexandria, or at any rate of those fashions of thought which moulded Abu Mina, extends in two directions. Westward, along the coast of Cyrenaica, the cathedral church at Apollonia still exhibits a cross form marked by elegant marble pillars, mounted on bases, all down the nave, and then by a wide transept. The high altar, set within its chancel screen at the crossing, is thereby allowed to dominate. Southward at Hermopolis, still in the first half of the fifth century, the arrangements devised for Abu Mina are repeated with greater faithfulness than at Apollonia (fig. 96). For here the ambulatory, with its galleries above, continues right round both nave and transepts, and the central altar within its chancel screen is more obviously embraced, in that the wings of the transept are not rectangular but rounded to match the apse in size and shape. At Hermopolis, however, the apse shows a certain resemblance to the Syrian fashion: it is enclosed within a massive wall and flanked by two sacristies.

The design of a trefoil head, enclosing the chancel at the east end of a basilican church, occurs impressively and rather surprisingly at Deir el Abiad, the 'White Monastery', near Sohag, still further south along the valley of the Nile. The monastery here was established by Shenoudi, a fierce ascetic hag-ridden by the desire not only for holiness but also for independent nationalism. It might be supposed that Shenoudi would have little use for urbane forms of architecture but he enjoyed the assistance of the count Caesarius, who held high rank as an official of the Byzantine court, so that the ruder methods of a debased Egyptian style are combined with classic grace. The church is hemmed about by the remains of the brick structures which housed Shenoudi's monks and, in the midst of this débris, the stone church rises grim and fortress-like. The walls, built in courses of white limestone blocks, are, like an Egyptian temple, slightly tilted inwards from the base; the unadorned outer surface is relieved only by two regular lines of window recesses and six very plain doorways. The formal entry on the west leads through a substantial narthex with columned apses at each end.[3] Thence a single opening admits to the nave with its elegant ground-plan of aisles forming an ambulatory along three sides where columns of marble or granite, with roughly carved but recognizably Ionic or Corinthian capitals, upheld the galleries above the aisles. The arrangement of the chancel at the east end is elaborate, with a massive triumphal arch opening onto a central square flanked by three nearly equal apses. Detached columns in two rows, one above the other, mark the curve of each apse and frame ornamental niches topped with triangular pediments; these niches are sometimes luxuriantly carved with a shell pattern or entwined foliage, while the stonework of limestone, marble or granite contrasts with the half domes of burnt brick which roof the apses. A cluster of miscellaneous rooms, including a baptistery and a small crypt, jostle in the background.

A secondary structure is attached to this well-proportioned basilica on the south side. It would be premature to speak of 'refectory' or 'chapter-house' in connection with monks so loosely organized as the Egyptian anchorites of the fifth century, but the annexed buildings were clearly intended to serve as places of meeting for members of the community. The chief room is a narrow rectangle, nearly as long as the nave, from which it is separated by a thick wall containing five doorways. The west end of this chamber displays, once again, the motif of an apse embellished with free-standing columns.

The Red Monastery at Sohag, situated about five kilometres from the White Monastery, exhibits a similar pattern though on a rather smaller scale. Here the walls are made of brick, there is no narthex, and the trefoil chancel with its domed lantern above is approached by an elaborate arrangement of columns designed to draw the eye from the wide nave to the narrow triumphal archway. The columns are more uniform in design than those of the White Monastery and the capitals elaborately carved in a fully developed Corinthian manner. With the Sohag monasteries may be classed the church built in the disused temple of Hathor at Dendera where a compact trefoil head, flanked by side chambers, is attached to a wide, rectangular hall.

The trefoil chancel established itself as a regular feature of Egyptian churches, but when apses are contracted in size they must have served a purpose quite different from the wide arms, equipped with ambulatory, that take the place of rectangular transepts at Hermopolis. The arrangement then becomes far more closely akin to a pair of side-chapels; at Sohag, however, there is no sign of altars in them, nor would it have been possible in any case to set altars there without violating custom by making these altars face north and south.

The apses at Sohag should probably be thought of as sacristies rather than as Mass chapels in the medieval manner, and comparison may be made with two churches built by the wealthy Paulinus at Nola, near Naples, about the year 400. One of these is described as having a triple apse, but the use of the apses is not described and there is reference to one altar only. A second church which Paulinus built nearby was also furnished with the trefoil apse. Paulinus explains[4] one of the side apses as the room where the priest made preparations for celebrating the Eucharist and the other as a 'place of prayer' to which the ministers and others could retire at the end of the service. The central apse at Nola, as no doubt at Sohag, contained the throne of the bishop, facing the altar.

Sites such as Hermopolis and Sohag exhibit churches of classic form modified by local traditions. Elsewhere in Egypt south of the Delta much of the ecclesiastical building is crude and squalid. One reason for this was the tendency of the Coptic Church, which followed the Monophysite heresy, to become isolated from the rest of Christendom. There was much ignorance and poverty, while timber and other suitable building materials were hard to come by in the lower parts of the Nile Valley. The rapid spread of the Faith had been accompanied by a tendency towards the 'most austere and rigorous discipline'[5] and a consequent distrust of beauty in any form. The great monastic founder Pachomius, for instance, made a chapel in his convent, and 'setting up pillars for it he covered the faces thereof with tiles and furnished it splendidly and was extremely pleased with the work because he had built it well.' Thereafter, however, regarding his artistic achievement as a snare and a delusion, he gathered his monks together, supplied them with ropes and pulled down the oratory, offering the advice 'Take heed lest ye strive to ornament the work of your hands over-much'.[6] When such scorn of artistic effort prevails, church-building is likely to be rudimentary and featureless. The material used is brick, made from mud mixed with chaff, and the smaller churches are no more than square boxes with a dome rather casually fixed on top, sometimes with an octagonal wall to assist the change from square to circle, more often with clumsy masses of brickwork acting as supports. This design is capable of limitless extension, and when the square cells are joined together they open easily into one another by means of arches supported on columns or rough-hewn piers.

Any developments were such as the liturgy required. Some Coptic churches, for example, had a row of altars, each free-standing behind a solid screen of wood or brick in its own chapel. Thus, at Medammot, near Luxor, there is an eastern row of five domed cells, each designed to contain its altar, and then a honeycomb of more cells running in lines of eight from north to south.

The church of Deir Abu Hennes, on the east bank of the Nile near Antinoë, shows the Coptic fashion of bays covered by unpretentious domes in combination with the basilican style. Entry to the church is by way of a low narthex, equipped with recesses to contain books, at the west end. This leads to the nave and narrow aisles, partitioned into three bays assigned respectively to the women, the men and the chorus. Each bay is roofed with a dome. Of these the western one is higher and narrower than the other two. In order to support the domes, however, piers were set up in so bulky and slipshod a manner that the interior is clumsily obstructed. Finally, at the eastern end of the nave, a pointed arch springing from pilasters with carved capitals leads into the domed apse, the *haikal* or sanctuary. This apse is equipped with ornamental niches, a characteristically Egyptian feature, and with doors leading into small chambers at either side. One of these rooms contains a font. It is sometimes held that Deir Abu Hennes, like a number of other Egyptian churches, was originally a basilica with a wooden roof. When domes made of rather poor brick were substituted for the timber, the slapdash props necessary because of the threat that a dome might collapse destroyed the long perspective of the basilica, in favour of what amounts to a string of boxes.

Those that remain of the early monastic foundations in Egypt display a casual arrangement of dwellings, storerooms and tombs clustered together around one or more churches showing greater refinement of both material and workmanship. The mud-brick tombs naturally reproduce, in the changeless conservatism of funeral custom, the techniques of a more ancient Egypt. The churches, however, usually belong to the basilican order found in all the Aegean coastlands, though with some local peculiarities, and, as time went on and doctrinal controversies sharpened, with a tendency to follow Syrian examples rather than Byzantium.

The sober plainness which marks the exterior of the churches provided a contrast to the lavish, sometimes crude adornment inside. The four main sites in Egypt of such early Christian monastic settlements are Saqqara, just south of Cairo, the convent of St Simeon at Assouan, and two communities of rather similar character that lie in the desert lands west of Sohag, namely El Bagawat (Khargeh) and Bawit. Of these Bawit may be taken as representative. It was established by a hermit named Apollo and grew with such speed that, even before the saint's death in 395 AD, there were at least five hundred monks living there. The oldest buildings, however, belong to a featureless style that can hardly be earlier than 450, while much of the decoration suggests a kinship with the period of Justinian.

Bawit occupies an enormous enclosure, nearly half a mile square, with a number of tombs in the mountains beyond. Most of the seventy buildings which have been uncovered from the desert sands are small barrel-vaulted chambers with a rectangular ground-plan. The barrel vaults are a fossilized survival of local practice in the time of the Pharaohs, when the tombs were set within pits, the sides of which served as buttresses to the vaults. At Bawit the vaults are struc-

turally detached, and are little more than canopies held in place by the thrust against massive outer walls, while the upper storey often present is supported not by the artificial vault but by beams fitted above it. The method of vault construction is also primitive, and consists merely of placing the courses of bricks edgewise one above the other until a rough semicircle is obtained.

At Bawit no human remains have been found within the cells. For, though the monk regarded his cell as a tomb, his body might after death be removed elsewhere, so long as a commemorative tablet or inscription hallowed the place and kept the dead man symbolically present when the funeral Eucharist was celebrated, from time to time, on his behalf. The upper storey, if one existed, could then be used as a place of assembly for those who gathered together to carry out the traditional ceremonies. That there was nothing essentially Christian about this arrangement is shown by the vaulted tomb chambers, with additional storeys above the vaults, that have been found in the cemetery of Tounah el Gebel, where most of the buildings date from the first century BC.

The two churches at Bawit are placed close together, and are similar to one another in their rectangular plan and general arrangement. The walls of the southern church are of brick but faced on each side with courses of well-cut stone, the monotony of which is broken here and there by a wooden frieze or by decorative sculpture in low relief. Entry was by way of the narthex, leading to a nave and aisles separated from each other by walls with doors in them. Four granite columns, the spoils of an earlier temple, decorated the west end; at the east, the sanctuary, of the same width as the nave, was marked by two further columns and a wooden screen set between them rather in the fashion of an iconostasis as found in Greek churches today. The apse of the sanctuary was enclosed in the rectangle of the building; above, a circular vault displayed the painted figure of Christ among his apostles, while a round window provided such light as was necessary in addition to the sparkle of lamps and candles. The external wall of the sanctuary was decorated with a frieze of intricate pattern while a cross upheld by two angels corresponded to the place where Christ's head was shown within. The north church, though a less elegant structure, had the advantage that the various parts of the building were separated not by walls but

by the less complete obstruction of woodwork strengthened by pillars.

At Bawit, as elsewhere in Egypt, the rough unpretentious style of the architecture contrasts with graceful,
even sophisticated, details of ornament, in which a
native tradition of decorative art, fostered by the
Pharaohs, survives to meet the needs of Christian
devotees. Examples of stone carving which may be
seen as forerunners of the typically Coptic style have
been discovered at Ahnas, 150 kilometres south of
Cairo. The sculptures here may be divided into two
styles, though these merge into one another. The
earlier fashion of 'soft' carving, with figure subjects
taken from Greek mythology, preserved such classic
forms as the acanthus capital and a pattern of 'egg and
dart' decoration together with a fondness for inter-
twined foliage which seems to be characteristic of
Egyptian taste. But round about 400 AD the sculptors
of Ahnas began to develop a 'hard' style, marked by
stiffer conventional foliage and capitals so finely cut
that thin wiry strands of stone appear in sharp relief
against a background of deeply incised shadow. The
traditional form of the Corinthian capital breaks down
in the sense that a stylized pattern of wide-spreading
leaves fans out to conceal the scroll ornament, and in
the end the acanthus is replaced altogether by basket-
capitals[7] of the sort found in Justinian's churches at
Ravenna. Whether through Asiatic influences or
because of a general failure of taste, such human
figures as are shown acquire a peculiarly Coptic look to
them, with clumsy posture and large wide-open eyes
set in a rigidly forward-looking gaze. Classic grace and
lightness of touch yield to a 'provincial' stiffness and
monotony well calculated to convey the monastic
interest in the mystery of death rather than the gaieties
of life.

Much of the carving from sites such as Bawit has
found its way into museums, where it may be said to
illustrate two things—the ability of Egyptian sculptors
to copy and adapt the Late Antique style of the Aegean
coastlands as well as a certain lack of power in their
efforts to infuse their interlaced acanthus friezes or
spiky capitals with vigorous life. But traditions of a
refined Hellenistic art were maintained side by side
with the rougher naturalism. One pillar from Bawit
(fig. 97), now in the Louvre, shows a charming design
of vine-scrolls and birds which invites comparison

97. Coptic carving: a pillar from Bawit.

98. Cairo Museum: naturalism and formalism in Coptic carving.

with Bishop Maximian's throne at Ravenna. Similarly, a carved wooden door from the church of St Barbara, in Old Cairo, offers a delicate, rhythmic pattern of vine tendrils while its pair of angels, floating in space as they support a laurel-wreathed bust, are the work of an artist skilful in expressing both the human form and the swirling folds of drapery. The unique cedar-wood altar from St Sergius, Cairo, with its fluted Corinthian columns leading up to shell niches marked with a cross, shows an equal dexterity. Such a contrast of styles may, however, mean only that the Copts, for all their rugged independence, were not afraid to import the work of artists trained in the methods of Byzantium (fig. 98).

As the tombs of the Pharaohs indicate, however, detailed narrative painting, rather than sculpture, was the achievement which came naturally to the Egyptian character. And, while Saqqara and El Bagawat both provide important examples of the art, it finds fuller expression at Bawit. The paintings are carried out in fresco, that is to say, by applying paint to plaster which is still moist, and, thanks to the dry sand which covered them for so many centuries, some portions at least remain fairly well preserved. The standard of

achievement varies. Sometimes the Hellenistic tradition dominates, of natural objects closely observed and human figures shown in lively and expressive movement, but more often Coptic stiffness and formality prevail. Partly in order to convey an air of timeless sanctity but also by reason of a certain carelessness or incompetence, saints and apostles are ranged woodenly in order, one matching another in rigid frontal posture, with dark staring eyes under arched brows, and wiglike hair. At El Bagawat, abstract personifications such as Peace, Justice and Prayer combine with a somewhat casual choice of Biblical scenes. Noah standing upright amidst his family in the ark, Jonah lying beneath his gourd and Daniel in the lions' den reproduce the standard salvation themes of the Roman catacombs, but a more general interest in historical narrative is shown by the disorderly sequence of scenes illustrating the departure of the Israelites from Egypt. There are also signs of influence from Palestine and thereabouts: Isaiah being sawn asunder appears together with a building which could be his shrine near Bethlehem, and incidents are depicted from the life of St Thecla, the martyr especially revered at Seleucia.

The more abundant and apparently rather later frescoes at Bawit, for all their content of mystical sincerity, retain some traces of a pagan heritage. There is, for example, a figure of Orpheus playing his harp as well as lively hunting scenes in which men, hidden behind trees, shoot at gazelles or youths attempt to harpoon a hippopotamus. The apses of the Bawit chapels, on the other hand, are usually decorated with a representation of Christ in triumph. Seated, youthful and beardless, on his bejewelled throne and flanked by angels and emblems of the Evangelists, he raises his right hand in blessing while with his left he clasps the open book which contains his saving message. The sun and moon, when they appear against the background of a star–spangled sky, are a reminder of eternity and thus of Christ's unending sovereignty. Below, the middle place in a line of close-packed figures is taken by the Virgin who, distinguished by a large halo and dark garments, raises her hands in the attitude of an *Orans*. At either side the apostles are ranged, each with halo of modest size and each, in a symmetry which is by no means lifeless, clasping a gem-studded book against his heart (fig. 99). This standard formula of Christian victory admits, however, of several variations.[8] Thus the throne may be duplicated, with Christ raised in glory above and the Virgin and Child, throned in almost equal splendour, occupying the central place below amid the conventional hierarchy of the Apostles. At times the stiff and contemplative postures are exchanged for a sudden ecstasy, as in Chapel 46 where, in a straightforward Ascension scene, the Virgin and certain of the apostles avert their gaze, in lively motion, from a spectacle of overwhelming glory.

Some of the Bawit chapels are decorated with narrative scenes drawn from the Bible record or from the rich crop of romantic lives of the saints which flourished with particular exuberance in the fertile soil of Egypt. Chapel 3, for instance, offers a series of incidents drawn from the life of Christ, though only four of them remain: the Massacre of the Innocents, the Baptism, the Marriage at Cana and the Last Supper. Of these the Baptism appears twice. On the north wall Christ is shown as beardless, standing in the water with John the Baptist on one side and, on the other, an angel holding the clothes. The river-deity of Jordan, represented as a young man, completes the picture. The painting on the east wall repeats the general formula but without any attempt to secure exact consistency. Christ stands, a stocky diminutive figure, between John the Baptist and the angel, but here he is bearded and mature. The river-sprite is a woman, and the boy kneeling on the bank seems to be no more than an attendant, with hand outstretched as if to recognize the importance of the occasion. A large duck standing nearby is in the ancient tradition of Egyptian painting with its close attention to creatures of the riverside. Of the Old Testament characters it is David who most obviously attracted the attention of the Bawit artists, and the chapel decorated, as an inscription records, by 'George the painter' offers a set of twelve scenes, each enclosed within a frame, drawn from David's early life. The style of these particular frescoes is lumpy and crude, but the colours are fresh and the movement vigorous. In one panel Saul, distinguished by a halo, is seated on a throne of which each arm is shaped like a dolphin. He brandishes the spear which he is about to hurl at David who, youthful and fair-haired, peacefully plucks his lyre in an attitude of unconcern. The last three scenes of the David cycle relate to the contest with Goliath; here the victory is emphasized throughout but the horror and bloodshed no more than hinted at in gentlemanly reticence. Pictures of David in other chapels include one, in Chapel 32, which shows him as a young man using a ladle to draw wine from a jar and pour it into Saul's cup. Another group of paintings displays the growing interest in apocryphal details of the life of the Virgin; this includes such unaccustomed subjects as the Return from the Visit to Elizabeth—in which Mary, mounted on horseback, is led homewards by the archangel Gabriel—and a Nativity where the Virgin is shown reclining on a bed with the midwife Salome standing in attendance at her side.

The funerary theme of remembrance is stressed by the repeated figure of a monk clothed in white garments and standing rather stiffly with eyes staring straight ahead. His head is framed in a golden halo and his name is written beside him to show that he is no imaginary being but a particular hermit of Bawit whose disciplined life has earned for him the lasting joys of Paradise. No less typical of the range of monastic interest are the saints, usually named, who are depicted at Bawit. Some, like the St George in military costume shown on a column of the north church, display a supple artistry capable of reproduc-

99. Bawit. Wall-painting: the Virgin, shown as an *Orans*, stands between two apostles.

ing free movement and delicate shades of expression. More often the style gives to the figures a wide-eyed impersonal air. A local peculiarity of Bawit is a fondness for saints riding on horseback. The most remarkable of these is Phoebammon, grandson of a governor of Antioch, who met a martyr's death in the Fayum district of Egypt during Maximian's persecution. Phoebammon sits astride a mettlesome charger but turns his body to face the spectator in the frontal Coptic fashion. With his right hand he clasps a long-shafted cross, with his left hand the martyr's jewelled crown. Floating down from the heavens an 'angel of the Lord' approaches with outstretched wings and offers another crown of victory, but the grave hieratic air of the composition is lightened by the flowering mallows which shoot up beside Phoebammon's path. Examples such as this show how far the art of Christian painting had travelled by the middle of the sixth century, from the Biblical symbolism of Dura towards a fully developed medieval outlook.

NUBIA AND ETHIOPIA

Further south, along the Nile Valley, the remote kingdom of Nobatia (Nubia) received visits from missionaries, but in no very systematic fashion until about 540 AD, when the determination of the empress Theodora led to the establishment of Byzantine influence and the adoption of Christianity in its Monophysite form. A number of churches, now being rediscovered after long neglect, were built during this period. Some of these churches, such as that of Abdallah Nirqi near Abu Simbel, appear, by virtue of their simple barrel vaults and eastern apses flanked by two auxiliary rooms, to belong to the period of Justinian, but they, and certainly such wall-paintings as those of the cathedral at Faras, can be more precisely assigned to the eighth or ninth century.[9]

Still further southwards, Ethiopia was evangelized by missionaries from Syria and a cathedral was erected at Axum early in the sixth century, but nothing seems to remain of that ancient foundation.

THE CHURCHES OF NORTH AFRICA

The coastlands of Northern Africa are thickly dotted with the sites of Christian churches now dilapidated and in decay. Excavations, however, leave no doubt concerning the character of the buildings which, throughout the whole area, stretching from the confines of Egypt to the Straits of Gibraltar, display a general similarity. Martyr-shrines of the centralized type scarcely exist and the churches follow the style of the civil basilica in its Latin form. Here and there, in the large towns, the workmanship is elegant and cultured, more often it is straightforward and simple enough; but in either case an instinctive conservatism ensures that little variation occurred during the three or four centuries preceding the Moslem conquest of North Africa. The country was earlier racked by bitter disputes between the Catholics and Donatists, roughly corresponding to the imperial and the intensely nationalist factions, but no such changes in building technique mark the difference of sentiment as were used in nineteenth-century England to distinguish Anglicanism from Nonconformity. By contrast with Egypt, there was no vigorous native culture capable of modifying conventional forms, and the standard church of North Africa was therefore a lofty basilica with nave and two aisles, ending in a raised semicircular apse, though four local peculiarities occur. In the first place, the number of aisles is sometimes doubled as at Orléansville, while at Tipasa the church developed into a forest of columns dividing the space into a nave and eight aisles. No very obvious ends either of worship or of architecture appear to have been served by this multiplication of aisles but simply a taste for a broad rather than a long hall of assembly. Next, the position assigned to the altar, while this may be the apse, is more commonly well down the nave, as in some of the Syrian churches. It is more or less in the middle of the church at Damous el Karita (Carthage), where local practice no doubt allowed it to be thronged about on all sides by the congregation.

Occasionally the apse is cut off from the rest of the building by low walls or, with greater elaboration, by a colonnade. More frequent, and more characteristic, is the device of the double column or pier and column used to separate nave from aisle. At Tigzirt, for instance, the columns were symmetrically paired: the outer ones supported the nave arcade together with its galleries and clerestory while the inner row upheld short rectangular pillars attached to the nave arcade and leading up to a second row of slimmer columns above. Each double set of capitals is topped by a bulky abacus stone, the side towards the nave being cut obliquely and decorated with rather rudimentary carving.

The splendid church at Tébessa shows a somewhat similar arrangement (fig. 100). Here, however, the outer range consists of a robust arcade supported by stumpy squared piers with very plain capitals. The inner range consists of tall marble columns taken, as so often, from an older building, and rising up to finish, at a higher level than the arcade, in richly carved Corinthian capitals surmounted by a cornice. Set on this cornice, a second row of columns framed the gallery and supported the timbers of the roof. A contrast with the simple Constantinian elegance of the standard North African church is presented by the 'fortress-churches', which display a type of architecture called for in remote country subject to tribal raids, but found also on the coast of Tripolitania. One such building, at Ptolemais (Tolmeita), gives an impression of massive solidity not only on the outside but by reason of the heavy, rectangular pillars which separate the nave from the low, dark, barrel-vaulted aisles.

The material from which the churches of North Africa are constructed is nearly always rubble or smallish squares of local stone bonded together by courses of larger blocks. Roofs were of wood, though occasionally, in the treeless desert lands of the south, brick vaulting came into its own. No attempt was made to construct a dome or sizeable cross-vault until the device was tried on a church at Leptis Magna, an elaborate building probably of the fifth century but remodelled by Justinian.[10] Transepts were not extensively favoured but the entrance portico may be substantial, at times presenting a face of blank wall to the west and having the doorways unobtrusively set at the north and south ends.

100. Tébessa: east end of the nave.

Martyrs were held in the highest regard throughout North Africa, and their resting-places were venerated on the grounds that, as St Augustine put it, 'one must not spurn or neglect the bodies of the dead and particularly the bodies of those just and faithful persons whom the Spirit used as instruments.'[11] The honoured relics were usually placed within what, from the beginning of the third century, were known as *areae*.[12] The word is a general term meaning a churchyard but, as excavations at Tipasa have shown, it could imply, or anyhow include, a portico set up to protect the rows of tables around which guests might recline at funeral feasts. As these commemorations fell out of favour and the tables disappeared, sarcophagi were lumped about the place instead. Sometimes, however, as at Orléansville in Algeria, the tombs were set in crypts beneath the apse, so that the parish meeting-place became hallowed by an aura of sanctity.

The apses of North African churches are so variable in design as to indicate a wide freedom of liturgical practice. There may be a simple semicircle, projecting or enclosed within a rectangle, and placed usually at the east but not seldom, in some districts, at the west end of the building. Two of the five[13] churches dis-

covered at Carthage have apses with no flanking sacristies and churches at Sabratha and Leptis Magna show a similar diversity in that, while some have an apse and no more, others are equipped with the conventional side chambers, the prothesis and diaconicon. In the 'fortress-church' of Ptolemais the two side chambers are quite differently constructed; that on the north being a trefoil of little apses while that on the south is a square emphasized by corner piers.[14] The church at Breviglieri seems to be unique in displaying a threefold apse, where the matching pair of semicircles at the end of the aisles suggest side–chapels rather than vestries.

About a dozen of the churches have a secondary smaller apse at the end of the building opposite to the main apse. At Sabratha and Leptis this feature came about for no ecclesiastical reason but simply because a judgement-hall, of basilica type, was adapted for use as a church (fig. 101). Elsewhere, as at Orléansville or in Bishop Alexander's church at Tipasa, the secondary apse was set up as a place of burial for some important personage, at Tipasa probably Alexander himself. At Junca the arrangements are of exceptional regularity. Here the building is a five-aisled basilica. Tacked onto

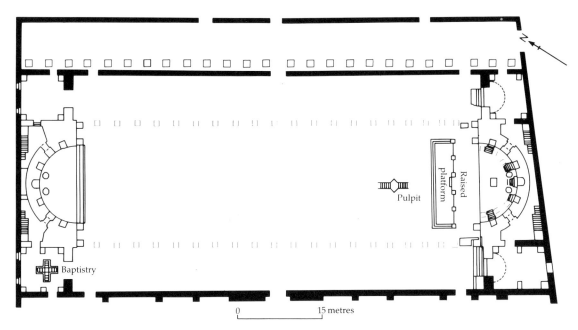

101. Leptis Magna, basilica I: ground-plan. A grandiose civic hall of the third century date, remodelled as a church by Justinian.

the entrance-porch, however, are three large rooms, the central one containing an apse precisely opposite the eastern apse and, though smaller, closely resembling it in shape. This counter-apse, with its seats for the clergy, is connected with a miniature crypt reached by a descent of six steps and marked by a cupola supported on four columns. So far as excavations have hitherto shown the crypt contained not a complete body but fragmentary relics enclosed in a round pyx. Such an elaborate form of martyr-shrine may seem hardly called for, but the cupola signified a sense of reverential awe and the apse fulfilled its primary purpose of providing seats of honour for whatever ceremonies took place. Half a dozen other churches, of which Henchir is the most remarkable, show a counter-apse of similar though simpler type.

A famous mosaic, found at Tabarca on the coast of Tunisia and now in the Bardo Museum at Tunis, offers a picture which supplements the results of excavation. An inscription records that this is MATER ECCLESIA, the typical 'Mother Church' of North Africa in the fifth century rather than any particular example. A row of six columns, with roughly sketched bases and capitals, indicates the division into nave and aisles. A

line along the top of the capitals looks like a straight architrave rather than the arches customary in North Africa, but the artist has combined inside with outside views, and perhaps he shows here the external face of the wall as it rises straight up from the aisle and, incidentally, provides him with space for the inscription. Above this appear the clerestory windows and a sloping tiled roof. The west end has steps leading up to a rectangular doorway with a round-headed window and two small circular openings to admit light in the pediment above. The altar stands well down the nave; it is furnished with three tall candlesticks and has its front surface, whether of marble or wood, decorated with a bold pattern of diagonals. Beyond the altar a flight of what St Augustine knew as 'sanctuary steps'[15] leads up to the three arches dominating the east end and onwards to the apse with its large round window, that has perhaps slipped down from the cornice above. The Tabarca mosaic thus shows a typical North African church, unambitious in design but neatly classical in feeling and well adapted for the purposes it had to serve (fig. 102).

The Tabarca mosaic concentrates on the church-building itself but the church stands for only a part of

102. Tabarca: the 'Mater Ecclesia' mosaic.

the activities carried out by the Christian community.

At Tébessa, where everything is on a grand scale, there have been discovered not only the church, but also a baptistery, shrines of martyrs and bishops, stores and offices from which charitable relief could be dispensed, meeting-halls, the bishop's house and inns for the reception of pilgrims. Djemila, as excavations show, was no less complex and varied (fig. 103). Here the central point is occupied by a pair of basilicas, one rather larger and more elaborate than the other. This was probably distinguished from its neighbour, any-how at first, as being the bishop's church, where the Eucharist was celebrated, by contrast with the hall where the catechumens received instruction. The ancillary buildings are clustered around these two. Even vaster arrangements distinguished Damous el Karita, on the outskirts of Carthage. Here the huge eight-aisled church extended to a length of over 65 metres, with a range of miscellaneous buildings run-ning onwards for more than double that distance.

Notable among these structures are the remains of a subterranean rotunda, its wall pierced by niches and strengthened by densely-packed columns. This rotunda is sometimes described as a mausoleum but was in fact originally a baptistery; a roughly laid circle of stones, still in place, indicates the footing for a font-bowl.[16] Changes in the masonry imply another circular building erected on the foundations of the underground baptistery, to allow for the instruction of candidates or, more probably, to provide a place in which the rite of confirmation might be administered. Relatively soon, perhaps because of a weakness in the walls, the upper rotunda was rebuilt and encased in a cube of masonry above which the top of the dome appeared. A smaller baptistery was at this time con-structed for the church and the rotunda diverted to other uses, perhaps as a reception hall. The civic splendour of Carthage in the first quarter of the fifth century was thus matched by a costly, even flamboy-ant, display of ecclesiastical magnificence.

103. Djemila (Cuicul): the forest of columns that bears witness to intense building activity in the 'Christian Quarter'.

NOTES

1. Particularly the Coptic *Encomium of St Menas*, of 893 AD (Pierpont Morgan collection M.590).
2. The slab which served as the background for the image still remains. A small marble relief in the Alexandria Museum, showing St Menas and his camels, is probably copied from the original at Abu Mina.
3. Or certainly the north end; the south is less clear.
4. Paulinus, *Epistle* 32, *PL* 61.338.
5. Eusebius, *Ecclesiastical History* 2.15.
6. *Paradise of the Holy Fathers* xiv, ed. Wallis Budge (1904).
7. This applies more particularly to the capitals of Saqqara and Bawit, which are allied to but generally later than those of Ahnas.
8. Dating is not very precise, and seems to range from about 450 AD to as late as the seventh century.
9. See Bibliography, p. 310.
10. Church 2. *Archaeologia* 95 (1953), 24. Perhaps there were one or two more, e.g. at Damous el Karita (Carthage).
11. *City of God*, i.13.
12. The expression is used as early as 212 AD by Tertullian (*ad Scapulam* 3), writing from Carthage.
13. This number can be increased if the suburban churches are included. See W. H. C. Frend, *The Early Christian Church in Carthage* (Ann Arbor, 1977).
14. Detailed plans by P. Romanelli in *ACIAC* IV (1938). The side chambers are included within the rectangle of the east end.
15. *Gradus exedrae*; see *On the City of God* 22.8.30.
16. The recent excavations are described in detail by S. Boyadjiev in *ACIAC* IX.

9

Greece and the Balkans: Spain

Despite its early contacts with St Paul, Greece, though tradition ascribes to it a few early martyrs for the Faith, was not one of the influential centres from which Christianity spread. The country was indeed characterized by a stubborn tendency to maintain pagan practices—to which Constantine and his successors thought it prudent to turn a blind eye. The Eleusinian Mysteries, in honour of Demeter, were in vogue until the end of the fourth century, and until its suppression in 529 AD the University of Athens taught a refined form of Platonism which could scarcely come to terms with the Gospel. Nevertheless throughout this time churches of considerable size and splendour were being built in Greece, sometimes on hallowed sites where a devout worship of the ancient gods could be transformed into impulses of reverence for Christian saints.

A series of anti-pagan edicts put forward by the emperor Theodosius I led to the closing of a number of temples round about the year 390. One of the places affected by these edicts was Epidaurus, famed for its shrine of Asclepios (Aesculapius), where an advanced technique of medicine was combined with the practice of incubation, or sleeping within the temple precincts, from which miraculous cures of disease were held to result. With praiseworthy enterprise the Christian authorities put up a church of substantial size to meet the religious needs of those who continued to visit so hallowed a spot. The remains now are unimpressive but the plan of construction can still be traced (fig. 104). Approach was by way of a large courtyard, with towered façade and a range of auxiliary buildings at

each side. The church itself, 36 metres in length, was entered not by a main central doorway but by matching portals to north and south leading into a long narrow narthex with wings projecting at both ends. The east wall of this narthex was pierced by five openings which gave access to the nave and each of the four aisles. The sanctuary at the east end received a transept-screen of columns, and the outermost aisles were so enclosed as to provide the twin chambers required for use as prothesis and diaconicon. A shallow semicircular apse projected at the east end. Along the whole of the north side a separate range of rooms was added, rather in the manner of the basilican halls tacked onto some of the churches of Egypt. Still further out on the north side came the baptistery. The Christian building at Epidaurus may thus be said to belong to the general type which spread, under the impulse of Constantinople, around the Aegean Sea, but with the addition of features which suggest the firmly individual style of places rather more on the outskirts of Empire, such as Milan and the Syrian towns.

From the end of the sixth century, Greece was ravaged by the onslaught of Avars, Bulgars and Slavs, who not only plundered but wantonly destroyed churches and other public buildings. Only Salonica was successful in withstanding such assaults. In consequence, Salonica can show very ancient churches still in use, while elsewhere only foundations remain, together with scattered capitals and portions of flooring in marble or mosaic. Enough, however, remains to prove

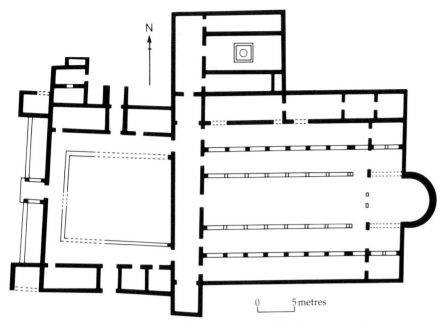

104. Epidaurus, the fifth-century basilica and associated buildings: ground-plan.

that the best of these churches were constructed with an instinctive regard for proportion and fine craftsmanship well in keeping with the traditions of Greek architecture in the Classical Age.

One example came to light as recently as 1955, when the harbour church at Corinth (Lechaeon) was excavated. The notable feature here is its length—127 metres not counting the elaborate forecourt with horseshoe colonnade which precedes the main building. An air of symmetry distinguishes the ground-plan. The slim narthex projects just so far beyond the external walls as does the broader transept at the east end. The nave is double the width of each aisle, from which it is separated by a row of twenty-three marble columns, set on bases, with a compound column at each end to give added stability. The eastern apse is furnished, in the fashion of some medieval chapter-house, with recessed seats for the clergy; as usual, however, the sanctuary occupies the space in front of this, at the centre of the transept. The position of the altar and chancel screens is well marked and the *solea* extends a long way down the nave. Slight differences in the floor levels give variety to the church and the splendour of its decoration is evident in the remains of

its marble floor: greenish slabs in the nave with a pattern of multi-coloured squares and lozenges in the aisles. The elegant capitals found lying about are of several types and of not very certain date. One has the Ionic corner-scrolls with an 'egg and dart' effect in between, the whole topped by a large impost-block, panelled with acanthus foliage swirling around a cross. Other capitals are more nearly Corinthian, with turned-back acanthus leaves set in two rows and the entire surface freely marked with the drill.[1]

Recent discoveries have made it clear that handsome churches of the same general type as the basilica at Corinth were relatively common in Greece. Nicopolis, on the west coast, is one such. A richly designed mosaic covered the floors, but the building as a whole, with its walls of brick, is thicker and stumpier than its Corinthian counterpart.

On the opposite side of the Greek mainland, at Nea–Anchialos or 'Little Thebes', a remarkable group of ruins has come to light. This includes four churches, the largest of which is distinguished for the elegance and variety of its capitals; some of these, being of marble from Proconnesus, near Constantinople, were presumably imported ready-made. They were of a

N

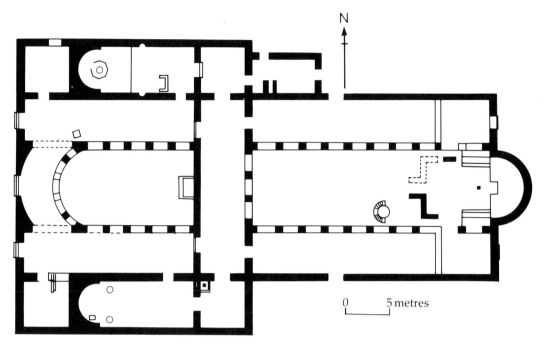

0   5 metres

105. Nea-Anchialos. Basilica and atrium of the main church, late fifth century: ground-plan.

piece with the marble panelling and with the delicately carved screens which must have given a refined air of metropolitan grandeur to the entire building. Even more remarkable, however, is the unusual pattern of the atrium. Entered by means of three formal doorways piercing the west wall, this courtyard contains not the usual right-angled ambulatory but a colonnade consisting of three parts, two being straight and in line with the nave arcades, while the western side is semicircular. The colonnade, in fact, though wider, corresponds on plan to a pair of rooms, one on each side of the courtyard, which are shaped like little basilicas with their apses to the west. One of these rooms contained the font, and the theme of purification was enhanced by a fountain with splendidly carved canopy set, as often, within the atrium. Two rectangular turrets completed this skilfully devised plan at the western end and matched the pair of storerooms projecting from the narthex (fig. 105).

On the upper shore of the Aegean, Philippi was also an ecclesiastical centre of much magnificence by the beginning of the sixth century. Until lately it was best known for three massive pillars (and the stump of a fourth) rising to a height of about five and a half metres above the ground. These pillars once supported the nave vaults of a church of ambitious design for which a site was prepared by the removal of a covered market and a gymnasium. Entry to the church from the large atrium was by way of a transverse narthex with three doors. The largest of these, leading into the nave, still remains, with walling built up in alternate bands of rubble and brick at either side. Over the narrow aisles were galleries, approached by an external staircase, of which a part remains beyond the north end of the narthex. The columns separating nave and aisles were taken from various buildings of the Roman period and do not match exactly, but the capitals are richly carved all over with swirling acanthus and other foliage. Lacking Ionic scrolls or any emblems, they invite comparison with those of Santa Sophia at Constantinople and seem to date from the early years of the sixth century.

The projecting horseshoe apse was buttressed by great chunks of masonry, the chancel area being plain and unencumbered since the columns did not invade it but turned north and south to enclose the aisles. At the centre of this rectangular space a low screen enclosing the altar was placed between two sets of clergy benches. But the architect was too ambitious. Not content with a straightforward basilica he attempted to cover the chancel with a brick cupola, but this dome collapsed almost before it was finished and the church was never restored to full use. To north and south of the chancel runs a symmetrical pair of structures, each composed of two slim rectangles with an eastern apse. The north chapel was a baptistery; the southern, originally designed as a sacristy, may have served as the sanctuary after the dome collapsed.

Excavation has also disclosed the ground plan of other churches nearby. The biggest of these, either the cathedral or a pilgrimage centre, was approached by way of a vast atrium equipped with fountains and porticoes. The building is a T-shaped basilica with a semicircular apse, sober regularity of design being combined with splendour of detail. The floor and walls of white marble from Proconnesus contrasted with the green Thessalian marble of the nave columns and the grey and black marbles of the sanctuary; the capitals were carved in a flamboyant version of the acanthus theme. Blocks of stone taken from disused Roman buildings served as bases for the massive columns of the nave, and, attached to the outer side of each, was a second block, not so wide but nearly twice as high, which supported a screen made of carved marble slabs effectively separating nave and sanctuary from the aisles. The narthex gave access on the north side to a baptistery, still well preserved, and beneath the church is a crypt, traditionally held to be the place where Paul and Silas were imprisoned.

Nearby a church of entirely different type has been found. Its octagonal form, set within a square precinct, suggests a martyr-shrine, and it has been compared to the shrine of St George at Ezra, in Syria, since both have a central chamber supported by columns and encircled by an ambulatory with niches at the corners. Nevertheless, the interior arrangement at Philippi points clearly to use as a parish church. The apse, projecting on the east side, connects with the bema, or platform designed to receive clergy seats and altar, and this conventional setting for eucharistic worship is continued in that the reading-desk is placed well to the west, not far from the centre of the building. Clearly by 500 AD the distinction between the congregational basilica and the martyr-shrine has become blurred and either shape might be adapted for general uses accord-ing to the lie of the land or the whim of patron and architect.

The number of churches at Salonica and the artistic vigour which stemmed from them gave the city its nickname of 'Paradise on earth'.[2] Church-building continued almost without a break from the fourth century to the thirteenth and, although much was destroyed during the Turkish occupation, enough remains to show in some completeness how East Christian ideas developed. The earliest period is represented by three churches in particular, of which the most ancient is the Rotunda of St George, orig-inally either a pagan temple of the same general type as Agrippa's Pantheon at Rome, or, more probably, a domed mausoleum connected with the palace of Galerius. It was built as a circle with eight niches in the thickness of the robust brick wall and had a low-pitched roof of timber to protect the dome. When the rotunda was transformed into a Christian church, the eastern side was extended to form a rectangular sanc-tuary with a small annexe at each end, circular on the outside and hexagonal within. An ambulatory, now removed, was constructed round the drum of the church while, both at the west and at the south, a porch was formed by opening up one of the niches and flanking the doorway on each side with a piece of straight wall surmounted by a turret. That the building was a martyr-shrine is confirmed by the triumphal character of the splendid mosaics, where martyrs in an attitude of prayer are ranged in front of an exception-ally rich architectural frieze.

The Council of Ephesus, in 431 AD, declared Mary to be 'Theotokos', the Mother of Christ in his divine as well as his human nature. By way of reaction to this event the citizens of Salonica, urged on by a combina-tion of piety, commercial success and jealousy of Constantinople, where the patriarch disliked the new doctrine, set about building the church of the Acheiropoietos. The word means a miraculous icon, 'not made with hands', but it was applied figuratively to the Virgin on the grounds that she was the 'Tabernacle not made with hands' in which Christ dwelt. The Acheiropoietos church, entirely different from St George's in design, is a handsome basilica with nave and two aisles separated by a long arcade of twelve high columns bearing 'Theodosian' capitals of a generally Corinthian type, surmounted by a large

106. Salonica, Hagios Demetrios: the variety of the carved capitals. Engraving by Charles Texier, 1864.

carved impost stone in the shape of an upturned pyramid. The capitals in this case are particularly elegant; each has two rows of acanthus foliage, heavily undercut and marked by a lavish use of the drill, with Ionic scrolls at each corner separated by a band of palmette decoration. The aisles are enclosed to form galleries with a bold and lofty arcade which repeats, in a quieter key, the pattern of the nave below. In harmony with this composition the side walls display a double range of round-headed bays designed to give light to the aisles and galleries; this feature, together with the lush arcading of the west front, has been thought to suggest Syrian influence. It certainly shows a free and inventive treatment of earlier models.

But local patriotism at Salonica centred on the figure of St Demetrius. A martyr of Galerius's time, he was transformed by popular acclaim into a warrior-saint who presided over the city as its 'patron and protector', and Demetrius' church, built near the centre of Salonica, was, before a disastrous fire in 1917, a basilica of exceptional splendour. Even today, partially rebuilt in a somewhat rigid manner, it combines classic order with the profound instinct for

grandeur and mystery which characterized the Byzantine approach to life. Preceded by a courtyard, with baptistery and formal staircase, the building extends to a length of 58 metres. An unpretentious narthex, with entrance doorways on both western and southern sides, gives access to the nave with its double aisles. The columns separating the aisles run in a straightforward line, but the larger nave columns, spoils taken from earlier temples and grouped according to colour rather than exact measurement, display a more ambitious rhythm—three, four, three, with piers set between the groups. The whole of this arrangement is matched by the arcade of the gallery above; still higher, a bold clerestory with round-headed windows placed singly, in pairs or in double pairs, admitted an ample flood of light. The outermost aisle on each side is continued round the large rectangular transepts, which compress the shallow apse between them.

This church as a whole is ascribed to the initiative of the prefect Leontius in about 412 AD, but this date has to be modified in two respects. The foundations show signs of earlier work, Roman baths in the main but including, beneath the altar, a small cross-shaped

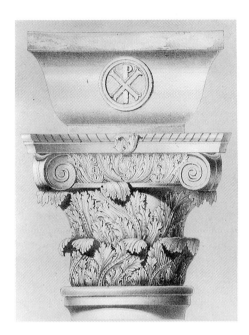

crypt that contains a flask of blood-stained earth. The crypt thus resembles the shrines of Palestine in that, though lacking the martyr's bones, it marked a hallowed site. Associated with the shrine was a fountain, protected by slabs of marble carved with a cross, from which holy water was administered to the faithful. At some point, in order to secure a more convenient and dignified access, the slabs were rearranged in their present form and surmounted by a semicircular arcade with five columns.[3] In the second place, extensive changes were made in Leontius's building after a fire which occurred early in the seventh century. This accounts for variation in the style of the carved capitals (fig. 106). Some of these precisely reproduce the capitals of the Acheiropoietos church while others are of the 'wind-blown acanthus' type and lavishly speckled with dots made by the drill. Still other capitals show, in place of the corner volutes, animal heads with stiffly projecting foliage between. Before the fire of 1917, the rich variation in columns and capitals was emphasized by panels of coloured marble filling the space between nave arcade and gallery. This brilliant decoration has now been lost as has much of the mosaic, though enough remains to illustrate its high

quality. The use of very small cubes in its construction allows of an attempt at finer gradations of colour and more delicately shaded portraiture than is usually found in mosaic work, and attractive design is matched by detailed excellence of craftsmanship. The subjects are not a coherent series of events drawn from the Bible or from lives of the saints but rather a number of pictures or 'icons', each enclosed within a mosaic framework, which seem to have been presented by individual benefactors. The Virgin enthroned or standing between angels was a popular theme. Appearing even more frequently is Demetrius himself, here shown as a high civic dignitary rather than as a warrior and accompanied by the diminutive figures of those who successfully sought his aid. The power of Demetrius to protect his city of Salonica is typified by an exceptional mosaic, attached to one of the pillars in front of the apse, which shows the youthful saint standing between the governor and the bishop and resting his hands on their shoulders. But the mosaic panels do not all belong to the same period, and this one dates from the seventh or eighth century. It is now in the Museum of Antiquities at Istanbul.

Tucked away amidst a jumble of buildings survives

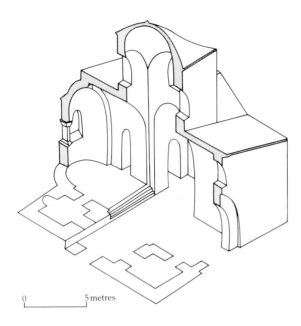

0 — 5 metres

107. Salonica, chapel of Hosios David: isometric plan.

in part the fifth-century chapel of the monastery of Zechariah. Differing markedly from the basilican churches of Salonica, it takes the form externally of a square with semicircular apse; within, however, it presents a cross with four equal arms and a square chamber filling each corner. Clearly demonstrating the domed, cross-shaped unit, this chapel, now known as Hosios David, is the oldest example in Europe of what was to become the characteristically Byzantine layout (fig. 107).

Hosios David is remarkable for a splendid mosaic described by an early commentator[4] as illustrating the visions of Ezekiel and Habakkuk.[5] At the left corner Ezekiel bows down, with hands raised and head averted from his vision, while at the opposite corner Habakkuk sits in meditation with a book open on his knee. Behind, a gentle Pompeian landscape of trees and buildings extends into the distance, but the central point of the composition is occupied by a large figure of Christ enthroned upon a rainbow whose brilliant colours radiate upwards to form an enveloping aureole of brightness. Christ is here a youthful, almost feminine figure, expressive of serene compassion. His halo is marked with a jewelled cross, his right arm is raised in blessing and his left hand clasps an open scroll inscribed with a paraphrase of Isaiah's words: 'Behold our God in whom we hope, our salvation in whom we rejoice. He will give us rest and hospitality in this house.'[6] From below Christ's feet flow streams of water, complete with 'little fish' immersed in the cleansing flood of baptism and a dejected river-god who realizes that his sway is at an end.

The ornate manner in which the early churches of Salonica were furnished is suggested by the fragments of the ambo found in the Rotunda of St George,[7] and which appears to be of fifth-century date. Because of the reverence attaching to the Book of the Gospels, which was held to contain the Word of God and thus to deserve a respect second only to that due to the Elements of bread and wine placed upon the altar, the ambo was sometimes treated in the grand manner. The St George ambo was composed of two vast blocks of white marble, cut on a semicircular line and joined together by a lintel. Within each block a stairway of five steps was cut, in the fashion of the ambo later made by Justinian for his church of S. Sophia at

Constantinople. The upper part of the Salonica ambo consists of a frieze delicately worked with bands of vine and acanthus, while below come scalloped niches flanked by columns. Advancing in lively manner, each within his niche, the Magi approach the enthroned Virgin and Child, whose figures present, by contrast, an early example of stiff and remote majesty in the Byzantine mode.

The placing of the ambo varied according to local custom before liturgical practice hardened into standard forms. In some churches the ambo was closely joined to the area, at the east end of the nave and in front of the apse, where the altar stood enclosed within chancel screens. Nave and transepts could then be well filled with worshippers. When, however, as often in Greece and Eastern Mediterranean lands, the ambo was placed a long way down the nave and approached by a raised pathway, two changes resulted. In the first place, at least half of the nave was so closely connected with the chancel that the general congregation was driven out in favour of the ministers; on the other hand, the people clustered in the aisles or in galleries above were able to hear better and thus to share more fully in awareness of mysteries dimly glimpsed behind screens and curtains. Even when the nave was unencumbered by the ambo it could not be left entirely free for public use, since it was the highway for solemn processions. According to the oldest form of Eastern liturgy,[8] the service began, while the catechumens were still present, with readings from the Prophets, Epistles and Gospels. The procedure, known as the Little Entrance, dictated that these Scriptures, at least the Gospel-book, should be carried with much ceremony to the ambo from a sacristy either adjoining the apse or, sometimes, forming part of the narthex.

Excavation has also brought to light a number of basilicas, for the most part in a very fragmentary state, situated in other parts of Greece. On the island of Thasos, for instance, there is a church shaped as a cross enclosed by a narrow aisle, and having wooden roof and apse, that closely follows the lines of St Demetrius. But the finds in southern Macedonia have been far more abundant. Stobi, about a hundred miles north-west of Salonica, was a flourishing local capital despite being ravaged by the Goths in 479 AD. Evidence of this prosperity is supplied by the surviv-

ing parts of the cathedral church. The atrium at the west was constricted by other buildings into an odd, triangular shape, but the basilica itself follows the pattern of the Acheiropoietos at Salonica. A rectangular chancel screen was carried well down into the nave. The arrangement of the apse, however, is less conventional. It consists of two parts: the outer section is a semicircular corridor from which the devout were able to peer through inset openings at the relics contained within the small, shallow crypt; the bema, with its seats for the clergy, was constructed as a higher storey, two metres above. Something of the kind was devised by Pope Gregory I for St Peter's in Rome, but the Stobi example is earlier by a century and more.

Fragments of wall-painting at Stobi display the loose, impressionistic technique of the catacombs combined with heavy outlining of head, nose and brows. The eyes have the ringed, staring look of Coptic faces, but the influence behind them is probably traceable to Syria and the Dura school of painting rather than to Egypt. The capitals, though varied in style, could all be described as 'Constantinopolitan' and the décor of the whole is that of Constantinople at the beginning of the sixth century, but rendered in a provincial idiom.

Knowledge of this same period has recently been enlarged by discoveries made at other far distant outposts of empire, in Spain. A complex of buildings at Centcelles, near Tarragona, includes a pair of burial-chambers which, whatever influences from Asia Minor may have played upon them, are arranged in an unusual, local style. One of the rooms is round, with four semicircular niches for sarcophagi and an entrance on the south. It is roofed with a cupola, made partly of tufa and partly of tiles radiating from the centre; beneath it lies a crypt with a secondary crypt below for draining off any water that might collect. A passageway links this domed building with another chamber, quatrefoil this time, which has no other entrance in its very thick walls. Mosaics, arranged in three horizontal friezes, adorn the cupola of the round building and, though on a humbler scale, invite comparison with those of S. Costanza at Rome. The first band consists of hunting scenes. By contrast there next are shown episodes from Old and New Testament, while above appear some sadly damaged figures seated upon thrones. The Biblical themes, set in a row within a framework of pillars, reflect the conventional fourth-century choice: Adam and Eve, Daniel in the lions' den, the three youths in the fiery furnace, the Good Shepherd and Lazarus. Fragmentary as they are, they appear to be the earliest known essay in decorating a dome with Christian subjects in mosaic and an attempt by some wealthy landowner to glorify his family with an almost imperial splendour.[9]

NOTES

1. The building of the church seems to have been completed in successive stages beginning at the middle of the fifth century, but all was brought down by an earthquake in 551 AD.
2. Gregory Palamas, *Homily* 43, *PG* 151, 548.
3. Dating is not exact. It is uncertain how much of the constructions in the crypt antedates Leontius (Grabar, *Martyrium* i. 450–457) while more recent studies (e.g. G. and M. Sotiriou, *He basilike tou Hagiou Dimitriou tis Thessalonikis* (1952)) tend to disregard Leontius and assign the whole of the original church to the middle of the fifth century.
4. Ignatius, an otherwise unknown monk of the early Middle Ages. *DACL* 15.1, 693.
5. Ezekiel 1 and 2, Habakkuk 2.1–4. But perhaps the second prophet is really Zechariah, in accordance with the primitive dedication. The whole scene would receive apt commentary from Zechariah 14, 'Living waters shall go out from Jerusalem . . . and Jerusalem shall dwell safely.'
6. 26.9–10.
7. Part of it was discovered in the Church of St Pantaleon.
8. *Apostolic Constitutions* viii.3, ed. F. E. Brightman.
9. All this in spite of the rule laid down by the Spanish Council of Elvira (306 AD): 'There must be no pictures in a church, nor should objects of worship and adoration be illustrated on the walls.' Elvira, however, was in southern Spain, a considerable distance from Centcelles.

10

Ravenna

It is Ravenna which provides the clearest survey of architectural style and decoration over the fifth and sixth centuries, and this comes about through the happy accidents of its history. Built on a marshy plain, about five miles from the sea, the town was connected by canals with its harbour, Portus Classis, which had formerly been used by Augustus to shelter his Adriatic fleet. The harbour fell into decay but the extensive system of canals remained and when, in 402 AD, the emperor Honorius judged it prudent to abandon Rome in favour of a stronghold with defences more secure from Gothic invasions, he chose Ravenna as his place of residence, 'Felix Ravenna', as the city proudly declared on its coins, 'Ravenna fortunata' by reason of its splendour and new-found importance. In 493 Ravenna fell into the hands of Theodoric and his Ostrogoths; they retained control until, some fifty years later, Italy was reconquered by the generals of Justinian who, though ruling from Constantinople, turned his gaze westwards and desired with a mystic's passion the complete unity of an empire which should extend right round the Mediterranean. Later on North Italy came to be controlled, somewhat remotely, from Constantinople by means of local governors known as exarchs. In the middle of the eighth century, however, the Lombard invasions brought all this to an end and reduced Ravenna itself to the status of a small provincial town, dreaming of past greatness and proud of its inheritance of fine buildings without having either means or ambition to transform them drastically under the influence of varying fashions in architecture.

Throughout the vicissitudes of fortune which Ravenna experienced the impress of a local style persists. The usual building material is a long, thin brick with a rough and sometimes mottled surface that subtly changes colour with the variations of sunlight and shade. The bricks are set in a pebbly cement, laid as a rule quite thinly but sometimes, as in the Church of S. Vitale, in bands as thick as the bricks. The straightforward basilican style, typical of the West but found commonly enough in the Eastern Empire, is that in which most of the churches are constructed, though special character is conferred by a liking for high naves, large aisle windows and internal walls carpeted with sumptuous, rather formal mosaic.

Two of the earliest of these basilicas are the churches dedicated to St Agatha and to the Holy Spirit. Both have been substantially modified over the years and have been subjected to a complex piece of engineering whereby pavement and columns were raised six or seven feet to avert the risk of flooding. They nevertheless retain their fifth-century pattern quite clearly. St Agatha's, preceded by an atrium of which only traces remain, is divided into nave and aisles by two rows of ten columns each (fig. 108). The bareness of the western façade is relieved by the vertical lines of pilaster strips, a device fairly characteristic of Ravenna, while the apse, seemingly built a century or so later than the nave arcade, has bold windows once surmounted by a mosaic representing Christ enthroned between angels. The Church of the Holy Spirit repeats the same general formula. This basilica, erected by Theodoric about 495 AD, was to be the

108. Ravenna, St Agatha, showing the ambo placed between columns at the centre of the nave.

cathedral of the Arian, as opposed to the Catholic, party, but was handed over to the Catholics in 561 after the expulsion of the Goths. Here again the building is approached by way of a large atrium. It is stumpier than the church of St Agatha, with a nave arcade composed of seven columns on each side, but gives the impression of great height. The columns are of marble with stone capitals of Corinthian type topped by rather lumpy imposts,[1] each marked with a cross. The row of six clerestory windows has been blocked up. More or less contemporary with the arcade, a marble ambo is now placed on a pillar set between two of the pillars half way down the south side. This ambo is of a pattern favoured at Ravenna: the straight line of a rectangular surface swells out in the centre to form a semicircular turret in which the reader stood. Another such ambo, taken from the church of St John and St Paul, is now in the Archbishop's Museum. Made of an attractive grey marble, it has animals and birds carved on the surface, together with a crude representation of the saints after whom the church was named. But the finest example is contained in Ravenna Cathedral, which otherwise has little of antiquity to show. This marble ambo was made, as a frieze inscription records,

by Bishop Agnellus and therefore about 560 AD. The surface is divided by a geometric framework into panels, twenty-four on the semicircle and six at each side. The subjects carved within the panels are, on the top, a row of sheep, then peacocks, followed by stags, doves, ducks and carp. In Western churches the placing of the ambo was a matter more of practical convenience than of liturgical correctness. The ritual of the Little Entrance never evolved there and, though other processions took place occasionally through the nave, this part of the church was less a stage for drama, which it tended to become in the East, than the Ark which sheltered the varied congregation of the faithful.

The church of St John the Evangelist, built in 426 by Galla Placidia in fulfilment of a vow made during a violent tempest, is a stately basilica much restored but still retaining parts of its fifth-century structure (fig. 109). The many large windows of aisles and clerestory, enclosed within a frame of blind arches similarly shaped, are, if not precisely in their original form, at least a very early adaptation, and have the effect of filling the church with light which at one time sparkled from a brilliant mosaic showing the empress and her

109. Ravenna, St John the Evangelist: the east end.

110. Ravenna, S. Apollinare Nuovo: the nave arcade from the south-west.

children delivered from the peril of shipwreck. The twelve columns of grey marble separating the nave from each aisle remain as in Galla Placidia's day, with Corinthian capitals topped by impost blocks of 'Theodosian' type. The most unusual feature of the building is the apse at the east end. This is a seven-sided polygon, lit by a continuous range of seven windows, separated one from the other only by a stone column. Three more windows, now blocked up, were set below this arcade. The apse was flanked by rectangular rooms, perhaps martyr-chapels rather than sacristies, which project from the aisles and are, again, lit by large windows with semicircular heads. The whole effect of this east end, bold and original as it is, suggests the Aegean coastlands rather than Rome. It thus serves as a reminder that sharp distinctions in architecture between East and West cannot be rigidly maintained. A fertile current of ideas flowed around the Mediterranean and, from Constantinople in particular, men, materials and designs passed to Ravenna and beyond, enriching and modifying local fashions with touches of lively and sophisticated splendour.

A more celebrated building in the same tradition is the church of S. Apollinare Nuovo, founded by Theodoric at some point between 494 AD and 526, the year of his death (fig. 110). Here the customary basilican plan is followed but with the addition of several of the characteristic variants which occur at St John's. Windows of nave, aisles and apse (restored) illuminate from all sides a building which gives the impression of height and space in spite of the dislocations caused by raising the columns slightly more than a metre above their original level. The capitals, with their wide-splayed acanthus leaves and chunky impost blocks, are of Greek rather than Roman type and were probably exported ready-made from Constantinople by businesslike merchants little concerned to find that they were providing for an Arian and therefore heretical church. The outer surface of the basilica, though varied by pilaster buttresses and bands of brick, remains austere and in marked contrast to the sumptuous decoration of the interior. The arches, with their panelled under-surface, are very rich; above them, a cornice of four slim orders leads admirably on to the glittering plate of colour which the mosaics provide. These were at one time even more ample and included an enrichment of the apse, whereas the mosaics remaining today are confined to

111. Ravenna, S. Apollinare Nuovo: the pattern of mosaic above the north arcade.

the side walls of the nave. Here they form three horizontal bands, one above the other, with the first running close against the ceiling, the second in the spaces between the windows and the third, much larger than the others, immediately above the nave arcade. In the topmost band occur scenes drawn from the Gospel story, miracles and parables on the north side, details from the Passion narrative on the south. The choice of events may reflect a sequence of passages read during Lent according to the local tradition of Ravenna, though the modest size of the panels and their distance of some 12 metres from the ground adapt them more to serve as parts of a bold decorative scheme than for easy instruction of the people. They could, however, be said to represent themes of popular interest, some of the subjects being those found in the earliest attempts at Christian art, others introduced by the beginning of the fifth century. Two styles are employed, but, since Theodoric summoned 'skilful workers in mosaic'[2] from Rome, both have points in common with Roman examples of mosaic and ivory-carving. The artist responsible for the Passion sequence has a liking for vigorous, sometimes crowded, compositions, for action rather than sym-

metry. By contrast the panels of the north side show never more than five figures and often only three, carefully balanced and firmly controlled. The manner in which Christ is portrayed differs also. The Christ of the Passion scenes is bearded and grave, whereas in the miracle mosaics he appears as youthful and beardless. But in either case he wears the purple robe of majesty, and a large halo, stamped with a cross, encircles his head.

Between each pair of historical scenes is set a panel which regularly depicts a golden canopy standing out against a blue background. Above the canopy two white doves face each other with a golden cross between them; while the canopy itself contains a double rope of pearls from which a diadem is suspended. The function of these panels is a twofold one: they break what would otherwise be a confused jumble of narrative and they form a connection with the range of mosaics below, since the crowns hang over the heads of the saintly personages shown on the wall spaces between the clerestory windows. These unnamed figures, statuesque but rhythmically poised, and clearly distinguished one from another, are prophets or perhaps apostles. All are clothed in the

112. Ravenna, S. Apollinare Nuovo: marble panel from the chancel screen.

conventional, hieratic fashion of a white tunic with black edging-stripes and a mantle stamped with the rectangular mark known as a gammadion.[3] With sandals on their feet and a large halo around their heads they each clasp a book or a scroll as emblem of their calling.

The lowest, and widest, bands of mosaic depict two stately processions. On the north wall a line of twenty-two virgin martyrs, preceded by the Three Wise Men, advances from the fortified port of Classis towards the Virgin Mary, enthroned, with the Child on her knee and attended by four angels. Parallel with these, on the opposite wall, a procession of twenty-five male martyrs, each carrying his diadem of glory, leaves the Palace of Theodoric to approach the calmly majestic Christ, seated on his bejewelled throne with two angels standing at either side. The whole composition is clearly the work of several artists. The double line of saints, at any rate, is a re-working carried out by Bishop Agnellus, about 560 AD, when the church was transferred from the Arian Goths to the Catholic party under the patronage of Justinian, who is shown, looking rather plump and mature, in a mosaic panel within the church. Agnellus, triumphing in the change, selected St Martin of Tours, renowned as the 'hammer of the heretics', to be leader of the procession advancing to the throne of Christ. Both rows of figures are rigid and statuesque. There is, however, with the men, a variation in age, hairstyle, hang of garments and position of the feet that the artists responsible for the women did not attempt, though the virgin martyrs exhibit enough difference in angle of the head and embroidery of the robes to avoid monotony. The mosaic showing the 'Three Kings of Orient', though patched and repaired, is of the highest quality (fig. 111). Clearly differentiated in age, in the cut and colour of their robes, and the type of vessel which contains the gold, the frankincense and the myrrh, the Magi press forward, with subtle variations of reverent eagerness, across a flower-strewn meadow, while palm trees in the background form a kind of arcade that frames each king from his companion. The general type of inspiration is the same as that shown by the artists who designed the rest of the mosaics half a century earlier: a sense of timeless mystery as the background of human endeavour, so that a somewhat conventional stiffness, quickened into rhythm by supreme artistry, presents truth more surely than a

113. Ravenna, S. Apollinare in Classe: interior.

realism which reflects no more than the mood of the moment.

S. Apollinare Nuovo has many things to offer in addition to its mosaics. An ambo of the usual Ravenna type, now repaired and lacking any steps, is set between two columns of the nave. Marble panels—three of them *transennae*, perforated in such a way that the carving shows up clearly against a dark background—survive from the chancel screen and display the sensitive quality of the best sixth-century work (fig 112): amidst grapes and vine-leaves, with their hints of the Eucharist, peacocks, the birds of immortality, face one another with the Cross between them. Four columns of porphyry, which formerly supported the ciborium over the altar, offer a contrast, deep red against white, with the marble of the screen nearby.

If the church of S. Apollinare Nuovo is pre-eminent for its mosaic decoration, the church of S. Apollinare in Classe, situated in the flat and swampy land three miles outside the city, provides a standard example of harmonious architecture. Founded about the year 534, at the expense of the banker Julianus Argentarius, it was built entirely of brick and reproduces some of the features already made known in the church of St John

the Evangelist. There is the same system of blind arches framing the windows of both aisles and clerestory. Again the apse, though later raised to allow for the excavation of a crypt beneath it, is circular inside but polygonal on the outer face. Moreover the sacristies, which flank the apse on either side, suggest those found in St John's, though they are neater and equipped with small polygonal apses that harmonize with the east end of the nave. The original west front, with its ample narthex ending in two rectangular towers, must have suggested Syrian models, but one of the towers has now disappeared and the other exists only in truncated form. The interior of the church (fig. 113) illustrates with much charm the typically Byzantine love of rhythmical proportion and of light, regarded not merely as a physical entity but as symbol and purveyor of life. The nave is just double the width of each aisle, from which it is separated by a line of twelve columns set on square bases and made of an exceptionally fine grey marble from Proconnesus. The capitals, carved in a white marble, are of mixed style with Ionic corner-pieces projecting above windswept acanthus leaves, deeply drilled, while the impost blocks are sharply cut back and thus avoid the

114. Ravenna, S. Apollinare in Classe: the mosaic of the apse.

lumpy appearance of those in S. Apollinare Nuovo. Light floods into the lofty building through the wide, round-headed windows: forty-eight in the nave and aisles together with a triple arcade in the west wall and five windows in the apse, but the carpet of floor mosaic, together with most of the marble panelling on the walls, has been completely lost.

The surviving mosaic is concentrated in and near the apse, and belongs to various dates and styles. The most celebrated panel is the seventh-century 'three sacrifices' mosaic, showing Melchizedek, Abel and Abraham making their offerings at a fully furnished altar. But the portion of mosaic which seems to be contemporary with the founding of the church is confined to the half-dome of the apse. The upper part alludes, in a manner half historical, half symbolic, to the Gospel story of the Transfiguration. The hand of God, appearing at the top of the scene, indicates the divine and mysterious nature of the whole occurrence. To right and left, half-figures of Moses and Elijah emerge from banks of cloud, while the central position is taken by a bejewelled cross with a tiny head of Christ at the intersection. This stands out against a background of blue studded with gold stars and makes an

effective substitute for the more usual figure of Christ the Ruler of all. Below the round medallion containing the cross three sheep appear, one on the left side and two on the right, within a rural landscape of formalized rocks, trees and plants. The sheep represent the three apostles, Peter, James and John, who were privileged to witness the Transfiguration. The hint is thereby subtly given that, just as St Peter at the Transfiguration wished to build three tents in order that he, together with James and John, might dwell within the unfailing radiance of God's power, so Christians build churches in the hopeful assurance that they will remain within the scope of never-failing salvation. The lower part of the mosaic shows the august, priestly figure of St Apollinaris set in the central place of honour below the Cross and raising his arms in the manner of an *Orans* (fig. 114). Facing him on either side are six white sheep separated from one another by flowering lilies. When placed in close connection with Christ, twelve sheep represent the Apostles naturally enough. Here the imagery is rather different and the sheep stand for the general body of the faithful, under the influence of such language as that of a fifth-century sermon[4] composed by Peter

Chrysologus in honour of St Apollinaris: 'Lo, he is alive: behold how, as a Good Shepherd, he stands in the midst of his flock.' The martyr 'fills up that which is lacking in the sufferings of Christ' and may therefore be shown in a manner more naturally appropriate to his Lord. Throughout the composition historical realism is subordinated to timeless abstraction.

While the basilica, plain and well ordered on the outside, light and brilliant within, is typical of Ravenna, the oldest church remaining in the city, the Mausoleum of Galla Placidia, is of a different character. Galla Placidia, sister of the emperor Honorius and regent for Valentinian III, combined practical vigour and good sense with a taste for mystical piety. She was responsible for the building of several churches at Ravenna, during her period of residence there about the year 425, and one of these churches, which may have served the purposes of her private chapel, is S. Croce. This was originally a cross-shaped structure of which only the nave, and that much remodelled, now exists. The west front of S. Croce received, where today a street runs, a long, low narthex to one end of which Galla's mausoleum was attached. This is an unpretentious but delicately balanced structure in the form of a Latin cross, with three equal arms and a rather longer arm forming the entrance (fig. 115). Constructed, unlike most of Ravenna's ancient buildings, of large, chunky bricks, it presents an outside surface embellished with a continuous range of blind arches, whose proportions have been somewhat marred by a rise of a metre and a half in the level of the ground. The four arms match one another perfectly. Each has a classical pediment concealing the vault inside, and, as though to preserve this particular harmony, the central member which binds the arms together takes the form of a low rectangular tower rather than of the dome which appears inside. The building is in fact a small but finely constructed example of a martyr-chapel. It may possibly have contained relics of St Laurence or other martyrs but Galla's main purpose in constructing it was to house the sepulchres of her brother Honorius, her husband Constantius and herself. Whether Galla was in fact buried there must, in spite of medieval tradition, be accounted as doubtful at best, but the funerary nature of the building is made obvious enough by its shape, its size, the three sarcophagi which it contains and a fitting choice of themes for the resplendent mosaics. These combine admirably with the architecture, in that the neat and closely related scheme of vaults and cupola gives space for a rich but compact display of refined artistry, while the mosaics in their turn emphasize the grace and poise of the architecture. The lower part of the walls, up to the cornice from which spring the arches of the vaults, is plated with slabs of a brownish marble, mostly restored; above the cornice line, however, the whole surface is given over to mosaic pictures or patterns. The prevailing background is dark blue against which the other colours, gold and a greyish white in particular, stand out effectively. On the other hand, the alabaster with which the small, rectangular windows are filled admits a light which is attractive but hardly bright enough, even when the sun is shining, to show the mosaics to full advantage; it may be supposed that lamps and candles were used to provide further illumination.

The cupola offers a scene of restrained majesty. The central point is occupied by a plain Latin cross, around which are ranged in circles over five hundred golden stars. Diminishing in size as they come nearer to the cross, these go to make up an early essay in the art of perspective, and suggest a timeless infinity. The pendentives of the cupola contain the lion, ox, eagle and man which served as symbols of the Gospel-writers who recounted the story of the redemption effected by the Cross, while below, in compartments marked off by a ribbon border, stand white-robed apostles with, at their feet, the repeated theme of two white doves beside a drinking-bowl, or, it might be, the souls of the faithful beside the waters of life. The same liking for exact symmetry is shown in the mosaic panels at the end of the building's short cross-arms. There, amid a balanced profusion of twining acanthus, two stags advance in eagerness to quench their thirst at a rush-fringed pool between them, thus illustrating the Psalmist's text: 'Like as the hart desireth the waterbrooks, so longeth my soul after thee, O God.' Above, within a similar pattern of acanthus and vine tendrils, prophets are set as lights of the world upon flower chandeliers at either side of a wreath enclosing the mystic symbol of the chi-rho cross and the letters alpha and omega.

The other two arms of the building are finished rather differently. Beneath a vault, decorated with red, white and gold flowers on a background of indigo, are two scenes in which a formal rhythm is

115. Ravenna: Mausoleum of Galla Placidia.

achieved without any loss of vitality. In the centre of one composition, flames coil about a gridiron towards which the deacon Laurence, clothed in the vestment of his order and holding a processional cross and open psalter, advances triumphantly. Balancing the figure of the saint on the other side of the gridiron is an open bookcase containing volumes of the Gospels which inspire his confidence and declare the principle 'no cross, no crown'.[5] The mosaic in the opposite arm of the building shows the Good Shepherd interpreted with an originality which differs sharply from the crude portrayals in the catacombs (fig. 116). At the centre Christ, in face like some youthful Apollo and wearing a golden tunic and a mantle of purple, is seated on a throne-like heap of three rocks. A large halo surrounds his head. With his left hand Christ grasps a long cross while his right hand is extended across his body to touch the uplifted face of one of the six sheep that are symmetrically arranged, three on each side of the Shepherd, amid the crags and bushes of the radiant 'Hellenistic' countryside which melts away into the far distance.

The carved fronts of the sarcophagi are in complete accord with the themes chosen for the mosaics, and continue to use the Bible symbolism of sheep and doves. The tomb of Honorius presents the 'Lamb standing on the mount Zion' from which flow the four mystical rivers of Paradise, while behind the Lamb is set a tall cross with a dove perched on each arm. Constantius' tomb repeats this subject with a difference. The Lamb, the mountains and the rivers are there, but a halo with chi-rho monogram takes the place of the cross and on either side a sturdy lamb, firm-set in the statuesque Syrian manner, faces inwards with, behind, a graceful palm tree bearing upon it the fruit of righteousness. No monument could exhibit more clearly than Galla's mausoleum the impressive nature of a wholly consistent symbolism allied with imaginative power.

Of all the churches in Ravenna, however, the most complex and ingenious is that dedicated to the local martyr, St Vitalis. The historian Agnellus, who wrote in Ravenna during the ninth century, regarded it as the most remarkable church in all Italy. Begun in 526, when Ravenna was still under the domination of the Goths, S. Vitale also received its funding from the mysterious Julianus Argentarius, who was perhaps

116. Ravenna, Mausoleum of Galla Placidia: mosaic of the Good Shepherd.

used by the court at Constantinople as agent in both religious and political matters. Most of the work may be assigned to the high noon of Justinian's reign, about 540 to 548 AD.

S. Vitale (fig. 117) is often described as the 'imperial church', and there is about it an air of grandeur which, contrasting with the practical form of a parish basilica, fits it to be termed a Chapel Royal. Those mosaics which depict Justinian and Theodora solemnly offering their eucharistic gifts may appear to support this suggestion, but it is more probable that the style and splendour of the church bear witness to lavish presents of money and materials from the imperial treasury, bestowed no doubt with an eye to practical advantage, than that S. Vitale differed in its functions from any other church in Ravenna. Influences from Constantinople are obvious enough. The marble of columns and capitals, and probably the craftsmen who carved them, came from the imperial quarries at Proconnesus, and the plan of the structure closely resembles that of SS. Sergius and Bacchus at Constantinople, which seems to have been started a few years earlier. But S. Vitale reveals the individual touch of a great, if unknown, architect, being somewhat higher-

pitched and admitting more light than SS. Sergius and Bacchus. Moreover, it is built of the long, thin, subtly-coloured bricks characteristic of sixth-century Ravenna, and shows to perfection the meticulous sense of rhythmical balance which marks the churches of that place and period.

The essential plan of the building is an octagon, the external face of which is divided vertically by buttresses and horizontally by a slim cornice to form panels, each containing a large, round-headed window. This pattern is repeated in the cupola, which takes the form of a smaller octagon having but one panel on each face; this is pierced by a window which exactly matches those below save that, by way of variation, it is set within a slightly recessed frame. The regularity of the main octagon is however interrupted, or enriched, by additions. There is in the first place the entrance-porch, a long narthex with apsidal ends and flanking turrets that extends across two sides of the octagon. At the other end of the building, though not precisely opposite the narthex, rise the carefully proportioned shapes of the complex sanctuary. This consists of a jutting, rectangular chancel completed by an apse that is semicircular within but presents an angled outer

117. Ravenna, S. Vitale: the interplay of wall and roof as viewed from the north-west.

face. At either side of the apse there is a round chapel, or sacristy, with two rectangular chambers, one taller and one lower, annexed to it. The varying play of shapes and angles thus produced draws the eye upwards in satisfying harmony. Inside the building a rich profusion of decoration is enhanced by the light which glances from the many windows. The central area is an octagon marked at every corner by lofty piers which lead up to the arches supporting the vault of the cupola (fig. 118). Within each of these main arches a semicircular bay contains a triple arcade repeated in two stages, giving respectively onto the ambulatory and the gallery that are bounded by the larger octagon of the enclosing walls. The mosaic pavement of the ambulatory, where it still exists, is like a patterned carpet designed to lead purposefully from the outer wall to the columns. It thus typifies the whole internal arrangement of the building, which is designed to lay emphasis on a central area enriched by the diversity of openings that, playing rhythmically around it, create a lively sequence of vistas, variously accented in light and shade. The grey marble of the columns is particularly attractive in both colour and texture, while the capitals are deeply drilled to form delicate patterns of

acanthus foliage and topped by impost blocks cut so sharply back that they avoid any suggestion of heaviness (fig. 119). The capitals of the presbytery are coloured and thus bear their share in the exuberant scheme of decoration which is concentrated in this part of the building. The dominant note here is an awe-inspiring majesty, but a fresh and lighthearted tone is given to most of the scenes by an abundance of light green colour and by the flowers, trees and chunky, formal rocks which appear as a rural background to most of the panels. Several craftsmen seem to have been employed and the style varies from a lively realism to more rigid and statuesque postures, but the variations may be due to difference of subject as much as anything else, since the rendering of clouds and springtime fields is similar throughout.

The 'arch of honour', which leads into the presbytery, has its lower surface decorated with the head of Christ: solemn, bearded and impressive. On either side of him are circles containing busts of the Apostles, clearly differentiated one from the other, and ending with a more local note, the figures of saints Gervasius and Protasius, patrons of Milan. The same theme of Christ as the centre-point of the Universe is

118. Ravenna, S. Vitale: the east end of the octagon.

119. Ravenna, S. Vitale; capitals.

twice repeated, with varying symbolism, inside the presbytery. The summit of the vault is occupied by a circle within which stands the sacred Lamb, white against the background of the starry heaven. In each of the four main panels of the vault an angel appears with arms uplifted to support the portrait of the Lamb, while the ribs, lavishly decorated with festoons of flowers and fruit, rise up to converge at the same point. The apse below illustrates the mystery in very different terms, by means of stiff, motionless figures shown against a golden background of timeless majesty, though, once again, there is the 'living green' of fields and plants underfoot. Christ, youthful and beardless, sits clothed in purple on the sky-blue globe which represents the created order; at either side an archangel, like some minister of the imperial court, attends upon him and introduces the suppliants. From the left St Vitalis, to whom the church is dedicated, advances with hands veiled beneath his mantle to receive the martyr's crown which is his due. From the right approaches Bishop Ecclesius, on whose initiative the building of the church was undertaken. The natural supporters of these august scenes are the four Evangelists and the Prophets, represented by Isaiah

and Jeremiah. Moses is shown rather more elaborately, first as loosing his sandals before approaching the bush 'burning with fire' and secondly as receiving the Law on Sinai's height. A sense of lively realism characterizes these mosaics as also the group which sets forth the theme of sacrifice. There are four such. In the great semicircle above the arches that open into the left wall, two episodes from the life of Abraham are displayed. First he reverently brings his offering of food, a calf on a dish, to the three angels seated beneath the oak of Mamre, while Sarah stands, puzzled and hesitant, within the door of the house. The angels, with their haloes and priestly vestments, are seated at a table bearing three loaves marked with a cross; hence the scene is rich in allusions both to the Trinity and to the Eucharist. At the end of the panel comes an illustration of Abraham restrained from sacrificing his son Isaac. The ram stands nearby, not caught in a thicket, as Scripture has it, but submissive and with head turned towards the altar on which Isaac crouches, thus freely accepting its destiny as Redeemer. In the corresponding semicircle on the other side the theme of sacrifice is again emphasized (fig. 120). An altar, fully veiled and supplied with

120. Ravenna, S. Vitale: the mosaic of Abel and Melchizedek.

patens and chalice, occupies the centre with the hand of God appearing over it. At one side Abel, clothed in skins and standing in front of a rustic hut, presents his offering, of a sheep, which proved acceptable in God's sight while, to balance him at the other side of the altar, Melchizedek the priest-king, resplendent with golden halo and pontifical garments, offers the loaf which is no ordinary bread but shines with unearthly lustre.

By those who examined mosaics of this kind with the 'comeliness of spiritual understanding', the figures, it was maintained, would be recognized as indicating not merely remote allegories but rather historical events leading up to and closely connected with the sacrifice of the altar which took place nearby. This same idea of a close relationship between the timeless realities of Heaven and their representation in events upon earth seems to have affected Byzantine views on the nature of kingship. The scheme of mosaics in the sanctuary of S. Vitale is completed by a famous pair of framed panels which so depict Justinian and Theodora as to hint that the earthly kingdom of the emperor in some sort reflects the heavenly rule of Christ. Justinian is attended by

guards and by dignitaries civil and ecclesiastical. Among these is Archbishop Maximian,[6] conspicuous alike by the position he occupies and by alone being named; he holds the large golden paten which is his offering to the newly-founded church. Justinian looks straight ahead in steadfast contemplation. Not only is he arrayed in the solemn splendour of imperial robes and diadem but his head is surrounded by the halo of reflected divinity. A similar impressiveness marks the approach of the empress with her gift of a golden chalice. Preceded by two officials and attended by a company of aristocratic ladies clothed in brilliantly coloured robes of silk, Theodora stands wearing a purple cloak that is embroidered in gold with figures of the Three Wise Men. Her long, pale face, beneath the pearl-encrusted diadem, is set in a motionless, forward-looking gaze. She is distinguished from her companions not only by her halo but by greater height—as though, by God's decree, she were raised above the normal run of mortals.

The S. Vitale mosaics thus offer, amidst a wealth of decorative detail, a fully-developed summary of Christian truth. No longer does the primitive symbolism of the catacombs suffice; instead the place of

Christ within and above the fabric of the Universe is three times stressed, his work as Redeemer is commented on with allusions to sacrifice and to the Eucharist, and the close relationship between Church and State receives unmistakable emphasis.

NOTES

1. The stone of the imposts differs from that of the capitals and appears to be a restoration.
2. Cassiodorus, *Letters* i.6, ed. T. Hodgkin (1886). Comparison may be made with the S. Maria Maggiore mosaics and the 'Andrews diptych' (p. 218).
3. It took the shape of a capital gamma. Four of them put back to back composed a Greek cross.
4. *Sermon* cxxviii, *PL* 52.
5. As Cyprian put it: 'The Gospel of Christ whereby martyrs are made' (*Epistle* 38). G. Hartel in *CSEL*, iii.580.
6. Maximian was promoted to his see in 546 AD.

11

The Foundations of Justinian

CONSTANTINOPLE

The Church of the Holy Wisdom at Constantinople, Hagia Sophia or Santa Sophia, stands out as one of the world's masterpieces and as the formative influence which finally settled the Byzantine style of architecture. The building has suffered curious turns of fortune, losing much that contributed to its glory and gaining additions not precisely adapted to it, but in substance the church remains as the emperor Justinian saw it when he attended the dedication service on 27 December in the year 537 AD. It owes its existence to a mishap. Constantine's basilica of the Holy Wisdom was destroyed during a revolution in 512. Justinian, impelled by pride and statecraft no less than piety, set forward with fanatical energy the construction of a new church. The ground-plan of this building (fig. 121) owes much to the great hall known as the Basilica of Maxentius erected early in the fourth century close to the Forum at Rome, but the emphasis becomes centralized by reason of the huge dome and the works necessary to support it. Originality was shown, moreover, in the vast size and exceptional splendour of the whole structure as well as in a certain breadth of sympathies resulting from the employment of men and materials drawn, with lavish disregard of cost, from every corner of the Empire. In order to realize his grandiose plan Justinian had to search for architects who combined scholarly taste with the highest technical powers. And so, as Procopius, a contemporary historian, records,

Anthemius of Tralles, the most learned man in that skilled craft known as the technique of building not only among all his contemporaries but also when compared with those who lived long before him, ministered to the Emperor's enthusiasm duly regulating the tasks of the craftsmen and preparing in advance designs of the future construction.[1]

Associated with Anthemius was Isidore of Miletus, a lecturer in physics who had made a special study of domes and vaults. The church aroused admiration for two reasons dear to sixth-century Byzantines: the perfect harmony of its proportions and the technical skill with which it was constructed. Height and light were amongst the qualities which amazed the beholder:

In height it rises to the very heavens and as if surging up from amongst the other buildings it stands aloft and looks down upon the rest of the city,

or, to continue the eye-witness account:

the church is singularly full of light and sunshine and makes you ready to declare that the place is not lit by the sun from without but that the radiance is produced within itself.

The walls of S. Sophia at ground level, 76 metres long and 71 metres in width, very nearly form a square. Inside, a central square is marked off from the aisles by four huge piers, one at each corner. Springing from these piers, arches span the aisles to connect with buttresses set against the external walls. Along the north and south sides of the central square runs a lofty arcade matched by the arcade of the gallery above where, however, the columns are smaller and the openings number seven instead of five. Rising higher still, over the gallery, the nave wall, pierced by rows of windows, fills the curve of the two great arches which are the less dramatic counterpart of the two open arches which sweep across the east and west sides of the square. Beyond the open arches the ground-plan develops in a trefoil manner. From each of the great corner piers a semicircular colonnade runs to form the link with another set of piers flanking the entrance to the narthex at the west end, and, at the east, the apse, which Procopius explains as 'the part towards the rising sun where the sacred mysteries are performed in honour of God'. The aisles are divided into three compartments covered by low vaults, while the galleries above are crowned by spherical vaults of a pattern which is continued over the divisions of the narthex, so that the entire building becomes an essay in the interplay of rectangular forms and circles or half-circles (fig. 122).

Nowhere is this more obvious than in the construction of the great central dome. Arising from the four main piers, the stones of which were specially strengthened with cement and metal cramps, the circle is set on the square with the help of concave triangles (pendentives), which extend the surface of the dome into the corners of the square. Procopius may again be called upon to supply his commentary:

Since the arches are so constructed as to form a four-cornered plan, the stonework between the arches produces four triangles. The lower part, then, of each triangle, being compressed where the arches unite, is slender, while the upper part becomes wider as it rises in the space between them and ends against the circle which rests upon them. A spherical dome, standing upon this circle, makes the structure exceedingly beautiful; yet it seems not to rest upon solid masonry but to cover the space beneath with its golden dome suspended from heaven.

The men of the sixth century may have regarded Anthemius's vast floating dome as miraculous, but it was in fact protected with extreme care. The four main piers were carried up through the roof to form buttresses resisting the sideway thrust while the material used for the construction of the dome was a variety of tile made from very light earth found on the island of Rhodes. Moreover, a certain amount of supporting counter-thrust was provided by the half-domes curv-

ing westwards to the narthex and eastward in the direction of the apse. But in spite of these precautions an earthquake, occurring in May 558, so unsettled the building as to cause a partial collapse:

The wide-flung shrine did not collapse to its foundations, but the eastern arch of support for the great cupola fell to the ground and a portion of the dome mingled with the dust.[2]

These words come from a long poem, written in Homeric verse by a court official named Paul the Silentiary. Paul gives a full and detailed account of S. Sophia as it was reconstructed, promptly and vigorously, by the emperor. Justinian strengthened the piers and, thinking the dome too flat for safety, raised it by six metres. Its base was surrounded by a rim of buttresses and the shell of the dome itself was strengthened by forty ribs running from the circumference upwards to the apex. The emperor was well entitled to the solemn triumph in which he proceeded, on Christmas Eve 562, to the second inauguration of the great church which had earlier caused him to exclaim 'Solomon, I have surpassed you.' Paul the Silentiary, in his florid but exact description, dwelt lovingly on the details of an architectural scheme 'whose mighty arches seemed to be set in the heavens'. 'The eastern side', he begins, 'expands in the form of three semicircles.'[3] Paul explains the central apse as the place where the clergy seat themselves, while the two semicircles flanking the apse are described by the name of conches, or sea-shells, a technical term equivalent to exedras. These columned recesses are a particularly happy device for widening the angles of a square underneath a dome and to Paul they seemed to be 'stretching out bent arms to embrace the people eagerly singing in the church'.[4] He was also much impressed by the boldness of the architect in being content, at ground level, with two columns of porphyry while placing six columns, 'bright flowers of fresh green Thessalian stone', above to support the arches of the 'fair upper galleries for the women'. The columns of this higher range thus had no counterparts to receive their thrust immediately below and gave the impression of having the bases 'fixed over empty air'.

Paul indicates that the west end of S. Sophia resembled the east end except that 'there is no circling curve to enclose it' but instead a 'vast elaborate entrance', 'not only one door but three'. Beyond this comes the

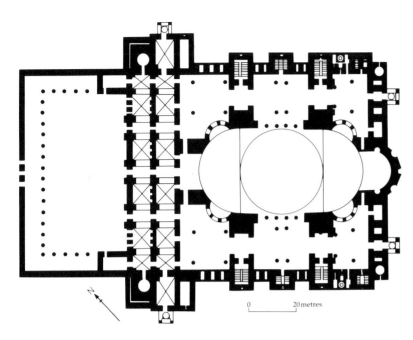

121. Constantinople, S. Sophia: ground-plan.

narthex 'as long as the wondrous church is broad' with 'seven sacred gates wide open and inviting the people to enter'. It is noted that 'here right through the night arises a melodious sound pleasing to the ears of Christ, Giver of Life, as God-fearing David's psalms of praise are sung in antiphonal strains.'[5] Outside, beyond the narthex, extended the atrium, 'an open court surrounded by four cloisters'[6] and containing a fountain. At this point in his exploration of S. Sophia, Paul hastens on to 'the wonders scarcely to be believed' of the middle part of the church. The four bulky piers are described as 'naked to look at in front, but on their sides and backs firmly held together by the supporting arches and resting steadily fixed on foundations of unbroken stone', while 'above them spring vast, rounded arches like the curve of the many-coloured rainbow'. Like Procopius before him, Paul gives a description, which has become classic, of the pendentives which fill the space between the arches:

For where the arches bend away from one another as the design required and would have left but empty air, a curved wall, like a triangle, sweeps up as far as need be until it connects with its fellow on either side. So the four triangles,

creeping upward, spread out until they become united and crown the circular expanse on high.

The cornice, or rim of the dome, is next described, with its 'narrow curved path, on which the torch-bearer may walk without fear as he kindles the sacred lamps'. Paul then tells of the dome itself:

Rising on high into the boundless air the great helmet enfolds all on every side, just as though the radiant heaven had become the church's covering. And at the topmost part is skilfully depicted the cross, protector of the city. And marvellous it is to see how the dome rises gradually, wide below but growing less as it reaches up higher.

Paul also gives a straightforward account of the side aisles with their dignified ranges of columns and their galleries above, but what really aroused his enthusiasm was the splendour of the decoration in all its forms. The capitals, which now assume the 'basket shape' typical of the age of Justinian, are praised in lush, full-blown language:

on the lofty crest of each column, where the marble impost rises up, a swirling tendril of acanthus clambers in supple curve—a wandering chain, golden, utterly charming as it twines its sharp-pointed spikes around.[7]

122. Constantinople, S. Sophia: view from the north-west.

Similarly the effect of the mosaics is summed up in terms of the impression made on the beholder:

Now the vaulting is covered with little pebbles of gold joined tightly together, and the sparkling flood of golden rays that strikes down from them is almost too bright for men's eyes to behold.

Apparently this decoration was made up of patterns and natural forms rather than human imagery.

While mosaic covered the vaults, the whole of the inner wall surface and much of the floor was plated with various types of marble. 'The hills of Proconnesus strewed the floor', explains Paul, referring to the marble, white with grey streaky lines, which was quarried near the sea of Marmora and became the material for most of the columns in the aisles as well as for capitals and the framing of windows and doors. Eleven other sorts of marble are named, in particular the porphyry, brought from Egypt and made into the columns of the conches, and the Thessalian *verde antico* used for the eight columns of the nave and extensively in other parts of the building (fig. 123).

Of the fittings which served the purposes of worship Paul selects three for detailed comment: the screen, the altar with its ciborium and the ambo. Church screens, in the sixth century, had not yet assumed the form which came to be characteristic in the East, with the solid partitions and curtained doors of the iconostasis entirely concealing the performance of the eucharistic rite. The screen erected by Justinian was lighter and of a pattern closer to the medieval chancel-screens of the West. There were the 'triple doors whereby the screen opens to the priests', the large central doorway in front of the altar and two smaller ones giving access to the sacristies; above the panelled base of the screen came an openwork section with six pairs of silver columns topped by a beam having a large cross in the middle and figures of angels, prophets and apostles on either side. These figures also were fashioned in silver and fell a prey to the rapacity of the Crusaders who sacked the church in 1204 AD.

The altar, according to Paul, was a gold slab 'standing on gold foundations and bright with the glitter of precious stones'. This masterpiece was very different from the simple altars of stone or wood, used at an earlier period, to which St Gregory of Nyssa,[8] writing about 380 AD, bears witness:

The altar whereat we stand is by nature only common stone, nothing different from any other stones of which our walls are made and our pavements formed.

The altar of S. Sophia was normally covered with a purple cloth and above it rose a magnificent canopy 'borne aloft on fourfold arches of silver'. Paul describes this canopy as a 'tower', but the word which came to be more often used was *ciborium*,[9] originally a tent-like structure set up over pagan shrines or over the emperor's throne on state occasions. The S. Sophia canopy was suitably elaborate: from a base set on top of the columns an eight-sided spire

rises to a single crest, where the form of a cup is skilfully set. And the edges of the cup are bent down to resemble leaves while in the midst has been placed a shining silver globe, and the cross surmounts it all.

The ciborium, in its early forms, was conveniently designed as a frame on which to fix decorative objects or from which lights, wreaths or curtains could be hung. At S. Sophia the ciborium had, fixed to the flat base from which sprang the octagonal spire, silver bowls containing rods which looked rather like candles but were in fact also 'made round with silver, brightly polished'. The curtains, suspended on all four sides, were, it would seem, normally kept drawn to emphasize the sacred character of the altar. But in themselves they were, as Paul indicates, remarkable works of art 'adorned with splendour'. Made of silk enriched by gold thread, they offered instruction along with beauty. The front veil showed Christ with right hand extended 'as if preaching the words of Life', with Paul 'full of divine wisdom' and Peter 'the mighty doorkeeper of the Gates of Heaven' standing on either side. The edges of the curtain were decorated with illustrations of Christ's miracles and of the emperor's works of piety in building churches and providing hospitals. The other curtains showed 'the kings of the earth' joining hands with Christ and the Virgin Mary, which in the Middle Ages would have suggested the Tree of Jesse showing Christ's descent from the Old Testament kings of David's line but in the sixth century must be taken as another variant on the theme of the close alliance between Church and State.

Fascinated as Paul was by the screen and the ciborium, he devotes far more attention to the ambo which, approached along its raised *solea*, was set well down the church. Two flights of steps, protected by balustrades made of variegated marble and ivory, led up to a floor which extended into semicircles on the north and south. The semicircles were enclosed by walls 'up to the height of a man's girdle' and made of stone with a lavish decoration of silver plaques. This body of the ambo was upheld by eight columns, while the marble floor, cut out and hollowed on the underside 'like the shell-back of a tortoise', provided space for the clergy who were to render the liturgical chants. The area on the ground floor was enclosed by columns made of rose-pink marble with white bases and gilded capitals. Between the columns were set marble slabs leaving only two narrow entrances, while above the columns ran a wooden architrave embellished with golden ivy leaves and a pigment the colour of sapphire. Two silver crosses 'with a curved spike above each, bending like a shepherd's crook' to form the chi-rho monogram, completed the splendid array which suggested a colourful island 'in the middle space of the boundless temple'. The passage leading up to it converted the island, as Paul thought, into an isthmus, and when the priest 'holding the golden gospel' passes along it on his way to the sanctuary 'the surging crowd strives to press lips and hands upon the sacred book, while great waves of jostling people swirl around.'

The Byzantines, skilled as they were in the science of optics, tried many devices in order to vary and increase the play of light upon brilliant colours. So, naturally enough, Paul, apart from his interest in the windows of the church, devoted minute attention to the artificial lighting which 'illumined the temple as with some midnight sun'. From the base of the dome, chains of brass, presumably attached to projecting arms, swept down to support a circle of metal equipped with flat silver discs. These discs were pierced to hold glass vessels filled with oil which burned like a bright candle. Alternating with the silver discs were crosses bored through with holes of a size adequate to hold similar lights, in a 'circling chorus'. Within this splendid candelabrum was hung a smaller 'crown with lightbearing rim' and, higher up, a great silver disc which acted as a reflector so that 'night was compelled to flee'. Apart from all this, lights of different kinds were dotted about in the greatest profusion. Single lamps, set in vessels of silver, were ranged along the aisles while others 'sweetly flashed in their airy courses' from twisted chains. The beam of the chancel screen was decorated with clusters of lights built up in ever-widening circles until they resembled fir trees flanking the central cross. Though Justinian's fittings have all disappeared, S. Sophia is still illuminated by a vast number of small lamps giving an effect of the greatest charm and brilliance. Paul therefore seems well justified in his claim that the lamps not only heartened all beholders but acted as a beacon by which the ship's captain sailing up the Hellespont might direct his course. Practical convenience was allied to mystic meaning, and the 'divine light' of S. Sophia could not only guide the merchant at night but also suggest to him 'the gracious help of the living God'.[10]

Paul dismisses the mosaics of S. Sophia in a few lines, and it appears that all the figures which came to take a prominent place in the decorative scheme were set in place after Justinian's day. For it would not be at all in character for Paul to omit from his description so remarkable a feature in the building which, to him as to many of his contemporaries, seemed to be without rival and of superhuman grandeur. The language of the poet-bishop Corippus[11] may sound fulsome but it is typical of the period:

Let discussion of Solomon's Temple now fall into silence, and let the wonders of the world yield pride of place. There are two shrines, founded under the guidance of God, which imitate the glories of Heaven: the sacred Temple and the splendid building of the new shrine of Wisdom. Here is the royal house, here is the House of God.

It may be noted, however, as a commentary on changes in artistic fashion, that the historian Edward Gibbon was less approving, remarking that 'the eye of the beholder is disappointed by an irregular prospect of half domes and shelving roofs'.

Justinian, a man of demonic energy and boundless ambition, was the true successor of Constantine in regarding himself as the 'equal of the Apostles' and in looking on Church and State as the two parts, closely interwoven, of the one Power ordained by God. His readiness to spend lavishly, as a token of power, fortunately occurred at a period when capable craftsmanship was allied to artistic sensibility. Even such utilitarian structures as water cisterns possess the graceful lines which inevitably arise from the touch of a master hand and, in particular, the vast cistern of Bin-bir Direk, the 'Thousand and One Columns', shows

something of the facility of invention and technical skill which distinguishes S. Sophia. On this site slim columns, set in two stages connected by nothing more robust than tie-beams, and crowned by impost capitals of a simple type, support the groined vaults which, though massive, are made lighter by the use of flattened bricks in place of stone.

On the evidence of the ancient records, however, it was the tangle of structures comprising the Palace of the Emperors that exhibited, naturally enough, the fuller riches of a symbolic architecture that had much in common with the churches of the period. Above all, the entrance-porch known as the Chalke, or House of Bronze, was admired as a masterpiece of architectural design and luxurious ornament. Entirely rebuilt by Justinian after the fire of 532, though along lines suggested by Constantine's earlier and simpler porch-way, it is described with much enthusiasm by Procopius.[12] His words imply a large rectangular hall surmounted by a dome upheld by four arches springing from four colossal piers built against the east and west walls, while the thrust was lessened by means of barrel vaults running along the north and south sides. The mosaics which encrusted the dome were a secular variant of those church mosaics depicting Christ and the Apostles victorious over the powers of evil. They exhibited conquests won for the emperor by his general, Belisarius, and the central position was occupied by Justinian and Theodora themselves receiving in solemn triumph the captive 'King of the Vandals and King of the Goths'. 'Round about', as Procopius records the scene,

stands the Roman Senate, all in festal mood. This spirit is expressed by the cubes of the mosaic, which by their colours depict exultation on every countenance. So they rejoice and smile as they bestow on the Emperor honours equal to those of God, because of the splendour of his achievements.

Thus, at the centre of the dome which represents the overarching canopy of Heaven is set not Christ but the anointed emperor, who was his counterpart here on earth.

Justinian supplied Constantinople with a very large number of churches, some built in the form of a basilica hall, others on the central plan, but nearly all have completely or in great part disappeared. The famous Church of the Holy Apostles, for example, was destroyed by the Turks to make way for a mosque,

123. Constantinople, S. Sophia: interior of east end.

124. Constantinople, SS. Sergius and Bacchus: capitals supporting the architrave.

but Procopius describes it as a cross-shaped building with an aisle, or ambulatory, marked by columns in two rows, first at ground level and then constituting the galleries above. The sanctuary, 'which may not be entered except by those who celebrate the mysteries', occupied the crossing. Above this rose a circular drum, pierced by windows, and a dome 'resembling that of the Church of Sophia, though inferior to it in size'. Each of the four arms of the cross was likewise surmounted by a dome which, however, lacked the windows beneath it. So Procopius says. But what seems to be a picture of the church in the tenth-century manuscript of Basil's *Menologion*[13] shows similar windows in all five drums, and this evidence is borne out by two twelfth-century manuscripts.[14]

The influence of this Church of the Apostles was widespread. Not only St Mark's in Venice, but buildings as far away as the twelfth-century cathedral of St Front at Périgueux reproduce the form of a Greek cross bedecked by five great cupolas. But in Justinian's own time the pattern was most closely followed in the remodelled church erected by Theodora and himself over the tomb of St John at Ephesus. All is now fragmentary, but the outline of the walls is easily

traced and attempts are being made to reconstruct parts of the building.

Here massive piers divided the body of the church into six nearly equal compartments, each surmounted by a dome. The sanctuary occupied the square at the crossing; this was the same size and shape as the projecting transept arms and as the square, forming the head of the cross, which framed clergy seats and sacristy. The two closely similar rectangles which composed the nave were slightly compressed to allow space for the passageway separating nave from sanctuary, so that the two domes thereby became elliptical rather than perfectly round as were the other four. The flowing rhythms of S. Sophia thus gave place to an imposing but formal cross-shape which could be analysed as six repeated units set one against the other.

Notable among the remnants of Constantinople's sixth-century churches, St Polyeuctus, built by the princess Juliana Anicia, who preceded Justinian, offers vast but jumbled foundations and some carved stones. The most famous of these is the pier now standing hard by St Mark's, Venice, on which Classical and Persian patterns combine. St Irene, though much altered in the eighth century, retains some of the walling that characterizes many of Justinian's buildings, in which bands consisting of about five courses of ashlar blocks alternate with layers of brick. But the church of the military saints, Sergius and Bacchus, has more to show. Since it was completed, perhaps by Anthemius of Tralles, at the very beginning of Justinian's reign, this church may be seen as an early essay in the ambitious style of S. Sophia, which in many respects it closely resembles. Built mainly of brick, but with thin bands of ashlar designed to vary the monotony and strengthen the walls, SS. Sergius and Bacchus is oblong in plan, measuring 28.5 metres by 25.5, with a semicircular apse at the east end. The site chosen was a difficult one, squeezed between the Hormisdas Palace and a basilican church with which it shared a long, colonnaded narthex.[15] SS. Sergius and Bacchus was thus built close to the heart of imperial power; means of access were provided from it not only to the neighbouring church of St Peter and St Paul but to the Palace itself. The rectangular body of the church was converted on the inside to form an octagon based on vast piers joined together, as in S. Sophia, by straight lines alternating with curved recesses. This pattern was continued, above the entablature, to form the arcade of the galleries, while, to crown all, rose the drum of the massive but low-pitched dome made up of sixteen panels, alternately flat and concave, with windows set in the straight panels. The purpose of the nave recesses, attractive though they may be in producing subtle and unexpected vistas, is at least in part to provide buttressing for the dome; in this respect they are the more sophisticated counterpart of the semicircles enclosed by the corners of the square in

such earlier Syrian churches as Bosra and Ezra. By contrast with S. Sophia, a narrow ambulatory rather than two bold aisles here encloses the central octagon, and the whole effect, even allowing for variations in the floor level, is stumpy and lacks the flowing, rhythmical lines of the cathedral. Nevertheless the carving of both capitals and architrave is of the highest elegance (fig. 124); bands of egg and dart pattern contrast with leaf tracery, of acanthus or swirling tendrils, that stands out with triumphant clarity against the black of the deeply cut background. The church of Sergius and Bacchus, in the mathematical exactness of its structure, in its abundance of arches and vaults and in its plain exterior contrasting with the richness and abstract patterns of the decoration within, represents a development from earlier, classic models that runs parallel with that of S. Vitale at Ravenna.

The recently (1939) discovered church of St Euphemia deserves mention here as illustrating the close structural connexion that exists between secular and ecclesiastical building. What had been originally planned as a hexagonal triclinium, or dining hall, was converted for use as a church at some point in the sixth century. The layout of the chancel closely suggests that of the earlier St John Studios. There are three entrances, one in front and one at each side; the central entry is connected with the pulpit by means of the raised *solea*. Traces exist not only of the post-holes for the altar canopy but also of the 'synthronon'—six narrow benches, with a wider section at the top, to provide steps and appropriate seating for the clergy. A delicate colonette[16] and fragments of glass inlaid in marble suggest a lavish scheme of decoration.

SYRIA

The exuberant vitality of Justinian caused the range of his building enterprises to spread throughout the Empire. The style set by the workshops of Constantinople was adapted to local influences which in their turn exerted a wide authority. Thus, features which might seem to reflect the natural tendencies of Syria or Egypt turn up in Italy also, while Roman forms reverse the trend, appearing in the Middle East. Most of these sixth-century buildings were destroyed by hostile invaders or by the piety of later generations who

sought to enlarge and develop them, so that it is often only the ground-plans together with fragmentary pieces of wall that have been disclosed by recent excavation.

Some of the best-preserved remains occur in the frontier outposts established to guard remote corners of the Empire. One such is Andarin, in central Syria. Though now in ruins, the building clearly followed the traditional lines, set by Qalb Louzeh, of a basilica with nave, aisles, a narthex in three compartments, and

125. Qasr ibn Wardan: west front of the church.

126. Mount Sinai: the fortified complex of buildings around the monastery.

apse. But Andarin, to which the date 528 may be assigned, is rather more squat than its predecessors, and the use of brick in the construction of the apse vault suggests that one of Justinian's military architects had imported ideas and material from Constantinople.

At Qasr ibn Wardan the remains are far more substantial (fig.125). Here was a military stronghold, with barracks, church and governor's palace all showing the typically Byzantine method of construction, in which bands of stone reinforce walls made with long, thin bricks laid in a careful and regular manner. Moreover, the plan of the church suggests that S. Sophia, rather than some Syrian prototype, served as inspiration.The short, compact nave was crowned with a dome, buttressed by massive corner piers between which, at all four sides, a large arch extended. Beneath this arch, to north and south, are included the two columns and triple arcade which mark off the nave from the aisles, this same formula being repeated in the galleries above. The capitals are in two parts, a circular band of acanthus leaves surmounted by a square head with animals decorating the corners and, here again, the influence of Constantinople seems dominant. The narthex presents a bold front, with three prominent doorways and a tower containing the staircase which leads to the galleries, but the barrel vault of its roof is squeezed into a narrow span as is the similar roof of the chancel in front of the semicircular apse. Two side chambers, entered from the aisles, flank the apse and enable the east end to take on a rectangular form. This feature is Syrian enough, but it looks as though workmen from Constantinople accompanied the soldiers and employed a technique which was, in general, metropolitan rather than local.

MOUNT SINAI

Justinian's efforts at establishing secure government and the imperial faith extended even as far as the outpost fortress of Mount Sinai 'in a barren land, unwatered and producing neither crops nor any useful thing'.[17] Here vast walls of red granite, flanked by towers and strengthened by buttresses, mark out a protecting rectangle within which is contained a jumble of buildings of varying date (fig. 126). But the great monastic church, situated in the middle of the enclosure, belongs at least in part to Justinian's own day. The plan is that of a straightforward basilica. Thus first comes the narthex, with an inscription over the entrance in the fashion of Syrian churches of the fifth or sixth century: 'This is the gate of the Lord: the just shall come in thereby.' Opposite the inner door runs a quotation of words spoken to Moses on Sinai's height: 'I am the God of thy fathers, the God of Abraham, the God of Isaac and the God of Jacob.'[18] The columns separating nave from aisles seem to be original. Their granite capitals, hard and awkward to carve, are yet worked somewhat roughly with crosses, sheep trampling on serpents, date palms and other emblems as well as rams' horns at the corners. Some of the roof beams, made of cypress, bear inscriptions such as 'For the commemoration and eternal rest of our late empress Theodora' which point to a date shortly after Theodora's death in 548 AD. The apse is equipped with side-chapels. Eastwards lies a low, semicircular sanctuary known as the Chapel of the Burning Bush, apparently part of a more primitive shrine. The walls of the church were plated with marble slabs, in the fashion of S. Sophia, but there was here no hesitation about including Biblical scenes, for the ceiling of the apse is decorated with a splendid mosaic of the Transfiguration. Christ, alone supplied with a halo, dominates the scene, but his pointed beard and graceful air of early manhood indicate a period before it became conventional to depict him as a figure stern, mature and remote. He is enclosed within an aureole of brilliant colour, the 'bright cloud' of the Gospel, and at either side stand Moses and Elijah, each with a long white beard and hand raised in a gesture of prophetic declamation. Meanwhile the apostles express their surprise in stagey, contorted attitudes: James and John kneel, while Peter grovels beneath Christ's feet. The whole composition is framed with a line of circular medallions that contain portrait heads of apostles, prophets and other witnesses to the transfigured Lord, who is thought of as fulfilling the Old Law, given at Sinai, by the manifestation of his royal glory on Mount Tabor. One or two local figures, Bishop Leontius among them, are included as though to proclaim that the Church, continuing down the ages, is the appointed guardian of these divine mysteries. By contrast with the formal, symbolic illustration of the Transfiguration in S. Apollinare in Classe, Ravenna, the Sinai example offers the realism, the boldly outlined figures, the stiffly sinuous curves and the vague yet resplendent background that mark the art of sixth-century Constantinople.

PAROS

Sixth-century architects seem to have taken keen pleasure in trying out as many combinations as possible of the two standard models, the basilica with aisles and galleries but no transept and the cross-shaped building surmounted by a central dome. One such example of imagination and enterprise is offered by the finest church of the Greek islands, the Church of the Hundred Gates[19] at Paros. A traveller, Niketas Magister, who visited it in the year 902 described it, though damaged by Arab raiders, as 'symmetrically built' and 'supported on every side by columns of marble'—the variety known as cipollino, 'little onion' —while the walls also were made chiefly of marble so skilfully cut that it resembled 'hangings of linen stuff'. A complication at Paros is that the diminutive church of St Nicholas has been incorporated into the main structure, being attached to its north transept, with a much smaller diaconicon serving as counterweight on the south side. The main church is cross-shaped, with nave and chancel longer than the transepts. The nave aisles, with galleries above, continue round the transepts which thus are drawn freely into the rhythm of the building. The central portion of the nave, from which the transepts spring, is roofed with a dome, on pendentives and supported by four stout pillars; transepts, aisles and galleries alike are equipped with barrel vaults. The lasting influence of Constantine's Church of the Holy Apostles is apparent. At Paros, however, the cross-arms are covered not by domes but by roofs with a double slope, and the elongated nave and chancel reflect the straightforward basilican style. In the apse is the synthronon, seven ranges of semi-circular marble steps on which the clergy sat. The bishop's throne rises up in the centre; at either side of it are single seats, elevated above the rest of the benches but not as high as the throne.[20]

A ciborium, or altar canopy, in the sanctuary is remarkable for this period if not unique. Constructed as a square, it has four corner-columns, roughly worked in a bluish veined marble apparently taken over from some less distinguished structure but with finely-carved capitals of grey unpolished marble supporting thin marble slabs, which make up a curved lunette on each side. Above all this rises a marble dome, now almost wholly restored.

The baptistery is tacked on to the south aisle and transept of the church. A cross-shaped font, made of Parian marble, appears at the east end of this subsidiary building, which is elaborately arranged as a nave with aisles, apse and central dome. The baptistery, however, seems to be an addition, in keeping with the work of Justinian's time but somewhat later in date.

TSARICHIN GRAD

On the mainland of Greece, the newly-excavated site at Philippi offers examples of the varied types of building that were adapted to the needs of Christian worship. Other instances occur in the remote districts that lie further north; among them is Tsarichin Grad, which may have been Justinian's birthplace and was certainly a key-point in the defence system which that emperor established against the inroads of Avars and Slavs. Round about the city lay a number of unpretentious churches designed for use by local congregations or by the frontier troops. Many of the soldiers were drawn from Anatolia, and it is not entirely fanciful to perceive Anatolian architectural features, such as the towered portico and the single, projecting apse, translated here from stone into brickwork. The buildings, often of very modest size, may take the form of a nave alone or of an aisled basilica. But cross-shaped buildings also were favoured, and these of two main types. One was a straightforward cross with short, dumpy arms to north and south. The other was

shaped as a trefoil, with a projecting apse usually
semicircular on the inside but angled on the outer face.
There was at first nothing peculiarly Christian about
such an arrangement. It was used as one of the more
elaborate forms of pagan tomb structure both in Italy
and in Syria, and it may have owed a certain prestige
to the use of the trefoil shape in fashioning the throne-
room of eastern palaces. More certain is the influence
of the trefoil shrines of Palestine that marked events in
the life of Christ, particularly since the doctrine of the
Trinity provided subtle overtones.

The acropolis of Tsarichin Grad, though strongly
fortified, seems to have been an ecclesiastical rather
than a military centre; it is at any rate abundantly
supplied with church buildings. The cathedral (fig.
127), preceded by an elaborate pattern of porches,
courtyard and ambulatories, was a basilica of conventional type, rhythmically arranged with a nave just
over double the width of each aisle, from which it is
separated by a range of four columns and a pilaster. At
the east end came a large apse with semicircular head.
Seats for the clergy were fixed to the north and south
walls of the apse as part of what seems to have been a
very open and unencumbered layout of the sanctuary,
while a matching pair of sacristies, also apsidal, was
approached one from each aisle. As at Ravenna, walls
were made of wide, flat bricks set in thick layers of
mortar, but the capitals, carved in a vaguely Ionic
fashion with acanthus decoration, reflect the taste,
crudely expressed, of Constantinople.

Attached to the north of the cathedral was a range of
administrative buildings or residences. On the south
side lay a martyr–shrine entered by way of a slim
narthex. Square on the outside, this shrine possesses a
circular inner room extended by four apses to make up
a cross shape; set by itself in each corner of the square
is a small rectangular compartment. Against the
curved walls of the central room stand the four piers
which at one time upheld a cupola; beneath this a
shallow, cross-shaped depression marks the place
where a martyr-relic was venerated. The quatrefoil
martyr-shrine at Tsarichin Grad, attached to the
cathedral church yet standing separately, is the
refined version of an arrangement which gained wide
currency. Excavations at Corinth have unearthed a
straightforward basilica with a martyr-chapel directly
annexed to the south aisle. This is, in effect, three-
quarters of the Tsarichin pattern. Even more closely

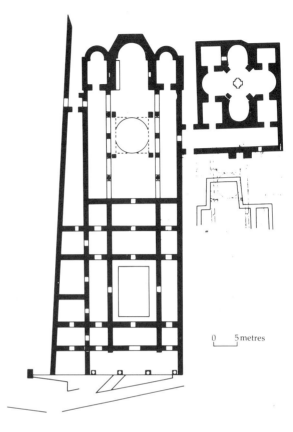

127. Tsarichin Grad. Cathedral with martyr-shrine
annexed: ground-plan. Compare figure 76.

akin is the martyrium built, partly within, partly projecting from, the aisle at Tébessa, for there the three
sides of the square include the three apsidal arms of
the cross together with rectangular sacristies which
occupy the corner spaces. The pattern of the circle,
inscribed within a square and having four cross-arms
that terminate in apses while rectangular chambers
occupy the corners of the square, extended its range as
far eastward as Armenia.[21]

Of the other churches on the acropolis at Tsarichin
Grad one, a modest basilica, is remarkable in that it has
a crypt extending beneath the entire structure and
presumably intended as a burial-place for citizens of
note. The 'South Church' is a basilica with projecting
transepts and a single apse shaped as a horseshoe but
angled on the outside. Here again the clergy seats back
onto the wall of the apse while in front of it are set the
bases of four pillars that once upheld the canopy over
the altar. A few capitals exist of Ionic type surmounted
by an impost block. Most of these imposts are stamped
with a cross, but one bears a monogram which may
indicate the name Justinian without reference to
Theodora, in which case a date within the period 548–
65 may be accepted for the building. But the chief
interest of the South Church lies in its mosaic floor,
where the differing schemes of mosaic accord with the
importance of the various parts of the church. There is,
however, little of specifically Christian import. A
shepherd, leaning on his staff and surveying his
sheep, might be intended to represent the Good
Shepherd, as in the early floor mosaic at Aquileia, but
he is shown in all simplicity and without a halo, so that
the scene could be interpreted simply as an element in
a pastoral landscape.

The church at Konjuh, to the south of Tsarichin
Grad, not only provides another example of a parish
church adopting the form of a martyr-shrine, but also
seems to indicate a readiness, in sixth-century
Macedonia and beyond, to accept influences widely
drawn from both East and West. Here occurs the
conventional narthex, ending in side chambers; from
it entry is made by three doorways into a horseshoe
aisle which encloses a circular, domed nave. The bema
is separated from the nave by a screen consisting of
stone slabs set between slim pillars. One of these is
finely carved with the motif of a bird pecking at
grapes, as on the sarcophagus of Bishop Theodore at
S. Apollinare in Classe.

THE ADRIATIC COAST

Further west, apart from the cemeteries and churches
of Salona,[22] remains are not very abundant along the
Adriatic coast, but recent excavation has disclosed a
fair number of what prove usually to be straightforward basilicas.[23] At Srima, near Sibenik, occurs a
pair of churches, one rather larger than the other. Each
consists of a rectangular nave, projecting semicircular
apse, long narthex that serves both buildings, and an
elaborate array of ancillary rooms between the two
churches and at each side. The church of St Thomas at
Zadar, apparently started as a Roman courtroom, was
transformed in the fifth century to become a three-
aisled basilica with, again, a semicircular apse. At
Sepen, near the north point of the island of Krk, stand
the walls, strengthened by pilaster buttresses, which
clearly mark out a substantial cross-shaped church,
this time having the apse concealed within a rectangle.

Near the top of the gulf, where lie the cities of Pola,
Parenzo and Grado, there is much more to be seen. At
Pola the cathedral, though now much restored, is in its
essentials a fifth-century basilica of standard type,
with two aisles extending to a squared-off east end.
The clergy seats behind the altar were arranged as a
raised, internal apse, leaving, eastward of them, a
rectangular hall probably intended for the reception of
relics. The notable feature is the triumphal arch,
springing from columns that back onto heavy pilasters
in the manner of S. Paolo fuori le mure in Rome. The
desire to provide adequate, indeed splendid, martyr-
shrines has led to a rich embellishment of the plain
basilica.

The cathedral at Parenzo has in large measure
retained its ancient form and decoration. Smaller than
the masterpieces of Ravenna, it rivals them in beauty
and is more complete, retaining many of the subsidiary buildings. Four stages have been traced in its
evolution. First there was the 'chapel of St Maurus',
probably part of the house in which Maurus, the first
bishop, had lived. When Constantine's victories
brought peace to the Church, this chapel was super-

128. Parenzo: interior of the Cathedral.

seded by a small basilica having a hall on the north side for the instruction of catechumens and, on the south, a martyr-shrine containing a mosaic of the symbolic Fish. Early in the fifth century the church was completely rebuilt as a basilica in the form of a long rectangle. On the foundations of this structure Bishop Euphrasius erected the present building about 540 AD. To the west lay a small courtyard enclosed by an ambulatory with three arches on each side; the marble columns here, topped with the basket-shaped capitals of Ravenna type, were spoils from some local building. Still further to the west an octagonal baptistery was set, and, to the north, a large structure with a dumpy nave, bold apse and apsidal endings to the two aisles. This has an ecclesiastical look about it, but is in fact the bishop's palace; the audience hall reveals the similarity in design which could exist between a large domestic or official building and a church. The façade of the church itself was originally ablaze with mosaic of which only the lower part remains, the seven candlesticks for the Seven Churches of the Apocalypse standing out prominently. Three marble doorways give access to the nave, where decoration is of the most sumptuous nature (fig. 128). Columns made of

marble from the imperial quarries at Proconnesus separate nave and aisles. The capitals are richly varied, the two most common forms being Corinthian with a strongly-marked abacus and a double row of acanthus below and, secondly, the type of inverted pyramid found in S. Vitale, the faces deeply drilled to give a delicate pattern of leaves and tendrils. The nave arches of the north side retain on their under-surface a decoration of stucco, gracefully moulded in geometric patterns with accompanying birds and flowers. It was at the east end of the church that Bishop Euphrasius introduced his major changes. He added a spacious apse, polygonal outside and circular within, lit by four windows. At the centre of this apse was a pillar against which the bishop's throne was set below a panel of marble and mother-of-pearl serving as the background for a cross of gold. Around the rest of the apse ran the tier of clergy seats, with, above them, a dado made up of porphyry and other marbles, glass and mother-of-pearl. Higher up again, between and beyond the windows, extends the brilliant mosaic which contrasts so happily with the restrained dignity of the architecture. Apart from saints and donors, the theme chosen is the Infancy narrative with which St

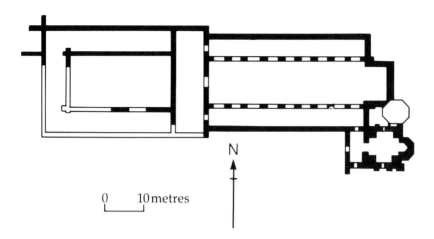

N

0   10 metres

129. Vicenza, Church of SS. Felix and Fortunatus: ground-plan.

Luke's Gospel begins. Zacharias and John the Baptist appear together with the angel who foretold John's birth. To these figures are added panels showing the Annunciation and Visitation; in the semi-dome, the Virgin, seated on her throne holds the Christ-child as he gives a blessing to the worshippers. From the clouds above, the hand of God appears bestowing a triumphal wreath. Parenzo here seems to offer the oldest example of the Mother of God occupying the place of honour hitherto assigned to the figure of Christ in majesty. But her close association with her Son in the work of redemption had been stressed by St Augustine, among others, and the figure of the Mother of God with the Child on her knee and attended by guardian angels occurs not only in the nave mosaics of S. Apollinare Nuovo but also in the apse of the slightly later church of Panagia Kanakaria at Lynthrankomi in Cyprus.[24] The long, slim aisles of the church at Parenzo end in neat semicircular apses, so that the whole ground-plan allows of comparison with such churches of Asia Minor as St Thecla at Meriamlik, built seventy years earlier. Attached to the north aisle is an independent building, of trefoil shape with entry porch, conventional enough as a martyr-shrine but perhaps in this case prepared by Euphrasius as his mausoleum. Here too the remains of floor mosaics testify to a wealth of decoration designed to enrich a building of graceful design but unpretentious local workmanship.

A little further north the city of Grado, to which the bishopric of Aquileia was transferred at the time of the Lombard invasions, preserves a remarkable group of sixth-century buildings. The cathedral, built by Bishop Elias about 575 AD, occupies the site of a small, apsidal basilica the foundations of which have been discovered roughly 1.6 metres below the floor which Elias constructed. The brick exterior has the look of a Ravenna church, with shallow buttresses framing the regular line of clerestory windows. The nave is separated from the narrow aisles by columns of uneven thickness and colour, most, if not all, being spoils taken from older buildings in Aquileia. The capitals also vary in shape and size. Some are clearly re-used, while others, of Corinthian type with deeply-cut acanthus leaves or 'Byzantine cubes' with leaves and crosses carved on the face, date from the time of Elias. Variation of this kind contrasts with the perfect symmetry of the rounded arches. The nave floor, 42 metres long, is carpeted with mosaic not particularly bright in colour but displaying an ingenious variety of geometric designs, while the central section, with its continuously undulating lines, suggests the flow of waters lapping the sea-girt city. Plain and lofty walls are panelled off by flattened buttresses similar in form to those which define the exterior while all is topped by a low-slung roof with tie-beams and exposed rafters. The pattern of the east end, as devised by Elias, is a variant of the scheme displayed at Tsarichin Grad and many another place: a bold apse, polygonal on the outside but semicircular within, is flanked by two side chambers. At Grado, however, these are not a matching pair. The sacristy on the south has the common shape of a rectangle ending in a tiny apse, but on the north side symmetry has been sacrificed in order to provide two burial-halls, one more or less rectangular, the other a trefoil. The south side has an additional annexe, rather casually tacked on, which seems to have been the *salutatorium*, or reception hall, where the bishop interviewed visitors. Standing very close to the north-east corner of the Cathedral, but independent of it, is the octagonal baptistry, constructed in brick with roofing of tiles arranged in eight panels.

Another building at Grado that dates from the early Christian era is the church of St Mary, a miniature basilica measuring 16 metres by 11. The form of construction is that of Elias' time, with flattened buttresses inside as well as out, semicircular arches ranged close together, and both columns and capitals carelessly assorted as regards material, size and style. The apse and the two minute sacristies which flank it do not protrude but are squeezed within the straight eastern wall, in a manner suggesting that here too influences from Asia Minor found ready acceptance on the shores of the Adriatic within the wide-ranging scheme of a common Mediterranean culture. An older church, belonging to the first half of the fifth century, seems to have been burnt down; Elias, using some of the earlier materials, rebuilt it on a level four feet higher than before. Some parts of the original church have been revealed once more, and include the presbytery with its clergy bench, a bishop's seat in the middle, and pavement taking the form of a repeated wheel pattern in a mosaic of marble and stone. A rare feature, at this period, is the chancel-screen,[25] which railed off the sanctuary from the rest of the church. Such things had not yet acquired the solid, enclosed look of an iconostasis. Approached by two steps, the screen consists of an engraved panel at either side of the entrance, together with four thin columns, one at each end of the panels. The columns, topped by small cushion capitals, support the *regula*, a wooden beam with moulded upper edge from which curtains might be hung and which, at a later stage of development, was used as a platform for portrait busts or statues.

NORTHERN ITALY

Grado has the privilege, shared with Ravenna, of presenting its early Christian buildings still used and in what is substantially their original form. Elsewhere in northern Italy churches of the same period exist mainly as fragments concealed beneath later reconstructions. But enough remains to indicate that as, in the fourth century, the imperial administration was transferred from Rome to Milan, much in the way of financial resources and artistic vigour also moved northwards to the neighbourhood of Milan and the district extending eastwards from that city to Aquileia.

At Vicenza, for example, the present cathedral stands more or less on the lines of the fifth-century basilica[26] of St Felix and St Fortunatus, which was in large measure destroyed by the Hungarians in 899 AD. The bases of the columns, however, remain along with much of the walling, so that the original plan can be made out exactly (fig. 129). Preceded by a substantial courtyard and entered by way of a conventional narthex, the slender and graceful building had nine arches on each side leading into aisles which measure exactly half the width of the nave. The walls were made of brick bedded in thick mortar and firmly based on a foundation of cement. The sanctuary at the east end protruded beyond the aisles but in a rectangular rather than rounded form. Attached to the south-east corner of the church is a building, now used as the sacristy, which has all the characteristics of a reliquary-shrine. Entered by way of a rectangular ante-room roofed with a barrel vault in brick, the chapel consists

130. Naples, S. Giorgio Maggiore: apse, with central doorway.

of two parts—a cross-shaped nave with cupola above it, and an apse, octagonal outside and circular within, of which each outer face is emphasized by a flattened buttress.

The martyrium at Vicenza seems to have been added about 500 AD, and the same date may be assigned to the chapel of St Prosdocimus, connected by a passageway with the vast Renaissance church of St Justina, at Padua. This chapel, now much transformed by restoration and lined with grey marble, was originally cross-shaped with four shallow arms. The central space was covered by a dome, masked on the outside by a squared drum of large bricks, and strengthened within by the help of four corner squinches. Light was given by a round-headed window set in the middle of each face of the cross. A fifth-century marble plaque in the chapel shows the bust of a youthful Prosdocimus contained in a circle between two palm trees denoting Heaven.

Verona, close neighbour to Padua, gives evidence of much activity in church-building towards the end of the fifth century. Northward of the present cathedral, the footings of the ancient cathedral have been discovered and show it to have been of conventional North Italian type, with a nave separated from aisles by columns set on bases. The chancel was apparently raised, and extended well down the nave by means of its passage to the reading-desk.

The Church of the Apostles, itself almost completely remodelled, repeats the fashion—set at S. Ambrogio, Milan, at Vicenza, Padua and elsewhere—of having a martyr-chapel attached to the south-east corner. This, the shrine of St Tosca and St Teuteria, is shaped as a cross with four almost equal arms, while the central portion rises as a tower with groined vault. Walls are made of pebble squeezed between courses of brick, and for windows there are loopholes with straight sides and curved top in the lower part and, in the tower, thin slit-like loopholes surmounted by a little cross-beam. The structure as a whole once more shows close connection with the Mausoleum of Galla Placidia, at Ravenna.

Verona's third ancient building is the church of S. Stefano, now returned, by the removal of plaster and other débris, to something like its original condition. The shape is a simple one: a large nave, 36 metres long by 11 metres wide, ends in a small transept with rectangular arms, beyond which extends an apse, semicircular inside but with straight arms and a flattened curve outside. Here again the walls are made up of brick and pebbles arranged in courses and bedded in thick layers of mortar. Such ancient capitals as remain inside the church are of a simplified Corinthian style, rather roughly executed and probably, in accordance with a common practice, taken from a disused building elsewhere. S. Stefano is, therefore, a church constructed in the shape of a long cross.

The sites of other ancient churches in northern Italy have been so worked over and transformed by later building that the shape of the original structure can hardly be discerned. At Rimini (St Andrew) it seems to have been a Greek cross, at Vercelli (S. Trinitá) a wide nave ending in a trefoil sanctuary after the fashion of the Red Monastery at Sohag, at Turin a basilican nave and aisles rising up from a firm floor of beaten brick and cement. At Como the church had the form of a long cross, and a very similar pattern, disclosed by recent excavation, is apparent in the fifth-century church of St Laurence at Aosta.[27] Cluttered as this is by a variety of tombs, it clearly shows in outline a Latin cross with unequal arms, each ending in an apse. The needs of worship, in this part of the world, were thus met by a number of variants on a simple and practical theme, with the influence of St Ambrose's Church of the Apostles seldom far away.

SOUTHERN ITALY

In southern Italy such remains as have been discovered tell the same story of capacity to adopt and adapt a wide range of differing forms. The church of St Saturninus at Cagliari (Sardinia) is of the cross type, four arms being attached to a central square roofed over with a cupola. At Brindisi, S. Giovanni al Sepolcro is a rotunda, built rather roughly on the pattern of a very early substructure. Here the frequent practice is followed of casually re-using capitals, both Corinthian and cubical, taken from other buildings. Several churches at Naples, though almost entirely reconstructed, preserve an apse of fifth-century date or thereabouts, which shows a local peculiarity in that the wall is pierced by one or more arcades (fig. 130). This type of apse could not have been used for seating the clergy. Adopted at S. Gennaro as a passageway that led to the graveyard, it continued in fashion as a decorative feature opening, in the case of S. Giorgio, onto a street. A striking example of early work surviving within a medieval frame occurs at the church of S. Restituta. Here, beneath the Angevin building, a primitive basilica has been traced but nothing remains above ground excepting twenty-seven majestic columns in grey marble or granite with their marble bases and capitals. These columns, perhaps originally spoils from an earlier temple of Apollo which stood on the site, were, with a rare sense of fitness and style, left standing almost in their original position and thus provide a classical element in an otherwise Gothic church. The baptistery,[28] square with a small dome, is set alongside the end of the right aisle. It is held to be the earliest example in Italy of this type of structure, and influences from North Africa have been detected.

NOTES

1. Procopius, *Buildings* I.i.24. Procopius says of Anthemius that he excelled in the art of 'mechanike'. But the word implies all that an architect is responsible for, and is used in a half-depreciatory sense to show that the emperor exercised supreme control. The standard text of Procopius is that of L. Haury (Teubner, 1905). This text is used by H. B. Dewing (Loeb, 1914–   ).

2. Paulus Silentiarius, *Ecphrasis*, ed. P. Friedländer (Teubner, 1912), 198.

3. *Ibid.*, 354.

4. *Ibid.*, 374.

5. *Ibid.*, 450.

6. *Ibid.*, 591.

7. *Ibid.*, 658.

8. *In baptismum Christi, PG* 46.581.

9. The word *ciborium* seems to be derived from the name for the hollow seed-pod of a species of Egyptian waterlily, but it appealed to some of the early Fathers of the Church because of its resemblance to *cibolus*, an ark, which recalls the Ark of Salvation.

10. *Ecphrasis* 920.

11. *In praise of Justin* iv.283.

12. *Buildings* I.x.10–20.

13. Vatican Gr. 1613.

14. Vatican Gr. 1162 and Paris Gr. 1208.

15. Procopius, *Buildings* I.iv.3. A graceful Turkish portico has now taken its place.

16. Now in the Archaeological Museum at Istanbul. R. Naumann and H. Belting, *Die Euphemia-Kirche am Hippodrom zu Istanbul* (Berlin, 1966), followed by T. F. Matthews, *The early Churches of Constantinople* (Pennsylvania, 1971).

17. Procopius, *Buildings* V.viii.

18. Exodus 3.6.

19. The name is a mistaken version of 'The Church at the foot of the Tower'.

20. The church has been subjected to several restorations, including a drastic one as recently as 1962. But the main structure of the Great Church dates from about 550 AD. The church of St Nicholas is some seventy years older. See G. Orlandos in *Studi* 26 (1965).

21. See p. 131.

22. See p. 92.

23. Described by N. Cambi and by A. Sonje in *ACIAC* IX (1975). To these must be added a group of small triconch churches, such as Pridraga, near Zadar. N. Cambi in *ACIAC* x.

24. At Lynthrankomi the place of the guardian angels is taken by a mandorla of glory.

25. The panels belong to the fifth century, the columns (restored) to the sixth.

26. This was itself built on the site of what appears to be an earlier funeral hall.

27. C. Bonnet in *ACIAC* IX (1975).

28. See p. 210. The church itself, attached to the north side of the vast cathedral of St Januarius, has been much restored and remodelled.

12

Fonts and Baptisteries

The practice of baptism, as a sign of renewed life and accepted salvation, was characteristic of the Church from the earliest days. But, though regarded as a necessary step in the Christian life, baptism was at first administered in whatever conditions chanced to be suitable. Christ himself had been baptized while standing in the river Jordan and it was deemed perfectly appropriate that converts to the Faith should follow a similar course. At the very beginning of the Apostolic Age Philip's exposition of Scripture so impressed the treasurer of the Ethiopian Queen Candace that he exclaimed 'Behold, here is water: what doth hinder me to be baptized?' whereat both men walked into the wayside pool and the rite was carried out.[1]

In the earliest handbook of Christian liturgical practice, the so-called *Teaching of the Twelve Apostles*, which dates from about 120 AD, much freedom is allowed in the manner of conducting baptisms. The words run:

After the preliminary instruction, baptize, in the name of the Father and of the Son and of the Holy Spirit, in running water. But if you have no running water, baptize in some other water. And if cold is unsuitable, use warm water. But if neither is to hand, then pour water on the head three times in the name of the Father, Son and Holy Spirit.[2]

Similarly, when writing from Carthage seventy years later, Tertullian declared that 'it makes no difference at all whether a man is baptized in the sea or a pool, in a river or a spring, in a lake or a tub'.[3] Literary evidence of this kind serves as a comment on those first pictures of baptisms, which are to be found in the Roman catacombs. Several occur within the Cemetery of Callistus, the oldest of them being a second-century example painted over a door in the Crypt of Lucina. Here the baptizer, clothed, extends his hand towards a naked figure stepping out of the water, while the Dove hovers overhead. Not far off, in the Sacrament Chapel known as A2, a similar scene is enacted. Here the officiant, clad in a long white toga, leans over from the bank and lays his hand on the head of a boy who stands with the water just over his ankles. In the adjoining chapel, A3, a baptism is again represented by the same formula. Once more the candidate is shown as youthful and naked, standing ankle-deep in water. Meanwhile the baptizer, a much larger figure, pours water, indicated by six large strokes of dark blue colour, over the candidate's head, while the Dove flies purposefully towards the group. This picture is flanked on three sides by scenes which, as types or symbols, hint at the necessity of baptism: a man fishing, Jonah, and the paralysed man cured at the pool of Bethesda.[4] An incident of Old Testament history,[5] often used in catacomb painting as on sarcophagi to prefigure baptism, is Moses striking the rock in the wilderness of Zin whereat water gushes out upon the rebellious people. No less significant was Noah's Ark, which had been drawn into service as early as the First Epistle of Peter.[6] Indeed almost any Biblical reference to water—the Egyptians overwhelmed by the Red Sea, the Samaritan woman at the well, the hart which 'desireth the water-brooks'—could be used with effect to illustrate the sacramental power with which water might be

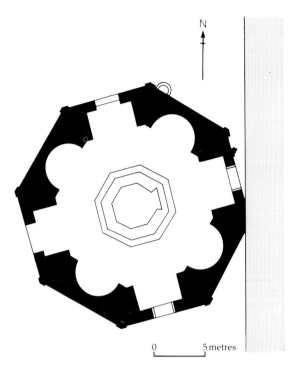

N

0   5 metres

131. Milan, baptistery underneath the Cathedral: ground-plan.

invested. The manner in which John baptized Jesus is nowhere explained, and the artists made the best of this by showing the scene in accordance with the earliest liturgical practice. It is therefore not easy to say whether the diminutive, naked figure over whose head the cleansing water is sprinkled represents, in any one instance, Christ or the Christian. Perhaps the distinction was not strongly felt; on St Paul's reasoning, the Christian was through baptism drawn into the cycle of Christ's experience.

Baptism publicly administered in some stream or pool could be inconvenient and, in times of persecution, hazardous, so that private houses soon became the natural place for such ceremonies. There was usually a fountain in the courtyard, but one of the often complex series of bathrooms well inside the building had clear advantages. 'From the parlour', writes Pliny about 100 AD,

you enter the spacious and splendid cooling-room belonging to the baths. The opposite walls of this chamber curve outwards to form semicircular basins (baptisteria).[7]

Pliny goes on to explain that these particular basins were not deep enough to swim in, and such evidence as is offered by early Acts of the Martyrs[8] indicates that quite small receptacles, like the base of a present-day shower-bath, were used. In this the candidate stood while the water 'which brings enlightenment and rebirth'[9] was poured over his head.

Though baptism in private houses continued for some time after the Peace of the Church,[10] a desire for the regular ordering of the sacrament under the bishop's control led to the construction of small buildings, placed near the churches, to which candidates might be conducted in order to receive baptism. As early as 314, when Bishop Paulinus built his cathedral at Tyre, a number of subsidiary buildings were annexed to the side of the basilica for those 'who still have need of purification and sprinkling with water and the Holy Spirit'. The description, given in a flowery sermon by Eusebius of Caesarea, is vague, but St Cyril of Jerusalem, writing in the middle of the fourth century, offers a detailed account of the baptismal rite and thus indicates the type of building needed for the ceremony. The candidates assembled in what Cyril calls the 'vestibule', or outer room, of the baptistery, where they renounced the works of the devil and made a solemn profession of faith in the

Trinity. Then, passing into the inner chamber, they removed their clothes and were anointed with consecrated oil, before being 'led to the holy pool of divine baptism', into which they descended three times, in commemoration of Christ's three-day sojourn in the grave. Thereafter followed another anointing and the putting on of white garments, appropriate to those whom God had 'covered with the robe of gladness'. There followed the Eucharist at which the candidates made their first communion, but this, Cyril implies, took place after all had proceeded from the baptistery to the church. Some such ideas probably lay behind the choice of a cross-shape, though this was more frequently adopted for the font than for the baptistery itself. A well-preserved example has been found at Emmaus. Within a square building that ends in an apse, the baptismal basin is formed as a cross with rounded arms of equal length. It is only half sunk into the ground, though the floor of the apse where the bishop stood for the service was raised to the level of the rim. On the west side two steps lead down into the font, the depth of which is little more than a metre. Another font of similar type occurs at Sbaita, in the Judaean desert, where the eastern and western arms, each containing three steps, are naturally longer than the transverse arms where the inner face of the stone is vertical.

That a cross-shape was appropriate for a place of baptism could be justified by reference to Scripture: according to St Paul, 'we were buried with Christ through baptism unto death' in anticipation of a sharing in his resurrection. Ideas of death and burial jostle therefore with the thought of baptism as 'illumination', and this duality of mood is well expressed by the Cape Bon font now kept in the Bardo Museum at Tunis. The font is shaped as a cross, lined and surrounded by mosaics which express, through such subjects as the Flood and Noah's Ark, the idea of deliverance from, or perhaps through, death, but which also repeat several times the hopeful themes of the Sun and the bright-burning candle of enlightenment.

The notion of baptism as being in some sense a solemn, almost funereal, occasion[11] made it reasonable enough that, when the civil basilica was adapted to the uses of a parish church, the domed mausoleum should serve as the type of the baptistery. However, the buildings erected to serve as baptisteries, no less

132. Vatican sarcophagus (174), showing a baptistery.

than the fonts contained in them, are far from uniform in shape. Some are squared, but the circular form and the octagon and the hexagon were commonly used, in imitation of the *frigidarium* and other chambers found in the baths of a Roman private house. The quatrefoil in various forms occasionally appears, while at Sidi Mansour and half a dozen other places in Tunisia a local fashion produced the more complex design of a central basin extended into six or eight branches, so that several candidates might be baptized at the same time in comparative privacy. Characteristically enough, certain of the early Fathers of the Church found themselves able to discover a symbolic meaning in these shapes and particularly in the octagon. The number particularly revered in the Hebrew Scriptures is seven, for after his work of Creation, God had rested 'on the seventh day'. But eight could be held to represent the New Creation, with all the vigour and hope arising from Christ's Resurrection. St Ambrose could therefore write of the octagonal baptistery that used to stand near the church of St Thecla at Milan:

Eight-sided is the lofty shrine to match its sacred use;
Eight-angled is the font to show its benefits profuse;
With such a number grace and life supplanted human guilt
And with such number must the hall of baptism be built.[12]

The building to which Ambrose refers has been identified in the recent excavations under Milan Cathedral (fig. 131). Within an octagon no more than 12 metres in diameter (19.3 metres to the outer face), the font, also octagonal, is centrally placed. Each face of the internal wall takes the form of a niche; rectangular entrance-ways alternate with semicircular dressing-rooms while the angles are marked by columns. The building appears to be a fifth-century restoration by Bishop Laurence but on precisely the lines of the Ambrosian structure which was itself, following the pattern of the emperor Diocletian's celebrated mausoleum, widely influential in the West.

The type of baptistery indicated by Cyril's references could be modified in two ways. Comparatively few of the surviving structures are equipped with an elaborate vestibule, but for such preliminaries as the recitation of the creed a convenient room of some sort was desirable. The baptistery of St Babylas at Kaoussie had attached to it a small chamber, described in one of its mosaics as *pistikon*, 'place of the creed', and some of the more elaborate fifth-century churches—at Salona, for instance, or Gerasa—possessed an even more ample arrangement of subsidiary rooms. At the same time it might be convenient to have an altar readily available without the necessity of proceeding to the main church, and thus it came about that, here and there, chapels prepared for eucharistic worship were constructed close at hand. A clear illustration of a baptistery, more or less contemporary with Cyril's description of its use, is provided by the carved end of one of the sarcophagi now in the Vatican Museum (fig. 132).[13] The little building is circular in form; its roof is a ribbed cupola topped by a stone bearing the chi-rho emblem, while the windows, all set high up in the walling, are divided by bars into panes of some translucent material. The heavy metal door,[14] laid out in panels showing trellis work above and a decoration of lion heads in the lower range, is screened by two long curtains. But these curtains are drawn back and held in place by rings fixed to the wall so that the lamp hanging near the font might be visible to passers-by who would thus be reminded of their own 'illumination', the custom of pagan worshippers who left open the doors of a hero-shrine being thus adopted and turned to advantage. The whole building, at least in its upper portion, is remarkably like conventional representations of the Holy Sepulchre, and the close connection that exists between baptistery and burial-chamber is thereby emphasized.

Water was introduced into the baptisteries, where possible, by pipes of lead or pottery, but some constructions are such that the font clearly had to be filled by hand. The style of equipment varied widely. Certain baptisteries were relatively humble, with little more than a depression in the ground where the candidate stood while water was poured on his head from a laver. Others were furnished with a tub into which the candidate was apparently expected to clamber, while a larger number possessed a cistern of fair size into which all might descend by means of seven or, more commonly, three steps. Some of the later baptisteries were marked by a taste for bizarre luxury; the courtier Ennodius of Pavia, at the beginning of the sixth century, wrote with gusto about the baptistery of St Stephen at Milan, where water gushed in jets from the top of every column with which the font was surrounded.

133. Nocera: the baptistery as it was at the end of the eighteenth century. Engraving by L. J. Desprèz, 1783.

A grandiose baptistery was included by Constantine among the buildings of his palace on the Lateran Hill. Completely rebuilt in the classical manner by Pope Sixtus III, about the year 435, it has been transformed by a series of subsequent restorations, but the original layout is preserved with fair exactness. Eight porphyry columns, apparently surviving from Constantine's original structure, divide the interior into a central octagon and an ambulatory, also octagonal, which surrounds it. The architrave, supported by the columns, serves as the base of a gallery. Above this, as the sixteenth–century engravings show, eight large clerestory windows led upwards to the curve of the dome. The original font basin has entirely disappeared, together with life-size figures of Christ and John the Baptist as well as a golden lamb and seven stags made of silver which poured water from their mouths into the basin.[15] But around the architrave are still inscribed elegiac verses, perhaps the composition of Pope Sixtus, which in ornate language provide a complete theology of baptism. The baptistery is hemmed in by a number of additional chapels and a large portico with apsidal ends which may correspond to the vestibule mentioned by Cyril of Jerusalem. But this Lateran baptistery was wholly exceptional in size and magnificence, and the ancient examples of such buildings still to be found in Italy, while graceful enough, are modest structures, certainly when viewed from outside.

Apart from a rather doubtful identification in the Catacomb of Priscilla, the only font to be found in the catacombs is an oblong trench hollowed out of the rock in the Cemetery of Pontianus. Some 1.2 metres in depth, it is approached by a flight of steps with a small level space left for the officiant. A painting in fresco shows Christ as an adult standing in the river Jordan while the Baptist in his ragged garment leans forward to perform the rite and an angel, with hands respectfully veiled in his garment, balances the composition on the other side. Both font and painting have been assigned, questionably, to the sixth century.

A somewhat earlier example, to be dated about 390 AD, is the baptistery attached to the church of St Restituta at Naples. Built in the shape of a square, it is transformed by squinches into an octagon supporting a dome. The mosaics of the baptistery, though much damaged and ineptly repaired with paint and stucco, give an effect of great splendour. The summit of the

134. Albenga: baptistery.

cupola represents the heavens as a blue disc with stars, golden or white, scattered over its surface. The central point is occupied by a large chi-rho monogram, flanked by alpha and omega, while, overhead, the hand of God appears holding a bunch of golden leaves bound with a coil of ribbon. Below, eight compartments, of curving triangular form, extend to the base of the dome. At the top of each appear blue hangings fringed with gold as well as clusters of foliage and fruit while, on the side ribs, fluted two-handled vases pour forth a further symphony of leaves, fruit and multicoloured birds. The Biblical subjects which follow, all much battered, include an unusual but appropriate scene in which a man stands by a lake peopled with enormous fish, an allusion to St John's account of the miraculous catch 'at the sea of Tiberias'.[16] The mosaics on the vertical walls consist of a series of well-modelled figures of saints clothed in the formal Roman toga and each clasping a crown of golden oak-leaves held in place by a square-cut jewel. At the four corners appear the emblems of the Evangelists, and space is found nearby for the obviously baptismal theme of the Good Shepherd with his sheep,[17] a dove and two harts drinking the water of life, all rendered here in the simpler, impressionistic style of the wall-paintings of the catacombs.

At Nocera, 50 kilometres east of Naples, the baptistery presents something of a contrast, and its lines have much in common with S. Stefano Rotondo at Rome and the rotunda of S. Angelo at Perugia. The cupola here rises directly from a cylindrical drum and is buttressed by the robust walls of the ambulatory (fig. 133). The inner face of the font is circular, with a diameter of 5.5 metres, while the outer face is an octagon surmounted by columns.[18] The circle around the font is marked off from the ambulatory by paired columns supporting high-pitched arches, the general effect being thus a forest of columns enclosing the central font. The rotunda is extended to form an apse at the point opposite to the entrance.

A variant on the same theme, and probably of the same sixth-century date, is provided by the baptistery squeezed against the walls of the Gothic cathedral of Albenga, on the Ligurian coast near Genoa. Here, however, the octagonal form prevails throughout, in the upper stage of the building and the more widely extended lower stage as well as in the font with its surround (fig. 134). Yet the octagonal lower stage is not arranged as an ambulatory; it is, in effect, a thick wall hollowed out on the inner face to form eight niches, marked off by angle columns and shaped alternately as rectangles and semicircular apses. The purpose of these niches, unless they served merely as dressing-rooms, is not very clear. One of them contains a mosaic which repeats a conventional theme in an unusual manner. The centre is occupied by the chi-rho monogram, flanked by the alpha and omega that symbolize eternity, but this device, complete in itself, is enclosed within two circular bands one inside the other, which repeat the same theme and thus suggest the threefold formula of the Trinity. Beyond this mysterious circle of divine power, the deep-blue vault of Heaven is marked by the sun and four stars but more prominently by twelve white birds shown rather stiffly, though with some variation of posture and all facing inwards. These represent the Apostles but, since a white dove commonly stands for the purified human soul, their appearance on the wall of a baptistery is specially appropriate.

The baptistery at Novara closely follows the precedent set by Milan and exemplified by Albenga, differing only in that the rectangular and semicircular shapes show themselves on the outside as well as on the interior surface.

The outburst of eager church-building characteristic of North Africa in the fourth and fifth centuries produced a number of baptisteries but no one regular style or form. Sometimes great originality was shown. At Castiglione, not far from Algiers, the baptistery is a crypt built immediately beneath the apse of the church and to precisely the same dimensions. The crypt had as its roof a low vault lightly constructed for the most part with tubes of pottery fitting into one another. The font itself was a robust square of stone projecting 30 centimetres above ground level and enclosing a circular basin, a metre in depth, with four small steps. So far as can be seen, water had to be brought and emptied away by hand. The baptistery is only part of a larger complex, for at each side lies a room entered by a round-headed door. That on the left is dark and unpretentious, while the room on the right shows more ambitious workmanship, at least in the ceiling with its barrel vault at each end and groining in between. This room communicates directly with the aisle of the church and, in addition, a small doorway leads outside the building. An aumbry was found to

135. Djemila: baptistery.

136. Qalat Siman: baptistery. Horizontal courses of large stone blocks in the Syrian manner.

contain a hollowed block of stone, covered by a lid, which may have held the consecrated oil. In that case the room is an early example of the *consignatorium*, the place where the bishop confirmed candidates immediately after their baptism.

North Africa supplies many other examples of the baptistery built as an independent unit but closely connected with a church. At Timgad the arrangements are elaborate. The baptistery here consisted of a rectangular hall, about 8 metres by 6, and approached by way of a vestibule. The floor was entirely paved with a richly decorative mosaic: a border of lotus flowers separated by semicircles and, at each corner, a giant vase from which acanthus leaves emerge to fill up, with their coiling tendrils, the entire space as far as the central font. This font takes the form of a hexagon, lessening in size since it is composed of three descending layers of steps. Mosaic ornament is applied to both inner and outer surface. Garlands of laurel, zigzags and squares, in a great variety of size and colour, provide delicate patterns which receive a touch of Christian dogmatism from the addition of chi-rho emblems, white on a rose-tinted background. To the south-east corner of the baptistery was annexed a

rectangular hall with a semicircular font attached to one of the walls. But this, like the remains of other subsidiary rooms nearby, suggests a bath-house rather than a baptistery.

At Tigzirt the baptistery, set to the north of the basilica and connected with the *diaconicon*, takes the form of a quatrefoil. The thick, rubble walls enclosed a groined vault covering the central compartment and a semi-dome over each of the four apses. The font in this baptistery is circular and furnished with three steps, while at one side a concrete platform reaches almost to the edge of the bowl, and provides a convenient method of access for the bishop. The bases of four columns, of which only two remain in place, point to the existence of a *baldacchino* covering the font and enclosing it with curtains. A well-preserved example of such an arrangement occurs at Djemila, to the south-east of Tigzirt (fig. 135). Here the canopy rises from an architrave supported by four channelled columns; their capitals are worked with a stiff and rather rough acanthus pattern and their bases form high, rectangular blocks of stone at the corners of the square font. A vaulted corridor runs the whole way round this large and splendid baptistery and provides, set along its outer wall, a series of arched recesses for use as dressing-rooms.

The baptistery at Tigzirt is usually assigned to the sixth century. That of Tipasa, 80 kilometres westward, is, for no very obvious reason, dated a century earlier, though stylistically the two have much in common. The building at Tipasa, square in form and detached from the church, is hemmed in by bath-houses and other subsidiary rooms. It contains a round font, not more than a metre deep, and is again made up of three concentric layers, lined with cement. The water was presumably brought in buckets but there exists, as at Tigzirt, a drain for emptying the font. A colourful mosaic of flowers and leaves decorates the floor of the baptistery and in the entrance-vestibule a mosaic inscription extols the grace and power of baptism: 'if anyone asks that he may live, let him ever recall that here he may be purified with water and glimpse the joys of Heaven.'

The remote situation and uneventful history of many churches in Asia Minor and Syria have caused their ground-plans at least to remain untouched by later development. It is common enough to find, attached to basilicas whether grandiose or diminutive, a baptistery which takes the form of square or rectangle, with or without a shallow apse. The standard form seems originally to have been an unadorned rectangle, standing by itself, but connected with the basilica by means of an ambulatory flanking a courtyard in the manner of a medieval cloister garth. An example of this type, apparently of fourth-century date, is supplied by the little church of Bettir. But development, uninfluenced from the West, followed a speedy and fairly regular course. As a first alteration, the rectangle was attached directly to the church; later a semicircular niche was hollowed within the thickness of the wall; finally this niche was extended to form a projecting apse. But variations were allowed. At Rheah, for instance, the diminutive apse is not set parallel with the apsidal sanctuary of the church but instead projects at right angles to it. The Rheah baptistery, however, accords with a type found elsewhere in Syria, whereby windows are few and set high while a band of carved decoration, about two-thirds of the way up the external wall, gives the impression of a second floor.

One of the best preserved of the Syrian baptisteries is that connected with the church of St Paul and Moses at Dar Qita. It has the advantage of an exact dating since the year 422 is inscribed on the lintel. The architecture is typically Syrian: walls composed of huge blocks of stone, rectangular doorways with a simple channelled moulding, similar carving around the semicircular window above the entrance, and a moulded cornice which once supported a wooden roof. The dumpy little apse reaches scarcely half-way up the building and is severely plain except for a moulding deeply cut in horizontal bands and marking, both inside and out, the point where the curve springs from the vertical wall. The font, semicircular and protected by a low parapet, is contained within the apse, and there are signs of a well-arranged system of water-pipes. This Dar Qita baptistery is oddly placed in relation to the basilica; indeed it is completely separate, lying opposite the south-west corner of the church.

While most Syrian baptisteries are right-angled structures, other shapes may occasionally be found. The baptistery at Deir Seta, for instance, is a hexagon, its prominent doorway flanked by round-headed windows and ornamented in the simple fashion of channelled lines which characterizes the district, though the six columns originally marking the font have disappeared. The large and elaborate baptistery found amid the complex of monastic buildings at Qalat Siman (fig. 136) was an octagon set within a square of wall so thick that deep niches could be recessed in it. An upper storey emerged as an octagon with a window cut in each face, whilst enclosing aisles, with steeply-pitched roof, acted as buttresses. Three hundred miles westward, at Side, in Pamphylia, another large baptistery occurs. Separated by a corridor from the east end of a stately basilica, it consists of three interconnecting rooms, each having its walls freely furnished with rectangular or semicircular niches. In the midst of the central, square room is set a marble-lined font framed by four marble columns, one at each corner.

A baptistery which may be said to link closely with Milan and the Mausoleum of Diocletian, as well as with the mystical use of the number eight, is the Baptistery of the Orthodox situated beside the cathedral at Ravenna. This is built as an octagon, with plain walls in the lower half. The work of Bishop Urso,

137. Aix-en-Provence: the baptismal basin, flanked by its columns.

and thus to be dated around the year 390, it was drastically remodelled by Bishop Neon half a century later. By then new stylistic influences were in the air, as well as a taste for enhanced luxury. Bishop Neon heightened the octagonal walls,[19] lightly marking the outer surface with recessed panels. He removed the flat roof, substituting a dome, while throughout the interior he executed a brilliant yet harmonious scheme of mosaic decoration, to supplement or supersede the earlier work in stucco.

The Baptistery of the Orthodox influenced not only the Baptistery of the Arians at Ravenna but also the development of the interesting group of baptisteries, founded at various dates from the mid-fourth to the late sixth centuries, which occurs in southern and central France. The original type is, however, a standard one, suggested by the conventional pattern of a Roman bath-house. Circular or, more often, octagonal in form, they consist essentially of the font with two or three steps running all the way along the basin and enclosed by columns formerly hung with curtains and supporting a cupola. Beyond this central area, where those 'who were naked as Adam in Paradise'[20] were partially screened, came the wide passageway with or without recesses used for such practical purposes as the storage of clothes.

The example at Aix-en-Provence is now an adjunct of the north aisle of the Cathedral. Here the octagon of the baptismal basin was discovered, in poor condition, as recently as the year 1929. The eight surrounding columns, of marble or granite, are topped by richly carved Corinthian capitals which appear to be spoils from an earlier, pagan temple; however, the structure as a whole is, in effect, a remodelling that dates from Renaissance times (fig. 137). A similar ground-plan is found at Riez, where more of the original fabric remains. The building, isolated on the outskirts of the town, is square on its external face but octagonal inside, with four little apses opening from the circular ambulatory. The cupola has been rebuilt, but here also the great columns upon which it rests are ancient spoils adapted to a Christian setting. The baptismal basin is small, little over a metre in diameter.

Fifty kilometres to the south-east, the baptistery attached to the cathedral at Fréjus repeats the main features of the Riez example (fig. 138). It is an octagonal room, furnished with four small apses, and constructed in colourful and varied brickwork. The eight granite columns which define the ambulatory are topped by white capitals carved in different versions of the Corinthian style and, once again, seem to have been imported from some older building. The octagonal font basin sunk into the floor is marked by a raised ledge and by the bases of small columns, the remnants of a canopy which at one time enclosed it. What makes the structure unique among the baptisteries of France, and recalls that of Albenga, is the continuation upwards to form an octagonal second storey, lit by eight windows alternating with niches set within the angles of the wall. This upper octagon develops into a circular drum surmounted by a cupola.

Another ancient baptistery in the same part of France is that of Venasque, which seems to have been originally a sixth-century reconstruction of material drawn from a ruined temple. The building took the form of a somewhat imperfect square, with a semicircular apse projecting from each side to make up an irregular cross. The walls were of rubble, with more substantial stones at the base. Inside, columns of red and white marble topped by Corinthian capitals marked the entrance to the apses, each of which was decorated by an arcade springing from slender wall-columns. The floor is paved with large stones which covered the octagonal font basin until recent excavation disclosed its outline.

But variations abound. The baptistery at Cimiez contains a rotunda with eight columns enclosing a hexagonal basin of the type more often found in North Africa, but Port–Bail, remotely situated in Normandy, favours the hexagonal shape for both building and font, while at Valence an octagonal font is set within a cross-shaped structure.

The oldest of the French baptisteries, however, is that of Poitiers which, as the 'Church of St John', stands out boldly not far from the cathedral. The building owes its present appearance, that of a lofty rectangular hall with ante-chapel in the form of an uneven pentagon, mainly to a twelfth-century reconstruction. But the outline of the original baptistery, which occupied the site of a Roman house, may be clearly traced and assigned to a period shortly after the great St Hilary, 'the Athanasius of the West', became bishop of Poitiers in 353 AD. Entry was by way of a western porch into a rectangular room separated by a wall and two wide doorways from the place of baptism itself. This was another rectangular hall of

138. Fréjus, baptistery: the arches of the ambulatory.

similar size and decorated, in the manner characteristic of the French baptisteries, with marble columns and capitals taken from some pagan temple. The eastern wall, in particular, was handsomely arranged with a row of six columns connected by arches to form three bays, the central one much wider and loftier than the other two. But some of the capitals seem closer in form to the Merovingian style than to classical models, and it may be that the details of this ornament should be assigned to a far-reaching restoration carried out in the seventh century. The font basin is recessed into the floor at the centre of the baptismal hall. Octagonal in shape, it was built in stages so that the candidate, descending four steps to a depth of 1.3 metres, found himself standing in a narrow space while the bishop from above poured water over his head and shoulders. The lower steps are reconstructions, but the upper two show that the inner surface of each step was treated with a hard, smooth cement. Channels made of terracotta provided for the supply of water and for draining it away.

The fate of the baptistery at Poitiers illustrates the changes that came over the practice of Christian initiation. The custom of baptizing infants gradually became the rule rather than the exception. Moreover, from the fifth century onwards, the part played by the bishop himself decreased and the local presbyters came to be regarded as the natural ministers of the rite. Even at the solemn Easter baptisms in the great cathedral cities the bishop was accustomed to baptize no more than a few of the candidates and leave the rest to priests, deacons and even those in minor orders, with the understanding that the sacrament would later be completed by the bishop through the laying-on of hands at confirmation. The effect of these changes was that every church acquired its font, usually a bowl of small size and raised on a pedestal, while the isolated baptisteries were abandoned. In the case of Poitiers, the font basin set in the floor was smashed and covered over at the time when the building was heightened and enlarged to serve the wider needs of a parish church.

NOTES

1. Acts 8.36.
2. *Didache* vii.
3. *De Baptismo* 4, *CSEL* xx.204.
4. St John 5.2–9.
5. Numbers 20.2.
6. I Peter 3.20.
7. Pliny, *Letters* ii.17.11 (Loeb), i.136.
8. E.g. Acts of Marcellus and Acts of Laurence. Reference is made in both these Acts to baptisms which took place in prison, where the supply of water would clearly be limited.
9. Gregory of Nyssa, *Catechetical Orations* 32, *PG* 45.84.
10. Sixth-century Church Councils forbade it except by reason of necessity, and the 'Quinisext' Council of Constantinople, in 692, ruled that such private baptism might be allowed only with the bishop's consent.
11. 'At the self-same moment (i.e. of Baptism) ye died and were born, and the water of Salvation was at once your grave and your mother.' Cyril of Jerusalem, *Myst. Cat.* 2.4, *PG* 33. Among the many patristic passages of similar import, Pope Leo I's *Epistle* xvi (*PL* 54.698) deserves particular mention.
12. This *inscriptio ad fontem S. Teclae* is given by Dölger in *Sylloge Laureshamensis* III (Monastery of Lorsch).
13. Inv. 174. Some have doubted the identification with a baptistery and prefer to describe the building as 'part of the general background'.
14. The door should probably be thought of as made up of two leaves, but only one is shown.
15. These details are given in the *Liber Pontificalis* 13 (ed. Duchesne).
16. St John 21.
17. Christ is seated in the attitude of the Good Shepherd in the Mausoleum of Galla Placidia, to which decorative scheme the Naples baptistery has many resemblances. See p. 176.
18. Originally eight columns, though only three remain.
19. R. Trinci, in *ACIAC* IX, stresses the exact mathematical principles, based on Plato and Pythagoras, which were used to control the building.
20. John Chrysostom, *Sixth Homily on Colossians*, *PG* 62.342.

13

Mosaic

'Mosaic' is the term applied to the art of constructing patterns or pictures from relatively small pieces of such materials as marble, polished stone or glass, and thus decorating floors and walls in a durable manner. Originating apparently in the East, where terracotta of various colours was used to enliven wall surfaces, mosaic was introduced into Greece by the fourth century BC. Early examples are uncommon, but, in the temple of Zeus at Olympia, a mosaic made up of river pebbles shows Tritons gracefully posed within a border of stylized palm-leaves. The mainland of Greece was not at first congenial soil, but the use of mosaic developed rapidly in North Africa and, in Italy, at Rome and Pompeii.

The choice of subjects was varied. Thus Sosus of Pergamum, one of the few craftsmen whose name is known, created a pattern, later taken over by Christian mosaicists,[1] of doves perched around the rim of a bowl from which one of the birds is drinking water while the others sun themselves. Sosus enjoyed experimenting with the form of realism which deceives the eye as being not only lifelike but appropriate to its setting. For instance, it was he who invented the 'unswept floor' technique, whereby the floor of a dining-room is inlaid with stone coloured to represent fruits, fish, and fragments of food that have fallen from the dishes. The most famous mosaic at Pompeii is that of Alexander leading his troops in battle against the Persians, but lighter themes were commonly in vogue and, elsewhere at Pompeii, musicians and actors are shown rehearsing their parts before the play begins. Distinguished among all the other mosaics of pre-Christian Rome are those of Hadrian's Villa at Tivoli, with such themes as a company of dancing Centaurs. Not much later, the use of mosaic had extended to the outposts of Empire; the pavement of a house at Woodchester, near Gloucester, depicts Orpheus charming the wild animals by the beauty of his song.

Several types of mosaic may be distinguished. The term 'slice-pattern' (*opus sectile*) is used when a floor is composed with thin plates of marble, of varying size, shaped and fitted together in geometric forms. Much more frequent, anyhow in the West, was the 'tessellated work', so called from the word *tessella*, meaning a small cube of stone. The cubes were firmly set in a well-grounded layer of mortar and, since their rectangular surfaces were of more or less the same size, they could be placed only in straight lines, offering scope for patterns bold but very restricted in range. The desire to produce more elaborate scenes, with an effect like that of painting, led to the evolution of the style known as 'vermiculate'—that is to say, resembling the tracks of worms in being curved and irregular. In this type of mosaic the marble cubes are not of one size and one shape only: they may be rounded or square, large or small, and thus, with their subtle gradations of colour, lend themselves readily to arrangement in complex and sophisticated forms. The contours of the human body could be followed without difficulty, while animals, birds and plants were reproduced with meticulous care. Delicate scenes, worked in this vermiculate style, were composed in panels known as *emblemata* and sent from the studio to be inserted into a tessellated background, so that the general effect became one of formal ornament serving as a symmetrical frame for an elaborate illustration. But the growing desire to lay vast surfaces of mosaic often led to a change of emphasis, when instead of a single composition within its formal border, the area was broken up into a number of medallions, each containing a figure or a small group.

Mosaic gained wider popularity from the third century onwards and was used to decorate not only walls, pavements and flat ceilings but curved surfaces as well until, in the words of a poet-bishop, 'the marble, with its many-coloured sheen, runs everywhere over dome and floor and around the windows.'[2] This description may be compared with the rather later comment of Cassiodorus, the praetorian prefect of Theodoric:

The variegated surface of the marble is woven into the loveliest variety of pictures, the value of the work, now as always, being increased by the minute labour that has to be expended on the production of the Beautiful.[3]

The first vault of any size to be decorated with mosaic seems to have been Diocletian's palace at Spalato, which thus set a fashion soon to be developed in great richness. The range of colour gradually widened. Whereas at first the cubes were cut from marble or natural stone and variation was given by subtle shading, brilliant contrasts became possible when glass cubes were extensively used. A medieval craftsman named Theophilus,[4] who wrote handbooks on technical themes, supplies a commentary:

In the ancient buildings of the classical period, the mosaics display glass of varied colour—white, black, green, yellow, blue and purple. The glass is not transparent but opaque like so much marble. In fact you might speak of little square stones.

The glass acquired its colour through the addition of metallic oxides and, with some of them, differences of shade could be obtained by varying the time during which the glass remained in a molten state. Little plaques of enamel, silver or mother-of-pearl might be occasionally introduced into a scheme of mosaic in order to heighten some particular effect.

The finest mosaics of the earlier period are made up of cubes set so tightly together that the smooth surface resembled a fresco painting; thereafter the fashion inclined towards larger cubes set with less exactness.

The reason for this change was not necessarily inferior workmanship but a growing interest in the properties of light and an awareness of the effects to be gained when a shimmer of light is reflected from the roughened surface of cubes set at varying angles. By the sixth century the convention had become well established that the size of the cubes varied according to the nature of the subject, small squares being used to illustrate faces and hands while larger pieces were thought proper for draperies.

The custom of using gold to enliven mosaics developed along fairly clear lines. At the start gold was employed hardly at all, perhaps because of a fear that it might overpower the rest of the work, and at Pompeii a bright sulphur yellow is tried out instead. But by the fourth century gold came into sparing, though very effective, use as a means of heightening such details as the rim of a drinking bowl or ewer when these vessels stand out against a neutral background of grey or buff. When, in the fifth century, gold comes to be used relatively often in bands that form the background of narrative scenes, its brightness is customarily toned down by an admixture of green or blue or brown, and it is only in the mosaics of Ravenna and S. Sophia that gold came to be freely employed to indicate majestic dignity or supernatural power. Whereas silver has a cold look to it and tarnishes easily, the brilliance of gold is warm and heartening—particularly when the gold leaf, always slightly transparent, is set on a red background.

Mosaic is little used in the Roman catacombs. The crumbling walls, lack of light and need for economy made such a scheme of decoration inappropriate, at least until the fourth century, when the activity of Pope Damasus led to unaccustomed splendours. In the mausoleum of the Julii[5] beneath St Peter's, the oldest existing Christian mosaic, lately rediscovered, shows both skilful construction and a choice of themes reflecting the same interests as are displayed on the sarcophagi. Moreover, it demonstrates a willingness to adapt pagan imagery, in this case the Sun at its rising, to Christian purposes without scruple.

The mosaics of Constantina's mausoleum bear witness to a similar readiness, persisting at the middle of the fourth century, to employ the conventional forms of pagan decoration in serving the purposes of Christian art, or at least without offending the sentiments of Christian worship. Mosaic covers the ceiling of the barrel-vaulted ambulatory around the shrine, the space on either side of the entrance, at one end, and the tomb, at the other, being filled with five matching zones. The first shows a geometric pattern which includes a repeated theme of four stylized dolphins with their heads together. Next, an intricate framework of red, white and green bands encloses in its compartments single figures of cupids and psyches alternating with birds—the mallard, mute swan, bustard, and the rest—shown in a style of the most delicate realism. The third zone offers a graceful, sinuous pattern of vine leaves twining around portrait-busts, perhaps those of Constantina and her husband. Here and there cherubs are picking the grapes, while below is a cruder representation of jovial husbandry: three men trample the fruit in the winepress and a fourth guides two disgruntled oxen who draw a cart loaded with more grapes. Beyond this, roundels enclose what seem to be stock portrait-busts alternating with formal flower-heads. Then, as Constantina's tomb is approached, a free and exuberant pattern of birds, plants and drinking vessels, touched significantly with the sheen of gold, hints at the joys of Paradise. There is nothing specifically Christian about all this, and early archaeologists had some excuse for interpreting S. Costanza as a temple of Bacchus, but the symbolism of lively movement connected with the vine was from the beginnings of Christian art eagerly accepted as being in harmony with the doctrine 'I am the Vine: ye are the branches'.[6] The mosaics of the central drum, destroyed in 1620, appear[7] to have displayed events from the Old and New Testaments rendered in a mood of easy-going classicism and accompanied by entertaining river scenes. But two small apses contained within the side walls of the ambulatory are religious in a detailed and specific manner. In one, Christ, with thick beard, is shown seated on the globe of the world and solemnly presenting his mandate to St Peter who humbly approaches with his hand covered as though to receive a holy object.[8] In the mosaic of the other apse, Christ, youthful and beardless, and standing with two sheep at each side, is a far less majestic figure. St Peter and St Paul approach to receive the scroll of the divine Law, which Peter grasps. But the apostles, with their large untidy beards, present an almost clownish appearance, while Christ's face is shown with a distinctly mawkish

expression. The apse mosaics seem to have been added twenty or thirty years after the original scheme of decoration had been completed; in any case, being low down and thus an easy prey for the restorer, they have obviously suffered a number of changes.

The mosaic of S. Pudenziana—begun, as inscriptions formerly explained, about 390 AD and completed a few years later—shows a remarkable advance in the direction of balanced, large-scale composition (fig. 139). Though heavily cut back when the apse was altered in the sixteenth century and subjected to much remodelling since that date, it remains well-proportioned and dignified in the classic manner yet touched by intimations of supernatural power. As such it presents an interesting contrast in taste to the lush eighteenth-century painting of the dome. The mosaic shows, in the centre, Christ seated on an elaborate jewelled throne, and extending his right hand in a gesture of authoritative teaching. His face is youthful but bearded, while his head is encircled by a large, golden halo. At each side five (originally six) apostles are ranged not in the motionless uniformity often found on the sarcophagi of the period but with marked differences of attitude and portraiture. St Peter and St Paul occupy the places of honour next to the throne, and a wreath of victory is extended over the head of each by two female figures, amply draped in formal, golden garments; these should probably be understood as the Church of the Circumcision and the Church of the Gentiles, as found, and clearly named, in the only section of mosaic that survives in S. Sabina. The background, at S. Pudenziana, consists of a colonnade topped by three rows of sloping tiles. Above appear various structures, including the Church of the Nativity at Bethlehem and the Church of the Holy Sepulchre at Jerusalem, shown with an almost photographic realism which suggests a copy of an original made on the spot, in Palestine. The sky, streaked with blue, red, brown and gold, bears upon its surface gigantic emblems of the four Evangelists. At the central point, a tall, jewelled cross[9] rises up from the hillock of Calvary. By contrast with the restrained symbolism of an earlier age, this great mosaic offers a wealth of imaginative detail, which almost suggests a painting by some Renaissance artist. The theme might be described either as Christ commissioning the Apostles after his Resurrection or, more suitably, Christ

139. Rome, S. Pudenziana: the mosaic of the apse.

attended by the Apostles at his Second Coming to reign upon earth for a thousand years.[10] Anyhow, in spite of the touches of historical realism, the scene belongs substantially to an ideal, eternal world where Christ presides, in triumphant majesty, over the heavenly Jerusalem.

But the most notable collection of mosaics surviving in Rome is that of the vast basilica of S. Maria Maggiore, built, or completely transformed, by Pope Xystus III about 435 AD. The mosaics may be divided into three groups. The first consists of twenty-seven panels, out of an original forty-two, set on each side of the nave as a kind of frieze, above the range of Ionic columns and below the line of tall, round-headed clerestory windows. Enclosed in the rectangular frames, which are eighteenth-century substitutes for their earlier housing, the panels play a by no means dominant part in the rich and harmonious scheme of decoration. But they show up well, particularly on the north side, when the conditions of light favour them. They consist of a series of historical scenes, often rather crowded, and it must always have been difficult from ground level to distinguish precisely what was happening. No longer are the scenes chosen primarily as hints and symbols of God's power unto salvation. They show instead a keen interest in the details of Old Testament narrative, and in the historical record for its own sake. Even when full allowance has been made for restoration and repair, carried out with varying degrees of skill, it remains obvious that several different artists were employed and that their methods tended now to a vigorous impressionism, now to a softer, flatter style more akin to painting than to mosaic. But all bear the Hellenistic stamp and have more in common with the historical scenes carved on Trajan's column than with the crude, linear figures of the catacombs. More closely, they invite comparison with the miniatures of such manuscripts as the Vatican Virgil, the Iliad in the Ambrosian Library at Milan and the Quedlinburg *Itala* and thus with a tradition of rather sophisticated de luxe book production.

Some of the panels offer one scene only while others, where two incidents are shown one above the other, provide the artist with a severe test if the effect is not to be jostled and indistinct. The first three panels on the south side, concerned with the story of Abraham, are among the best examples. The easternmost of these illustrates the return of Abraham victorious in battle over the four kings (Genesis 14). Abraham rides a warhorse, with a cluster of mounted warriors, lance in hand, behind him. Meanwhile Melchizedek, 'priest of God Most High', advances with the mysterious tribute of bread and wine which theologians took to prefigure the Eucharist. The next panel concerns the hospitality offered by Abraham to the three angels by the oaks of Mamre. In the upper register, the patriarch, in an attitude of submissive reverence, approaches the three angels, whom, again, the Church Fathers came to invest with solemn significance as suggesting the doctrine of the Trinity. Clothed in shining white, they are wingless but each has a halo and a subtle shading of gold and red makes their faces shine with superhuman radiance. Below, Abraham appears twice. On one side of the panel he chides Sarah who, standing in front of her house at the kitchen table, concentrates her efforts on making bread for the visitors. On the other side sit the three angels, solemn, rapt and dignified while Abraham places the dish before them on a table already furnished with three loaves. The next panel illustrates the importance of human choice as colouring, for good or ill, the pattern of history. The foreground is occupied by the figures, clothed identically in tunic and pallium, of Abraham and Lot, while behind each is clustered a retinue—wife, children and servants. Between the two groups, a vertical shaft of space indicates the separation of their destinies. Lot, with one hand extended in the direction of Sodom, half turns, as he sets forth on his journey, to look back at Abraham with a glance in which determination mingles with foreboding. Abraham, however, remains with feet firmly planted on the ground and his hand protectingly placed on Isaac's head, assured but, as his look seems to declare, conscious of the dread workings of divine providence.

The rest of the panels on the south side show episodes from the life of Jacob. There is a lively sense of historical detail yet, on the whole, both style and condition are less satisfactory than is the case with the mosaics of the north side, which record the life of Moses and Joshua. The first of these is as remarkable as any. Here Pharaoh's daughter occupies a throne set beneath a gorgeous canopy. She wears the elaborate apparel of royalty and one of her five attendants holds a casket of jewels before her. Another conducts the youthful Moses, himself arrayed like a prince, into her presence, the whole scene being characterized by a brilliance of colour making for luxury and splendour. In the lower half of the panel the figures are somewhat smaller. Moses, shown as a boy, stands in the centre of a group of men seated on the steps of an amphitheatre. They wear the pallium, which leaves their right shoulder bare, in token that they are philosophers, the wise men of the Egyptian court. To one side clusters an attentive crowd. Moses is, no doubt, displaying the profound wisdom with which such commentators as Philo[11] credited him, and this in a fashion suggested by the New Testament[12] story of Christ disputing with the doctors to such effect that 'all who heard him were amazed at his understanding and his answers'.

The other panels vary to some extent in artistry and power. The battle scenes, which tend to be crowded and confused, are sometimes transformed into poetry by the attitude of the spectators. Thus, when Pharaoh's troops are overwhelmed in the Red Sea, Moses stands motionless at the head of a cluster of Israelites whose faces express a vigorously personal response of awestruck amazement at their miraculous deliverance.

A fine example of disciplined arrangement is provided by the panel which shows the appearance of the angel to Joshua near Jericho (fig. 140).[13] Israelite soldiers, equipped with helmets, shields and spears stand well grouped to the left of the scene. In front of them Joshua advances, bowed in reverence and with both hands covered beneath the folds of his orange-red garment. A significant space separates him from the angel, who remains poised, motionless and upright, against a contrasting background of wavy mountain crests. The angel's costume matches that of the soldiers, for he wears a cloak over armour and clasps a spear, but his head is surrounded by a blue halo, while his countenance expresses the composed but purposeful air of an immortal spirit intervening in the chancy affairs of mankind.

The close-set group of mosaics that encircle the triumphal arch show a similar interest in historical detail but the subjects are treated, in the mood of the Middle Ages, as ministering to sound doctrine. The style, however, is still that of the classical world, with a strongly marked concern for robust modelling and individual character. Here again several artists seem to have been employed and given freedom to develop

140. Rome, S. Maria Maggiore. Mosaic panel: Joshua.

their subjects with a fair degree of independence. By comparison with the nave panels, the mosaics of the triumphal arch are designed with a more lavish use of gold as background and a rather calmer and more majestic arrangement of the figures. Such contrasts might perhaps be explained as due to the nature of the subjects, but a variation in the technique of laying the cubes points to a difference in artistic convention and therefore a likely difference in date. Whereas the nave panels are worked in a smooth, regular way with the cubes evenly squared, the mosaics of the triumphal arch display a studied casualness and a nearer approach to impressionism in the variable, almost rough, manner in which the cubes are shaped. The subjects seem to be chosen with the clear-cut end in view of emphasizing the divinity of Christ, apparent from his earliest childhood. They thus served to refute the speculations, condemned at the Council of Ephesus in 431 AD and twenty years later at Chalcedon, of those who 'corrupt the mystery of the Incarnation and shamelessly pretend that he who was born of the holy Virgin Mary was a mere man'. Above the highest point of the arch all this is hinted at symbolically. A richly jewelled throne has set upon it a

crown, a cross and the Lamb's book of life, 'sealed with seven seals'.[14] As supporters, at either side, the apostles Peter and Paul clasp the volume of the sacred law with their left hand while, with their right, they make a gesture of acclamation.

The rest of the mosaic shows the teaching thus hinted at transferred into historical terms. In the top register—on the left—appears a double event linked by the presence of angels, who betoken the divine Providence. On one side the Virgin, attended by three of these solemn and statuesque ministers, sits enthroned. Her costume is a jewelled brocade such as some princess might have worn at court, and her hands are occupied in spinning a veil of purple wool for the Temple,[15] but her gaze is one of awed amazement. The scene is an elaborate rendering of the Annunciation, and the archangel Gabriel together with the dove typifying the Holy Spirit, hover overhead (fig. 141). In the corner is a shrine with closed doors; this may indicate the end of the old religious order and the beginning of the new, for at the other corner of the tableau is shown a temple with curtains drawn back and a lamp hanging in the entrance as though to emphasize the brightness and sanctity of

141. Rome, S. Maria Maggiore. Mosaics of the triumphal arch: the Annunciation and the Visit of the Magi.

the fuller Faith. Near this temple stands Joseph, the picture of dismayed astonishment, while two angels strive to convey to him something of the mystery which is being enacted.

The scene in the register below is a scarcely less remarkable version of the visit of the Wise Men. The central figure is the Christ-child, seated on a disproportionately large throne of extreme ornateness. His form appears lumpy, partly because of some inadequate restoration, and he extends a hand of the curiously clawlike type which the artist of this panel often introduces. Behind stand four angels, again with expressive faces and again clothed in dalmatic and pallium; here, however, a different effect is produced by the white highlights chosen in preference to the folded draperies, furrowed with black lines, of the Annunciation panel. Above the head of the infant Christ shines the star, while at his right hand the Virgin sits enthroned in great splendour. To his left sits another female figure, clad in a dark mantle and with hand to chin in pensive contemplation. She is commonly described as a symbol of the Church, but such is the sophistication of this set of mosaics that it might even be maintained that the Virgin appears

twice, first in the glory of her destiny and then in the dismay and wonder which it brought upon her. From the direction of a walled city two Wise Men approach, richly dressed in a Phrygian fashion and bearing their gifts on dishes.

The curve of the arch much reduces the size of the third panel, which gives a dramatic representation of Herod's command to slay the innocent children. The power and brilliance of the military knights contrast with the uniformity of the crowd of mothers. The round faces, black straggly hair and sameness of doleful expression which the artist assigns to them give the general effect of an anonymous chorus in some Greek Tragedy.

Below all this comes a picture entitled 'Jerusalem', where the city is represented by half a dozen buildings enclosed within a turreted wall. The entrance gate is wide open, and a golden cross hangs from the summit as if to declare the reason for the easy access made available to all. The walls are studded with precious stones in the manner of the new Jerusalem 'made ready as a bride adorned for her husband'.[16] On the green foreground appear six white sheep, corresponding to six more sheep on the other side of the arch, standing before the 'little town' of Bethlehem. The 'Apostles of the Lamb',[17] twelve in number to match the twelve tribes of the old order, are thus appropriately shown as lambs who harkened to the voice of the Shepherd.[18]

The upper register on the right offers an extended panorama with the backcloth of an arcade leading up to the Temple. Once more, angels are present to indicate the divine overtones of the transaction, but they are calmer and more composed than the ecstatic figures who attend on the Annunciation. The scene is the Presentation as recorded in St Luke's Gospel.[19] Mary, again clothed as a princess, holds the Christ-child in her arms while Joseph extends his hand, in a gesture of greeting and acclamation, to the prophetess Anna. Simeon makes a movement of profound obeisance and behind him is ranged a line of the elders of Israel, their faces brilliantly expressive of deep emotion. In the corner a somewhat obscure subject, an angel standing before a reclining figure, may be the warning given to Joseph to flee into Egypt.[20] The next panel, at any rate, concerns Egypt, and is remarkable as offering the first pictorial example of an incident, drawn from late apocryphal Gospels,[21] which occurred at Heliopolis. When the Holy Family entered the temple there, Isaiah's prophecy 'the idols of Egypt shall be moved at his presence'[22] was fulfilled; the images fell from their pedestals and were smashed in pieces. The local ruler, Aphrodisius, accompanied by his bodyguard and a philosopher, is shown reverently approaching the Holy Family, while a group of angels lend superhuman lustre to the scene. In the band below, Herod, indicated by name, is represented in conversation with the Wise Men and two scribes of whom he had enquired 'where the Christ should be born'.[23]

These mosaics of the triumphal arch represent not only artistic imagination of the highest quality but also a notable essay in proclaiming a fully-developed doctrine of Christ's divine nature and worldwide dominion. The point would not be lost on the fifth-century spectator that the pope, as Christ's vicar on earth, was claiming a sovereign authority and power of leadership in the affairs of civilized life.

The third group of mosaics at S. Maria Maggiore, those which decorate the apse, is a splendid example of the late medieval style, designed by the Franciscan Jacopo Torriti. But the artist seems to have retained, or

at any rate reproduced, some of the work which existed before. Certainly the curving scrolls of acanthus leaves and the border of riverside scenes with swans and ducks, fishermen and little cupids sailing their boats in the breeze suggest the playful love of nature which marked the end of the classical period and found its way into the earliest productions of the Christian Church.

Most of the other mosaics in Rome which may be assigned to this period have been so extensively restored that the original pattern is in some doubt, but the church of St Cosmas and St Damian retains, within the apse, substantially unaltered mosaics that still reflect classic grace and vitality combined with the sense of majesty and timelessness that are the hallmark of Byzantine style (fig. 142). The figures convey a solemn dignity without being frozen into stiffness: though all face the spectator with the wide-open eyes appropriate to those in touch with divine mysteries, they form a group rather than a series of unrelated, statuesque units, and their posture is lively and varied. The likeness of Christ dominates the scene. Clothed in mantle and tunic of gold, and with a golden halo framing his long black hair and beard, he stands out majestically against a background of the indigo heavens streaked with vermilion or bluish lines of formalized cloud. His right hand is outstretched in a gesture of command while, with his left, he clasps the scroll of his Law for mankind. The composition at each side is effectively balanced, in the fashion of a triangle with Christ as the apex. On the extreme right a palm tree and the eager figure of St Theodore, a soldier-martyr from Pontus, offering his martyr-crown, are touched with the glitter of gold which is repeated at the opposite end in another palm tree. In this tree perches a phoenix, the bird of immortality, while nearby Pope Felix IV[24] presents the church which he had founded. A contrast in colour is provided by the apostles Peter and Paul, in their white tunics and mantles. They are shown as introducing, respectively, Cosmas and Damian, dark-robed and each holding his crown, into the presence of the Redeemer. On the ground at their feet, beside the river Jordan, flowering plants cluster around diminutive rocks. Below this scene are ranged the customary twelve sheep representing the twelve Apostles, each one individual in expression and posture, while the lamb *par excel-*

142. Rome, SS. Cosmas and Damian. Mosaic of the apse: Peter, Damian and Theodore.

143. Salonica, St George. Mosaic: St Leo of Patara and St Philemon the flute-player.

lence, the Lamb of God,[25] stands in their midst on a mound from which flow the four rivers of Paradise.

Above the triumphal arch are further mosaics which comment on, and in some degree repeat, the themes put forward in the apse. Defined against a golden background the Lamb of God occurs again, reclining this time on his altar-throne, together with angels in wind-blown tunics, emblems of the Evangelists and what is now rather an odd fragment: arms of the Four and Twenty Elders upholding the crowns assigned to them in the Book of Revelation.[26] The mosaic as a whole, however, is an impressive study in the art of combining realistic portraiture with the complex symbols of apocalyptic imaginings. Time is animated by eternity.

The mosaics which still survive from the fifth century in the church of St George at Salonica exhibit to some degree this same combination of clear-cut portraiture and symbolism. But the detail is entirely different from anything found in Rome. In preference to scenes directly suggested by passages from the Bible, the artists have taken delight in a lavish display of framework, acanthus scrolls, balustrades and the like divid-ing the cupola into eight large panels each of which contains an elaborate, indeed fanciful, study of an architectural theme. Lamps, candlesticks and curtains confer an air of holiness on the buildings but their forms, standing out against a golden background, suggest the backcloth of a theatre rather than any attempt to reproduce particular shrines of the Holy Land. Prominent in the foreground, the figures of saints are grouped in twos or threes (fig. 143). For all their marked individuality, the saints are alike in that their stance is upright and formal while their hands are outstretched in the prayerful posture of some primitive *Orans* of the catacombs. Apart from Cosmas and Damian, they are little-known personages and what they have in common is that all suffered martyrdom in the East, for the most part during the persecutions of Decius and Diocletian. Their cult was a local one, perhaps suggested by the fact that St George's contained their relics. The character of the mosaics is very reasonably claimed as Hellenistic, but the subject seems to be linked with Eastern ideas and certainly with the notion of the dome as representing the vault of Heaven where Christ, 'image of the invisible God',[27] reigns supreme.

The Christian scheme had its pagan counterparts. In a temple at Palmyra, for example, Bel, ruler of the world, occupies the centre of the dome; circling below him are the gods of the planets and signs of the Zodiac. Still further below are four sirens, upholding the Universe, whose harmony is matched by the charm of their song. A similar division into zones marks the cupola of St George's. Though the upper part is badly damaged, enough remains for the subjects to be clearly made out. At the summit of the cupola Christ appears as the triumphant Ruler of the Universe. His figure is enclosed within a large, rounded shield having a rich border of flowers and fruit. This *clipeus* could serve as the obvious emblem of the world in its wholeness, and was regularly used as a frame for portraits of the emperors, conceived of as Christ's earthly counterparts in sovereign sway. The second zone is occupied by the Apostles.[28] Below them, next in rank among this celestial hierarchy, the saints appear in front of the splendid and complex system of architecture which hints that, after their warfare of martyrdom, they had obtained a place within the Heavenly City.

The themes found in the cupola of St George's were developed in the mosaics of other churches at Salonica. Even where the figure of Christ as victorious Pantocrator is not explicitly displayed, it seems to be alluded to in the extreme luxuriance of natural forms rejoicing in the 'deliverance from the bondage of corruption into the liberty of the glory of the children of God'.[29] In the wall mosaics of the church of the Acheiropoietos, both colour and design point to an apocalyptic exuberance. Vine branches coil from magnificent vases while octagons in sequence contain birds or serpents or bunches of flowers and leaves shown in the brightest colours and touched with the supernatural radiance of gold and silver.

The Acheiropoietos mosaics date from about 470 AD,[30] thirty years or so later than the earliest Ravenna mosaics, found in the Mausoleum of Galla Placidia[31] and in the Baptistery of the Orthodox. In this baptistery the summit of the cupola is occupied, appropriately enough, not by Christ in majesty but by Christ receiving baptism in the river Jordan, while around this central medallion the rest of the composition turns like the spokes of a great wheel, suggesting the endless continuity of infinite time (fig. 144)[32]. The style of the mosaics is typically Ravennate, lying midway be-

tween the almost casual impressionism of some of the S. Maria Maggiore subjects, in Rome, and the precise, well-ordered figures of the saints at St George's, Salonica, where the faces are meticulously patterned in small *tessellae* and the garments strongly marked with vertical lines running parallel to the columns in the background.

The design of the baptistery mosaic, for all its imaginative power and deeply religious overtones, follows a conventional pattern. In the Baptism scene itself Christ stands submerged to his waist in the river while John the Baptist, holding a long cross in his left hand, takes up his position on a rocky bank, amid stiffly decorative flowering plants, and pours the water over Christ's head by means of a small silver dish. Over them the Spirit, as a dove, sweeps downward in gentle, purposeful flight. At the other side the personification of the Jordan, rendered unselfconsciously in terms of pagan mythology as an elderly, bearded man, extends what looks like a green cloth composed of weed or rushes for Christ to use as his towel. The whole picture is enclosed within a frame, and from this hangs a looped curtain, perhaps intended to suggest mysterious power hovering over the twelve Apostles who, regularly spaced around the circle, are separated from one another by floral candlesticks of gold standing against a dark-blue background. The Apostles are distinguished not only by name but by a strong impress of individual character that contrasts with the uniformity of their action in raising a jewelled crown in hands veiled ceremonially by the folds of their garments. The artist avoids the monotony of the unvarying white vesture found in some compositions of similar nature by giving the Apostles light and dark tunics alternately and by touching their mantles here and there with gold. Below the Apostles is a band of rich though somewhat stiff and repetitive symbolism. Framed by strong lines of decoration which emphasize the vertical, downward thrust of the dome, two scenes are identically displayed four times over. One of the repeated panels shows an altar with a book of the Gospels open upon it and flanked on either side by an empty chair with shell ornament above. The other motif consists of an empty throne surmounted by a cross and flanked by little gardens enclosed within an openwork screen. Christ's dominion is the theme, exemplified by the throne set within the luxuriance of Paradise and, on earth, by the

144. Ravenna, Baptistery of the Orthodox: the mosaics of the cupola.

altar placed between the two seats reserved for the emperors who, by divine decree, wield civil authority in the East and the West.

In the semicircles above the windows decoration is continued in the well-tried form of acanthus leaves, peacocks significantly perched in the branches of vine-shoots, and small, formalized crosses. Mosaic here is reinforced by a decoration of moulded plaster as, with the light of day pouring in through the windows, the prophets, 'lights of the world holding forth the word of life'[33] clutch their scrolls of office. Below these figures, densely coiling foliage, that seems to spring from the columns, provides a contrast with the cool and geometric beauty of the marble facings which cover the walls behind. The whole conception is an impressive commentary on the hope of enlightenment to be obtained through baptism, and must have been still more effective before the floor was raised several feet and something of proportion[34] thereby lost.

At a rather later period in the history of Ravenna's mosaics, about 495 AD, the Baptistery of the Arians was erected by Theodoric. The pattern of the earlier baptistery was closely followed both in its octagonal, brick construction and in its mosaic decoration, though here the artistry is less inspired and the effect has been marred by damage and some inept botching by restorers. All that remains is the central medallion and the zone where the apostles are displayed. The scheme of the Baptistery of the Orthodox is followed closely but not slavishly, in accordance with what may be termed Byzantine practice; the aim is not to innovate but to reproduce customary themes with an endless variety of minor adjustments owing their origin to differences in taste and skill.

The Baptism scene in the cupola of the Arian Baptistery closely resembles its earlier counterpart, save that Christ appears as a decidedly boyish figure while the river-god of Jordan is shown as a dominant personage seated above the waters (fig. 145). He displays as his insignia not only the water pot from which the current of the river flows but also a reed as his sceptre and the bizarre embellishment of two lobster claws on top of his head. The Apostles have a distinctly stilted look to them. Clothed uniformly in white and separated from one another by palm trees that show up vividly green against a background of gold instead of indigo, they advance in two files, headed respect-

145. Ravenna, Baptistery of the Arians. Mosaic: the Baptism in the Jordan.

146. Ravenna, the Archbishop's Chapel. Mosaic: Christ triumphant.

ively by Peter and Paul, towards an elaborate throne on which has been laid a cross in token of Christ's redemptive effort close linked with majesty.

Another group of Ravenna mosaics which seem to belong to the age of Theodoric and thus to the end of the fifth or beginning of the sixth century are those of the Archbishop's Chapel.[35] This chapel, dedicated to St Andrew, is a little cross-shaped building. The vault provides the central motif of the mosaic decoration in the form of a symbolic essay on the theme of Christ's divine authority. As though rising from the four corners made by the supporting arches, angels ascend, stretching out their arms to uphold a round medallion containing not the figure of Christ but the chi-rho sign which is his emblem. The angelic forms are thus gracefully elongated and there is room, in the spaces between, for the lion, ox, eagle and angel, equipped with haloes and clasping richly bound books, that represent the Evangelists. The lower surfaces of the arches exhibit a taste for regularity and detail. Each displays a line of portraits enclosed within circular frames, a method of commemorating the deceased that was frequent in pagan as well as Christian funerary art. Christ occupies the central position in all the arches, being shown twice as a young man, beardless and handsome, and twice by means of the symbolic chi-rho flanked by alpha and omega, the beginning and the end. Twelve other medallions present busts of the Apostles, depicted in the forms that had become conventional by the end of the fifth century. St Peter has his hair cropped and in a fringe; St Paul is bald, with long face and thick beard; St Andrew's hair is a fuzzy aureole. The north and south arches display martyr-saints instead of apostles. The six men show considerable variation in age and feature, while a certain sameness is, pleasingly enough, conferred on the women by the device of adorning them with a long white veil that runs down from the top of their head over their shoulders. The approach to St Andrew's Chapel is by way of a vestibule that retains a fair amount of its original mosaic decoration. The little barrel vault is most attractive: ducks, choughs, peacocks and other birds are set within a regular pattern formed by white trefoils and stylized red flowers which make no pretence of being copied from nature. The effect produced is a happy combination of floral design with a moderate impressionism resulting from the varying sizes of the *tessellae* and from the use of pale green to soften the brilliance of the gold background. Above the door is a striking, though much restored, figure of Christ as a warrior, in the act of trampling the lion and serpent underfoot (fig. 146). Such an application to Christ of the Psalmist's words,[36] 'Thou shalt tread upon the lion and the adder: the young lion and the dragon shalt thou tread under thy feet' is quite often found in medieval miniatures, but at this early period it is so rare as to cast some suspicion on the dating of the mosaic. It may however be remarked that Christ's attitude has much in common with the figure of St Laurence in the undoubtedly original mosaic in the Mausoleum of Galla Placidia.

Two chance survivals of early Christian mosaic elsewhere in Italy again illustrate the theme of Christ's authority. Both, however, are somewhat earlier than the Ravenna examples, and may be assigned to the period of artistic revival which marked the reign of Theodosius I. In the Baptistery of Soter, at Naples, the scene is enclosed within a wide border showing peacocks and other birds, together with a variety of fruits, rising from a two-handled tankard; this rich abundance suggests the joys of Paradise. Within the frame a palm tree continues the theme and near it St Peter, carrying not his keys but a staff topped by the chi-rho emblem, stoops with hands reverently covered to receive the scroll of Christ's Law. Christ, standing on the globe of the Universe, stretches out the scroll with his left hand and raises his right arm in blessing.[37] The brightness of his halo contrasts with the dark colour of his hair, sketchily indicated beard and large, wide-open eyes.

The other example is contained in the chapel of St Aquilinus attached to the basilica of S. Lorenzo in Milan. Here the Saviour is shown teaching the twelve Apostles. He is seated upon a rock and thus dominates his companions who appear ranged in two groups, one on each side. Christ has been imagined here as young and beardless, with a halo containing the alpha and omega, but the same dignified convention is observed whereby he raises his right hand in a gesture of benevolent authority while his left hand clasps a book upheld on a fold of his garment. Some of the Apostles also clutch scrolls containing the message entrusted to them, while at Christ's feet is laid a red case of the kind used for containing such written records. The other compartment of the apse contains a pastoral scene with shepherds and a flock of sheep. But there seem to be chests and feet of horses in the heavens above, and it may be that the ascension of Elijah is illustrated.

The style of the St Aquilinus mosaics is clear, straightforward and somewhat clumsy by contrast with that of the chapel of St Victor, which survives as a remnant of the early structures attached to the basilica of S. Ambrogio in Milan. Known as the Chapel of the Golden Heaven, by reason of the brilliant golden *tessellae* with which the ceiling is covered, it is lit from large, round-headed windows between which solemn, hieratic personages clothed in white garments stand out prominently against a blue background. These figures represent Ambrose himself together with the local martyrs Protasius, Gervasius, Maternus, Nabor and Felix. Their faces may display the marks of individual character, but the artist has been concerned less with external appearances than with the attempt to convey an impression of spiritual vitality. Higher up, amidst the golden mosaics of the dome, the bust of St Victor himself stands out within a garland of flowers and fruit. Victor holds a cross and an open book inscribed with his name: this is the Book of Life, and the garland suggests the laurel wreath accorded, as a sign of triumph, to victorious emperors.

Pavements of mosaic dating from the early Christian period are found throughout the Roman Empire, but with particular frequency in Phoenicia and North Africa. These were likely to experience much rougher usage than wall mosaics, so that the use of enamels was ruled out. But the artist with an eye for the decorative effect of marble and stone had great opportunity for showing his skill, since the naves of churches were little encumbered by furniture of any kind and the mosaic could be spread out for all to see.

The style had been set by the Alexandrines in the second century BC. The most usual arrangement at first was to choose a figure subject and place it within a border of geometric patterns or repeated forms of flowers and fruit. As the fashion developed for covering a large area, floor mosaics came to be divided up into several compartments, each containing an elaborate framework of medallions within which single figures or small groups could be set. Pagan convention had favoured the more dramatic incidents of legend, such as the warfare between Hercules and the

Amazons,[38] or the lighthearted acrobatics of cupids and dolphins. On a smaller scale, animals, birds and fish, observed with affectionate care, are often shown within a coiling pattern of vine-stems. Art–forms of this order the Church took over without hesitation. It appears that Christian mosaicists tried their hands at illustrating the New Testament narrative, but such efforts led to distress at the thought of sacred scenes trampled underfoot, and a law of Theodosius II and Valentinian III, passed in 427 AD, prohibited, under severe penalties, the placing of 'Christ's image' on the ground.[39] Of pagan themes some, at least, could be neutral and others even edifying. The phoenix, for instance, was held to 'live for five hundred years and then to make its sepulchre of frankincense and myrrh and die whilst from the ashes of its body sprang a worm which, nourished by the corrupt remains of the dead bird, puts forth wings and flies off to Heliopolis, city of the Sun, in Egypt.'[40] Naturally enough, this suggested the Resurrection, particularly with the support of a verse from Psalm 92—'the righteous shall flourish like a palm tree'—which could in the Greek version be construed 'the righteous shall flourish like a phoenix'. Literary use of the phoenix story was made in the Christian interest as early as the beginning of the second century[41] and thus the phoenix came to be adopted in Church art as an emblem of peculiar significance and power. The noble pavement from Daphne, near Antioch, now in the Louvre, shows a phoenix, like a long-legged crane, standing alone in the glory of a five-rayed halo within a field studded by flower-buds and enclosed by a wide border of rams' heads with flowers between (fig. 147).

Heathen deities could be, so to speak, neutralized and adapted to a Christian environment when they were transformed into signs of the Zodiac or the 'Labours' distinguishing the twelve months of the farmers' year. Thus they found their places in the floor decoration of churches where brilliance of colour and design were commonly looked for rather than detailed reminders of Bible history.

However, remarkable mosaics of a Biblical type have been found at Mopsuestia, a lively centre of theology and the arts when, at the end of the fourth century, Theodore came there from Antioch to be bishop. It was in his time that a famous martyr-church, dedicated to Nicetas the Goth, or possibly the martyrs Tarachos, Protos and Andronicos, was built just out-side the town walls. In addition to a rich ornamentation of birds, fruit and flowers, together with cups, candles and other ritual objects, the mosaic floor offers two rare themes. One is the story of Samson, and presents the only complete cycle of his fortunes that exists from the early period, its doctrinal importance being that, shown as the Jewish counterpart of Hercules, he is also the symbolic forerunner of Christ in his achievements and in his Passion.

The second theme in the Mopsuestia mosaic is a composition centred on Noah's Ark. A variety of beasts and birds, accurately observed and shown with much delicacy of colour and arrangement, throng about the Ark, but there is no attempt at a realistic setting-forth of the Bible story. Noah and his family are absent; in their place are two doves, one sidling in through a hole in the Ark and one seated inside, plain for all to see as the lid of the Ark is open. An inscription, 'The saving Ark of Noah', drives home the lesson, obvious enough in any case, that the Ark, illustrated in this purely symbolic fashion, stands for the Church. Unlike a fifth-century mosaic at Gerasa, which treats the subject historically and shows the animals leaving the Ark as well as the thank-offering of Noah and his sons, the Mopsuestia mosaic compactly displays the Ark in its allusive character, as also represented in wall-paintings of the catacombs. Here, however, the subject is enriched by the kind of artistry, current in Antioch about 400 AD, of which the Battle with the Amazons, found at Daphne nearby, is a classic example. It looks as though cultured and scholarly Theodore availed himself eagerly of the skill of these Antiochene craftsmen. The tradition continued, less vigorous and less inspired, in rather later mosaics at a few other places in Cilicia and particularly at Ayas, where the ritual objects appear once more together with animals, stiffly and sketchily ranged, without light or shade, on a monotonous white background. The inspiration seems to have been rather different in Palestine itself, where the finest mosaics occur in the Church of the Loaves and Fishes at El Tabgha.[42] Here two framed panels bear scattered upon them a wide variety, accurately delineated, of the birds and plants characteristic of the Nile Valley. Some craftsmen, or at least their patterns, must therefore have been imported from Egypt rather than Antioch, with the aim of decoration only rather than sermonizing.

It is the harmonious effect of a vast carpet, displayed in the splendid, though rather late, example found almost intact at Kabr Hiram, that is especially characteristic of Antiochene mosaicists who seem to have travelled in search of work right round the Mediterranean. At Sabratha in Tripoli, for instance, the pavement of the 'Second Church' may be seen as oriental in design and execution. The sixth-century building is roughly constructed, but the mosaic, now kept in the local museum, is one of the finest that remain. It used to cover the whole floor, and was divided into a number of panels each resembling a tapestry, with a simple pattern enclosed by a cable moulding or some equally effective framework. In the body of the nave is set a large, pictorial scene, also within a formal border consisting this time of a double row of trefoils, half of them pointing inwards and half outwards. Here a slim and delicately designed vine-scroll includes within its branches a wide variety of birds—peacocks, a phoenix, a caged quail, and flamingoes among them. Some of these might claim to be of symbolic import; others find their place simply because of their beauty or quaintness.

Much further west along the African coast, at Rusguniae, another great mosaic pavement, now much mutilated, displays an ingenious variety of geometric patterns in the aisles and three large rectangular panels in the nave. One of these is filled with a curious pattern of fish scales, lightly tinted in rose pink, while the next continues the same line of thought in the illustration of fish and sea-shells arranged loosely in seven rows. The eastern panel has rather more to it. Treated with much freedom of design and variety of colour, it shows rams, sheep and goats roaming in a flowered pasture and watched over by two shepherds who wear purple mantles with hoods. One of the men walks across the foreground bearing a pail; the other, whose head is encircled by a halo, milks one of the sheep. The scene recalls the vision of the North African martyr St Perpetua:

I saw a vast expanse of garden and, in the midst, a man sitting, a tall man, with white hair, in the dress of a shepherd, and round about were many thousands clad in white.[43]

Elaborate symbolism of this nature is rare, at least in the pavements of North Africa, where the whole surface often consists of no more than an intricate and charming geometric pattern. But the heroes of Church

147. Daphne, near Antioch. Mosaic pavement: the Phoenix, emblem of the Resurrection. Now in the Louvre.

history or the Bible story may be sparingly introduced, as in the mosaic floor found at Sfax, in Tunisia. The church here is a simple affair consisting of a nave and rounded apse but the pavement, composed with no particular elegance in cubes of limestone and brick, offers an imaginative design. The prevailing pattern is a succession of cross-shaped rosettes followed by branches, within which are set the customary subjects illustrating Nature's bountiful variety: baskets full of fruit, as well as animals, fish and birds, one holding a snake in its beak. But there are also human figures. A rider on horseback, clutching a palm-branch, may be intended to represent the popular military hero, St Theodore. Standing below a wide border embellished with white doves, Daniel too may be seen—not naked, as he is usually shown, but richly clothed in the formal garments appropriate to one who had been appointed 'the third ruler in the kingdom'.[44] That this is an oriental refinement seems to be indicated by such examples of local craftsmanship as the crude, childish carving on a stone capital from Tigzirt, in Algeria, where Daniel appears in his traditional attitude, with hands uplifted in prayer, between two lions. This roughness in regional African work finds its parallel in the mosaic floor at Tabarca and other churches. And it was not only a question of skill and finesse. Cost was a factor also; whereas the splendid wall mosaics were invariably the gift of bishops or highly placed officials, inscriptions, found in several parts of the Empire, show that sections of church pavement were proudly presented by the lawyer, the soldier and the shoemaker.

Another group of mosaics, recently discovered in and near Cyrene, testifies to a burst of vigorous building activity in Justinian's time. Some of the work is of a rough-and-ready, home-made variety, but most displays the metropolitan elegance of craftsmanship imported, together with much Proconnesian marble, from Constantinople. Nearly all the subjects are drawn from the classical stock-in-trade to make up, here again, a formal, rather than symbolic, scheme of decoration. Scenes taken from rural life are popular: in Cyrene Cathedral, for instance, a farmer clutches the tail of his cow whose nose has been seized by a lifelike crocodile. The Central Church at Cyrene, a straight-forward sixth-century basilica, has a spirited sequence

of human and animal figures bordering the mosaic, now fragmentary, which once carpeted the entire floor. Such episodes as a stag killing a snake are typical, but the Christian note is struck with a cross set between two peacocks. At Gasr el Lebia nearby the stag and snake theme recurs, as do the cow and crocodile, and the peacock from the Christian repertory. The unexpected appearance of a naked satyr illustrates the casual manner in which pagan formulae may be introduced into Christian churches. Allegorical figures in the classical manner are included also, as when the gate and towers of this 'new city of Theodora' are shown flanked by the personified forms of Foundation, Renewal and Embellishment, or where the four rivers of Paradise appear in the guise of water nymphs.[45]

In the cemeteries of North Africa dated tomb mosaics sometimes occur, the oldest, at Setif, being that of a certain Honorata who died in 378 AD. Nearly all are plain, framed inscriptions, accompanied only by geometrical decoration in red on brown, but fish are added in the mosaic commemorating the physician Rozonus, at Ténès.

Another method of illustrating Biblical scenes, less remarkable than mosaic but widely adopted in and around Antioch at the end of the fifth century, was by means of marble panels. Some of those recently found at Seleucia Pieria are carved in low relief, but others are treated more in the manner of an engraving. The design is first traced on the flat surface and then cut out in sharply-defined v-shaped grooves; the background was roughly hacked to receive coloured plaster. The examples which have survived are for the most part fragmentary, but they indicate a cycle of both Old Testament and New Testament subjects related to the patterns used for manuscripts. Among the themes illustrated are Saul's contest with the Amalekites and Joseph's conversation in prison with the chief butler and the chief baker. On the New Testament side, Lazarus appears and an undamaged figure of St Paul, bald and with rounded beard, raising his right hand in a stiff and formal gesture while with his left he clasps a book. The series is rounded off by representations of angels in attendance on Christ in majesty.

NOTES

1. The best example is in the Capitoline Museum at Rome.
2. Sidonius Apollinaris, II Ep.10. (Loeb), i.464.
3. *Letters* i.6, ed. T. Hodgkin (London, 1886), 148.
4. *On the various Arts* II.xi, ed. C. R. Dodwell (London, 1961).
5. See p. 41.
6. St John 15.5.
7. H. Stern, *Les mosaïques de l'Église de Sainte Constance*, *Dumbarton Oaks Papers* XII (1958).
8. The scene is not entirely clear. Some have interpreted St Peter as a female saint.
9. The jewelled cross was perhaps suggested by the silver-gilt cross which Theodosius II set up on Golgotha.
10. Revelation 20.
11. *Life of Moses* i.5, ed. Cohn and Wendland (Berlin, 1902) 4, 124.
12. St Luke 2.
13. Joshua 5.13–15.
14. Revelation 5.1.
15. This detail is drawn from the Infancy Gospel of James (10.1), a work which also told of Joseph's disquiet. M. R. James, *The Apocryphal New Testament*, 43.
16. Revelation 21.2.
17. Revelation 21.
18. St John 10.3.
19. 2.22–39.
20. St Matthew 2.13–18.
21. E.g. Pseudo-Matthew 23. M. R. James, *ibid.*, 75.
22. Isaiah 19.3.
23. St Matthew 2.4.
24. Felix was pope from 526 to 530. He adapted a large rectangular hall, built by the emperor Vespasian, and added an apse to it. His figure in the mosaic is mainly a seventeenth-century restoration.
25. The Lamb's halo provides an example, very unusual during the early period, of the use of silver.
26. Revelation 4.4. Most of the imagery of the upper mosaic is suggested by this chapter of Revelation, but the effect is marred by injudicious botching, much of it carried out when the arch was altered in the seventeenth century.
27. Colossians 1.14.
28. Perhaps the Virgin Mary was originally there also, as in later adaptations of the same design.
29. Romans 8.
30. Some attempt at precision has been made by reference to a fragmentary inscription in the mosaic which refers to 'the humble Andrew'. There was an archbishop Andrew at Salonica from 491 to 497. But there was also an Andrew from Salonica present at the Council of Chalcedon (451). Some commentators, however, have doubted whether a prominent ecclesiastic at either time would refer to himself as 'humble'. See C. Bakirtzis in *ACIAC* IX.
31. See p. 175.
32. The upper section of the mosaic is in large part an eighteenth-century restoration and some of the details, such as the cross in the Baptist's left hand, may not follow the original scheme.
33. Philippians 2.15.
34. The octagonal font also was reconstructed in medieval times.
35. The question of date has been much argued. The chapel was built by an archbishop named Peter, and probably he is to be identified with the second of that name (494–519 AD).
36. Psalm 12.13.
37. This part of the mosaic is much damaged, and another figure, presumably St Paul, has almost disappeared.
38. Louvre 3463, 3464.
39. *Codex Justinianus* i.8.
40. The story is found in Herodotus 2.73 and Pliny, *Natural History* 10.2.
41. *The First Epistle of Clement* 25. *The Apostolic Fathers* (Loeb) i.52.
42. See p. 100.
43. *Passion of SS. Perpetua and Felicitas* iv, ed. E. C. Owen, *Acts of the early Martyrs* 81. The lettering of the mutilated inscription on the Rusguniae mosaic has been held to denote a fourth-century date.
44. Daniel 5.29.
45. For the topographical mosaics, e.g. Madaba, see p. 103.

14

Carved Ivories

The use of objects made of carved ivory spread westwards from centres of oriental craftsmanship at an early date. Even in Homer's time, ivory was a recognized sign of luxury and, in the heyday of Roman prosperity, Horace,[1] as a pretended devotee of the simple life, felt called upon to boast that 'no ivory and no golden ceiling glittered in his house'. The chairs of Roman officials[2] were sometimes made of ivory and the consul's sceptre provided with an ivory tip,[3] while elephant tusks were among the most highly prized booty borne in a Roman triumph. And, after Caesar's assassination, his body was laid, in sombre dignity, upon an ivory bed covered with gold and purple. To such associations of splendour was added the fact that ivory, being extremely hard and awkwardly shaped, required on the part of the craftsmen skilful handling of chisel and saw as well as a whole collection of files and gravers used for the detailed ornament.

A guild of ivory-carvers existed at Rome in the second century AD and was regarded with imperial favour, but its members, capable artisans rather than artists, were well content to follow the technique and the models adopted by the stonemasons. While the capital cities could occasionally produce work of the greatest elegance, much of the ivory that survives is carved with the rough competence of travelling craftsmen. It is therefore not easy to distinguish local styles. Egyptian ivories have about them the archaic air which characterizes Coptic art, and a certain primitive stiffness seems to mark examples originating in Gaul. Elsewhere the style of ivories is a matter of date and the use to which they were put rather than geography.

Ivory offered itself as an excellent material from which to fashion combs and various other aids to personal adornment. As good an example as any is the ivory comb from Antinoë, now in the Coptic Museum in Cairo. On one side the teeth are coarsely set, on the other they are very fine. The central portion makes up two plaques. On the first, Christ is shown clasping his scroll of authority as, with a strangely distorted right arm and hand, he touches the eyes of the man born blind. Next to this, Christ again appears, holding a scroll and a long cross, in front of a roughly represented tomb in which stands Lazarus, tightly swathed from head to foot. The reverse side displays a vigorous carving of two angels who support a wreath of victory enclosing a saint mounted on horseback or, possibly, Christ entering Jerusalem on the donkey.

More substantial creations from ivory were jewel-boxes, book-covers and carved tablets joined together in pairs to form 'diptychs'. A diptych was originally a pair of wooden writing-tablets fastened by rings in such a manner that the inner sides, covered with wax, lay one against the other. They formed the equivalent of a briefcase and were used for recording letters and documents. Under the Empire, wealthy persons liked to indulge a taste for magnificence, and diptychs of ivory, elaborately carved, were sent to friends in order to announce the steps of promotion in an official career or, rather less frequently, to record a marriage or some other event of family importance. Attempts were made, not with complete success, to check this extravagant habit and to confine the use of such costly

148. Aosta, the diptych of Probus: the emperor Honorius.

149. Brescia: the diptych of Boethius.

diptychs to the consuls who, on entering office, were entitled and perhaps expected to send ivory diptychs, mounted in metal, to provinces, cities and 'persons of the highest influence and one's dearest companions'.[4] The largest and most splendid diptychs were those intended for the emperor himself; in these cases each leaf was often made up of four or five separate parts.

The consular diptychs are of value not merely in their own right, but because, since the calendar year bore the consul's name, they can be exactly dated and thus provide a firm framework from which to judge the evolution of style. An early example is the consular diptych of Probus, now preserved in the cathedral of Aosta (fig. 148). This diptych was carved at Rome in 406 AD and imitates the long-established forms of Roman statuary. The emperor Honorius is represented on both leaves: a stumpy, bovine young man as he was in life, standing alone beneath an archway decorated with ribbon ornament. His costume is that of a soldier, but halo and diadem symbolize his imperial dignity. Looking almost straight ahead he clasps, on one leaf, shield and staff and, on the other, a military banner and an orb. These two emblems illustrate the nice balance an emperor might have to

maintain between Christian and pagan ideologies. For on the orb is poised the winged goddess Victory, eagerly holding out towards Honorius the conqueror's wreath; the banner, on the other hand, is surmounted by the chi-rho monogram which, whatever its origins, had by the fifth century become a symbol of Christianity. The banner itself proclaims the moral in a more obvious fashion by bearing the text: 'Mayest thou ever conquer in Christ's name.'

Rather more frequently the consuls offered portraits of themselves. Asturius,[5] consul in 449, is shown seated upon his ornate chair between two attendants. Each figure, again in obedience to Roman convention, is enclosed within his own niche, here formed by pillars with channelled shafts and heavy Corinthian capitals. Clasping the sceptre and scroll which betoken his office, Asturius gazes with a trance-like expression into space. Behind him are architectural features which could be thought to represent his house, but the solemn and balanced elaboration of pediment, shell and garlands half suggests a shrine before which the consul is set in mystical awareness of his calling. The Asturius diptych leaf is often thought to have a Syrian look to it and the chain-like decoration

150. The diptych of Anastasius. Probably from Constantinople. Paris, Bibliothèque Nationale.

of the frame is in keeping with this judgement, but, if this is so, the Asiatic carver had travelled a long way round the Mediterranean in search of work, for there is little doubt that the ivory comes from Southern Gaul and probably from Arles.

Towards the end of the fifth century the method of showing of a consul became stereotyped, in that he invariably appears presiding over the Games and holding the napkin which he raised as a sign that the performance was to begin. A lower register might depict scenes from the Games or, no less often, the money-bags which hinted at the consul's generous expenditure on public entertainment. By this time the artistic style shows a certain falling-off from classical ideals. Carving tends to become shallower, and thus to resemble etching rather than statuary, while there is a finicky obsession with minute details of costume. The diptych of Boethius,[6] consul in 487, places him, once again, within a pedimented niche, but his large, flattened head is set stiffly upon what is less a body than a formalized swathing of garments (fig. 149).

Something like the same formula is maintained in the diptych of Anastasius[7] (517 AD), a masterpiece which may be attributed to the workshop at Constantinople (fig. 150). The consul is enveloped in the folds of his heavily embroidered clothing, but he has none of the crabbed and morose air about him which characterizes Boethius. Clearly he will enjoy the Games, and their excitements are hinted at by the vigorous contests shown on a small scale in the lower part of the panels. Anastasius, naturally enough, is seated on his splendid chair of office which occupies the entire width of the conventional archway and indeed seems to merge with it. The only architectural feature to be stressed is a graceful pediment decorated in egg and dart pattern; from this pediment the shell which is to be seen in the diptych of Asturius has descended, as it were, to form the halo with which the wide-eyed dignity of Anastasius is emphasized. Portraits of Emperor and Empress appear, attended by winged genii, and figures symbolizing Rome and Constantinople contribute, along with much other detail, to a lively and luxurious, if somewhat overcrowded, composition.

The importance of the consular diptychs in the history of Christian art is that they put forward a type and pattern of authoritative rule easily adapted to the figures of Christ and the Apostles. Moreover, the practice of devising and sending round leaves of ivory carved with what might be described as propaganda offered certain hints to church dignitaries: it has been suggested, but not proved, that bishops of the more important sees were expected to follow the custom of the consuls and supply diptychs on their accession to office. What is certain is that diptychs found their way quite early into the ceremonies of the Christian liturgy. One of the two leaves was then inscribed with the names of local benefactors, but such names were soon outnumbered or superseded by emperors, bishops and others in authority. The second panel, the diptych of the dead, recalled saints and martyrs together with the departed bishops of a particular church. Sometimes, as in the case of St Chrysostom, a name was pointedly removed from the diptych leaf on the ground that only those whose orthodoxy was above suspicion might be included.

It may reasonably be asked whether a diptych offering scenes or figures drawn from classical mythology illustrates the survival of a tradition whereby gods, nereids and satyrs play their part for convention's sake, or whether it reflects a sincere desire to keep alive the ancient pieties. To introduce such stock romantic figures as Hippolytus and Phaedra[8] might well be no more than a graceful method of announcing a betrothal, but when Aesculapius appears, as on the Liverpool diptych which shows the God of Healing along with the emblematic figure of Health, the choice of subject marks a determined stand on behalf of paganism, whether on religious grounds or as a sign of respect for a social order threatened by new currents of thought. The same type of argument may be applied also to the Christian emblems, whether crosses or something more elaborate. A leaf of the 'Barberini' diptych, a product of the early sixth century and now at the Louvre, shows an emperor, Anastasius or Justinian, on horseback and attended by such figures as winged Victories, conquered barbarians, lions and the fruit-bearing Earth. This splendidly balanced composition is completed by a top panel in which Christ appears, curly-haired, with cross-sceptre and right hand raised in blessing. The figure of Christ is contained within a medallion upheld by two flying angels, but whether it is to be regarded as a piece of conventional ornament or as a clear proclamation of faith is a question which perhaps did not occur to the artist. The last of the consular diptychs, dated 540 AD, the diptych

151. Ivory panel: the Ascension. North Italian, now at Munich.

of Justin which is now at the State Museum, Berlin, shows Christ bearded and with a halo. But the bust is set within an oval medallion of exactly the same size as those of Justinian and Theodora who flank Christ on either side: little distinction is here made between divine and imperial sovereignty.

The theme of ascension into Heaven was developed in both the Christian and the pagan interest. The most remarkable of the early Christian examples is the Munich panel, probably of North Italian workmanship and early fifth-century date (fig. 151). This ivory, while bearing a formal relationship to the style of the sarcophagi, displays a wholly unusual lightness and grace in its composition. There is no undue crowding, and the sense of space heightens the effect of mystery proceeding from each of the balanced scenes. Moreover, the artist's sensitivity is such that he invests his figures with strongly-marked character. At the foot of the panel the three women, posed in attitudes of mournful questioning, approach the tomb which, by contrast with the airy impressionism of the rest of the plaque, is carved with minute elaboration. In front of the tomb a wingless angel, seated with outstretched hand as he addresses the women, derives both form and posture from the best classical models; behind him grows a tree in which birds pecking fruit are symbolic of eternal life. Skilfully placed at the side of the tomb stand two soldiers, one gazing before him in hesitant surprise, the other asleep with his head bowed on his arms. Above, on a rocky hillside, are two apostles, one crouching in stupefied awe, the other with palms outstretched and face uplifted in gratitude and amazement as he contemplates Christ. Unlike the pagan deities or such Old Testament figures as Elijah, Christ has no need of a chariot. With his cloak swinging behind him in the wind he is the embodiment of victorious eagerness as he strides up the mountain. His face, encircled by a halo, expresses the charm of youth allied with resolute purpose, and in his left hand he clutches the scroll of authority. Meanwhile his extended right hand is clasped by the hand of God emerging from the clouds. This particular indication of the Father's power to intervene is a novelty. The hand of God is sometimes to be seen on sarcophagi, restraining Abraham from the sacrifice of his son or presenting the Law to Moses, but its appearance at the time of the Ascension seems not to occur elsewhere before the seventh century.[9]

The pagan counterpart to the Ascension motif is provided by a diptych leaf now in the British Museum. The subject is an emperor, raised after death to become a divine being. At the bottom of the panel four elephants and their riders draw an effigy of the emperor, so full of life as almost to suggest an enhancement of the human powers, enthroned beneath the triangular pediment of a little shrine. Nearby, in the centre of the panel, a diminutive, naked figure—the emperor in the likeness of the Sun, whose rising represents his own—is borne aloft in a chariot drawn by four prancing horses and preceded by two upward-surging eagles, disproportionately large. Above, the emperor, seated in the arms of two angels, is carried to Heaven where other deities, five men of varying age, await him. In a corner, signs of the zodiac appear and a bust of Phoebus, the sun-god. The ivory has a markedly eastern look to it, and the angels, with their robust human bodies, upturned eagles' wings and flamelike hair swept back by the wind, suggest Assyrian rather than classical models. But the monogram on the frame is usually interpreted as standing for the Symmachi, one of the great families of Rome, and it seems that the diptych was carved there, in about 450 AD, to proclaim defiantly, and with an overpowering wealth of symbolism, that pagan beliefs had not yet been entirely superseded by the triumphant upsurge of Christianity.

Naturally enough, certain ivories plead no cause but seek to express delight in paganism's lush sensuality. Such examples are, for the most part, of Egyptian origin. They include a small panel, now in the National Museum at Ravenna, which, with all the crude, rhythmical vigour of Coptic art, shows Apollo playing on his lyre while Daphne, extending an ill-proportioned right arm in a gesture of dramatic despair, clasps with her left hand the tree into which she is being transformed. In general, however, the history of carving in ivory closely follows that of carving in stone. As Christian themes come to predominate, the style of the pagan sarcophagi is adopted unselfconsciously as the mode of expression natural to the age. And the themes are uniform, whether on ivory or on stone: a limited range of Biblical subjects, rooted in the tradition of the catacombs, gradually expands to include both an ampler series of New Testament scenes and matter drawn from the Apocryphal Gospels.

The most abundant supply of such carvings in ivory is provided by the pyxes—small boxes, usually cylindrical in shape, that were at first used as jewel-cases. For a century or two after the Peace of the Church, pyxes ornamented with pagan or purely decorative motifs continued to appear. Several display Bacchic scenes; others show Orpheus charming the entire world of nature—animals, satyrs, centaurs and the rest—by playing on his lyre.[10] The best of these is at the Abbey of St Columbanus, Bobbio.

Pyxes were not confined to ladies' dressing-tables, since they could also be used, in connection with sacrifices, as incense holders. Thence they passed into the service of the Church, to contain relics or, more frequently, eucharistic bread. As early as the middle of the third century St Cyprian[11] had spoken of 'the box in which was the sacrament of the Lord', and the frequent choice for illustration on a pyx of Abraham's sacrifice of Isaac, typifying the sacrifice of Christ, well suits the eucharistic theme.

One of the earliest and finest of the ivory caskets on which Abraham and Isaac appear is a pyx, probably from a town on the Moselle, which is now in the Berlin Museum (fig. 152). Here Isaac stands, an almost babyish figure, cross-legged and with his hands behind his back, before a lofty and elaborate altar. Abraham has placed his left hand on his son's head while with his right he clasps the sacrificial knife. But he turns to perceive the hand of God appearing from a cloud, while an angel with hand outstretched in urgent entreaty is, in effect, a repeated sign of God's power to intervene. At the angel's feet crouches the ram with his horns caught in a thicket. The composition, though dramatically conceived, is somewhat mannered and may owe its form to pictures of Calchas slaying Iphigeneia, a classical counterpart to the Abraham story in which redemption, in this case the safety of the Greek fleet, is secured by the offering of an innocent victim. The other side of the box offers a representation of Christ enthroned amidst the twelve Apostles. This scene, too, has a classic air. Not only is the balance of the figures regular and restrained, but Christ displays that blend of benevolence with complete authority so dear to the political theorists of the Roman Empire.

Somewhat older than the Berlin pyx, and unsurpassed for excellence of design and craftmanship in ivory, is the rectangular casket preserved at Brescia, in northern Italy. This is sometimes described as the *lipsanotheca*, or reliquary, of Brescia, since it was for many years used, and perhaps originally intended, to contain the bones of saints. The form of composition, the manner in which Christ is represented, and such minor details as the women's hairstyle point to the Theodosian epoch and a date near 380 AD. Though arguments continue regarding its place of origin, it appears to be an Italian piece possibly carved by a craftsman, or craftsmen, from Asia Minor. The detail of the panels has much in common with the sarcophagi of the later fourth century and, though the sources from which the artist drew his models cannot be clearly established, it appears that he had before him an illustrated Bible or a series of standard cartoons from which a Bible could be composed. His chosen method was to work in panels of two sizes, large for the New Testament scenes, small for the Old Testament. To these was added a third order consisting of fifteen well-differentiated portrait-busts representing a Christ of markedly juvenile appearance, together with the Apostles and Evangelists. The top of the box is taken up by two of the large panels displaying a narrative sequence of the Passion story. On the front appear examples of Christ's benevolent activity: the healing of the woman with an issue of blood, the unfolding of the scroll of his teaching before the elders in the synagogue at Nazareth, and the Good Shepherd standing beneath a gracefully arched portico and surveying his sheep. The panel at the back contains two scenes. The first is often described as the Transfiguration, and at any rate it depicts a recognition by apostles of Christ's unique calling, so that it is odd to find that the companion piece in this particular panel shows St Paul seated on a stool and raising his hand in solemn warning as Ananias and Sapphira meet the doom which their deception had warranted. At each end healings are demonstrated. On the right side occur two favourite themes, the cure of the blind man and the raising of Lazarus, curtly set forth in the conventional attitudes, while on the left is a fuller and most attractive portrayal of Christ raising Jairus's daughter from her bed while four graceful spectators, closely grouped without crowding, express their awe and amazement at this display of supernatural power (fig. 153).

The Old Testament scenes include the established favourites which exemplify salvation in time of stress,

152. Ivory casket: Abraham and Isaac. Probably from the district of Trier.

together with a number of new and original choices. The earliest stories to be reproduced concern Jacob: the ladder of his dream with an angel climbing it, his wrestling-match with the angel, and the quiet, pastoral picture in which he waters Rachel's flocks for her at the well. Moses receives a fuller treatment continued over three panels; there are also two scenes of feasting, one showing five people seated round a table bearing loaves and a fish. This is the posture often adopted in early Christian representations of the Eucharist, and looks back to the Passover meal from which the Christian Eucharist developed. The popular theme of David and Goliath occurs, together with two odd and unusual topics drawn from the Book of Kings: the old prophet slain by the lion, and the heathenish sacrifice of King Jeroboam which caused his hand to be withered as he withdrew it from the altar. A more obvious choice of subjects is provided by Jonah, Daniel and Susanna, three standard examples of heroic constancy justified by God's effective intervention on their behalf. On the corners, and as an addition to the carvings on the lid, is a miscellaneous collection of emblems. There are, for example, doves caught in a net, to represent the capture of human souls in the net

of salvation, as well as a cross, a lamp, a fish, Peter's cock perched on a column, and a balanced pair of subjects: Judas hanging in disgrace, and, by contrast, the strong tower which represents the Church.

The series of carvings on the Brescia casket has passed far beyond the concise symbols present in the catacombs to a delight not only in classic form but in narrative for its own sake, and to an awareness of the marvels surrounding human life which characterizes the art of the Middle Ages.

The cylindrical pyxes, few of which are earlier than the sixth century, show a similar liking for the record of the sacred history and the apocryphal details that accompany it, but, apart from anything else, considerations of space preclude the wide variety of the Brescia casket. The standard scenes recur again and again, sometimes tamely reproduced, sometimes shown with graceful artistry. The Gospel miracles are a frequent choice, but certain pyxes are devoted to one or other of the Old Testament heroes.

The four pyxes in the collection at the Hermitage, Leningrad, may serve as typical examples. All are of North Italian workmanship and, in spite of individual touches, belong in general style and iconography to a

153. Brescia, Ivory casket: the 'Lipsanotheca'. The raising of Jairus's daughter.

closely connected group. It is the Moses pyx which offers the most striking variations from the norm, though two of the three scenes are among the most frequent in which Moses appears. The first shows Moses receiving the tables of the Law. The hand of God emerges from the clouds and extends to Moses a book which he reverently clasps in the folds of his mantle. Nearby, for all that Moses is said in the Bible record to have been alone with God on Sinai's height, a spectator raises his hand in token that a mystery is being enacted. Moses is here shown as young and beardless; in the next scene, where he strikes the rock to obtain water for the faithless Israelites, he appears as old, bearded and without shoes. The third incident is unusual, and perhaps unique, in its details. Moses is shown participating in a religious ritual charged with allusions to the Old Testament. A rectangular altar-table, or Torah shrine, bears on it the book of the Law, beneath a canopy formed of two twisted columns supporting a sea-shell from which a lamp hangs. On the ground nearby is a vase containing foliage. The dignified figure of Moses is placed to the left. He raises his hand in a gesture expressing readiness and authority; on his right an elderly man approaches holding a

basket of loaves, no doubt the shewbread to be 'set before the Lord'. Behind, a younger man, simply clad in a short tunic, advances bearing a horned goat on his shoulders.

The Jonah pyx, worked in high relief and with a wealth of naturalistic detail, has no more than the customary pair of scenes: Jonah is shown first being hurled into the water, and then asleep under the gourd tree. Similarly, the Daniel pyx, a cylinder 9 centimetres high with a low, conical cover, offers conventional subjects, but with much picturesque detail. For instance, an angel, without halo, advances towards the flames of the fiery furnace, which he extinguishes by plunging the shaft of a cross into them.

The next of the Leningrad pyxes is given over to a series of Gospel stories which had, by the fifth century, come to exert the widest popular appeal. Though not to be seen as a miracle of healing, the narrative of Christ's meeting with the Samaritan woman at the well was felt to be of special significance. On the Leningrad pyx she appears, clothed in a sleeveless tunic and with a row of curls along her brow, sitting by the elaborate structure which the artists liked to offer

154. Panels of a book-cover: scenes from the life of Christ. North Italian, about 430 AD. One of the panels is now in the Louvre, one at Berlin.

as an image of her well. Before her Christ stands between two pillars. He is young, with an abundance of curly hair. Clasping the roll of authority in his left hand, he raises his right in blessing given—and perhaps herein lay the attractive power of the event—to a representative woman of the world who yet had faith to enquire and the wisdom to accept revelation. The other incidents shown on the Leningrad pyx, and repeated on several others,[12] unite in offering a message of hope and healing to the afflicted: the blind man of Jericho, the paralysed man with his bed, and the Gadarene demoniac. These were felt to be episodes in history of such import that they deserved their place on sacred vessels just as they did in the solemnities of burial. For the ivory-carvers closely followed examples set by the makers of sarcophagi both in the subjects and in the details of attitude and expression.

It is, however, extremely difficult to make the most of any scene on the curving sides of a cylindrical box. Thus the flat panels, rare survivals that once made up diptychs or book–covers, display these favourite Gospel incidents to best advantage. The supreme example of artistic sensitivity is supplied by a pair of panels of which one is preserved at the Louvre (fig. 154), the other in Berlin. Each panel contains three scenes, separated by frames of egg and dart pattern, and all gain their effect from a refusal to crowd restricted space and from a delicate touch endowing simple gestures with profound emotion.

The first scene shows the Massacre of the Innocents in the presence of Herod, seated impassive and resolute on his throne. Here the matter-of-fact brutality of the soldier contrasts with the passionate grief of the distracted mother. Next follows the Baptism: a vigorous Baptist, his every action denoting the prophet's awareness of his call, lays his hand on a diminutive Christ standing in an impressionistic version of the river Jordan with, overhead, the Spirit descending as a dove. The remainder of the panels is given up to four miracles, conventional in choice but masterly as interpretations of well-loved themes. The turning of water into wine at Cana differs from the rest in that Christ is shown in an attitude of command, standing with right hand raised and a scroll betokening authority in his left. No more than two other characters are included: the master of the feast who, by a certain compression of the Gospel account, looks

on in wonder, and the servant pouring water from a two-handled vessel into one of four large pots. The artist here reproduces the spirit of St John's summing up: 'this miracle at Cana of Galilee is the first of the signs whereby Jesus revealed his glory.'[13] The three other scenes, that is to say the whole of the Louvre panel, offer as their theme the compassion of Christ shown in response to the varieties of human need. Christ's appearance and costume are identical throughout: he is the youthful, beardless, curly-headed Son of David's line.

The primitive custom whereby Christ was felt to be most aptly symbolized by the miracles which occurred during his ministry gradually yielded in some measure to an interest in the cardinal events of his life. Details of the Passion, for instance, are dramatically set forth in four panels now at the British Museum. The style is very different from that of the Louvre and Berlin leaves, and still more remote from the light, airy, well-spaced arrangement of the Munich Ascension. The stumpy, compact figures with their large heads stand out in high relief from the background. Action is realistic to the point of becoming over-dramatic, reflecting a tendency towards rough brutality which existed in Roman art side by side with the easy restraint of classicism. The first scene is a composite one. Pilate washing his hands, at one end of the panel, is balanced at the other by St Peter, seated to warm himself at the fire and stretching out the palm of his hand to emphasize his denial of the maidservant's accusation 'This man also was with him'; the cock sits, ready to crow, on his perch above. At the centre Jesus appears, carrying his cross, but with an air of purpose rather than pathos which is repeated in the scene of the Crucifixion itself (fig. 155). Here too the artist aims to compress much detail into a restricted space. Judas is hanging from a tree, with the pieces of silver spilled on the ground beneath his feet. The principle of balanced antithesis comes once more into play: Christ also hangs from a tree, but the tree of the cross has salvation as its fruit by contrast with the hideous ignominy of Judas. This representation of Christ on the cross is closely related to the door-panel of S. Sabina in Rome. Naked except for a loincloth and, once again, shown as a graceful youth, Christ remains free of suffering, the conscious master of his fate. Beneath the extended arms of the cross people of various types are gathered: the Virgin, Joseph of

155. Panels illustrating the Passion of Christ: a. Christ carrying the cross; b. the Crucifixion. North Italian, fifth century.

Arimathaea in puzzled melancholy clutching his casket of spices, and the Roman soldier making as though to thrust his spear into the Lord's side.

The Resurrection panel offers a stylized tomb, complete with circular drum and conical cap. At the side the two Marys are crouching, while in the foreground two Roman soldiers are seated in theatrical attitudes which might be interpreted either as the abandon of sleep or as amazement at the tomb's opened door. Finally Christ, still a boyish figure, stands triumphant on a raised plinth which might be thought to hint at the Mount of the Ascension, at the mid-point between four apostles who, in their several ways, exhibit the stock dramatic postures of joy, amazement and, in the case of St Thomas, incredulity.

In such fashion the ivory-carvers of the fifth century continued the tradition, set by the rough and ready paintings of Dura, of concentrating on the Bible narrative shown forth with vivid action and economy of detail. Development from this point took the form of a reflection on Christ's nativity, wherein myth is called upon to offer its tribute to mystery, and marvels drawn from the apocryphal writings supply a commentary on the bald records of Scripture.

Two ivories from North Italy—one carved just before the middle of the fifth century, one about 480 AD—serve as examples of this tendency. The first of these consists of three panels, now preserved in London at the Victoria and Albert Museum and known as the Werden casket. The scenes shown on these panels merge into one another in a densely packed sequence of vigorous movement. The artist proves himself able to render a conventional New Testament subject with freedom and sensitivity; this skill is evident, for example, in the contrast between Virgin and Child seated in unruffled calm and the Three Wise Men, each bearing an enormous dish and hastening forward in an attitude of eager excitement. The Werden casket may be said to look backwards as well as forwards. Acceptance of the old pagan deities as part of the decorative furniture of a Christian scheme continues in the elaborate figure of the river-god Jordan set against St John in the Baptism scene. On the other hand, some of the incidents in which the Virgin plays a part are direct anticipations of themes worked over repeatedly in the Middle Ages, such as, for instance, the earliest representation of Mary about to ascend the steps of the Temple to undergo the trial by bitter water which was to decide the strength of her claim to chastity.[14]

The Werden panels, for all their interest, bear a somewhat confused and smudgy look. This is entirely absent from the meticulous artistry of two leaves of the ivory cover for a Gospel-book that are now kept at Milan Cathedral. Both style and subject have much in common with the Werden casket, but each scene is separate and enclosed within the border of its frame. The two central panels are the largest. One shows the Lamb of God, set within a wreath of fruit and flowers. Matching this, the other leaf has a cross composed of metalwork in a pattern of ovals, rectangles and circles (fig. 156). The cross stands on a mound in front of the entrance to a temple shrine from which the curtains have been drawn back in token that the death of Christ provides access for all. The corners of each leaf are occupied by the emblems of two of the four Evangelists and with two nearly identical busts representing the Evangelists themselves. Between these medallions, at the top, are a Nativity scene and the coming of the Wise Men, both closely following the formula adopted on the Werden casket. At the bottom are shown the Massacre of the Innocents and a dramatic rendering of the Marriage Feast at Cana, with Christ in the role of the youthful wonder-worker amid a number of spectators. The half-dozen side panels on each leaf resemble the larger ones in that a style of clear and graceful narrative is adopted, and the figures are so well spaced that there is no blurring or awkwardness in conveying the message. The Gospel miracles of the blind man, the paralytic, and Lazarus closely follow the tradition set by the sarcophagi of Italy and southern Gaul, and such incidents from Christ's history as the Baptism, the Teaching in the Synagogue and the Triumphal Entry likewise follow the patterns of western iconography. There is also an illustration of the Last Supper, compactly represented, in the primitive fashion, by four figures reclining around the 'sigma' couch. But here, as with the illustrations on the Werden casket, the widespread influence of the apocryphal writings is apparent as supplying details for which the stern restraint of the Bible record failed to allow. The Annunciation therefore takes place not in a house but close to the spring from which the Virgin was filling her pitcher when the angel called her; opposite this scene, an attractive vignette shows Mary hesitating at the foot of the Temple staircase

156. Milan: panel from the ivory cover of a Gospel-book. The cross, in metalwork, stands before a shrine.

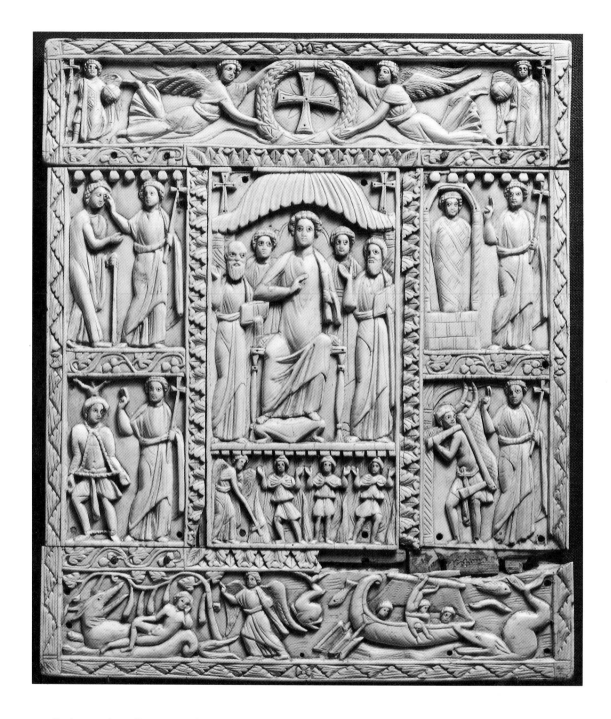

157. Book-cover from Constantinople: the 'Murano ivory'.

which the angel bids her ascend in confidence that she will emerge triumphant from the trial of the bitter water.[15]

The Milan Gospel-covers present Roman art at its best, disciplined yet vivid, drawn into the service of the Church. The 'Murano ivory', also a book-cover and now at the National Museum, Ravenna, is worked in a very different style. The choice of scenes is conventional enough, but the figures are elongated, stare straight in front of them with fixed gaze and, though stiffly posed, show in the hang of their garments something of the flowing, voluptuous line commonly described as 'Eastern'. The Murano leaf has therefore been ascribed to Egypt or, with greater likelihood, to Constantinople, early in the sixth century. The surface is divided into seven panels. The largest, central one is assigned to Christ, shown as youthful and curly-headed but enthroned, in solemn authority, beneath a mushroom-like canopy (fig. 157). Peter and Paul, clasping gospels, stand with hands raised in acclamation at either side, with two attendant angels in the background. A small subdivision of the panel, beneath Christ's feet, is occupied by the three men in the fiery furnace. The topmost panel, extending across the whole width of the cover, shows two angels, floating in an almost horizontal position with one leg raised at the knee. They support a Maltese cross enclosed within a wreath, while at each corner the somewhat martial figure of an archangel stands with long-shafted cross and orb. The four side panels display the well-loved miracles of healing: the blind man, the demoniac, the paralytic and Lazarus. Except that he stretches out his hand to touch the blind man, Christ appears in every scene as precisely the same personage. There is not the least pretence of realism or adjustment to varying circumstances. Rather Christ's figure embodies the concept, popular in the sixth century, of remote but benevolent majesty, with hair so tightly curled that it resembles a diadem, his right hand raised in blessing and a long processional cross, copying that of the archangel above, held in the left hand. The lowest panel of all brings in the favourite scenes of Jonah's deliverance.

The Murano leaf is deeply carved in a firm, clear line and thus presents a contrast with another pair of sixth-century Gospel-covers, now kept at Paris.[16] Here the workmanship is of a rough, provincial character, with clumsy, sometimes distorted figures, and a good deal of fussy cross-hatching in the background gives a general effect of smudginess. However, the craftsman, perhaps an Asiatic who had migrated to Gaul, was familiar with patterns which were by his day becoming standardized. For the arrangement of the scenes follows that of the Murano leaf; each cover is divided into seven panels—horizontal bands at top and bottom with a large central panel double the size of each of the four supporting panels at the sides. The upper register of both covers is occupied by the conventional form, found on the Murano leaf as well as on a number of sixth-century sarcophagi, of two angels, with one leg straight and the other bent, floating horizontally in the heavens and upholding the broad wreath which encloses a cross with arms of equal length.[17] The central panels match one another precisely. No longer is the artist content to follow the Milan example of symbolic Lamb and Cross. Here there are two figures, seated on identical thrones: Christ holding the book of his teachings, with two apostles in the background, and the Virgin, holding the Child and attended by two angels. The four subsidiary panels offer scenes appropriate to each central figure. Christ, again with the long cross of victory in one hand, performs his miracles of healing on the blind man, the paralytic, the woman with the issue of blood and the Gadarene demoniac; complementing these illustrations on the other leaf, the Virgin is shown in the episodes of the Annunciation, the Visitation, the trial by bitter water and the journey, on donkey-back and supported by Joseph, to Bethlehem. On the narrow strip at the foot of the former cover Lazarus and the Samaritan woman appear, while the Triumphal Entry occupies the corresponding panel of the second cover. Here, as throughout, dramatic postures of excited movement combine with a certain lumpiness of execution. The manner in which Christ is shown presents an odd inconsistency. Six times he appears as a beardless young man; in the central panel, however, he is shown with long hair and a full, pointed beard, a figure no less venerable than the two apostles standing in respectful attendance behind his throne. While the artists might well be undecided between the traditions of Christ the ever-youthful wonder-worker and Christ the awe-inspiring Judge and Ruler of the Universe, the contrast here is carried to the point of paradox.

While the Paris Gospel-covers may not be a dis-

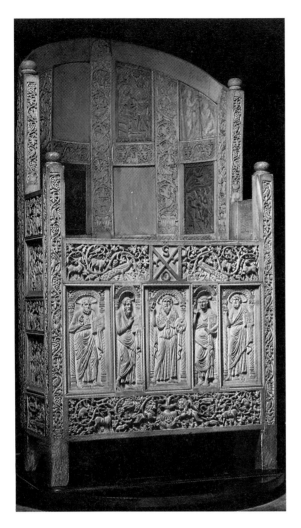

158. Ravenna: the chair of Bishop Maximian.

tinguished work of art, they clearly reveal the trend of Christian interest at the beginning of the sixth century, and they have a further importance as showing certain points of likeness, in both technique and arrangement of subject, to the finest of all early Christian works in ivory, the chair of Bishop Maximian, now in the Archiepiscopal Museum at Ravenna (fig. 158). This chair owes its attractiveness in part to its simple and finely proportioned lines. Raised up on four plain feet, the seat has a rectangular, panelled front with corner posts, simple in design but elaborately carved. Similar posts higher up join the seat to the curved back. The carving is remarkable not only for the grace and vigorous personality of the figures but for the bands of decoration, exuberant yet controlled, which separate the panels. On the front of the seat, for instance, curving vine-stems enclose pairs of animals and birds. In the lower border two lions guard the vase from which the vine emerges, their dominant place being taken, in the border above, by a pair of peacocks, the birds of immortality. Between the peacocks is a rectangle containing the monogram of Bishop Maximian (and thus indicating a date between 546 and 556). Within the borders are set five panels, three rectangles separated by two niches; each of these contains an Evangelist with his Gospel-book or, in the case of the central panel, John the Baptist holding his emblem of the Lamb. Draperies are somewhat stiff and conventional, but the figures, carved in deep relief, are full of character and well differentiated one from the other.

The chair back formerly possessed twenty-four panels, sixteen of which remain or have been restored to their position. At least two artists were employed; indeed the chair as a whole suggests the work of a school of craftsmen rather than one individual. Yet despite the apparent variations in technical skill, there is unity of inspiration and a general acceptance of sixth-century conventions (fig. 159). The New Testament miracles occur once more, together with apocryphal scenes from the life of the Virgin—among them Joseph with the rod which burst into flower to show that he was Mary's intended husband, and Mary herself with the bowl of bitter water for her trial. The Annunciation is shown in a particularly attractive manner. Mary sits in a chair not unlike that of Maximian, with a large basket of wool beside her, but she lays her spinning needles aside and clasps her right hand to her breast in wondering acceptance of the message delivered to her by the archangel, who stands on tiptoe before her with right hand raised and left hand holding the staff of authority. Both faces are expressive of a calm solemnity which is enhanced by the only object in the background, the corner of a pedimented shrine.

Vestiges of this same stylized temple corner appear in some of the other panels, such as that showing the Triumphal Entry, as well as in the Baptism scene. This last contains five figures, but so well arranged that there is no suggestion of crowding, while the elongation of both Christ and the Baptist adds a touch of graceful charm. The Baptist takes up almost the entire length of the panel as he stands, a patriarchal character, with one foot in the water and one raised on Jordan's bank. His hand is laid upon the head of Christ, a slim, naked boy attended by two angels who reverently cover their hands with the folds of their ample garments. Overhead the Dove descends; below the river-god crouches, wearing his crown, but raising his hand in amazement as though to declare that the dominion of pagan powers has now reached its end.

The panels on the sides of the chair, illustrating events from the story of Joseph in the Book of Genesis, represent a contrasting current in sixth-century style and are distinguished by their sketchiness and a certain slapdash vigour. Yet their dramatic power is undeniable, and such figures as that of Jacob, raising his arms in anguish at the news of his son's death, display a genuinely artistic sensibility.

The connection of the Joseph scenes with Egypt has been thought to indicate Alexandria as the place of origin for Maximian's chair, and this view is reinforced by the stylistic link between the carving of the chair and that of a sixth-century pyx (now in the British Museum) which shows not some New Testament happening but the execution of St Menas, the Alexandrian saint, and, secondly, Menas as an *Orans*, standing beneath the arch which represents his shrine. However, the cult of St Menas was by no means confined to Egypt, and there was a famous church dedicated to him in Constantinople. The imperial workshops at Constantinople are a far more likely source than Egypt for a piece of such distinction as Maximian's chair, unless indeed it was made at Ravenna itself by craftsmen from Constantinople who drew on the common stock of New Testament episodes, eking them out with copies from some picture-

159. The chair of Maximian, panel: the Angel's message to Joseph and the Journey to Bethlehem.

book that illustrated events recounted in Genesis. The excellence of the chair indeed suggests that it may have been a personal gift from the emperor to encourage the not always popular Maximian and strengthen his authority.

NOTES

1. *Odes* ii.18.1.
2. Livy, *History* 5.41.2.
3. Tacitus, *Annals* iv.26.
4. Symmachus 7.76, *PL* 18.301.
5. This diptych is now in the Darmstadt Museum.
6. Brescia, Museo Civico Cristiano.
7. Paris, Bibliothèque Nationale.
8. A diptych preserved in the Christian Museum at Brescia shows Hippolytus on one leaf and, on the other, an episode drawn from the loves of Diana as recounted by Ovid.
9. Suggested by Ezekiel 37.1.
10. For the Christian connotations of this scene, compare p. 32.
11. *Concerning lapsed members* 26, G. Hartel, *CSEL* iii.256.
12. A pyx in the Cluny Museum at Paris has four scenes: the Samaritan woman, the man born blind, the paralytic and Lazarus. A rather later example in the Louvre illustrates the Samaritan woman and the healing of the paralytic.
13. St John 2.11.
14. *The Infancy Gospel of James* xvi. M. R. James, *The Apocryphal New Testament* (1924), 45.
15. *op. cit.*, xi.
16. The so-called St Lupicinus Gospel-book. Bibliothèque Nationale.
17. The classic example of this motif, notable for its grace and balance, is provided by the Sarigüzel sarcophagus, now in the Archaeological Museum, Istanbul.

160. Ivory panel: St Paul. Probably German, early sixth century. Metropolitan Museum of Art, New York.

15

Arts and Crafts

METALWORK IN SILVER

In the Classical Age of Rome, as of Greece, personal ornament depended upon gold and silver rather than a lavish use of precious stones. But, under the influence of eastern ideas imparted from Assyria and Egypt, a taste for splendour and the bright colours of contrasting gems developed rapidly. When St Paul recommended that women should adorn themselves 'in modest apparel, not with braided hair and gold or pearls or costly raiment',[1] he no doubt had in mind such instances of fashionable extravagance as the array worn by a certain Lollia Paulina[2] which was encrusted with emeralds and pearls worth a fortune. Gospel simplicity, however, was qualified by the remembrance that jewels find an honoured place in Scripture. Bezalel had designed the high priest's breastplate to be set with four rows of gems engraved with the names of the Israelite tribes[3] while, according to the Revelation of St John,[4] the foundations of the Heavenly City are adorned with sapphire, emerald, topaz and amethyst. There was therefore some excuse for desiring brilliance of colour as an accessory of worship and, when Constantine brought the Church out of obscurity to vie with the splendours of the secular world, he indulged his penchant for magnificence to the full. The churches which he built in Rome received the most sumptuous decoration. St John Lateran had its entire apse plated with panels of gold while the ciborium standing over the altar was made of solid silver. Gold studded with pearls and a variety of precious stones was the material used for the altar-vessels. Nor was the basilica of St Peter on the Vatican any less splendid, for here too the apse was covered with sheets of gold and the altar composed of gold and silver embossed with jewels, in a fashion later repeated at Constantinople and in the churches of the sacred sites in Palestine.

In spite of protests made by such austere moralizers as John Chrysostom, Christian women whose circumstances allowed it liked to bedeck themselves with bracelets, earrings, necklaces and jewels sewn into the fabric of their clothing until, as the Ravenna mosaics indicate, they were almost weighed down by an abundance of precious stones. Of all this prodigal adornment, whether owned by private individuals or consecrated for use in churches, very little has been spared by the double assault of the Iconoclasts, who disapproved of religious imagery, and the barbarians, whose lust for booty was insatiable. There have nevertheless been remarkable finds of treasure, often lumped together higgledy-piggledy and hidden from barbarians by owners who never returned to claim it. Much of this treasure, though emanating from Christian households, has few characteristics that distinguish it from pagan counterparts. Even where the chi-rho symbol or some Biblical scene occurs, it may be in close connection with figures drawn from classical mythology. Artistic convention prevails over strict logic—just as, today, Father Christmas may jostle a Nativity picture in the row of cards that adorns the mantelpiece.

161. Silver statuettes from the Esquiline treasure, now in the British Museum: a. Rome; b. Alexandria.

One of the most famous discoveries of decorative silver was made in the Esquiline quarter of Rome in 1793. Almost all this assemblage of miscellaneous objects, which may be assigned to the latter part of the fourth century, is now housed in the British Museum. It includes dishes, spoons, knife-handles, horse-trappings and four statuettes, intended as ornaments for a ceremonial chair, which represent the cities of Rome (fig. 161a), Constantinople, Antioch and Alexandria (fig. 161b). One shallow dish with scalloped rim shows the emperor or some civic dignitary clasping the scroll of authority in his left hand and offering sacrifice at an altar. A graceful vase is richly embossed with figures of animals and with four naked genii busying themselves over the grape harvest,[5] while a jewel-casket with domed cover exhibits the Muses, differentiated from one another by the emblems of their art. All in all, the Esquiline hoard represents the treasure of a well-to-do family of refined taste. That the family was Christian is indicated by some of the spoons, marked with a cross alongside the names, Alexander, Faustus and the rest.

More remarkable, however, as showing how the Christian faith could exist happily enough in companionship with the old, pagan themes is the silver casket given as a wedding present to Secundus and Projecta (fig. 162). The casket is oblong in shape and consists of two matching but unequal parts, both formed like the lower half of a pyramid. The cover consists of five panels. On the flattened top, busts of the husband and wife appear within a wreath supported by two winged cherubs. One of the supporting panels shows Venus gracefully seated within a cockle-shell and dressing her hair with the help of attendant tritons and cherubs. Two other panels continue the easy progression of naked figures, this time nereids and sea monsters, while the fourth panel illustrates the departure of a bride for the marriage ceremony. The figures of friends and servants bearing the wedding presents are rhythmically arranged on each side of a stylized palace: the façade is a gallery upheld by piers and twisted columns, with a large central dome behind and a number of lesser domes roughly indicated at each side. The scenes thus far are of a conventionally pagan character, but at the base of the lid space is found for the chi-rho monogram and an inscription: 'May you, Secundus and Projecta, live your lives in Christ'. The decoration of the casket itself

162. Wedding casket of Secundus and Projecta.

consists of an architectural frieze made up of arches with tops alternately rounded and triangular. Within the arches appear the figures of youths and maidens waiting on the bride and helping with her preparations; superfluous corners are occupied by peacocks. The method of composition, with a medallion of husband and wife together and other figures ranged in an arcade, recalls the style of the fourth-century sarcophagi and, even though it cannot be taken for granted that Projecta is the matron of that name for whom Pope Damasus composed an epitaph, this highly finished and sophisticated example of the silversmith's art can be assigned with certainty to a Roman workshop, even if the craftsmen were perhaps of Asiatic origin.

Several other collections of silver from Christian households give proof of refined taste without much obtrusive piety. A set of pieces found at Carthage but now in the British Museum resembles the Esquiline treasure in character as well as date. Two bowls offer pastoral scenes with shepherds and animals ranged in the mannered simplicity of a Hellenistic idyll, but one of an almost identical pair of silver dishes combines Christian symbols with proverbial wisdom of a noncommittal type (fig. 163). The pattern of the dishes consists of hammered flutings, straight at the rim and sinuous below; at the bottom, an arrangement of gilded concentric circles leaves space for an inscription. One of the inscriptions merely indicates that the silverware belonged to the Cresconii, a prosperous family well known in North Africa at the turn of the fourth and fifth centuries. The other offers the advice *Loquere feliciter*—'take care how you talk'—but the chi-rho monogram, accompanied by alpha and omega, adds a Christian flavour.

In the year 1919 a notable discovery of miscellaneous metalwork, mostly silver,[6] was made at Traprain Law, in the Lammermuir Hills 25 miles east of Edinburgh. Here the pieces, not all of one type or period, were twisted, crushed and generally hacked about. They gave the impression of booty, stolen from various sources in Gaul or Britain, and carelessly dumped by robbers during the disturbances which attended the departure of the Roman legions in 410 AD. Of the hundred and seventy objects some reflect pagan influences and some are clearly of Christian origin while others display a neutral decoration of animals, birds, fishing boats or geometric patterns.

163. Silver dishes from Carthage, now in the British Museum.

The greatest abundance of the Christian plate consists of spoons marked with the cross or alpha and omega. Spoons have been intermittently used in the eastern churches for administering the Eucharist to communicants. But there seems to be no clear evidence of this practice before the sixth century, and the spoons often found in early collections of silver, even if they are to be classed as gifts charitably offered to a church, were perhaps applied to no other end than acting as a financial reserve.

Three other objects in the Traprain Law treasure were certainly made for Christians and probably set apart for liturgical purposes. There is an attractively shaped vase, bearing a chi-rho emblem, which may have been used to contain oil that found its place in the ceremonies of baptism as early as the third century. There is a wine-strainer[7] and, more important, portions of a vase bearing a figure decoration in two ranges (fig. 164). The upper part displays the regular series of rustic motifs—rams facing one another, a peasant leading his donkey back to a cottage shown with minute exactness of architectural detail, and a conventional countryside indicated by hillocks and stylized trees. But beneath this upper zone of ornament is a wider band of figures, more deeply cut, to suggest incidents drawn from the Old and New Testament. Adam and Eve come first, with, between them, a tree from which Adam is plucking the apple. Next in the series is a scene defaced and difficult to interpret, but there follows the Adoration of the Magi, wearing their characteristic Phrygian caps and offering their gifts on large plates toward which the Christ-child, seated on his mother's knee, stretches out an eager hand. Finally Moses is shown, clean-shaven and swathed in a long robe, holding out his hand to strike the rock; two little Israelites collect the water in circular vessels. The artistic skill shown in this work may not be of the highest order, since some of the figures are rather squat and dumpy, but the interest of the vase is that it faithfully repeats, in silver, standard themes of the stone sarcophagi and carved ivories produced in the period around the year 400. Great originality was not looked for, and the craftsmen in silver, as in other metals, were often content to reproduce drawings and models which had already seen much service.

More homogeneous and in much better condition, the treasure found at Mildenhall, Suffolk, in 1946 resembles the Traprain Law hoard in the design of

164. Vase from the Traprain Law treasure.

165. Spoons stamped with the chi-rho emblem. Found at Mildenhall, Suffolk, now in the British Museum.

fluted bowls and the use of round, hollowed beads as a method of decorating the rim of the vessels. A fourth-century date may be assigned to the Mildenhall pieces, and their excellence suggests that the craftsmen had been trained in Rome or Trier even if they did not live there. An impressive dish, weighing just under 8 kilograms, displays the conventional themes of Neptune and Bacchus and the various bowls and goblets are similarly decorated with pagan subjects. But three out of the eight spoons have, clearly stamped on the bowl, the Christian emblem of the chi-rho between alpha and omega (fig. 165). These may be compared with the two spoons marked with a cross and the name 'Paulos' that form part of the Sutton Hoo treasure.

There is nothing very ecclesiastical about the Mildenhall treasure, but the hoard discovered more recently at Water Newton (Durobrivae) can properly be described as church plate made for a thriving community and concealed at some time of crisis towards the end of the fourth century. Of the four bowls, wine-strainer, cup, dish and two jugs, five objects are plain and four decorated with the chi-rho. Two of the bowls have dedicatory inscriptions, the

vessel given by Publianus (fig. 166) offering a line of hexameter verse: 'Firm in my faith I honour thy shrine, O Lord.'[8] Particular interest attaches to a group of triangular plaques, veined like leaves. Some of these plaques are plain, some decorated with the chi-rho between alpha and omega. Their purpose is made clear through the inscription borne by one of them: 'Iamcilla has fulfilled the vow which she promised.'[9] They are votive tablets offered in thanksgiving for answered prayer, and, though such things were common enough in pagan circles and are referred to by Christian writers of the fifth century,[10] their occurrence as early as the Water Newton hoard has no parallel elsewhere.

Another collection of church plate, dating from about a century later than the Water Newton treasure, has come to light at Canoscio, Umbria.[11] The vessels include four chalices, plain and without handles. Just as churches developed from private houses, so the vessels used for the Communion seem at first to have been indistinguishable from household utensils, even though the growing taste for magnificence was soon to substitute heavy chalices, varied in shape and often studded with jewels. Also found at Canoscio are

166. The Publianus bowl from the Water Newton treasure.

several patens of varying size inlaid with niello, a form of enamel made up of silver, lead and sulphur. The *Liber Pontificalis* points to the use of massive salvers, weighing up to fourteen kilograms each, as patens, whereas the rare examples of early date that are still to be seen are of more manageable size and suitably engraved.[12] One of a number of spoons, with long handles and pear-shaped bowls, found at Canoscio bears on it a fish, an appropriate symbol if the spoon was in fact used at the Eucharist. Finally a wine-strainer (*colatorium*), with loop handle, has its surface pierced in such a manner as to make up a monogram-matic cross set between the alpha and the omega. The names of African martyrs inscribed on two of the patens suggest that the Canoscio treasure was made in Rome for export to Numidia.

Several other collections of silver illustrate what might be found in a sacristy about the middle of the sixth century. Among recent discoveries at Kamluca (Korydalla) in Lycia is a dish, 64 centimetres in diameter, marked with an eight-branched cross, as well as three flattish candle-holders elaborately worked in perforated silver. Still more interesting is a circular silver-gilt censer, engraved with the usual Gospel scenes and having an inscription, that mentions Bishop Eutychianus as the donor, running round the rim. Although Constantine presented the basilica of St John Lateran with 'two censers of the purest gold, weighing thirty pounds', the Kamluca example seems to be as early as any that now remain.[13] Two cup-shaped censers from Luxor, now in the Cairo Museum, may belong to about the same period, but the splendid hexagonal censer from Kyrenia (Cyprus), with its portrait-busts of Christ, the Virgin and apostles, cannot be earlier than the seventh century. The same is probably true of another hexagonal cen-ser, found at Crikrine in Dalmatia, which has an elaborate top framed as a cupola with twelve ribs.

A hoard of silver found at Lampsacus on the Hel-lespont and now in the British Museum includes a circular dish ornamented with a formal pattern between six recesses made to hold candles. This sanc-tuary light was suspended by means of three silver bars attached by rings to a star-shaped knop. Also from Lampsacus comes a variety of lampstand that, with its baluster stem, hexagonal base widening towards the bottom and three hollow feet, closely resembles a Jacobean candlestick.[14] Underneath are two cross-shaped impressions, bearing the name 'Sestos'. Stamps of such a nature are commonly found on the underside of silver objects from the beginning of the sixth century. The names, those of emperors, donors and officials, may be accompanied by the roughly formed bust of some saint and the stamps are to be classed as an early essay in hallmarking which indicates, if not the quality of the silver, at least the date when the piece was made. The Kamluca censer, for instance, bears the five stamps which became customary—circle, square, hexagon, horseshoe and cross—and the date-mark in the circle shows that the vessel was produced in the reign of Justinian.

The Kyrenia (or Lambrousa) treasure is remarkable for a collection of dishes that display, in high relief, scenes from the life of David. Four of these are small, with a diameter of six inches: David killing a lion, killing a bear, holding a harp as he welcomes Saul's messenger, and talking to a warrior armed with a spear. The five which make up a group of larger size, mostly with a diameter of eleven inches, illustrate David's anointing, his presentation to Saul, preparation for battle, his marriage to Michal and his fight with Goliath. Of these, all except the last have as their background a formal architectural theme consisting of a central arch flanked on each side by a horizontal pediment supported by two channelled columns with vaguely Ionic capitals. On the ground in front are weapons, money-bags and other objects suggesting opulence and success. Some of the figures are statuesque and the draperies hang rather heavily, but such details as the flute-players attending David's marriage provide an agreeably pastoral touch and the combats with the wild beasts are treated in a dramatic and vigorous manner.

These Kyrenia dishes belong to the seventh century, and are marked with the control stamps of the emperor Heraclius, who reigned between 610 and 641 AD. They are relevant to the earlier period, however, in that they show in full development a cycle of subjects which seems to have been in formation by the fourth century.[15] This is the date usually assigned to a wooden panel in St Ambrose, Milan, in which David, wearing a shepherd's costume, is seated amidst his flock with his feet on a dead lion, while a bear crouches before him and a messenger from Saul approaches. Such reminiscences of David's life were widely diffused and occur, for instance, in sixth-century frescoes

at Bawit. The designs on the Cyprus dishes closely influenced the artists who later produced illuminated manuscripts of the Psalms, unless indeed it was some very early Psalter which inspired the silversmiths.

Dishes made of precious metal represented a form of wealth which could conveniently be used for purposes of barter. They also formed that part of the endowment of a church which was readily seized on as plunder during the barbarian invasions, so that silver marked with Christian emblems and apparently made at Constantinople or in Syria during the sixth century turns up surprisingly in remote districts of Russia. The dish[16] of Paternus, Bishop of Tomi in 520 AD, offers the conventional symbol of the chi-rho monogram together with the alpha and omega, all contained within a decorative border based on an undulating vine-stem. But the most notable example is a plate, found in 1867 at Berezovo in western Siberia, which shows two curly-haired angels, stylized but lively in their windswept garments, standing one on each side of a tall cross. The cross is marked with geometric figures suggesting the cloisonné gems and enamels which distinguish the period of Charlemagne and already make their appearance on the gold cross which Justin II presented to St Peter's, Rome, about 570 AD. The cross of the Berezovo[17] platter is poised on a golden orb set on ground from which flow four little tongues of water representing the four rivers of Paradise.

Platters of this kind have a certain kinship with the larger dishes known as missoria, which could be used for washings in connection with religious rites, whether Christian or pagan. The dishes were sent as gifts to mark the emperor's favour, and were useful as propaganda on behalf of the imperial authority. None of the extant missoria bears a markedly Christian character, though the life guard on the dish of Constantius II (the Kertch dish, now at the Hermitage) has a shield prominently stamped with the chi-rho sign. But the missoria display a number of emblems and motifs which the artists readily adopted into the Christian scheme and they also indicate a determination to stress the majesty of the emperor as one who had been divinely chosen for his exalted office. Such matters are especially well illustrated in the missorium of Theodosius I for, unlike his immediate predecessors, Theodosius seems to have regarded his claim

167. The 'Missorium' of Theodosius.

to be 'the most holy Christian prince' from the stand-point of conviction rather than convenience. The dish (fig. 167), now kept at Madrid, indicates the date 388 AD and marks the point when, at a crisis of his fortunes, Theodosius took strong measures in defence of orthodox churchmanship against both heresy and paganism. The embossed design covers nearly the entire surface of the dish, 79 centimetres in diameter, and is divided into two unequal parts. The upper section is dominated by the emperor himself. Seated on a backless throne with his feet on a stool, he wears a tunic and the chlamys—a variety of cloak, originally Phrygian and worn by soldiers, but adopted, in a rather lengthened form, as part of Byzantine court dress. Its colour, the deep reddish brown known as 'purple', suggested the life-blood of one who was dedicated to the mystic duty of worldwide govern-ment. A large jewelled brooch holds the chlamys in place, and the theme of triumphant consecration to a high purpose is continued in the jewelled diadem, another eastern adornment that had been drawn into service by Constantine. Theodosius' face may reason-ably be claimed as an attempt at genuine portraiture, though the large eyes gazing heavenward customarily denote concentration on things of the spirit. The nimbus circling the emperor's head likewise indicates contact with the divine while the background consists of an arch offset at each side by a lintel supported on channelled columns—the regular fourth-century device for bestowing supernatural dignity on a scene. Because, in the Byzantine world, size can be used to indicate rank, Theodosius is shown as considerably bigger than his two colleagues in authority; on the same principle, the emperor of the West, Valentinian, is shown on a larger scale than is Theodosius' son Arcadius, and holds a long sceptre. But both wear the splendid diadem and the chlamys fastened by a glitter-ing brooch, and both hold in their left hand a globe signifying widespread dominion. Many of the attributes of empire displayed on the dish of Theodosius and regularly appearing on fourth-cen-tury coins were, by a natural transference of symbols, used in ecclesiastical circles to emphasize the dignity of Christ and his Apostles. The lower segment of the silver dish shows a half-clothed woman, representing the fruitful Earth, reclining amidst the 'bowed ears of the corn', with a horn of plenty by her side. She gazes pensively in the direction of Theodosius while three

little cupids fly up towards him bearing gifts in token of thankfulness and prayer for continued prosperity.

An example of the way in which patterns originating in domestic use moved on to meet ecclesiastical needs is provided by the silver jewel-boxes or perfume-boxes transferred from the dressing-table to serve as caskets containing the relics of saints. John Chrysostom, writ-ing about the year 390,[18] referred to the practice of enclosing fragments of the True Cross in gold and hanging them about the necks of both men and women. What Chrysostom had in mind was indicated by the discovery in the Vatican cemetery of two small, square boxes made of gold and supplied with rings to hang on a chain. These boxes are marked on one face with the chi-rho monogram together with the alpha and omega. Their date is uncertain, but the traditional view that they belong to the end of the fourth century may well be correct.

The caskets, however, are a more elaborate affair. Perhaps the finest is the large casket found beneath the floor of S. Nazaro in Milan and often claimed as contemporary with the founding of that church in 382 AD. This example still reflects a free and lively Hellen-istic style adapted, with its figures cushioned on air and its softly curving folds of drapery, to the Theodosian idiom. The casket is worked over with repoussé figures which reproduce favourite scenes of the fourth-century sarcophagi. On the lid Christ is shown enthroned among the Apostles, while water jars and loaves of bread in the foreground allude to the Marriage Feast at Cana and to the Feeding of the Five Thousand. On one side the shepherds are shown bringing their gifts to the Virgin and Child formally seated before them. The other sides show the Judge-ment of Solomon, Daniel rebuking the elders for their behaviour towards Susanna, and the three men in the fiery furnace. It has, however, to be noted that doubts have been cast[19] on the genuineness of this attractive casket, which may be a skilful reproduction made by some Renaissance silversmith.

One of the oldest reliquaries, now in the Vatican Museum, is an oval casket found at Ain Zirara, in Numidia, and ascribed to a Syrian craftsman of the fifth or early sixth century (fig. 168). On the lid is portrayed a martyr, holding his crown, while above his head the hand of God appears setting another crown of life eternal upon his head. At each side a tall,

168. The Ain Zirara reliquary.

lighted candle burns, in a manner characteristic of paintings in the cemeteries of Naples. On the oval surround scenes occur which might be paralleled in contemporary fresco painting or mosaic. To one side a stag and a hind drink from four streams which could be described as the rivers of Paradise or, to judge from palm-trees and two little shrines which may indicate Jerusalem and Bethlehem, the water of life flowing out from Palestine. On a hillock above the four streams is set not the expected Cross but the chi-rho emblem shown with the six equal arms of its early, Constantinian form. On the other side of the box, long-tailed sheep advance towards the Lamb of God, distinguished from the others by the small cross set just above its back. As Paulinus of Nola puts it in one of his hymns: 'Beneath the blood-stained cross stands Christ the Lamb upon a snow-white field.'[20]

The chi-rho monogram in two different forms alternating with geometric patterns makes up the sober decoration of a rectangular silver box found in a tomb at Sofia, but the date of this reliquary is uncertain. On the early examples a full display of Biblical scenes is usually preferred. The Brivio casket, now in the Louvre, combines rhythmical vigour with coarseness of detail. Elliptical in form, it is divided by cable ornament which frames the illustrations. On one side the Virgin, seated in a basket-chair, holds the Christ-child on her lap as he eagerly stretches out his hands to receive the offerings of the Magi. All three are shown wearing their Phrygian caps and in precisely the same posture as they hasten forward with right knee bent. Their faces are only roughly indicated, apart from their disproportionately large eyes. Matching this scene on the other side of the box are Shadrach, Meshach and Abednego in the fiery furnace. The three men stand in a row, as *Orants*, behind a long, low wall pierced by two doors. They, too, wear Phrygian caps, and neatly indicated tongues of flame jump up between them. Thus far they conform to the arrangement found in the frescoes of the catacombs; in place of the comforting angel, however, the hunched figure of an executioner appears, stirring the fire with a poker. At each end of the box a fortified city-gate represents Jerusalem and Bethlehem respectively, while on the lid the Raising of Lazarus is shown conventionally enough save that Lazarus is made to look like an Egyptian mummy and Martha crouches, with large, coarse hands extended, beneath the long wand which Christ stretches out towards the tomb. The casket may be assigned to the fifth century; of its origin little more can be said than that it is probably the work of a Syrian craftsman or, at any rate, of someone familiar with Syrian models.

A plaque from one such relic casket, now at the Louvre, shows St Simeon Stylites squatting on top of his pillar while the Devil, in the form of an enormous snake, coils round the pillar below him. But more closely comparable with the Brivio casket is another of fifth-century date which forms part of the treasure of the 'Sancta Sanctorum', the ancient chapel of the Lateran where the popes at one time kept their most precious relics. The Sancta Sanctorum casket is, again, a lengthened oval, edged with cable moulding. On the sides are engraved medallions containing busts. At one side Christ is shown with cross-nimbus and rounded beard, his hand raised in blessing, between two saints, each with a long, pointed beard. On the other side Peter and Paul appear, and another saint stands at each end. All the figures are rendered in the same style. Their cheekbones are prominent, and they have large, staring eyes, with a hollow point pierced in the centre.

The notion that Syria was the province where these caskets, together with similar examples found at Grado and Pola, originated is given support by a large silver vase, used for containing wine or oil, which is now in the Louvre collection (fig. 169). The vase was found at Emesa (Homs) on the banks of the Orontes, and, though less extensively decorated than the caskets, resembles them in the particular type of cable ornament which encloses the repoussé heads of Christ, the Virgin and four apostles. These heads, even if of finer workmanship, are uniform with the caskets in general style. Whether this silverware of widespread provenance but similar type comes from one or two Syrian workshops or is the product of wandering craftsmen can hardly be determined. All one can affirm is that this crude, vigorous, rather primitive fashion characterizes the metalwork of the fifth century before the jewelled elaboration of the next period.

The high point of the Syrian style was reached, about the year 570, in two magnificent patens discovered one at Riha[21] (fig. 170) and the other at Stuma.[22] Here a new theme is introduced into Christian iconography: not the Last Supper, or any meal held in the pastures of the Blessed, but the

169. The Emesa vase.

170. The Riha paten.

171. Palestinian oil-flask, now at Monza: the Ascension and the Visit of the Magi.

Communion of the Apostles, where Christ presides at the altar as the eternal High Priest 'after the order of Melchizedek'. On both these patens Christ is in fact shown twice, offering the bread to six apostles on the north side of the altar while from the south six other apostles advance, in attitudes of reverence and ecstasy, to partake of the wine. The whole composition, though it could be described as stylized, succeeds in denoting intense emotion while the repoussé figures of the apostles are markedly individual and arranged with an instinctive sense of harmonious order. The artistic effect is enhanced by a discreet use of gilding. The Riha paten shows several vessels on the altar, one being a chalice with deep bowl and short stem having a rounded knop. This is the form not only of the chalice held by Theodora in her Ravenna mosaic but also of several chalices found in Syria within fairly recent years. One of these, the 'Antioch chalice', now in the Metropolitan Museum at New York, is unique in having an elaborate decoration of grapes and vine-leaves applied to the surface of the cup. Within this rich but fussy pattern of foliage there appear two rows of figures including Christ, who is represented twice, and certain of the apostles. The cup may be assigned to

the fifth or early sixth century but some doubts have been cast on its genuineness.

No such suspicion affects a large, plain chalice[23] found at Riha. This bears on the underside of its foot the control stamps (not very clear) of Anastasius I or Justinian, while around the bowl runs a Greek inscription 'Thine own out of thine own do we offer to thee, O Lord.' These words are drawn from the consecration prayer in the liturgy of St Chrysostom—the form of worship which, adopted by the imperial court at Constantinople, gained predominance among the service forms of the Near East. A similar chalice, from Aleppo and now in the British Museum, is inscribed around the rim with an invocation of 'Sergius and John' but lacks the hallmarking, while a chalice, now in the Cleveland Museum of Art, again bears a dedicatory inscription to St Sergius and is remarkable as exhibiting a portrait-bust of Christ.

The custom of hanging round the neck medallions (*encolpia*) with brightly coloured representations of Christ on the cross or some Gospel miracle is witnessed to both by discovered examples and by literary sources.[24] But a special set of such scenes occurs on the ampullae preserved in the cathedral of Monza, just north of Milan (fig. 171). Ampullae are small flasks, round and flattened, which were used to contain a few drops of oil hallowed by contact with a sacred place or the relics of a sacred person. The Monza ampullae, made of silver and other metals, are said to have been brought to Queen Theodelinda from Rome by a priest named John, 'a worthless sinner', at the time when Gregory the Great was pope. Whatever may be the historical truth of this statement, the flasks were clearly made not in Rome but in Palestine. Works of the late sixth century, they yet may reflect a changing pattern of iconography characteristic of Palestine at a somewhat earlier date. For the Monza flasks, together with some examples, made from pewter and rather battered, at Bobbio, are marked by a unity of style and subject which shows them to be the product of one workshop. The subjects engraved upon them have no very great range. They recall the miraculous events connected with the sacred sites which the pilgrim had visited, and their special interest is that they are undoubtedly inspired by the frescoes and mosaics which decorated churches at Jerusalem or elsewhere in the Holy Land.

The Church of the Nativity at Bethlehem, for instance, had an altar of the Three Wise Men, and associated with it there seems to have been a mosaic which served as a pattern for several closely similar reproductions. The Magi are shown ranged rather stiffly on one side of the Virgin and Child, with the group of three shepherds balancing the composition on the other side. The Virgin is seated on her chair gazing forwards and holding the Child straight in front of her. In the foreground there may be a flock of goats while, above, a star in the form of a wheel bears, in Greek, the legend 'Emmanuel, God with us'. One of the flasks adds the sentence 'The Lord's blessing from the holy places of Christ'.

The Crucifixion scene is remarkable in that, while the two robbers are fast bound, Christ stands free and unfettered in front of the cross. But on some of the ampullae the same event is shown in an even more refined and allusive manner. For the two robbers appear, with hands outstretched and feet bound, on crosses of which only the extreme ends are visible, while the central cross is either absent or, set on its hillock, becomes a leafy Tree of Life, with Adam and Eve kneeling in worship at either side and the bust of Christ in glory above. The Resurrection is interpreted with the help of a simple formula: two women squeezed close together beside an elaborate little shrine, its pediment surmounted by a cross, and, on the other side, an angel standing with hand outstretched towards the open door of the shrine or holding a lamp above it. Another favourite scene, drawn from the common store of Christian art-forms and resembling one of the panels on the door of S. Sabina, shows four angels, floating horizontally with wings outstretched and upholding the oval frame in which Christ, victorious and enthroned, ascends to heaven. In the lower zone the Holy Ghost, in the shape of a dove, alights on the Virgin Mary as she stands amid the eager Apostles. Such themes are stereotyped and regularly repeated, but modifications are not unknown. One of the Bobbio flasks, for instance, introduces a subject not found in the Monza collection and shows Christ, a dominant figure with his head encircled by a large cross-halo, rescuing Peter from sinking beneath the waters while two densely packed lines of the eleven Apostles look on from a diminutive boat.

On a leaden flask, found in Egypt but clearly derived from Palestine, the Resurrection theme with the women at the Tomb is complemented on the other side by doubting Thomas.

Other ampullae combine a New Testament event with representations of saints. Thus one flask, again made of lead, shows a building with three arches above which appears a gabled roof flanked by a cupola and turret. Beneath the largest, central arch Christ lies in his manger, with the head of an ox nearby. But on the other side two military saints are displayed, each holding spear and oval shield. Inscriptions identify them as St George and an otherwise unknown St Aetius.

172. Bronze lamp: gryphon head, with chi-rho and dove.   173. Bronze lamp-filler from Upper Egypt.

METALWORK IN BRONZE

During the earliest periods of Christian art, the use of bronze is fairly widespread for a variety of objects serviceable at home or in church, Egypt being an especially productive source. For the most part such things repeat the shapes found in examples made of silver, glass or pottery. A whimsical originality could, however, be shown in the fashioning of bronze lamps during the fifth and sixth centuries. Constantine is said to have presented to the Lateran a number of lamps in the form of a dolphin,[25] and later craftsmen tried their hand at making lamps that were models of a duck, a peacock or the ship of the Church, while the chi-rho monogram occasionally appears. A remarkable instance of this latter type is provided by a boat-shaped lamp in the British Museum which has its handle curved to resemble the forepart of a gryphon bearing on its head the chi-rho emblem surmounted by a dove (fig. 172).[26] Another lamp has the handle elaborated to form a circular top; here Jonah lies under his gourd tree with a wreath enclosing the chi-rho above. More grotesque is a lamp shaped realistically like a sheep but with two tubes projecting from the front thighs to support octagonal plates into which oil flowed from the little reservoir in the animal's body. A cross is stamped on the sheep's chest and another cross, on which a dove is perched, rises from the head. Such bronze lamps, whether graceful or bizarre, represent the domestic counterparts of the richer examples, fashioned in silver, along the most varied patterns, which, with their countless points of gentle brilliance, turned a church into the 'likeness of a heavenly constellation'.

Some lamps were designed not to hang by chains but to be supported from below. One example, probably Egyptian, is set on a stand which, with its baluster stem and sturdy disk, might pass for a seventeenth-century candlestick were it not for the restless elaboration of the tripod base. The lamp itself is of conventional shape except that the handle extends in two spirals united at the centre to form the figure, once again, of a dove perched on a cross.

It is to be supposed that not all these ingeniously wrought lamps were intended for private households, since bronze was clearly drawn in to serve a variety of

174. Bronze incense-burner from Asia Minor, about 550 AD. Metropolitan Museum, New York.

175. Nubian patera.

church uses also. Five examples may be chosen. There are first the 'crowns', or wheel-like discs, which have their spokes separated by symmetrical ornament and terminate, usually within the wheel but sometimes beyond the circumference, in cup-like openings designed to carry the small glass vessels which held the oil for a 'circling chorus of bright lights'.[27]

The Museum at Cairo contains a plain corona with ten projecting arms in the form of dolphins; a large and much finer example of this type of lamp was recently discovered at Aquileia.[28] Elliptical rather than perfectly circular, this corona is decorated with a cable pattern at top and bottom, and again, but more lightly, over the twelve arched openings pierced in the surface. Each opening is partially filled by a symbol of some sort: the chi-rho motif in two different forms as well as the lamb, the cock—Prudentius' 'winged messenger of the dawn'—and the phoenix. The upper rim of the corona is interrupted by twelve rectangular openings; behind each of these is fixed a socket into which one of the twelve light-holders (only ten now remain) may be inserted. These light-holders are upward-turning stems, decorated with formalized leafage and ending in the heads made for the oil-

glasses. The whole candelabrum is hung by three chains to another circle of six lamp-holders formed by bronze dolphins.

A still rarer object than a corona-style lamp is the bronze lamp-filler. One such,[29] found at Medinet Habu in Upper Egypt, is shaped as a semicircle with scroll decoration along the edge and a long, straight spout (fig. 173). The flat handle is ornamented with a palm tree and the popular theme, originally Persian but adopted into Christian uses, of birds facing one another beak to beak.

More narrowly ecclesiastical are the paten, the censer and the patera. Bronze patens of the early period are few in number, but Cuicul, in Numidia, has furnished a notable pair which seem to be of fifth century date.[30] They are round, with small handles attached; one bears the Latin inscription *Deo Gratias* while the other has stamped on it the two Greek letters with which the name of Christ begins. Bronze censers of the sixth century are to be found in many of the great museums (fig. 174). Most of these incense-burners resemble little bowls suspended by chains; there is a small, dome-shaped cover for the burner itself. A group of particular interest, originating in

176. Lead coffin fron Sidon: the decorative pattern.

Asia Minor, offers scenes, rough and primitive in execution, that are drawn from the Gospel narrative. One example, now in the British Museum, comes from the convent of Mar Muza, between Damascus and Palmyra, and is a censer with low, circular foot, bulbous central portion, and rim. Around the middle of the vessel runs a frieze of raised figures, crudely worked, representing the Annunciation, the Baptism (where Christ is shown as a tiny figure scarcely larger than the Holy Ghost hovering overhead), the Crucifixion and the Resurrection. Christ on the cross appears as a stiff, unemotional figure, wearing the long robe known as a *colobium* and with feet firmly set on the ground. Beneath the arms of the cross, and therefore shown on a diminutive scale, stand the Virgin and St John, while the sun and the moon above bear witness to the universal importance of the event. The Resurrection is indicated by the Maries at the Sepulchre and here, as often elsewhere at about this same period, the tomb is represented by a small, well–built shrine, roofed with a dome and having a single entrance wide open.

The patera, a vessel resembling a concave saucer with a handle, was used in pagan libations and later adapted to the Christian ceremony of hand-washing in the course of the Eucharist. The few examples that survive are usually wrought in bronze and come from Africa. One of these,[31] said to be Nubian, has a bowl decorated on the inside with concentric circles and on the outer rim with bosses (fig. 175). At the base of the handle is a star monogram; the handle itself ends in a grotesque face, topped however by two equal-armed crosses of differing size. At a point opposite the handle is a ring fixed in the mouth of another monstrous head, so that the whole object is a strange, unselfconscious mixture, in the medieval manner, of sacred and profane.

The series of small bronze crosses with figures of saints roughly engraved on them as mementoes of a visit paid to some renowned shrine seems to begin with the seventh century. Long before this, however, bronze was thought to be a material well adapted for the manufacture of sacred knick-knacks. Some of these display a particularly delicate artistry. One example is a statuette,[32] made in the Angora district in about 500 AD, of an ox with a cross set between his horns; this is inscribed with the names of St Raphses and St Ctimon.

Rectangles of bronze, sometimes inlaid with silver, were used as weights particularly in testing the gold coinage. These weights (*exagia*) normally bear the names of the Roman prefects or other officials and sometimes the bust of the emperor or a trusted subordinate is added. But, with the easy mingling of politics and theology which characterizes the sixth century, crosses or figures of saints might often be substituted for the earthly rulers. One relatively large rectangular weight, now in the British Museum, shows two military saints standing side by side, each holding shield and spear. One of the saints raises his spear to threaten a spotted animal that looks like a not unfriendly panther but is no doubt intended to be a dragon. Above the dragon's head is a curving tree from which hang large fruits; below are the Greek letters which stand for one pound. With a similar touch of religious feeling, bronze stamps for use on seals might bear such sentiments of conventional piety as 'Christ grant his help' or 'Life and health be yours'.

METALWORK IN LEAD

Lead was used fairly extensively in Gaul and in Rome for both burial urns and coffins. At Rouen, for example, a dozen lead coffins were found in a cemetery which contained a number of skeletons lying in the bare earth. These coffins were normally covered with lids not soldered down but kept in place with the aid of an overhanging rim. One of them is adorned with three lions' muzzles and a human face, but neither there nor at Arles nor at Salona are such coffins clearly marked with Christian symbols, though there are a few rather ill-defined crosses. In a class by itself for interest and technical excellence is a lead coffin found at Sidon and transferred to the museum at Cannes (fig. 176). This example is decorated with a border of undulating vine-stems weaving around human heads and pairs of doves perched on the edge of fluted bowls. A similar pattern, classical in style, is found on the two longer sides of the coffin; but on the upper face the dominant motif consists of three monumental archways, each containing the chi–rho emblem and the letters ΙΧΘΥC (Fish) which mystically represented Christ. Between these archways the field is decorated with rosettes. At the two short ends the same type of archway is repeated, but one arch contains not the Christian symbols found in the others but, instead, the figure of someone wearing the philosopher's cloak and presumably representing the dead man for whom the coffin was made.

A group of leaden tanks recently found at Icklingham (Suffolk) and elsewhere in Britain seems to be connected with baptism rather than burial. These tanks are circular in form, two or three feet in diameter and between one and two feet high. Some are entirely plain, others bear the chi-rho emblem usually within a simple type of cable decoration. The most remarkable example, the 'Walesby cistern', is ornamented with three panels separated by columns. In the centre a female candidate is being presented for baptism while the flanking panels show figures who may represent members of the local church. Some of the lead tanks are equipped with handles, and it appears that, in keeping with some peculiarity of local practice, they may have been portable fonts.

Lead was used in making not only a few ampullae but also seals, commercial tokens and decorative medallions, that are at times marked with the conventional Christian emblems. But the heavy texture and dull colour of the metal make it ill-suited for ambitious works of art, and a fifth-century vase found at Carthage[33] is exceptional. Affixed to its surface are fifteen roundels, also of lead, showing figures in relief. The choice of subjects represents a curious, but by no means exceptional, mixture of Christian symbolism and the customary pagan themes. The Good Shepherd, an angel bearing a wreath, the palm tree and the peacocks facing one another over a wine-jar jostle against hunting scenes, combats of wild beasts and a young man clasping a bunch of grapes under one arm and, with his other hand, holding a wreath over a pagan altar. But none of the Christian subjects is exclusively so, and it may be questioned whether the craftsman did other than collect a group of miscellaneous themes drawn from any source that lay to hand.

GLASS

Between the end of the first century BC and the fourth century AD the art of glassmaking steadily developed within the Roman Empire as craftsmen, mostly Egyptian or Syrian, made full use of the opportunities laid before them by the invention of the blowing-tube. But glass, unlike metal, was not looked on as particularly luxurious, and most of the objects made from glass were designed for everyday, domestic use. This applied even in the Rhineland where a local school of glassmakers, probably under the direction of oriental masters, flourished just at the time when elsewhere the craft had begun to sink into decline and the use of glass was almost restricted to the mass production of bottles, cups and bowls, greenish in colour and of straightforward design. Some of the more ambitious pieces were engraved by means of the wheel or the diamond point, with subjects drawn from Greek mythology or from the store of Christian themes. A good example is supplied by the dish found at Homblières, in north-eastern France, and to be dated about 400 AD.[34] Here the engraving has been completed on the outside of the dish by the laborious method of drilling little holes that vary in size and depth, thus giving the required emphasis to the lines of the illustrations, which are then viewed from the inside of the bowl through an attractive sheen of lightly coloured transparency. In the centre of this dish appears a large chi-rho emblem accompanied by half a dozen stars, while around it are worked the conventional subjects of Adam and Eve, Daniel in the lions' den and Susanna beset by the elders.

A much rougher dish, of approximately the same period, has been found at Podgoritza,[35] in Yugoslavia. The casual and artless style of the illustrations, here engraved on the inside, and the illiterate jumble of the inscriptions suggest the product of a nursery school rather than the work of a serious artist. In the centre is a medallion which crudely indicates the sacrifice of Isaac while around the circumference are ranged scenes of deliverance: Jonah, Daniel and others.

The sacrifice of Isaac proves to be a favourite subject on these shallow cups or dishes. An example from Trier,[36] closely resembling another found at Boulogne, shows an altar with fire on it at the centre. To one side Isaac stands, naked and with hands bound behind his back; on the other side Abraham appears, clutching a

177. The Boulogne glass dish: the sacrifice of Isaac.

178. Gold-glass: 'Good luck to Severa, Cosmas and Leah.'

179. Gold-glass: Daniel feeding the dragon of Babylon with poisoned cake.

180. Gold-glass: portrait of the youthful Christ.

fearsome knife and with the ram nearby. Meanwhile from a bank of clouds the hand of God appears, bringing deliverance, a theme which is taken up by the inscription running round the edge of the dish: 'Mayest thou live in God' or, on the Boulogne example, 'Mayest thou live for ever' (fig. 177). It appears that these dishes were placed in graves or used at commemorations of the departed, in general accord with the ancient service for the dying which included the petition 'Free his soul O Lord, as thou didst free Isaac from becoming a victim at the hands of his father Abraham.'

Vessels made of glass were used in the services of the Church from very early times. The *Liber Pontificalis*,[37] not an infallible witness, records that Pope Zephyrinus, at the beginning of the third century, sanctioned the making of 'glass patens'. These may at first have been little more than round disks serviceable as covers for chalices, but two eucharistic patens found at Cologne and now in the Museum at Trier, show a fairly cultivated taste and vigour of invention. The paten from a tomb near the church of St Ursula has the shape of a flattened cup. Made of a milky white glass, it is decorated by means of gold and silver leaf touched up in blue, red or green paint to represent water, foliage and the detail of costume. The paten of St Severinus, Cologne, differs in that the glass is transparent and the decoration takes the form of little medallions, worked in gold on a base of blue and emerald green, which were made separately and inserted while the glass was still in the molten state. The medallions vary in size, the larger containing the usual figure subjects drawn from the Old Testament while the small ones display an ornament of eight-petalled flowers.

The Severinus paten belongs in effect to the extensive series of 'gold-glasses', a product characteristic of Rome or Cologne, and including examples both pagan and Christian. These gold-glasses are the bottoms of bowls or drinking cups that survive when the rest of the vessel has been smashed. They are medallions of gold leaf, engraved with the needle point and protected by a layer of glass fused, sometimes with the help of a fixative, on the under surface. Glass vessels ornamented in this manner are sometimes found in burial-niches, partly in order to mark the location but also with the idea that they might ward off evil spirits. More often they were used as wedding presents or

181. Adam and Eve hesitant between good and evil. Engraving on a fifth-century goblet found at Cologne.

gifts made within the domestic circle. This accounts for such expressions of good wishes as *'Pie, zeses'*, 'drink and prosper', and explains the frequent occurrence of stylized family groups. Conventionally the husband is shown wearing a toga over his tunic while the wife, clad in a mantle, has her hair dressed in a succession of curls round her forehead and wears round her neck a collar ornamented with jewels. Sometimes the figure of a gladiator is added, or some such mythological reminder as Hercules with his lion-skin and club. One gold-glass offering a message of good wishes to Severa, Cosmas and Leah (fig. 178)[38] shows the parents and a daughter who is clothed like her mother but has her hair rather differently styled, with a knot on top of her head. Even if of Jewish ancestry, as the girl's name implies, the family was evidently Christian, for the chi-rho emblem appears, surmounted by a wreath.

Sometimes, in place of the married couple, a picture is chosen from the Bible. One, with bitter-sweet allusion to conjugal happiness, shows Adam and Eve, the latter decorated with diadem and necklace, standing beside a luxuriant tree round which the serpent coils. The bottom of another drinking vessel[39] offers a crude

picture of Daniel killing the dragon of Babylon by means of a poisonous cake (fig. 179). As Daniel offers the cake he turns his head back towards a figure of Christ shown as protector of the righteous, with the rod of authority in his hand; thus a scene from the Old Testament Apocrypha receives a New Testament gloss.

The Good Shepherd is a popular choice for illustration on the gold-glasses, while Jonah and the three men in the fiery furnace also occur with frequency. A rather more elaborate sequence on a 'man and wife' glass, now at the Ashmolean, Oxford, displays Adam and Eve, the sacrifice of Isaac, Moses striking the rock, the healing of the paralytic and the raising of Lazarus. Another notable example, from the Vatican collection (Inv. no. 750), shows Christ in tunic and pallium pointing with his right hand to seven baskets full of loaves. For the glass-blowers worked within the mode of artistic fashion as set first by the catacomb paintings, then by the sarcophagi and finally adapted to mosaic. References to Pope Damasus point to the latter part of the fourth century as the period of greatest production.

Figures of saints are sometimes introduced, with

Peter and Paul being by far the most frequent. One of the finest examples is the bottom of a bowl on which are shown busts of Peter and Paul with their faces turned towards each other.[40] The usual distinction between the two apostles is not made; both alike are bearded and have hair receding from their forehead. They wear mantles fastened with large, circular brooches; behind them hovers a small figure resembling a pagan genius but proving in fact to be Christ, shown with long, straight hair parted down the middle and extending his arms to hold a wreath over the head of each apostle as, on other gold-glasses, he does over bride and bridegroom. Christ is not often shown realistically and alone, but the base of one drinking vessel made of very thick glass reveals, within a lozenge enclosed by a square, a bust of Christ, beardless and youthful, with hair cut in a fringe across his forehead and falling in curls over his shoulders (fig. 180). He wears tunic and mantle, fastened with a brooch, and the inscription *Cristus* is added.[40] At each angle of the square framework a smaller bust appears, exactly resembling the central figure except that the long curls are omitted.

The gold-glasses survive in fair number because, though some appear to have been made as separate amulets, most represent the durable part of a larger vessel. Complete glass vessels exist only as rare and scattered examples: no one type prevails. A fifth-century goblet,[41] found at Cologne, has sides, increasing in width from base to rim, that are roughly engraved with conventional reproductions of Moses striking the rock and the raising of Lazarus. Adam and Eve appear also, but in this case they differ from the usual formula: not only are the tree and the serpent included, but Adam turns his head away in the direction of a figure, clad in tunic and mantle, who must be either Christ or possibly an angel, investing the scene with supernatural lustre (fig. 181). An earlier example,[42] also from Cologne, is a bowl, elaborately if rather roughly gilded, which offers scenes from the life of Jonah as well as portraits of Constantine's sons. The cantharus type of vessel, frequently illustrated on the sarcophagi, is shown in the S. Vitale mosaics as placed on the altar and therefore presumably a chalice. Thus it is possible that a glass vessel of this nature, said to come from Amiens and now in the British Museum,[43] served at one time as a chalice. It is made of bluish glass with a wide lip, two handles, a fluted circular bowl and fluted foot—but is now usually held to be a Renaissance reproduction.

Surviving quite abundantly from the sixth century are little money-weights, made from dull green glass of poor quality. They are small discs, stamped on one face only with a monogram or bust together with the name of the prefect then in office. But sometimes Christianity is proclaimed by substituting a cross for the monogram.

POTTERY

An unpretentious earthenware, 'the clay which the thumb moulds while the spirit soars elsewhere',[44] was used all round the Mediterranean in making objects for everyday use and thus naturally pressed into service by Christian households. Just as Victorian families decorated their walls with edifying texts of Scripture, so, at an earlier period, the Faith was proclaimed with equal frankness by stamping appropriate emblems or inscriptions on this commonplace material. While much has perished, a copious supply of small lamps still remains. Most are of an elongated heart shape, with handle at the thick end and oil spout at the other, the upper surface being often stamped with a rough pattern, a cross or an inscription such as 'Mayest thou find life in Christ'. North Africa is especially productive of these lamps, made as a rule in a bright red ware. Further east, in Egypt, Syria or Asia Minor both shape and colour, as well as quality, are more variable; some examples are made of pale material with the decoration outlined in black. Dating is not always easy, but most of the lamps may be assigned to the fifth and sixth centuries. The choice of subjects for illustration is straightforward enough: Jonah lying under the gourd tree, Daniel in the lion's den, the spies bearing the grapes of Eshcol and such other Bible themes as lay ready to hand. One of the North African lamps shows Christ holding a long cross and standing on a dragon (fig. 182).[45] Peacocks, emblems of immortality and therefore connected with light, were a favourite choice; thus a lamp from Beirut

182. Typical North African lamp. This one shows Christ overpowering the dragon.

183a. The Bowl of Constantine: engraving of Christ in majesty.

183b. The Bowl of Constantine: restored on one side.

has as its ornament a concave circle with a hole in the centre and a cross and, at each side, two peacocks facing a tree from which the fruit has fallen to the ground.[46]

Pottery was used in making the oil–flasks (ampullae) when cost was a consideration outweighing the charm and greater durability of metal. Many of these earthenware flasks come from the shrine of St Menas at Alexandria and have the flat circular sides decorated with designs executed in relief. A typical example shows Menas, arrayed in tunic and cloak, standing between his two camels[47] within a border of roughly executed decoration. On the reverse side the design is repeated save that the border is supplied by an inscription: 'We have received the blessing of St Menas.' The Menas inscription came to be something very like a magical formula which could be associated with other saints, as on a large but rough two-handled flask where, within the customary words, the named figure of St Thecla[48] is shown standing composedly with hands on hips between a lion and a panther.

The Asiatic flasks seem on the whole to be of even cruder workmanship than the Egyptian examples. Usually they lack handles and are simply an oval extended at the top to form a stumpy neck. The commonest type, well represented in the Louvre collection, shows a bearded personage clothed in a tunic with many folds and supporting on his crossed arms a book which covers his chest like a breastplate. An inscription, not always very lucid, is added, indicating that the effigy was originally intended for St Andrew.

Other rather more ambitious flasks from Asia Minor show St George, or possibly St Theodore,[49] standing on a dragon or riding on horseback and piercing the dragon with a lance. A large and rather splendid ampulla of red ware exhibits, within a border of dots, two arches, with the Virgin and Child[50] seated beneath one of them and an apostle, holding his book of sacred learning, beneath the other. A cock perched on a column nearby suggests that the figure is intended for St Peter, but that identification fails to explain the three goats below. Perhaps they are no more than a motif casually introduced to fill up space; at any rate, when the design is repeated on the reverse side, the three goats are transformed into a goat and two cocks.

Other objects made in pottery for common uses include bowls and plates, fragmentary for the most part, that are marked with the chi-rho emblem. Glazed pottery is, however, very rarely found and the Bowl of Constantine (fig. 183), now in the British Museum, is unique for its high quality and technical skill—so much so, indeed, that some have regarded it as a forgery. The bowl, part of which has been broken and lost, is made of buff ware covered with a clear glaze; the outside, decorated with a chequered pattern of squares, blue alternating with white, frames the figure, formed by lines cut into the paste, of Christ in majesty. His attitude is important as setting a type that often recurs in the history of Byzantine painting. Seated, and wearing a richly embroidered tunic and mantle, he extends his right hand in a gesture of compassionate greeting rather than sheer authority. The left hand, now missing, seems to have been differently angled and may have held a book. Christ is shown with beard and long, flowing hair and his head is surrounded by a large halo, cross-shaped within a circle. Behind Christ's shoulders run three horizontal lines, and above them at either side are round medallions containing profile heads which, to judge from the inscription set round the rim of the bowl, represent Constantine and his wife Fausta. Since Fausta died in 329 AD the bowl was presumably in existence before that date. Alexandria is claimed as a likely place of origin, but the argument here depends primarily on the success of Egypt in ceramic art at a much later date, and Constantinople might be suggested with no less justification.

NOTES

1. I Timothy 2.9.
2. Pliny, *Natural History* 9.35. 58. (Loeb iii.242.)
3. Exodus 39.14.
4. Revelation 24.19.
5. A vase, formerly in the Strozzi collection at Rome but now in the British Museum, is similar in shape but dumpier. Worked in low relief, it shows Christ healing the blind man of Bethsaida and an apostle receiving the scroll of the Law.
6. Now in the Museum of Antiquities, Edinburgh.
7. A strainer, similar in general type but later in date, was found, together with chalice and paten, at Derrynavlan in south-western Ireland (1980). *Journal of the R. Society of Antiquaries of Ireland* cx. This strainer is, however, divided into two parts, one half for straining and one half for pouring.
8. *Sanctum altare tuum Domine subnixus honoro.*
9. *Iamcilla votum quo(d) promisit complevit.*
10. Theodoret, *PG* 83.922. Paulinus of Nola, *Carmen* xiv, *CSEL* 30.7.
11. *R.A.C.* 12, 313–28.
12. Nearly all patens are circular. An exception is the oblong dish, with raised cross in the centre and, at the corners, formalized locket shapes indicating the rivers of Paradise, that was found at Gourdon (Provence) and is now in the Bibliothèque Nationale, Paris. The date, however, here is open to question.
13. N. Firatli. *Studi* 27 (1969), illustration ccliv. The Kamluca collection is now partly at Dumbarton Oaks, partly retained in Turkey, the censer being in the Archaeological Museum, Istanbul.
14. The only comparable example, in the Dumbarton Oaks collection, is marked with the place-name 'Antioch' and date-stamps of Phocas I (602–610 AD).
15. Some of these David dishes are now in the Metropolitan Museum of Art in New York, others are in the National Museum of Cyprus at Nicosia.
16. In the Hermitage, Leningrad.
17. More often called the Strogonoff platter, as it formed part of the Strogonoff collection, now in the Hermitage.
18. *Quod Christus sit Deus, PG* 8.826.

19. E.g. C. R. Morey in the *American Journal of Archaeology* xxiii (1919).
20. *Epistle to Severus*, 32, *PL* 61.539.
21. Dumbarton Oaks Collection, Washington.
22. Now in the Archaeological Museum, Istanbul. The date-stamps on both patens indicate the reign of Justin II.
23. Now part of the Tyler Collection at Dumbarton Oaks, Washington.
24. E.g. Nicephorus, *Antirrheticus* iii.36, *PG* 100.434.
25. *Liber Pontificalis* i.34.
26. BM EC 7.25. The three following examples are also in the British Museum.
27. Paul the Silentiary, *Description of S. Sophia, PG* 86.2151.
28. L. Bertacchi in *ACIAC* IX, 71.
29. BM EC 1–47.
30. Illustrated in *DACL* xiii.2399.
31. BM EC 3.44.
32. BM EC 1.48.
33. Now at Tunis Museum.
34. Now at the Louvre. J. Morin-Jean, *La Verrerie en Gaule* (1913) p. 244.
35. Transferred to the Hermitage, Leningrad.
36. Now in Trier Museum. For the Boulogne example, transferred to Rouen, see J. Morin-Jean, *op. cit.*, 123
37. I.139.
38. BM CG 1–12.
39. BM 3.38. EC 619.
40. BM EC 636 and EC 2.1.
41. EC 7–9.
42. Cologne, Wallraf–Richartz Museum.
43. BM EC 3.105.
44. Gautier, 'L'Art', *Oxford Book of French Verse*, 296.
45. BM EC 60.10–2.34.
46. EC 835.
47. BM EC 860.
48. An early and perhaps influential example of this theme is provided by a marble relief from the monastery of St Thecla and now in the Greco-Roman Museum, Alexandria. For Thecla, see Grabar, *Martyrium*, 344 note.
49. BM EC 914.
50. BM EC 903.

184. Coins which demonstrate the alliance between Church and State. a. Constantine: solidus, 326 AD. Constantinople. b. Magnentius: bronze follis, 350 AD. Amiens. c. Olybrius: solidus, 472 AD. Rome. d. Justinian: solidus, 538 AD. Constantinople.

16

Coins and Gems

COINS

The use of coins in the early years of the Roman Empire was twofold. Apart from the business of buying and selling, paying taxes and storing up wealth, coins served as a means of advertisement and propaganda, reminding everyone of some political or military success and adding, in the inscription, a slogan that was often more akin to a prayer than to a statement about the social conditions of the day. Rome had taken over the idea of coinage from the Greeks and saw little need for innovation either in the technique of punching out the coins or in their general design. The successors of Alexander in the Hellenistic kingdoms had commonly set their portrait-head on their coins in the place hitherto reserved for a god, and this practice was adopted by Julius Caesar and the emperors who followed him. The vigorous realism of the Hellenistic portraits was, however, purposely toned down to become something rather closer to a type, conventional and generally accepted, of anyone who wields sovereign power. Originality was less sought after than a stability that concealed personal rivalries and impressed the inhabitants of a far-flung empire with the sensation of permanence and power. Even so, the art of the engraver did not entirely disappear; when Diocletian, at the end of the third century, reformed the monetary system in a desperate effort to control inflation, his portrait-head, with its wide eye, wrinkled brow, small, tight-lipped mouth and bull neck, constituted a vivid essay in the art of representing imperial authority even if it could not be claimed as an exact likeness.

The head of Constantine illustrates the same theme of mastery and determination. The various issues of the Antioch mint, for instance, show him with short hair, laurel wreath or diadem, straight nose and thick neck; his gaze is fixed resolutely ahead. The coins of such other mints as Nicomedia allow more variation of posture and, on some of the later solidi[1] of his reign, Constantine's head is tilted up and his eye and whole bearing become those of the mystical dreamer waiting for the spark of illumination to fall from heaven. Appalled by treachery and strife amongst his own relatives, Constantine at the very beginning of his reign turned away from his accepted patrons, Jupiter and Hercules, and placed himself instead under the protection of the 'Unconquered Sun'. This change had two advantages. It called to mind the glories of Constantine's ancestor, Claudius II, victor over the Goths, who had been a devotee of the Sun; secondly, a convenient basis for widespread political unity was provided by the sun, which shines over the whole earth as its source of light and healing.

Constantine had been emboldened to hazard his fortunes against the tyrant Maxentius by the vision of a cross standing out against the sun's disc and, beneath, the words 'In this, conquer'. Thereafter the God of the Christians, who had inspired and directed at the time of crisis, became his God and, even though he delayed baptism until he lay on his deathbed, Constantine from the outset took the view that a church united in harmonious worship would ensure the divine favour. The emblem of the Unconquered Sun fitted in naturally enough with this new-found faith. For the sun's daily resurrection from the prison of the dark offered obvious similarities to Christian teaching, while Christ had been identified, by some of the earliest Fathers of the Church, with the prophet Malachi's 'Sun of righteousness who should arise with healing in his wings'.[2]

Constantine refrained, however, from pushing the claims of Christianity in any extreme manner and even retained the office of pontifex maximus, charged with the duty of presiding at the solemn celebrations of pagan worship. But the Olympian deities disappeared from the reverse side of his coins. Instead, the inscription 'Glory of the Army' may be accompanied by the figure of a woman holding a leafy branch and supported by a column, or the figure of Victory is shown with outstretched wings and laurel wreath in hand, as on a solidus minted at Trier in 315.[3] Another favourite type was the fortified city-gate, surmounted by turrets with cupola tops. The frontier walls were no longer a firm defence and the city-gate, accompanied by some such legend as *Prudentia Augusti*, was a token of the care which the emperors took to keep civilized life secure against barbarian onslaught.

Signs of Christianity work their way onto the coinage by means of a discreet and gradual symbolism. A bronze follis, struck at Trier in 317 AD, has, on the obverse, Constantine wearing armour and a laurel wreath, while the reverse side shows the Sun God, crowned with radiance and extending his right hand in blessing. With his left hand this half-naked Apollo supports a globe, and he stands between a star on one side and a small cross on the other. It may be doubted whether the cross here has any great significance, but on another coin, struck at Siscia in the same year, the chi-rho emblem appears for the first time—as a personal badge on the emperor's helmet. Three years later this monogram of Christ was set straightforwardly on the field of coins struck in Italy, Greece and Spain but it was only after the Council of Nicaea, in 326, that the newly-established mint at Constantinople produced coins which freely and officially proclaimed the Christian faith. Here the obverse bears the customary portrait of the emperor while on the reverse occurs the *labarum*, the military standard surmounted by chi-rho emblem, with the lower end of its shaft transfixing the dragon of wickedness (fig. 184a). Even so the inscription *Spes Publica*, 'Good hope for one and all', is neutral enough to commend itself to any right-thinking person.[4] For Constantine, though patron of the Christians and feeling assured of Heaven's favour through the offering of Christian worship, had not the slightest wish to provoke resentment from his pagan subjects. The convert's zeal was tempered by political wisdom and a philosophic detachment which accepted Christianity as growing out of the older faiths, their natural successor and crown rather than a hostile opponent to them.

The emperors who immediately followed Constantine kept to the style of coinage he had established. Thus the imperial portrait of his successor Constantius, with elongated head and prominent eye, is an essay in remote, impersonal, even priestly, contemplation. But the troubled nature of the times and the desperate efforts made by the emperors to keep alight the torch of civilization are revealed, on the reverse side of many fourth-century coins, by savage and jarring themes: barbarian armies are crushed and captives dragged away by their hair. Christian aspirations continue to be muted until, in 350 AD, the usurper Magnentius struck at Amiens a bronze coin with a bold chi-rho monogram set in conjunction with the significant letters alpha and omega (fig. 184b).[5] The inscription—'Safety'—is neutral enough, but a year later Gallus Caesar is shown on his coins holding the *labarum*, and crowned by Victory with, as comment, the words of faith: 'In this sign thou shalt be conqueror.'

After Julian's ill-starred attempt at reaction in favour of the old pagan deities, clear but unemphatic allusions to Christianity recur on many of the coins. Invention in this particular art seems to fail and the emblematic figures become stiff and stereotyped, with a wealth of vague allusions to military prowess. In accordance with this mood, coins of the eastern half of the Empire, particularly from the time of Theodosius II, tend to show the emperor not as a head in profile but clad in helmet and armour and facing toward the front, thus giving the beholder a sense of alertness as well as personal contact. The Christian element in the design is commonly restricted to the chi-rho emblem, either dominant in its field and enclosed by a wreath or else a tiny object oddly associated with the Britannia-like figure which stands for the City of Rome or with such vestiges of ancient patriotism as Romulus and Remus suckled by the she-wolf. A fairly popular motif found on solidi of the period is a winged figure, explained by the legend 'The Safety of the State', seated and clasping a shield on which the chi-rho is prominently displayed.[6] This theme was modified in the direction of a more explicit Christian witness to become a winged angel standing upright and holding a tall cross. But only on rare examples, as on a solidus struck by Olybrius in 472 AD,[7] does a truly medieval point of view emerge, and a plain cross, surrounded by the legend 'The Salvation of the World', occupies the whole of the field (fig. 184c).

The artistic enterprise which marked the reign of Justinian did not extend to any particular enrichment of the coinage. But from this time onwards the close interlocking of Church and State was emphasized by the solemn posture of the emperors (fig. 184d). Richly bedecked with jewels and holding cross, orb or sceptre, they proclaimed that they owed their office to the divine election and that they were charged with the task of safeguarding not only the fortunes of the state but religious orthodoxy as well. And, if the conventional symbols of paganism persisted, that was entirely in accord with the conservative spirit always evident in such matters. Similarly the Urtuqid princes of twelfth-century Turkey, though they represented the victory of the Moslem world, yet retained on some of their coins ancient Byzantine figures of Christian import.

GEMS

The Greeks excelled in the difficult art of engraving precious and semi-precious stones, and it was Greek colonists who carried this particular skill and technique to Italy. Here gem collecting became a popular pastime, encouraged by the example of Pompey who, in 62 BC, returned to Rome with a great treasure of carved gems seized from Mithridates, king of Pontus. Gems were regularly used for the practical purpose of sealing documents besides being highly regarded as a form of decoration. But men who acquired large numbers of gems in the early years of the Empire tended to value their possessions not merely for the aesthetic pleasure they gave but also for the potency of the emblems or mottoes engraved upon the stones in warding off disease or poison or the shafts of misfortune. The Olympian deities—Jupiter, Juno, Minerva and the rest—appeared on gems as they did on coins; the Egyptian gods Isis and Sarapis were also much favoured, as were outlandish figures derived from the magic cults of the Middle East.

A particularly Roman contribution to the art was the choice of personified figures of Africa, Antioch or Rome and the appearance of portrait heads and busts, whether of the emperors or of private individuals. Scenes from daily life brought in the actor, the fisherman and the shepherd, as well as athletes of various kinds, while animals and birds also were shown. There was, moreover, a fashion for grotesques known as grylli, in which comic masks are worn by strangely hybrid creatures. One example, a red jasper now in the British Museum, [8] has a head composed of two human heads joined together, a body made up of a human face and a ram's head with ears of corn projecting from the ram's mouth, while a lizard curls nearby. The inscriptions on gems are apt to be wistful or cynical: 'They say what they like. Let them talk. I don't care.' But the most popular emblems were those which have about them the air of a lucky charm, such as a winged Victory or the goddess Fortune.

In the sixth century BC Pythagoras had forbidden his followers to bear the image of a god on their rings and, in their turn, the leaders of Christian thought were obliged to consider what devices were appropriate on rings and gems: dove, fish, ship, anchor or fisherman, according to Clement of Alexandria's classic recommendation.[9] Thus a fish, often associated with the anchor of hope, and, even more frequently, the chi-rho emblem, came to be a favourite subject for engraving on gems used in Christian households. But dating these objects is not always easy, and the matter is complicated by the existence of spurious antiques produced with great skill at the Renaissance and in more recent times.

One of the more remarkable essays on the theme of the fish is provided by a large chalcedony now at Berlin. This shows a throne of robust yet simple design, furnished with a footstool and a garland of honour. The throne is empty, but the back is engraved

185. Christian emblems on gems. a. Oval sard: The Cross steers while the Apostles row the ship of the Church. b. Gold signet-rings showing Christ attended by angels.

with the Greek letters for the word 'Fish' together with six little circles which, to judge from other examples, are meant to indicate eucharistic loaves. At each side of the throne occurs a compressed monogram that conceals the name either of the owner or of St Paul.

The fisherman occurs less commonly, but one substantial cornelian[10] shows a boat in which the steersman, seated at the stern, gives instruction to three members of the crew who are equipped with rod and line. Beneath the boat lurks a fish and IXΘYC is written in bold characters. If this scene is to be analysed, it must apparently be connected with baptism rather than Eucharist.

A variant on the same theme is provided by a ship rowed by oarsmen who represent, no doubt, the Apostles guided on their course by Christ the steersman. An oval sard in the British Museum (fig. 185a) compresses this scene to the extent that there are three oarsmen only and a cross is substituted for Christ in person as steersman.

The dove, with an olive branch in its beak, appears fairly often and is usually associated with the chi-rho which, in one or other of its forms, is the most popular of all the Christian symbols on the early gems as it is on the coins.

Of the emblems not mentioned by Clement of Alexandria, the Good Shepherd, linked with the most primitive strain in Christian devotion, is a favourite choice. Sometimes the Shepherd stands alone, clutching a disproportionately large lamb across his shoulder, but other artists preferred to crowd the field with every variety of supporting allusion. Thus, on a scarab found at Capua,[12] the Shepherd, clothed in his short tunic, advances towards the left with the lamb on his shoulders while two smaller lambs leap up at his knees. Overhead curls the Tree of Life with three doves, representing the spirits of the redeemed, perching on the branches. A fish is set in the field at each side; in a compartment of its own at the bottom appears a eucharistic loaf marked with a cross.

The restricted space available on gems makes the use of compound subjects difficult and inartistic, but the thought of uniting the Good Shepherd with the theme of Jonah was too attractive to avoid entirely. A circular sardonyx in the British Museum is divided into two registers. The upper scene depicts the Good Shepherd and Jonah lying under his gourd tree, on which a dove perches, while in the lower half comes an unruly composition in which fish, anchor and Jonah's whale all find a place.

Another sardonyx from the same collection, though not divided, suffers likewise from the desire to include as much symbolism as possible within the oval frame. To the left a small figure, placed with hands upraised beneath a tall tree and in the company of two sheep, suggests an *Orans*, someone maintained in life everlasting by the Good Shepherd, who occupies the centre of the stone. To the right the Jonah story is doubly indicated, for Jonah is shown both as he is swallowed by the monster, and then lying at his ease under the gourd tree. As if this were not enough for one cameo, still other emblems are scattered about: star, dove, fish and a roughly sketched chi-rho impaling a cross.

Amongst the most interesting of the engraved gems are those which illustrate the Crucifixion. A cornelian intaglio[13] from Costanza, in Romania, offers a rough, ill-designed figure of the naked Christ standing with arms outstretched in line with the cross-beam. No upright stake is visible, and the attitude typifies dominance rather than humiliation: beneath each arm are grouped six little figures, less than half the size of Christ, which represent the Apostles. Along the top edge of the cornelian are boldly inscribed four of the five letters of the word ΙΧΘΥC which came to be used as a summary of Christ's nature and thus as an all-purpose charm. A third- or even second-century date has been claimed for this stone, but it is better described as a crude, provincial piece to be placed somewhere between 300 and 500 AD. A rather more elegant version of the same theme is found on another oval cornelian,[14] on which Christ, with arms outstretched, stands against the upright shaft of the cross, with his feet some distance from the ground. The diminutive Apostles are a little more lifelike here, and the two who stand nearest the cross put out their hands to touch Christ's feet. The Greek inscription runs 'Jesus Christ', the last two letters being set within

a separate compartment at the bottom of the cornelian, one on each side of a lamb. In this view of the Crucifixion Christ's head is surrounded by a halo, as it is in a casual, impressionistic sketch found on a red jasper from Gaza.[15] Christ here has his arms outstretched, but body and legs curve freely and no cross is shown. A little man kneels at one side and, on the other, a woman wearing robe and mantle stands in an attitude of devotion. On the back of this stone runs an inscription in three lines of undecipherable lettering held no doubt to confer an added potency to the amulet.

The art of engraving gems spread to Persia, and in spite of their dislike of the Persians, the Byzantines keenly patronized this manifestation of Sassanid art. Nothing compares for splendour with such pieces as the cameo showing the emperor Valerian taken prisoner on the battlefield by King Sapor I,[16] nor had the Persian craftsmen any impulse to do other than copy well-tried themes. But the sacrifice of Isaac, Daniel in the lions' den and the Triumphal Entry are amongst the standard scenes, competently executed, which may be traced to Persia and even to north India.

The larger and more handsome stones illustrating the Annunciation and the Nativity mark a revival of the jeweller's art in the West and the inspiration given, at a somewhat later date, by illuminated manuscripts. Similarly gold signet-rings develop from the display of a straightforward monogram set between crosses into scenes of much elaboration. One gold signet,[17] which may be as old as the sixth century, consists of a plain rounded hoop to which an oval setting has been applied (fig. 185b). The oval is engraved with the bust of Christ, his head encircled by a large halo. A cross is shown at each side; below, angels with upward-sweeping wings appear while the legend 'Holy, holy, holy, Lord God of Sabaoth' runs round the bezel. The full splendour of medieval panoply has by this time arrived.

NOTES

1. The solidus is the standard gold coin, weighing about 70 grammes.
2. Malachi 4.2.
3. Constantine's coins of the Trier mint are discussed in E. Baldwin Smith, *Architectural Symbolism of Imperial Rome* (Princeton, 1956), 49 ff.
4. An example is BM PCR 1309.
5. BM PCR 1365.
6. Solidi of Eudoxia and Pulcheria. J. B. Bury, *History of the Later Roman Empire* i.138.
7. BM PCR 156.
8. Graeco-Roman Gems 2578. See Dölger, *Das Fischsymbol*, 272.
9. Paedagogus, *The Tutor* iii.2. See p. 2.
10. *DACL* VI, fig. 5047; G. W. King, *Engraved Gems* (1885) XIV. 4.
11. BM, Dalton Catalogue, fig. 40.
12. Illustrated in *DACL* VI, 5042, from *Bull. di arch. crist.*, 1891. The BM examples of this theme are 25 and 26.
13. An intaglio has the figures cut into the stone while, on a cameo, the figures stand out from it in relief. This example is in the British Museum: Dalton Catalogue, fig. 43.
14. *DACL* VI. 816, fig. 4944.
15. Kraus, *Realencyklopädie* II. 241. *DACL* vi.818, fig. 4945.
16. Paris, Bibliothèque Nationale.
17. BM EC 120. The second example is 189.

17

Textiles

A taste for luxury in textiles, as in the other arts and crafts, marked the reign of Constantine and his successors. But, since textiles easily perish and disappear, knowledge of style and colour depends to a large extent on literary allusion supported by the evidence of painting and mosaic. Constantine himself acquired a ceremonial tunic made from cloth of gold enriched by woven flowers[1] and, after some hesitation, he presented to the Church of the Nativity in Bethlehem 'hangings wrought in various colours'.[2]

Thus, in spite of scruples, the use of splendidly decorated material for altar cloths and curtains in churches began in the fourth century and gradually superseded plain linen. The apocryphal *Acts of St Thomas*, written about 250 AD, mention merely a 'linen cloth', such as was wrapped round candidates for baptism, being used to cover an unpretentious altar: 'he set forth a stool which they found there and spread a linen cloth upon it and made ready the bread of blessing'. It was with this tradition in mind that Pope Silvester I forbade the use of silks and other coloured material during the liturgy and prescribed the use of linen instead.[3] But it proved impossible to resist the tide of fashion, though the more austere among the Fathers of the Church lamented the tendency of the faithful to seek after luxury. John Chrysostom, for example, accused his flock of reserving their admiration for jewellers and weavers while Asterius, bishop of Amasea in Pontus, composed a classic diatribe on the subject, in his 'Homily on the Rich Man and Lazarus'.

There are certain people [he lamented] who are quite infatuated with vain desire. They discover some flashy and elaborate textile which, with the interweaving of upright and cross threads, copies the manner of painting and displays on garments the forms of every kind of animal. They skilfully produce for themselves, their wives and their children flowered clothing adorned with patterns of countless variety. When, therefore, they dress up and make their appearance in public, they resemble painted walls, so that children stand around them grinning and pointing at the coloured design on the garments. There you may see lions and panthers, bears and bulls and dogs: there are woods and rocks and huntsmen and every device of artistry used to reproduce the forms of nature. For it seems that they felt bound to decorate not merely their walls and their houses but their tunics and cloaks as well. However the more devout of the wealthy folk among you make choice of the Gospel story to set upon your woven garments—I mean Christ himself together with all his apostles, and each of his miracles recorded in the narrative.[4]

Mention is then made particularly of the Marriage Feast at Cana, the paralytic man, the woman with the issue of blood, the woman 'who was a sinner' prostrate at the feet of Christ, and Lazarus.

Asterius' description of the fabrics used by Christians for clothing at the end of the fourth century is borne out by the fragments which remain. Of these there are two groups. The first consists of tiny pieces, preserved in the treasuries of such western cathedrals as Sens and Aix-en-Provence. Far more abundant, however, are the curtains, winding-sheets and clothes which have been recovered, usually incomplete, from Antinoë, Akhmim and other places in Egypt. Objects of this nature not only give an idea of contemporary fashion throughout the Roman Empire but bear witness to the continuity of Mediterranean culture in their repeated wave, circle and lozenge patterns, found on the earliest Greek vases but here competing for favour with the 'palmette', the 'sacred tree' and other clearly Oriental designs.

The most usual type of fabric is a straightforward linen cloth in which single horizontal threads of the weft are drawn alternately over and under the single threads of the warp. Onto this background, quite plain or consisting of a simple pattern constantly repeated, were often fixed bands or medallions of hand-worked tapestry, and the few tunics,[5] used for burials, that have been found almost complete, are embellished in this way. Embroidery, or 'inlaid weaving', where the decoration is not applied but worked into the material, also occurs but less commonly.

The hoards of material found in Egypt vary in subject as in design. There are hunting scenes of Persian inspiration, as well as Greek gods, such as Orpheus or Apollo with his lyre, and illustrations drawn from Greek mythology: battle against the Amazons, it may be, or Vulcan forging the armour of Achilles. When Christian themes appear they often have to jostle with the conventions of paganism in an atmosphere of casual tolerance. Over most of the human figures brood some traces of an Egyptian or Coptic style, shown in the enormous, bulging eyes, heavily marked brows and uncouth, rounded limbs; but inscriptions, on the early pieces, are in Greek, and it would seem that the craftsmen of the fourth to the sixth century were Greek-speaking artisans, of varied origin, offering their provincial version of Byzantine art.

Precise dating of these textiles is not easy, but the tendency over the years was away from delicate shading in two or three tints of red and green towards gaiety and brightness of colour, applied in rather rigid bands and often accompanied by indifference to the proportions of the human body or the accurate representation of historical scenes. But intricate and charming patterns persist, together with animals, birds and plants which testify to careful observation of natural forms. The hare and the duck are special favourites, but lion, panther, deer and quail are stock subjects also, together with vine, acanthus and the tall rushes typical of earlier Egyptian art. Touches of religious symbolism may work themselves into the oft-recurring theme of the curving vine-stem, in which birds picking at the grapes alternate with an arrangement of leaves, but it is a light-hearted feeling for pretty decoration which prevails.

Perhaps the finest of all the Egyptian wool tapestries is the example, in the care of Harvard University, showing an august figure identified by a Greek inscription as 'Vesta all-blessed'. The goddess is seated in an attitude of sovereignty, looking straight before her. Her head is encircled with a halo and she is sumptuously attired in a costume which includes a vast necklace. Attendant genii hover nearby. A certain casual dignity stamps the composition as Hellenistic, while an almost studied neglect of anatomical detail adds the Egyptian flavour. A date early in the sixth century seems likely for the Vesta tapestry, as for a square purple panel now at the Hermitage, Leningrad, which shows in the centre the triumph of Bacchus and, round the border, the labours of Hercules. The view can no longer be maintained that pagan themes must belong to a period earlier than the end of the fourth century, when paganism was officially suppressed in the Empire. For the triumph of the Church came to mean a correct participation in the Christian liturgy, which did not exclude either the wistful scepticism of popular poetry or a lasting affection for the heritage of classical legend. Thus the figures of Greek mythology, no less than dancers, warriors with shields, cupids and the rest, continued as part of the artistic stock in trade, along with the crosses or the peacocks facing one another which mark the earliest attempts to indicate the Christian faith. These signs of Christianity were introduced in a quiet and even furtive manner. A small cross might appear on the shoulder of a tunic or in one of a sequence of medallions which otherwise exhibited animals or trees. Yet sometimes there are no hesitations. A British Museum tapestry, for instance, shows a boldly designed cross in yellowish brown standing out against a background of natural colour and surrounded by a blue circle displaying white flowers each set on a red heart-shaped field (fig. 186). By way of variety, two crosses might be combined, as on a tapestry panel from Akhmim, where the eight branches join in the centre at a circle which itself encloses a small cross.[6] The chi-rho monogram also occurs, both in the ordinary fashion of the Constantinian coinage and in a modified form where the loop of the rho exhibits a double curve, like a shepherd's crook, and does not finish attached to the shaft. But the novelty is the use of the ankh, the old Egyptian emblem of immortality. The ankh consists of a circle laid on top of a т cross, and thus lent itself admirably for adaptation as a Christian symbol (fig. 187). One piece of tapestry-woven cloth, rather more than a foot square, displays a horizontal row of ankh figures: within the circles are, in turn, the chi-rho monogram, a double cross and two crosses with dots in the angles. Above this band another ankh cross appears to the left, and, further to the right, a small equal-armed cross with angle-dots completes the reiterated theme.[7] The alpha and omega motif, too, is found on textiles as elsewhere in contemporary Christian art, a notable example being the tapestry-woven ornament of a linen curtain, now in the Victoria and Albert Museum, which may be assigned to the first half of the fifth century. Here a pagan genius, richly clothed in red, yellow and green drapery and wearing a splendid diadem and earrings, is transformed for the occasion into a Christian angel. He clasps a wreath of flowers enclosing a jewelled cross which has the alpha and omega below the arms and a dove in each of the angles above.[8]

At about this same period, heads or busts within roundels became popular, and in this mode of representation the saints were sometimes included. A large bust of St Theodore (fig. 188), attached to other fragments which are all parts of a wide curtain decorated with figures of the military saints, is in the Fogg Art Museum and shows an overall family likeness to the more famous Vesta tapestry in the same museum. Theodore's black hair is held back by a white band; he has a long, curved nose, cat's eyes and the severe, abstracted gaze of sanctity overlying a natural sophistication. The bust is enclosed within a sumptuous frame of pearls and precious stones and anticipates the fully developed type of Byzantine portrait.

Detailed illustrations of Biblical scenes on textiles were infrequent until the seventh century. But two matching roundels on a tunic in the British Museum, which may be as early as 550 AD,[9] illustrate the Adoration of the Magi, with birds rather irrelevantly set here and there in the field. The figures in this scene, with their swollen heads and large, round eyes, are rendered without the least regard for proportion in impressionistic, almost cubist, fashion.

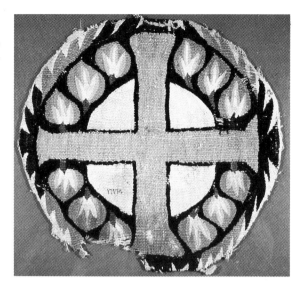

186. The cross boldly displayed on an Egyptian tapestry of the fifth century.

187. Tapestry panel from Egypt: the ankh used as a Christian emblem. British Museum.

188. Tapestry: bust of St Theodore.

Some of the earliest and best representations are boldly traced on the natural surface of linen curtains. When the picture had been completed, a layer of wax or clay was applied to protect it and the rest of the cloth was dipped in dye, usually indigo. The whole surface was thus coloured except for the piece protected by the adhesive wax, which could then be removed by melting with a hot iron. Bacchic themes, worked in this style, were favoured; a large printed textile, now at the Louvre but found in an undistinguished tomb at Antinoë, shows a fine Triumph of Bacchus in which the design stands out well against the customary surround of dark blue. The border of vines, inhabited by birds and edged at the top with a line of rosettes, has something in common with the rich decoration of the Antioch chalice, while the naked bodies are still treated with a concern for accuracy and grace. The style of the hair, coiled in regular spirals, and the prominent eyes resemble the figures of Rome and Constantinople on an ivory diptych now at Vienna which seems securely dated in the middle of the fifth century. At the top left corner of this large, gay and essentially pagan textile, scenes appear illustrating the birth of Bacchus: Semele, half reclining on a couch, is

approached by Zeus in the form of a hovering angel of light. Comparison is inevitable with a rougher and perhaps slightly later textile[10] where the Christian theme of the Annunciation is shown. The Virgin, her head surrounded by an enormous halo, lies back in the manner of Semele on a couch unambitiously indicated by rows of 'pothooks' but the angel, instead of hurtling down from on high, is standing calmly poised before her. Once again, both Virgin and angel have the huge eyes, strongly marked above and below, which express the gauche yet intense religiosity of monophysite Egypt. The name 'Maria' and a star are seen above, while an ox, standing close to the manger, indicates that originally the Nativity was attached. This part of the textile is, however, by now severely damaged.

Also from Akhmim is another Annunciation scene set within bands of vivid decoration. Here the Virgin is spinning: she holds the distaff and a basket lies at her feet. Gabriel, curly-headed and long-winged, is viewed from the front but turns his head sideways toward the Virgin (fig. 189).

A fragmentary curtain of the same period, also included in the Victoria and Albert collection, displays

189. Printed textile from Akhmim: the Annunciation.

a somewhat confused array of Biblical scenes. Moses is shown receiving the Law and two of the Gospel miracles of healing are illustrated: the man suffering from dropsy and the woman with an issue of blood. In the centre Christ appears as the youthful and curly-haired 'Son of David', though rather incongruously wearing an elaborate robe, in the act of raising Lazarus from the tomb. Once more the large eye, heavily defined, is a striking feature. Into the same class of printed linens falls an Akhmim panel showing three apostles named as Thomas, Mark and Peter. Each has a large, double halo and is wearing a pearl-studded cloak, as he advances—perhaps towards Christ as the Giver of Communion. The picture, fragmentary as it is, smacks of the deep liturgical interest reflected in the Ravenna mosaics.

Silk was greatly appreciated as a material in the early Christian period, but it was rare and extremely expensive. Efforts had been made to produce a substitute from the cocoons of caterpillars kept on oak and ash trees on the island of Cos, but the raw silk spun from the cocoons of caterpillars feeding on the traditional mulberry was for many years a monopoly of the Chinese and the Persians. It was used in the West mainly to add sheen to coarser substances or, more luxuriously, to provide tunics of 'half silk'. The emperor Elagabalus, whose extravagance was notorious, had clothes of pure silk made for him in about 220 AD, but his successor Aurelian, fifty years later, complained that ten ounces of silk cost seventy-two gold coins. Justinian is said to have obtained the eggs of silkworms from monks who smuggled them out of China.[11] At any rate he caused extensive mulberry groves to be planted in Syria and strictly controlled the silk trade in the imperial interest. Though he ruined some of the merchants by the strictness of his measures, Justinian was lavish in the use which he made of silk in Santa Sophia. The curtains hanging from the columns of the ciborium over the altar were, in the words of a contemporary witness,

a form of decoration not produced with the help of a needle threaded through the warp by toiling hands but by the shuttle changing from moment to moment the colour and thickness of the threads which the insect from foreign lands supplies.[12]

The cloth laid on the altar itself was a magnificent piece

of embroidery, showing Christ in a golden mantle and tunic of purple and attended by the apostles Peter and Paul; the border illustrated both Gospel miracles and the charitable activities of Justinian and his empress Theodora.

Silk fabrics from the early period which still survive are nearly always fragmentary. The Egyptian weavers had used silk mainly to form small, decorative panels on a background of linen clothing while, in the West, patterned silks testify to zealous travels in search of relics of the saints. For such prizes, 'more excellent than gold',[13] were carefully wrapped up in the most precious material which lay to hand. Antinoë has furnished a number of these often rather scrappy pieces of silk material. They are notable for their delicate arrangement of flowers combined with lozenges, squares or heart-shaped patterns, as well as for a lighthearted treatment of animal scenes. The zebras that stand face to face on a fragment now at Berlin have the same comic air as the lion heads that turn towards one another on a bright-coloured silk, preserved at Lyons, which shows, in addition, two crowned heads in medallions. The historian Ammianus[14] mentions the 'multiform figures of animals'—by which he means the gryphons, seahorses and other mythical creatures—which were copied from barbarian fashions and used on civil costume.

But, to judge from the fragments that still exist, the most popular theme to adopt was the Persian hunting scene, in one or other of its variations, used for decorative effect rather than with any overtones regarding the conquest of evil. Sidonius, bishop of Clermont,[15] who died in 482 AD, describes a foreign robe which had worked upon it Parthians looking behind them as they ride and shooting arrows at wild beasts. In reasonable accord with this description is a silk in the treasury of S. Ambrogio, Milan, which shows, against a background of green medallions, two horsemen drawing a large bow of the type used until quite recently in the Middle East, and shooting at a lion which hurls itself at a wild ass. A similar piece was discovered in a chest at the church of St Cunibert, Cologne; in both, the horses have the large, curving head characteristic of the four chargers which stand, pawing the ground as they prepare to draw a chariot into the circus, on the bold, repeated pattern of a silk from Aix. Discoveries at Akhmim have provided three separate silk panels where the riders, doubled one

against the other in the interests of symmetry, prance in a formalized manner across the field, with the name 'Zacharias' inscribed overhead.[16] Since no Christian saint bearing that name was either a horseman or a warrior, it appears that this was a design, perhaps rather casually repeated, intended to honour an official or renowned cavalryman of the time. But the pattern could readily be adapted to Christian ends, as shown by a pair of panels, now much defaced, on which a victorious figure, presumably Michael, holds a small cross in one hand while with the other he thrusts his cross-topped lance into a dragon's mouth.[17]

The more elaborate Christian scenes find their place readily enough on the silks as on other fabrics. The Metropolitan Museum in New York contains five small pieces of silk which illustrate the Nativity. Dating from about 500 AD, they are tinted in a rather harsh crimson, with touches of green and black. The largest piece shows the Virgin sitting on a throne-like chair with the Christ child at her knee. Jesus, distinguished by a prominent halo, stretches out his hands towards a figure on the left, a shepherd or one of the Magi, who wears a Phrygian cap and holds a crook. The faces of both mother and child are squared and formal. Another fragment has the strongly-defined heads of ox and ass facing each other over a stone crib in which the infant lies clothed in criss-cross swaddling-bands.

It can be plausibly claimed that the silks from the treasuries of Western Europe represent a rather more restrained and sober version of 'Eastern' art than do the Egyptian examples, and that they may therefore be attributed to the workshops of Constantinople itself rather than to provincial craftsmen. But they too draw on the common stock of imagery and represent the same type of artistic expression, somewhat slapdash but vigorous and decorative. The largest collection of such silks is contained in the cathedral at Sens. Some are charming little pieces of decoration in which the field is studded with quatrefoil flowers. These, and some pictorial fragments which include a tiny figure of Elijah being fed by the raven, suggest manuscript illustrations rather than textiles. Hints of classical scenes may also occur with such furnishings as a pagan altar and, in what appears to be a Bacchic subject, a man is shown being felled to the ground by a panther. This has a more graceful, Hellenistic look to it

190. Fragment of woven silk: Joseph being encouraged by an angel.

than the comparable fragment from Aix of a panther-slayer where the artistic value lies in the vigorous thrust of the panther as it springs with head turning backward and mouth open to expose the fangs.

On the Sens fragments Christian emblems are frequent, both crosses and 'gammadia'.[18] When figures are introduced, they are nearly always worked in a greyish yellow, against a background of deep purple, but this rather grand and simple colour scheme is seldom matched by the details of the composition. The most important of the silks at Sens offers part of the cycle of events connected with the life of Joseph (fig. 190); by the fifth century, these were accorded the dignity of prophesying incidents of Christ's Passion.[19] The figures are arranged quite well and in an unpretentious manner, but there is no attempt at elegance or subtle characterization. All, including an angel, are dressed alike in long tunics and have the large, heavy heads that recall the consular diptych of Boethius. In addition, the scenes are squeezed far too tightly together. But interpretation is helped by the fact that each scene is repeated on a second level and written commentary is provided. The initial scene is fragmentary, but seems to illustrate

Joseph's farewell to his father, as he set off on his journey. Following this is an apocryphal addition to the Bible record: the meeting of Joseph, as he was advancing towards his brethren, with an angel who enquires about Joseph's purpose and, by implication, assures him of divine protection. Next are shown Joseph's brothers and their flocks, represented by three animals clustering around a small tree. The need for compression results in the fact that only two brothers appear, one turning to the other with the remark 'Here comes the dreamer.' Two other small fragments of silk, of the same colour and technique but rather different in scale, bear witness to the popularity of the Joseph story but are so worn that they would be difficult to identify if it were not that the words 'angel' and 'Joseph' are supplied.

The cult of relics caused pieces of silk worked by Asiatic weavers to be transported to places much further afield than Sens, and one very early fragment was found in the coffin of St Cuthbert, at Durham. Within a border where vines are the main decorative theme stands a boat-shaped vessel with a richly jewelled foot and bunches of fruit together with fringed ceremonial cloths hanging down from its side. This splendid object is shown standing on the surface of a pool, with a pair of ducks swimming at each side and large carp below.

The fragments at Sens, Durham and elsewhere, for all their interest, give little indication of the grace which silk-weavers were able to express later on in such works as the Annunciation found in the Sancta Sanctorum at Rome, and now in the Vatican.

NOTES

1. Eusebius, *On the praises of Constantine*, PG 20.1337.
2. Eusebius, *Life of Constantine* iii.43, PG 20.1104.
3. About 320 AD. *Liber Pontificalis* i.34. 171.
4. *Homilia de Divite et Lazaro*, PG 40.166.
5. Such as the examples in the Victoria and Albert Museum and in the Musée Guimet.
6. Victoria and Albert Museum 308.
7. Akhmim. V. and A. 309.
8. Only part of this fine composition has survived.
9. The date is variously estimated. Some would put it two centuries later.
10. V. and A. 786.
11. Procopius, *Anecdota* 25.13 (Loeb vi.296). The matter is discussed by J. B. Bury, *History of the Later Roman Empire*, ii.331.
12. Paul the Silentiary, *Description of S. Sophia* (*Ecphrasis* 765), PG 86.2148.
13. *Martyrdom of Polycarp* 18, in *The Apostolic Fathers* (Loeb), ii.336.
14. *Histories* xiv.6.9 (Loeb i.40).
15. *Epistles* ix.13, PL 58.631.
16. V. and A. 794 and 800. BM P 592.
17. St Michael here is on foot. V. and A. 819.
18. For gammadia, see p. 182.
19. Even earlier, Tertullian writes in his *Against Marcion*, iii.18 (*CSEL* 47.406), 'Now Joseph is the man who figuratively stands for Christ.'

18

Writings and Illustrated Books

The early Christians inherited from their Jewish ancestors a keen awareness of the value of the written word. 'Lord, what love have I unto thy Law: all the day long is my study in it'[1] may have been applicable only to the professional scribe, but 'Search the Scriptures'[2] was advice offered to all, and a large part of the first mission-preaching consisted in explaining incidents of Christ's life in terms of Old Testament prophecy. Within the Church a 'canon', or 'rule' of Scripture, was drawn up almost from the beginning, in order to define the accepted books and to exclude unworthy competitors.

These works were written on papyrus, in accordance with the practice universal throughout the Roman Empire, or at any rate in the Greek-speaking part of it. Papyrus was manufactured in very large quantities from the pith of the papyrus reed which at that time grew abundantly in the waters of the Nile. The method of preparation, as explained by the naturalist Pliny,[3] was to cut the papyrus pith into thin strips. Those with the fibres running lengthways were set out side by side in a row and strips with the fibres running horizontally placed on top of them. The two layers were then flattened by hammering to form a single sheet of papyrus usually twenty to twenty-five centimetres wide—though some were larger and a number of sheets of poor quality did not exceed twelve centimetres. A single sheet would suffice for a letter, but works of greater size were written out on sheets glued together to form a roll. Some of the Egyptian rolls are enormous, but the customary Greek practice was to make them between six and eight metres long.

When the roll was made up, the scribe settled to his task of writing on it in a series of columns five to eight centimetres wide, using, as a rule, only the side of the papyrus which had the fibres running horizontally. When the roll was finished a label (*syllabus*) was attached to it by way of a title and it was laid on a bookshelf or placed upright in a bucket (*capsa*). Each roll might be expected to comprise a volume about the size of a full-length Gospel. The rolls were not particularly easy to use, for they had to be held in the right hand while the left hand unrolled and rolled up again as the reading went on. Words were not separated from one another and punctuation hardly existed, nor was there any index or means of looking up references. Script, as with modern handwriting, varied from the graceful to the atrocious.

The use of papyrus rolls for book production came eventually to be modified in two ways, as regards first material and then form. The competing material was calfskin or vellum, a term which is extended to include the skin of sheep or goat and thus becomes identical with parchment. The story[4] ran that Ptolemy Epiphanes, king of Egypt and a keen collector of books, became so jealous of the library owned by Eumenes II, king of Pergamum, that round about the year 190 BC he forbade the export of papyrus to Asia Minor. This obliged Eumenes to develop the manufacture of vellum, which in turn acquired the name 'pergamene', now changed to 'parchment'. In fact the Persian kings had made use of parchment for their chronicles two or three centuries earlier, and the success of Eumenes probably lay in improved preparation of the skins and in gaining a wider acceptance for them. Thereafter papyrus and vellum continued side by side, with papyrus long remaining the more popular material and parchment looked on, anyhow at Rome, as particularly serviceable for making high-class notebooks.[5] It was under the influence of these writing tablets, where several wax-covered boards or, later and more conveniently, sheets of parchment were held together by strings passed through holes at the side, that the codex, or volume in the form of a present-day book, developed as a rival to the roll. The Roman poet Martial,[6] commenting at the end of the first century AD, mentions works by Homer, Virgil and others written out on this type of parchment codex, and he refers to an edition of his own poems which, being in codex form, can be held, neatly and readily, in one hand.

A codex, whether of parchment or papyrus, might contain a much longer text than could be inscribed on a roll and it was a great deal easier to handle, but a conservative respect for the roll as a dignified method of book production made the change-over to the codex a slow and hesitant process. In Christian circles, however, the codex seems to have been popular from the very beginning. The evidence for this is the papyrus manuscripts, often fragmentary, which, preserved in the warm, dry atmosphere of Egypt, have been found within recent years at Oxyrhynchus and elsewhere. It is possible, on the ground of style in handwriting, to assign to these a reasonably exact date. At least a dozen portions of the Christian Bible must belong to the second century, and in each case the manuscript is a codex, whereas pagan literature was preserved for the most part on rolls until about 250 AD, when the codex gradually became the more fashionable form everywhere.

While the Jewish writings, such as those found in the Dead Sea Caves, are set out on rolls, the books of the Christian Bible, together with associated sayings and stories whether authentic or fanciful, display, right from the start, a remarkable degree of uniform practice which favours the codex and, in addition, follows an agreed system of abbreviating such hallowed words as God, Jesus, Son of Man and Spirit. The reasons for so clearcut an arrangement can only be guessed at; but, in any event, the Christian papyri testify not only to the rapid transmission of the Gospel text but also to close relationships and a vitality of common purpose within the Church from its earliest beginnings.

The method of producing a codex gradually underwent a certain refinement of technique. At first the sheets of papyrus were placed on top of one another and then folded over in notebook fashion down the middle, but the result could be awkward and lumpy if the sheets were numerous. To avoid this, it became customary to build up the codex by means of a number of separate quires, each quire consisting of between two and twelve sheets folded over to make a more manageable unit. From the beginning of the fourth century, parchment tended to supersede papyrus as the material from which the Bible codex was made, presumably because parchment was thought to be more durable and to provide a more elegant surface for fine script. When, therefore, in 331 AD, the emperor Constantine wrote to Eusebius, bishop of Caesarea, ordering him to supply 'fifty copies of the Sacred Scriptures', it was laid down that the books should be

written on prepared parchment, in a legible manner and conveniently portable form by professional scribes thoroughly practised in their art.[7]

Some twenty years after this the volumes in the great library of Pamphilus, the scholar patron of Eusebius, were replaced by copies on parchment, since the earlier books, written on papyrus, were showing signs of decay.

It is to this period, in the middle of the fourth century, that the earliest of the great Bibles now extant may be assigned. Written in columns of 'uncials',[8] or capital letters, they contained the whole of the canonical Scriptures in a single volume of no inordinate size. Pre-eminent for age and state of preservation are the Codex Vaticanus, in Rome, and the Codex Sinaiticus, formerly possessed by the convent of St Catherine on Mount Sinai but kept since 1934 in the British Museum. Both are written on thin, fine parchment, at one time thought to be the skin of antelopes but now more usually described as sheepskin alternating with goatskin. Their place of origin was probably Caesarea, a great centre of Christian scholarship and enquiry in the fourth century, but Alexandria, or some other place in northern Egypt, cannot be ruled out. The script, an elegant, bookish hand very different from the scribbling of some of the contemporary papyri,

191. Codex Sinaiticus: the ending of St John's Gospel.

seems to mark a conscious following of classic, first-century examples.

The slightly later manuscripts, such as the Codex Alexandrinus, normally follow a settled convention of having two columns on each page; but the Vaticanus has three columns, while Codex Sinaiticus varies in accordance with the type of literature being transcribed. For the most part it bears four narrow columns on each page (fig. 191), but this number is reduced to two when the poetical books of the Old Testament, from Psalms to Job, are in question. Codex Sinaiticus is built up in the manner which was coming to be generally accepted at least for the Greek manuscripts, through a number of quires nearly all composed of four sheets, or, when folded, eight leaves. Horizontal lines were ruled right across the page to guide the scribe, and vertical lines were added as guides to indicate the width of the columns. No ornamentation was attempted, but the wide margins, a gracious feature often adopted in the later manuscripts, seemed to invite either pictures or explanatory notes or both. The great codices, such as Vaticanus and Sinaiticus, were the work of several hands, uniting in an effort of dignified calligraphy eminently suitable for the transmission of sacred texts. No covers or bindings of any kind have survived, and it is uncertain whether these noble volumes were kept in carved boxes, or in leather satchels of the type which was found containing the Gnostic writings of Nag Hammadi.

Roll and codex both continued in use and, on sarcophagi of the fifth century and after, Christ is regularly shown as clasping the scroll of his authoritative teachings. Once adopted, however, the codex established itself firmly in favour not least because of the greater ease with which illustrations could be composed for it. Pictures were not added to the text of books until the fourth century, and the earliest of them continue, in miniature, a graceful, easy, style that recalls the wall-paintings of Pompeii. Perhaps the oldest piece of book illustration on a large scale is the Calendar of 354, produced in Rome but by an artist from the Near East. This, though by now extant only in late copies of the original, offers a series of lively and attractive essays in the neo-classical manner. A lavish arrangement of architectural motifs serves as a frame for cherubs and the personified Seasons—the month of November, for instance, appears as a priest of Isis,

192. Dioscorides's *Materia Medica*. Constantinople, 512 AD. The Princess Juliana Anicia seated among allegorical attendants.

with rattle, goose, a snake on a dish, and the jackal Anubis in attendance. But a desire to advance the cause of Empire brings in touches of somewhat heavier allegorizing. The great cities of Rome, Constantinople, Alexandria and Trier make their appearance in forms of dignified imagery while Constantius II, splendidly arrayed, dispenses largesse with unsparing hand.

Appropriately enough, in view of the pre-eminence that Homer and Virgil enjoyed within the late classical world, an illustrated manuscript of each survives from the fourth century. The Vatican Virgil[9] displays fifty miniatures varying in size and framed in three thin bands of colour, black, white and red. The pictures are of unequal merit, but most of them reveal a charming, if conventional, landscape upon which figures have been superimposed with differing degrees of appropriateness and skill. Colour is not very delicately arranged; the prevailing tints were laid on, as a rule, in horizontal sections, green or pale yellow at the bottom, pink or rose colour in the middle and blue or green on top, the whole being enriched here and there with touches of gold. Efforts at perspective were very halfhearted and geographical details received casual treatment. The island of Sicily, for example, is represented as little more than seven buildings and a harbour, with a disproportionately vast ship approaching it. The common ground that exists between pagan and Christian art-forms is indicated by the scene where Dido and Aeneas recline at a sigma couch, in front of a three-legged table bearing a fish.

The Milan Iliad, another parchment codex, is of much the same character as the Virgil. The fifty-eight miniatures which survive out of four or five times that number display a poetic vigour in the battle scenes and a delicate charm in depicting the countryside which, again, carry the classic grace of Pompeii through to the closing years of the fourth century.

Illustration may be valued for the pleasure it gives or as commentary in some important narrative, but its use is almost essential in a scientific textbook. Dioscorides, an army physician of the first century, made a systematic study of medicines and the sources from which they were obtained, and a splendidly illuminated copy of his *Materia Medica* was produced about 512 AD for the princess Juliana Anicia in commemoration of her wisdom and piety in founding a church at Honoratae, a suburb of Constantinople. The book, now kept at Vienna, offers charming illustrations, executed with a delicate accuracy worthy of Leonardo or Ruskin, showing hemlock, shepherd's purse and other serviceable plants, together with a group of snakes, beetles and birds. The whole is preceded by portraits of the author and other physicians, while there is an elaborate miniature, enclosed within a plaited border, of Princess Juliana herself (fig. 192). She sits enthroned between two allegorical personages who represent Prudence and Magnanimity. Meanwhile 'Love of the Foundress' hands her a book, while a kneeling figure in a posture of grovelling thankfulness proves to be 'Gratitude of the Arts'. All these illustrations in the Vienna Dioscorides, while they may owe something to earlier copies, mark the survival into the sixth century of the classic, Hellenistic style[10] of painting. If 'Byzantine' touches are to be distinguished, they consist of an extended use of gold and bright, lively colours.

It was amidst influences such as these that the Church developed its taste for book illustration, though examples belonging in the earliest period are now extremely rare. First in chronological order is a portion of the Itala, the Latin version of the Bible that preceded Jerome's Vulgate, discovered at the monastery of Quedlinburg but now at Berlin. Here the well-developed uncial letters and the scarcity of abbreviations point to a date about the beginning of the fifth century. Only five leaves remain, with a text written in very black ink on thin, white parchment, and, as the passages are all drawn from the books of Samuel and Kings, it appears that the volume was confined to the historical books connecting the Pentateuch with the Prophets. The method used for the illustration is not entirely consistent. Each leaf has two columns of text, and on one leaf there are no pictures at all. Three of the others have the picture area divided by broad strokes of red into four compartments while one leaf is separated by a diagonal line into two long fields. Thus there are fourteen pictures, all similar in style and colouring and apparently the work of one artist. Against a tinted background, brownish green below and sky-blue above, the figures, in their garments of red-brown touched with gold, appear in sketchy straightforward compositions. There is no hint of any elaborate symbolism, and simple notes are added with the pious aim of adding to the knowledge of the beholder, while here and there instructions are jotted down by the scribe telling the artist which parts of the scene to illustrate. Thus, the episode in which Saul is told that his lost asses have been found[11] is shown, in no very close accord with the Biblical text, as an announcement made by two messengers near Rachel's tomb. 'Put in a monument here', the artist is told, and the words 'Rachel's Monument' serve for the reader to identify a lofty pillar with its jutting centrepiece crowned by a steep roof. Saul himself appears as a distinguished, royal figure in anticipation of the later part of the story where he is anointed king by Samuel.

Another well-preserved and impressive scene is that of Saul sacrificing at Gilgal in defiance of Samuel's commands.[12] Samuel stands in a chariot drawn by one grey and one chestnut horse, while in the background a building indicates the fortress of Gilgal. Samuel, clad in a long, white robe, holds the reins in his left hand; his right hand is raised in admonition as he addresses the king, who is in the act of pouring a drink-offering onto the flaming altar. Saul turns his head in surprise. He is an imposing figure in leather jerkin, fringed mantle and diadem and, though awestruck, conveys an air of imperial authority which suggests that the artist had copied some medallion of Alexander Severus or Constantine. Moreover, the details of the sacrifice, as of Samuel's chariot, seem in these, the earliest Christian miniatures, to have been closely modelled on the standard, classical forms represented on Trajan's Column or the pages of the Milan Iliad. There is no sign of Byzantine panoply in this example of 'Western' book production. The general aesthetic mood is that of the Junius Bassus sarcophagus or the Brescia casket: firm, clear and simple, where the characters, however august, express youthful vigour no less than dignity.

The illustration of the Bible seems to have begun with separate books or a group of closely related books which, in the course of time, were combined to form a single volume. But it was the Pentateuch, and the book of Genesis in particular, which attracted the attention of the miniaturist. Though designed both to record and to instruct, such pictures may present a lightness and ease that go beyond the traditions of the rather more public arts of wall-painting and mosaic. The earliest of the Greek illustrated manuscripts is the Cotton Genesis, held in the British Museum. This parchment codex, acquired by King Henry VIII, was so badly burnt by a fire in the year 1731 that it now exists only in small pieces. But the style may to some extent be checked from facsimiles made for the French bibliophile Peiresc and from thirteenth-century mosaics in the vestibule of St Mark's, Venice, which appear to have been drawn from a cycle of Italianate illustrations very similar to that used by the Cotton miniaturist. The pictures are set within a wide, dark frame and usually against a background of blue. One of the best of the existing fragments shows Hagar, with a coiffure of fringe and side-curls, sitting in a composed attitude beside the well and stretching out her hand as the angel approaches.[13] This is one of the occasions when it is left to the Venice mosaics to supply missing details: the angel's youthful countenance and long wings.

Another resemblance between miniature and mosaic, to judge from Peiresc's facsimile, is provided by the scene in which God stations the cherubim before the Garden of Eden. Here God resembles a youthful Christ, with a cross-shaped nimbus behind his head. The three cherubim turn their heads to face the Lord, raising their right hands in obedience and extending their left arms in readiness. There are comic suggestions here of a theatre chorus, and the illustration of God's promise to Abraham, found only in Peiresc's facsimile, may be judged a more impressive composition. Here a vast hand of God extends in a luminous glow from the cloud; below Abraham stands all alone, the picture of austere dignity, clutching the long, dark mantle which almost covers his white, ankle-length robe.

One of the few existing fragments of any size shows the separation of Abraham from Lot,[14] characterized by an artistic grouping of the figures. This scene occurs in the S. Maria Maggiore mosaics and, though the treatment is not particularly close, the similarity between the two sets of illustrations is clear enough to show a common range of interest, during the fifth century, in the decisive incidents of the Old Testament story.

The same tradition of classical narrative is maintained in the Vienna Genesis, by far the noblest and the best preserved of the very early group of Christian manuscripts. It consists of forty-eight pages, out of an original number at least twice as large, and the writing is executed in silver on a purple parchment of fine

193. The Vienna Genesis. Constantinople, sixth century: a. the Flood; b. Rebekah's meeting with the servant of Abraham.

quality. The work may safely be assigned to a date within the period 500–550 AD and, though its place of origin has been disputed, the royal purple colour[15] suggests scribes working for the emperor at Constantinople even if they probably drew into service a standard cycle of illustrations originally composed at Alexandria a century earlier.

The text of the Vienna Genesis is that of the Septuagint, the Old Testament as officially translated from the Hebrew for the benefit of Greek-speaking Jews, but, in order to find room for the pictures, which occupy the lower part of each page, this version has been subjected to some rather casual abridgment. The normal arrangement is to have the scenes set out in two rows, forming a double frieze in which the events, shown in full or lightly suggested, make up a continuous narrative. An exception to this practice is the picture of the Flood (fig. 193a), which occupies the whole space of one of the panels. This is a weird and horrifying essay. The dominant colour, standing out brilliantly against its purple background, is blue, and the torrential rains match the flood-water rising around the half-submerged ark. Beneath the waters human beings and a few animals lie still or writhe in agony as they are engulfed while, at each side of the ark, light from above plays on a face and pair of arms raised in a last despairing gesture of supplication. No attempt is made at scale or perspective which might lessen the sense of the vast and overwhelming nature of human tragedy. The illustrations of the Vienna Genesis are, however, the work of several different artists, each following his chosen fashion. The aim on the whole is to secure unadorned narrative as opposed to any compressed symbolism, but success varies as regards composition and colour. One ingenious arrangement, which is in effect a two-level frieze without any distinct demarcation, occurs in the scene of Rebekah's meeting with the servant of Abraham.[16] At the top right of the picture (fig. 193b) is shown a walled town from which leads a road marked by milestones. But the road turns sharply left, dropping to a lower level and there, as the connecting figure, is Rebekah in her long, pink dress and blue veil as she carries her empty pitcher down to the well. The well, however, resembles a bright blue stream and by it, as though drawn straight from some Pompeian wall-painting, reclines the half-naked figure of a river-goddess. Rebekah then appears a second time, stoop-ing gracefully as she supports the pitcher on her right hand in order that Abraham's servant may drink. Behind, a clustered group of ten camels await their turn at the water trough. In this scene, once again, the refinements of artistic proportion are sacrificed to vivid and memorable story-telling.

Special attention is paid, in the Vienna Genesis, to the incidents of Joseph's life, with their happy combination of exciting detail and educative value. Not all, however, are treated in identical manner. The escape of Joseph from Potiphar's wife, for instance, is shown as a colourful piece of stagecraft, with the two figures in postures of dramatic movement before a standard set of theatrical properties comprising a colonnade, entirely out of scale, and an open door that leads nowhere. The episode is continued in a series of charming, if somewhat irrelevant, pictures as Joseph, glancing back hesitantly, finds himself among the queen's attendants, all engaged in such placid pursuits as spinning or minding the children.

This series of delicately tinted vignettes presents a marked contrast with the sketchy, impressionistic style of the picture in which Joseph is shown seated in prison with the chief butler and the chief baker. The prison is roughly indicated by a large grey tank with the roof taken off so that Joseph can be seen with his right hand raised in prophecy while the butler and the baker express in their every gesture the joy and the despair belonging to their respective dooms. The trees behind the prison are merely indicated by streaks and blotches of colour, but the gaoler, in his white jerkin and blue trousers, is a well-defined figure. He sits on a stone beside another Hellenistic stage property, the sundial on top of a column; in order to enliven the picture still further, his wife is introduced as a personage additional to the Bible story in order that she may lend a ready and astonished ear to the gaoler's account of Joseph's prowess. The patriarchal narratives, it has been said, make a timeless and unfailing appeal to the human heart, and the Vienna Genesis shows vividly how their powerful charm caught the imagination of sixth-century artists and was translated into visual form.

The later historical books of the Bible could also be a joy to the inventive artist, as is shown by the Joshua Roll now in the Vatican Library. This is in effect a long pictorial frieze running continuously over joined sheets of parchment, in which the vigorous, military

194. The Rossano Gospels: the Communion of the Apostles.

scenes drawn from the first half of the book of Joshua are varied by cities, trees and pastoral deities attractively delineated in a consciously classical style. Unlike Trajan's column, with its tight-packed run of incidents so closely interwoven that they can only with difficulty be separated, the artists of the Joshua Roll arranged their pictures in clear-cut sections. It was at one time believed that the Roll had been composed in the fifth or sixth century, but it now seems certain that, while there may well have been a prototype belonging to this period, the work as it stands at present is a product of the tenth century, and of the renaissance inspired by Constantine Porphyrogenitus. This emperor liked to think that the Constantinople of his day recapitulated in its buildings and statecraft the glory and greatness of ancient Rome, while a gratifying parallel could be drawn between the reverence due to a victorious monarch and the respect inspired by the military successes of Joshua.

Coming from the same artistic background as the Vienna Genesis and attributable also to the period round about the beginning of the sixth century are two Gospel-books, the Sinope Fragment and the Codex of Rossano. Both may be said, in their rather differing fashion, to show Hellenistic charm gently transformed by oriental solemnity. The picturesque touches of landscape painting almost disappear, and neither symbol nor impressionistic fancies are felt to be particularly fitting. Clear, historical narrative, suffused by the dignity appropriate to God's gracious self-manifestation, is the artist's aim; thus the Gospel manuscripts offer the same lessons and the same type of aesthetic experience as do the mosaics of a richly decorated church. The Rossano Gospels, so called from the Italian city to which the book was transported, is, like the Vienna Genesis, written in uncial letters of silver, or occasionally gold, on a fine purple parchment. The text (imperfect) is that of St Matthew's Gospel, together with part of Mark and, just as the medical treatise of Dioscorides included portraits of the author, so St Mark is shown, sitting beneath an elaborate framework of architecture and writing his Gospel upon a long roll while a female figure standing nearby represents the inspiring force of the Divine Wisdom. Another page has a frontispiece of the Canon of Eusebius—that is, the rules for ascertaining the parallel passages in the four Gospels—together with formalized busts of the Evangelists, each within a gold circle.

The surviving miniatures of the Rossano Gospels offer a series of events concerning the life of Christ from the healing of the blind man to the trial before Pilate. Into this historical cycle the parables of the Wise and Foolish Virgins and of the Good Samaritan are inserted. Beneath the miniatures, in most cases, occurs a second painting to confirm that the event accords with Old Testament prophecy. Along the lines of a stereotyped pattern four prophets appear, holding with their left hands an unfolded roll which makes them appear to be standing in waist-high pulpits.[17] Turning their faces towards the centre they raise their right hands in declamation. The usual costume is a blue-bordered tunic and white mantle, but when the prophetic voice is that of David or Solomon, these are shown as kings, wearing deep-blue mantles offset by great golden breastplates, and with gem-studded crowns perched insecurely on top of their hair. The prophets have their names written above their heads and suitable texts are supplied which fit the particular occasion.

Bright, harmonious colours and the effective grouping of figures are characteristic features of the Rossano Gospels; so, too, is a facility for compressing into one moment a wealth of consecutive detail. The Lazarus episode illustrates in masterly fashion this power of combining many elements into one simultaneous scene. The ground, as in all the miniatures, is marked by an undulating line. Near the middle stands Christ in a long, sleeved tunic and mantle which leaves his right arm and raised hand free. Behind his head is a large cross-nimbus and his right foot is lifted up as if in eager movement. Christ is followed by a group of people before whom stand two apostles, grave and elderly. Meanwhile two women kneel near Christ; they are enveloped in their garments and their outstretched hands are reverently covered with their mantles, to show that they are in the presence of something holy and mysterious. Behind the crouching women appears a mixed group. One man wearing a purple garment turns in amazement towards Christ, but the others have their eyes fixed on the cave, at the right of the picture. Here, three servants are shown. Two are bowed in awestruck hesitancy while the third, his red tunic swathed about his face to guard nose and mouth from the stink of corruption, leads

Lazarus out. Lazarus himself, closely swathed in white bands, seems to await, in motionless silence, the touch of the Saviour's power.

The miniature showing Christ before Pilate is no less impressive, and here, whether by accident or design, the figures are rather more elongated, almost in the manner which El Greco adopted to convey dramatic intensity. Christ, in his customary garments of blue and gold, stands alone. Of the two accusers, one, an old man, looks back enquiringly at Christ while the younger raises his hand in vigorous expostulation to Pilate. The governor, an elderly, bald man with tufts of white hair, is an impressive figure of remote dignity upon his throne, while at each side is set a guard holding the standard which bears the imperial portraits.[18] The general populace is represented by five men in Roman costume, watching the course of events with concentrated attention. This scene lacks the prophets and their forecasts. In their place, the result is displayed: the repentance and the hanging of Judas.

In only two of the Rossano miniatures do liturgical interests triumph over a scrupulous respect for historical realism, and that is where the Communion of the Apostles is shown as a theological essay on the theme of Christ the eternal High Priest (fig. 194). Apart from its occurrence on the patens of Antioch and Stuma, this scene found much favour with workers in mosaic from the ninth century onwards, but it is the Rossano manuscript which introduces the subject as an addition to the simple record of the Last Supper. Christ here appears as a majestic figure clothed in deep blue and gold, and distinguished by a large halo. At the distribution of the bread, the first apostle stoops with hands extended; just behind him the second apostle lifts up his arms in ecstatic prayer. The third veils his hands in token of reverence, while the other three adopt a uniform attitude, half bowed yet with hands partly raised in wonder. The distribution of the wine is shown according to the same formula. Christ extends the cup, which in fact looks more like a bowl, to an aged apostle with a white beard, while the other five stand in a row, their whole attitude expressing watchful adoration. The two scenes, now separate, must originally have been parts of one composition.

The Sinope Fragment, found in 1899 and transferred from the shores of the Black Sea to Paris, is closely similar in style and date to the Rossano Codex. It consists of five leaves of purple vellum, with illustrations of Herod's banquet, the two multiplications of the loaves, the healing of the two blind men and the cursing of the fig tree. Here the miniatures are not grouped together at the beginning, as in the Rossano manuscript, but are interposed in the text near the words to which they refer. The pictures are somewhat simpler and rougher than those of Rossano, and the figure of Christ, with a halo too large and arms too short, shows less composure and restraint. The method of simple, historical narrative is again followed, with vigorous emphasis on the significant details and disregard of background. Thus, in the fig tree scene, Jerusalem is indicated in the sketchiest manner, and emphasis is laid on two figures, an apostle who looks on amazed, and Christ shown in an attitude of purposeful power, his right hand raised towards the tree while his left hand clasps the scroll of authority.

The Sinope fragment also resembles the Rossano manuscript in that the prophets bear expectant witness to the New Testament events. There are only two accompanying each picture and they stand, one at either side, in their scroll-pulpits. They can thus be shown as rather larger figures, and more attempt is made at suggesting individual character. Moses, with long hair and full black beard, bears close resemblance to the face of Christ, while Daniel's princely rank is indicated by the splendour of his blue cloak and pearl-studded diadem.

The Vienna Genesis, together with the Gospel manuscripts of Rossano and Sinope, firmly set the fashion in which Biblical illustration was to develop after Justinian's reign. Whether produced in Asiatic monasteries or in the imperial workshops, the successor manuscripts, such as the Mesopotamian Gospels of Rabbula, display, amid an ever-growing wealth of decoration, the debt that they owe both to Hellenistic grace and to the vivid sense that the stuff of history possesses unique and unrepeatable value.

NOTES

1. Psalm 119.97.
2. St John 5.37, cf. Baruch 4.1.
3. *Natural History* 13.22 (Loeb iv.142).
4. Told by Pliny, on the authority of Terentius Varro, one of Cicero's friends.
5. Martial, *Epigrams* 14.7. (Loeb ii.442).
6. *Epigrams* 14.184 and 186.
7. Eusebius, *Life of Constantine* iv.36, *PG* 20.1185.
8. This word is taken over from its use by St Jerome in his Latin translation of the Book of Job. The original meaning was apparently 'inch-long'.
9. Vatican Gr. 3225.
10. Some would prefer to describe the Princess as exemplifying the Theodosian mood. See p. 259.
11. I Samuel 9.
12. I Samuel 15.
13. Genesis 16.
14. Genesis 13.
15. The earliest of the Gothic versions, the Gospels of Ulfilas, now at Uppsala, belongs to this period and is written on purple parchment in gold and silver inks. O. von Friesch and A. Grape, *Codex Argenteus* (Uppsala, 1928).
16. Genesis 24.
17. Perhaps this arrangement was drawn from a church, decorated like S. Angelo in Formis in a later period, where the prophets were placed on brackets beneath the main pictures.
18. Josephus (*Antiquities* 18.3.1) records that Pilate was the first to bring standards marked with the imperial portraits into Jerusalem.

Epilogue

What mean ye by these stones?
Joshua iv.6

THE STYLE OF EARLY CHRISTIAN ART

Style in art is a subtle compound, the product of countless minds feeling after truth as it is displayed to them through the shimmer of the elusive and ever–changing spirit of the age:

> For last year's words belong to last year's language
> And next year's words await another voice.[1]

Ruskin may have been right in supposing that beauty has been appointed by God as one of the elements by which the human soul is sustained, but a desire to instruct will often be conjoined with the aim of pure aesthetic pleasure, and the result must in any case be affected by the material which lies to hand and by the conventions in which eye and ear have been trained.

The early Christians had no hankering after novelties. Their wish, in artistic matters as in philosophy, was to adapt the recognized forms of their own age to the insistent task of proclaiming the Gospel: 'the old coin is made to bear the new stamp.'[2] St Paul, when he found himself called upon to address the men of Athens on the Areopagus, had made ready use of the commonplaces of Stoic philosophy. Though his speech, as it runs in the Acts of the Apostles, is to be regarded less as exact reporting than as a dramatic summary of Christian ideas, it clearly stresses the point that, if the new religion were to be comprehensible, it would need to be clothed in established thought-forms. And the thought-forms which, providentially enough, lay to hand were those, urbane and unemphatic, of Greek civilization in its later,

Hellenistic form which had, since the times of Alexander the Great, been widely diffused throughout the Mediterranean lands and as far east as the Euphrates. Something like the same spirit breathed through the art-forms also, characterized as they were by balanced refinement and charm rather than by heroic efforts at creativity. But the earliest essays in Christian art can hardly be compared with the landscapes, the rhythmical groupings or the still-life scenes of Pompeii. There is, indeed, little beyond the decoration of catacombs from which to judge the very early Christian style at all and, apart from the lively grace of a few figures, such as the 'veiled woman' in the Catacomb of Priscilla, the paintings are workmanlike productions quite lacking in artistic nicety. Choice of subject was rigidly limited by convention to a restricted series of incidents illustrating God's powerful acts of charity which save in time of need or, in the seventeenth-century language of Sir Thomas Browne:

The cemeterial Cells of ancient Christians and Martyrs were filled with draughts of Scripture stories, not declining the flourishes of cypress, palms and olive and the mystical figures of peacocks and doves . . . The portraits of Lazarus and Jonas are hopeful draughts and hinting imagery of the Resurrection, which is the life of the grave.[3]

Thomas Browne rightly thought that such scenes hint at the Resurrection, but the Resurrection itself is left to be imagined. Still more notable is the reluctance to portray the Crucifixion. St Paul had laid down the principle that 'the Jews ask for signs and Greeks seek after wisdom, but we preach Christ crucified',[4] and the sign of the cross was eagerly looked for in the world of nature and used in the affairs of everyday life. Of churchmen in North Africa about 200 AD it could be said:

At coming in and going out, dressing or putting on our shoes, on washing or eating, at lighting the lamps and going to sleep, on meeting anybody we touch our face with the sign of the cross.[5]

Yet the only attempt, before the end of the fourth century, to represent a figure on the cross is a bitter caricature, scratched on the wall of a house in the Palatine quarter of Rome, which shows a man raising his hand in a gesture of devotion towards the victim whose arms are outstretched on the cross but whose head is that of a donkey. By way of commentary a few words are added: 'Alexamenos is worshipping his god.'[6]

The earliest Christian art may be rough, compactly symbolic and narrowly restricted in range, but the vigorous patronage of Constantine transformed the fortunes of the Christian Church and led at once to a flurry of building on a grand scale and with ever richer embellishment. But there was no sharp separation in style of the religious from the secular. Ruskin may again be called upon for his testimony:

Wherever Christian church architecture has been good and lovely, it has been merely the perfect development of the common dwelling-house architecture of the period. Churches were larger than most other buildings because they had to hold more people: they were more adorned than most other buildings because they were safer from violence and were the fitting subjects of devotional offering; but they were never built in any separate, mystical and religious style, they were built in the manner that was common and familiar to everybody at the time.[7]

So much may be true, and no doubt the basilica and the martyr-shrine are ingenious adaptations rather than novelties, but the subjects of Christian art and the manner in which they are handled present a unity based on the Bible and marshalled with sufficient clarity and skill to win over, or at any rate to compete with, pagan opponents.

The stability brought about by Constantine was the result of an autocratic rule, rather on the pattern of the eastern empires, buttressed by a rigid court ceremonial, a powerful army and a civil service with far-reaching authority. Artistic effort was sensible and thorough, firmly and self-consciously based on the classical heritage which Rome had taken over from the Greek genius. At the same time there was no prejudice against the use of forms drawn from the Orient. Just as Palmyra accepted without scruple the graceful lines of Hellenistic drapery, so the statuesque figures of Palmyra, solemnly gazing straight ahead, found their way into Western art first as the embodiment of majesty and then as indicating 'the comeliness of spiritual understanding' in saintly persons.

There was a tendency among the Church Fathers, even in the fourth century, to distrust the value of beauty. St Basil, for instance, though charmed by the scenery of the place which he chose for his monastic retirement, had little use for any works of art on the supposition that they are bound up with the ephemeral nature of the material world. Paintings, however, Basil agreed, gain value when they offer instruction in spiritual matters which defy the march of time, and this view Basil's brother, Gregory of Nyssa, emphasized when discussing mosaic decoration:

the art has told the whole story by the skilful use of colours, as in a book which possesses a tongue. For mute design is able to speak from the walls upon which it has been placed and thus renders a very great service.[8]

Splendid buildings which pointed to the triumph of the Church were, at least in the opinion of the scholar-politician Eusebius, to be received with gratitude and amazement, but there are only the faintest echoes of the doctrine, put forward at this time by the New Platonists, that beauty is a property of things which the human soul recognizes as akin to its essential nature and the mode whereby the creative energy of God stamps his own impress upon matter:

This ken we truly that as Wonder to Intellect
So for the soul desire of Beauty is mover and spring.[9]

But, though Christian philosophers in the days of the Roman Empire felt no call to produce a theory of aesthetics, and in spite of an undercurrent of Puritan feeling which regarded beautiful things as something like an impediment to goodness, the artistic achievement carried out by, or for, the Church during the reigns of Constantine and his successors provides a notable chapter in the history of civilization. In some respects new wine was being poured into old bottles, but the classic forms nevertheless received an infusion of vigour and new joyfulness. Modes of expression in painting and sculpture remain symbolic, for when lofty themes are being dealt with, 'the divine ray cannot reach us unless it is covered with poetic veils.'[10] Yet the crabbed impressionism of the catacombs is loosened, and such buildings as S. Costanza's mausoleum in Rome show a delight in varied and graceful forms. As Bishop Westcott used to point out,

the painful literalism which debases many of the monuments of the fifteenth and sixteenth centuries found no place in the fifth and sixth, still less in earlier times.[11]

Fiery North Africans like Tertullian might trumpet out appalling descriptions of the sufferings in store for those who persecuted the Christian faith, and St Augustine might draw on the apocalyptic imagery of the tormented Jewish people to illustrate the horrors confronting the wicked, but the art-forms of fourth-century Christianity observe the classic precepts of dignity and restraint, concentrating, as the very first Christian art had done, on the hopeful theme of deliverance. The ancients, it has been observed, 'have a natural taste for the decorative arts', but, whereas the pagan mood inclined towards a stress on the fleeting and insecure nature of human happiness, the Christians proclaimed, now skilfully, now crudely, a confidence springing from 'joy whose grounds are true'.

The upheaval caused by the emperor Julian's attempt to put the clock back and base his tottering authority on the revival of an antique Hellenism was closely followed by the effort of Theodosius I to establish a Catholic Empire in which the Church should play its decisive part in a system of rigid orthodoxy. The menacing pressure of barbarian hordes quickened the resolve to present a united front, with an aura of sanctity surrounding both the 'most holy Prince' and the 'most holy City of Rome'. It became a kind of sacrilege to question the emperor's judgement, and the lifeless forms of paganism, dear only to a nostalgic circle of disillusioned conservatives, were suppressed in favour of an upsurge of power founded in a Church itself rigidly controlled in the direction of orthodoxy by statesmen bishops such as Ambrose of Milan.

We desire, wrote Theodosius, that all peoples who fall beneath the sway of our imperial clemency should profess the faith which we believe to have been communicated by the apostle Peter to the Romans and maintained in its traditional form to the present day. And we require that those who follow this rule of faith should embrace the name of Catholic Christians, adjudging all others madmen and ordering them to be designated as heretics.[12]

The emperor's determined effort to secure national unity failed, partly because of intrigue and corruption, partly because the onrush of the Germanic invaders proved irresistible. The Eastern Empire, centred on Constantinople, broke away and when, in the year 410, Alaric the Goth 'captured Rome, the city which had captured the whole world', it seemed that the end of an epoch had arrived and that the new-found prosperity of the Church had suffered eclipse. St Jerome, and no doubt many another, expressed his wretchedness in the Psalmist's complaint 'O God, the heathen are come into thine inheritance: thy holy temple have they defiled and made Jerusalem an heap of stones.'[13]

Nevertheless, the work of church-building and decoration continued. It was some while before the final collapse that the poet Ausonius wrote to his imperial patron: 'The basilica used to be a building given over to buying and selling, but now to prayers offered for your welfare.'[14] In other words the typical basilica hall was a church rather than a market, and although, at the beginning of the fifth century, North Africa was being not only ravaged by the Vandals but also torn by dissension between rival groups of Christians, it was at precisely this period that the coastlands were being thickly dotted with such churches. The vast basilica of St Paul in Rome, half built when the Goths pillaged the city, was steadily completed in the next twenty years or so, while the church of S. Sabina, a work of exceptional grace, was founded by a Dalmatian priest named Peter at a time when much of the city lay still in ruins. One reason for this remarkable combination of political collapse and artistic enterprise is that, not for the only time in history, rugged conquerors were charmed by the lure of a sophisticated civilization shot through, for all its weaknesses, with a deep religious impulse. The power of the State might decline with the departure of the Western emperors from Rome, but the authority of the Church tended thereby to increase under the leadership of popes, such as Sixtus III and Leo I, who tempered their taste for autocratic rule with a sensitive patronage of competent artists. Many of these seem to have arrived from Constantinople which, now largely isolated from the rough and chancy circumstances of the West, preserved in a grand if somewhat rigid manner the ideal of a State Church and the traditions of Hellenistic art in that solemn, brilliant, rather abstracted form which could thereafter be described as Byzantine.

As in any period of history, the early Byzantines produced much run-of-the-mill work, but even here certain principles may be observed. There is a proud, self-conscious backward glance at the past and a keen appreciation of the classical art-forms, together with acceptance of a calling to fill these forms with new life. There is moreover a sense of reverential awe permeating affairs both secular and religious. The domed, rectangular room known as the Chalke, which Justinian rebuilt along with most of his palace, was decorated with mosaics showing the overthrow of enemies and then, in the centre, the emperor and his queen in attitudes of serene triumph and thronged about by their privileged officials. Hence the characteristic representation of Christ in the sixth century is not the Good Shepherd but the Ruler of the Universe, isolated in majesty or attended by an adoring company of angels or apostles.

But beside this tendency to modify Hellenic grace in the direction of stilted magnificence lay a more profound awareness that the function of art is to draw out from behind the bare face of events some glimpses of their spiritual reality. Coleridge was later to declare:

> Thou mayst not hope from outward things to win
> The passion and the life whose fountains are within[15]

and the aim of the Byzantine artist was not so much straightforward imitation as to 'catch like a shower in the sunshine the impalpable rainbow of the immaterial world'.[16] Hence the preference for a rhythmical composition as opposed to photographic realism. Hence the joy in light which seemed to reflect the illumination diffused throughout mind and heart by the ever-shining Word of God.

The first crude and stumbling efforts of Christian art were symbolic on the grounds that 'while we are veiled in with mortality, truth must veil itself too, that it may the more fully converse with us.'[17] And, amidst all the pride, self-glorification and display of the later period, the sense never entirely failed that skilful design and refined technique are means appointed to convey that which is timeless to the jostling generations of mankind.

NOTES

1. T. S. Eliot, 'Little Gidding'.
2. Philo, 'The Worse attacks the Better' (*Quod deterius*) i.292 (tr. Loeb, ii.24).
3. *Urne Burial*.
4. I Corinthians i.22.
5. Tertullian, *On the Crown* 3, *PL* 2.80.
6. The Palatine 'crucifix' is illustrated in *DACL* iii.3051.
7. *The Stones of Venice* iv.53.
8. *Oration on St Theodore*, *PG* 46.737. So, a little later, St John Damascene (*Oratio de imaginibus*), *PG* 94.1248: 'The picture is to the eye what the word is to the ear.'
9. Bridges, *Testament of Beauty* iii.795.
10. Dionysius the Areopagite, as explained by Egidio da Viterbo, *In librum primum Sententiarum*. Cf. E. Wind, *Pagan Mysteries of the Renaissance* 14.25.
11. 'The Relation of Christianity to Art' in *Thoughts on Revelation and Life* (1887).
12. *Theodosian Code* xvi.i.3, standard edition by T. Mommsen (Berlin, 1905).
13. Psalm 79,1.
14. *Gratiarum actio. A rhetorical address to the emperor Gratian, PL* 19.937.
15. 'Dejection: an Ode'.
16. Lytton Strachey, *Life of Manning*, in *Eminent Victorians*.
17. John Smith, the Cambridge Platonist, *Select Discourses* (1821), 406.

Bibliography

The Historical Background

The best, and certainly the most readable account of the history is still Edward Gibbon, *The Decline and Fall of the Roman Empire*, vols. 1–4, ed. with valuable notes by J. B. Bury (London, 1909).

Cambridge Ancient History, vol. 12 (Cambridge, 1939); especially chapters 6, 9, 12–16, 18–20.

Cambridge Medieval History, vols. 1 and 2 (Cambridge, 1911–).

A. Alföldi, *The Conversion of Constantine and Pagan Rome* (Oxford, 1948).

N. H. Baynes, 'Constantine the Great and the Christian Church', in *Proceedings of the British Academy XV* (1929).

N. H. Baynes and H. Moss, *Byzantium* (Oxford, 1948).

L. Bréhier, *Le monde byzantin* (Paris, 1947).

P. R. L. Brown, *The World of Late Antiquity* (London, 1971).

J. B. Bury, *History of the Later Roman Empire* (London, 1923). This covers the period 395–565 AD.

H. Chadwick, *Early Christian Thought and the Classical Tradition* (London, 1966).

A. Fliche and V. Martin, *Histoire de l'église*, vols. 1–4 (Paris, 1964–).

W. H. C. Frend, *The Rise of Christianity* (London, 1984). A notable survey, with a synopsis of events and detailed bibliography.

A. H. M. Jones, *The Later Roman Empire: 284–602 AD* (Oxford, 1964).

N. W. King, *The Emperor Theodosius and the Establishment of Christianity* (London, 1961).

R. A. Markus, *Christianity in the Roman World* (London, 1974).

A. Momigliano, ed., *The Conflict between Paganism and Christianity in the Fourth Century* (Oxford, 1963).

G. Ostrogorsky, *Geschichte des byzantinischen Staates* (Munich, 1940). English translation: *History of the Byzantine State* (Oxford, 1956).

H. M. D. Parker, *A History of the Roman World from 138 to 337 AD* (Oxford, 1935).

A. Piganiol, *L'Empire chrétien 325–395* (Paris, 1947).

S. Runciman, *Byzantine Civilization* (London, 1933).

A. A. Vasiliev, *History of the Byzantine Empire*, revised edition (University of Wisconsin, 1958).

J. B. Ward-Perkins, 'The Roman West and the Parthian East', in *Proceedings of the British Academy LI* (1965).

Reference Books

F. Cabrol and H. Leclercq, eds., *Dictionnaire d'archéologie chrétienne et de liturgie* (Paris, 1907–53). Very detailed treatment of the various subjects, though the earlier volumes are (naturally) somewhat dated.

Dumbarton Oaks Bibliographies (Washington, D. C., 1973–). Series I, Vol 1 'offers a cumulative topographical classification of art historical literature listed in volumes 1–60 of the Byzantinische Zeitschrift.'

T. Klauser, ed., *Reallexikon für Antike und Christentum* (Stuttgart, 1950–).

F. van der Meer and C. Mohrmann, *Atlas of the Early Christian World*, tr. M. F. Hedlund and H. H. Rowley (London, 1958).

K. Wessel, ed., *Reallexikon zur byzantinischen Kunst* (Stuttgart, 1963–). This supersedes the earlier handbooks.

Primary Sources

Eusebius of Caesarea, *Ecclesiastical History*. Text of E. Schwartz (*GCS*, Leipzig, 1903) in Loeb, tr. K. Lake and J. E. L. Oulton. Also translated, with notes and commentary, by Oulton and H. J. Lawlor (London, 1928). Eusebius makes copious quotations from earlier sources and carries the history down to 323 AD.

Socrates Scholasticus. Ed. (unsatisfactory) W. Hussey (Oxford, 1853), tr. in *NPNCF* (1890).

Sozomen. Ed. (excellent) J. Bidez (Berlin, 1960). This and the preceding work give parallel accounts continuing the history from Eusebius's record for the next century. Both are entitled *Church History*.

Procopius of Caesarea. Tr. H. B. Dewing, Loeb (1914–40). A careful eyewitness of events in Justinian's reign. Passionately opposed to the emperor in his *Histories*, excessively laudatory in *The Buildings*.

Paulus Silentiarius, *Description of Hagia Sophia*, PG 86. Tr. (inaccurate) of some extracts in W. R. Lethaby and H. Swainson, *The Church of Sancta Sophia* (London, 1894). Notes in the edition of P. Friedländer, (Leipzig, 1912).

Constantine Porphyrogenitus, *The Book of Ceremonies* I, chs. 1–83, *PG* 112. Ed. A. Vogt (Paris, 1935). The work of a tenth-century emperor, but reflects earlier ritual in vogue at S. Sophia and the imperial court.

Liber Pontificalis, L. Duchesne (Paris, 1881, reprinted 1952). A collection of papal biographies, but with much incidental information.

E. Diehl, *Inscriptiones Latinae Christianae Veteres* (Berlin, 1961).

General Studies on the Art Forms

J. Beckwith, *Early Christian and Byzantine Art*, chs. 1–5, revised ed. (Harmondsworth, 1980).

B. Brenck, *Spätantike und frühes Christentum* (Frankfurt, 1977).

O. M. Dalton, *Byzantine Art and Archaeology* (Oxford, 1911) and *East Christian Art: a Survey of the Monuments* (Oxford, 1925). Classic studies, even if to be modified in the light of more recent researches.

C. Diehl, *Manuel d'art byzantin* (2nd ed. Paris, 1925).

F. Gerke, *Ideengeschichte der ältesten christlichen Kunst*. Reprinted from *Zeitschrift für Kirchengeschichte* (1940).

A. Grabar, *Martyrium* (Paris, 1943–46). A fundamental study of the influence exerted on art and architecture by the cult of the martyrs and their relics.

A. Grabar, *The Beginnings of Christian Art, 200–395* (London, 1967) and *Byzantium, from the death of Theodosius to the Rise of Islam* (London, 1966).

R. Kautzsch, *Kapitellenstudien: Studien zur Spätantken Kunstgeschichte* (Berlin, 1936). Capitals from the fourth to the seventh century are examined in great detail, with the help of admirable illustrations.

E. Kitzinger, *Byzantine Art in the Making* (London, 1977). The main lines of stylistic development in Mediterranean Art are traced from the third to the seventh century.

R. Krautheimer, *Early Christian and Byzantine Architecture*, parts 1–5, revised ed. (Harmondsworth, 1975). Authoritative survey, with detailed bibliographical references.

G. Mathew, *Byzantine Aesthetics* (London, 1963).

C. R. Morey, *Early Christian Art* (Princeton, 1941).

A. Rumpf, *Stilphasen der spätantiken Kunst* (Cologne, 1957).

W. F. Volbach and M. Hirmer, *Frühchristliche Kunst* (Munich, 1958). English edition: *Early Christian Art*

(London, 1961). Introductory essay followed by superb photographs.

Signs and Symbols

D. Atkinson, 'The Origins and Date of the Sator Word-Square', *JEH* 2 (1951).

B. Bagatti, *Excavations in Nazareth* (Jerusalem, 1969).

B. Bagatti and J. Milik, *Gli Scavi del 'Dominus Flevit'* (Jerusalem, Franciscan Press, 1969).

J. Daniélou, *Les Symboles chrétiens primitifs* (Paris, 1961). English translation by D. Attwater (London, 1964).

E. Dinkler, 'Kreuzzeichen und Kreuz', *JAC* 5 (1962).

E. R. Goodenough, *Jewish Symbols in the Graeco-Roman World* (New York, 1953–8).

R. Houston Smith, 'The Cross Marks on Jewish Ossuaries', in *Palestine Exploration Quarterly* (1974).

E. Testa *Il simbolismo dei giudeo-cristiani* (Jerusalem, 1962).

House-churches

C. Hopkins and P. V. C. Baur, *Excavations at Dura Europus* (New Haven, 1934).

E. Junyent, *Il titolo di San Clemente* (Rome, 1932).

C. H. Kraeling, *Dura, the Christian Building: final report* (New Haven, 1967).

Britain

S. S. Frere, 'The Silchester Church', in *Archaeologia* 105 (1976).

G. W. Meates, *The Roman Villa at Lullingstone* (Kent Archaeological Society, 1979).

C. Thomas, *Christianity in Roman Britain to AD 500* (London, 1981).

J. M. C. Toynbee, *Art in Britain under the Romans* (Oxford, 1964).

The Catacombs

An enormous volume of work has appeared since the pioneer study by G. B. de Rossi, *Roma sotteranea* (Rome, 1864–77). Special mention may be made of:

P. du Bourguet, *La peinture paléo-chrétienne* (Paris, 1965). English translation: *Early Christian Painting* (London, 1968).

O. Marucchi, *Le Catacombe romane* (Rome, 1933).

J. Stevenson, *The Catacombs* (London, 1978). A convenient summary of recent discoveries.

P. Styger, *Die Römischen Katakomben* (Berlin, 1937).

P. Testini, *Le Catacombe e gli antichi Cimiteri cristiani in Roma* (Bologna, 1966).

J. M. C. Toynbee and J. B. Ward-Perkins, *The Shrine of St Peter* (London, 1956).

J. Wilpert, *Roma sotteranea: die Malereien der Katakomben Roms* (Rome, 1903).

F. Wirth, *Römische Wandmalerei* (Berlin, 1934).

More recent discoveries concerning both structure and decoration of the catacombs are discussed in articles by H. Brandenburg, U. M. Fasola, P. Testini, F. Tolotti and others in *ACIAC* IX (1975–8).

Sarcophagi

G. Bovini, *I Sarcofagi paleocristiani* (Rome, 1929).

F. W. Deichmann, *Repertorium der Christlich-Antiken Sarkophage* (Wiesbaden, 1967).

F. Gerke, *Die christlichen Sarkophage der vorkonstantinischen Zeit* (Berlin, 1940).

J. Kollwitz, *Die Sarkophage Ravennas* (Freiburg, 1956).

M. Lawrence, *The Sarcophagi of Ravenna* (New York, 1945).

E. Le Blant, *Les Sarcophages chrétiens de la Gaule* (Paris, 1886).

J. Wilpert, *I Sarcofagi cristiani antichi* (Rome, 1929).

Church Buildings

Beit Alpha

E. L. Sukenik, *The ancient synagogue at Beit Alpha* (Jerusalem, 1932).

Rome

F. W. Deichmann, *Frühchristliche Kirchen in Rom* (Basel, 1948). Short but very pertinent notes on individual churches, with illustrations.

R. Krautheimer and others, *Corpus basilicarum romanarum* (Rome, 1937–   ).

G. Matthiae, *Le Chiese di Roma dal IV al X secolo* (Rome, 1963). Summarises the early development of the churches and their furnishings.

C. Pietri, *Roma Christiana* (Rome, 1976).

Milan

G. Traversi, *Architettura paleocristiana milanese* (Milan, 1964).

Germany

R. Egger in *Frühmittelalterliche Kunst in den Alpenländen* (Lausanne, 1954).

T. Kempf and W. Reusch, *Frühchristliche Zeugnisse in Einzugsgebiet von Rhein und Mosel* (Trier, 1965).

W. Kramer, *Neue Ausgrabungen in Deutschland* (Trier, 1958).

R. Noll, *Frühes Christentum in Oesterreich* (Salzburg, 1954).

Adriatic Coast

G. Brusin and P. L. Zovatto, *Monumenti paleocristiani di Aquileia e di Grado* (Udine, 1957).

E. Dyggve, *History of Salonitan Christianity* (Oslo, 1951).

E. Dyggve and R. Egger, *Forschungen in Salona* (Vienna, 1914–39).

H. Kaehler, *Die spätantiken Bauten unter dem Dom von Aquileia* (Saarbrücken, 1957).

B. Molajoli, *La basilica eufrasiana di Parenzo* (Parenzo, 1940).

For Julia Concordia, see P. L. Zovatto in *Studi* 26 (1965).

The articles in *ACIAC* XI (1985) offer a number of corrections and amplifications as regards knowledge of buildings in and around Dalmatia.

Syria

H. C. Butler, *Early Churches in Syria* (Princeton, 1929).

J. Lassus, *Sanctuaires chrétiens de Syrie* (Paris, 1947).

G. Tchalenko, *Villages antiques de la Syrie du Nord* (Paris, 1953)

Armenia

J. Strzygowski, *Die Baukunst der Armenier und Europa* (Vienna, 1918).

Strzygowski's views are modified here and there by A. Khatchatrian, *L'architecture arménienne du IV au VII siècles* (Paris, 1971).

Palestine

J. W. Crowfoot, *Early Churches in Palestine* (London, 1941).

W. Harvey, *Holy Sepulchre* (London, 1935).

L. H. Vincent and F. M. Abel, *Jérusalem nouvelle* (Paris, 1925). Recent excavations, still continuing, have thrown doubt on the reconstructions found in this and the preceding work. See V. Corbo in *Liber Annuus* (Franciscan Studies at Jerusalem) XII, XIV, XV, and particularly XIX (1969), 'La basilica di S. Sepolcro a Gerusalemme'.

Bethlehem. L. H. Vincent's article in ACIAC. IV is modified by P. B. Bagatti, *Gli antichi edifici sacri in Bethlemme* (Jerusalem, 1982).

C. Kraeling, *Gerasa, City of the Decapolis* (New Haven, 1938).

Asia Minor

Ephesus has been well served by J. Keil and others in the publication *Forschungen in Ephesos* (Vienna, 1932–   ).

For Meriamlik and other churches in the district, see E. Herzfeld, S. Guyer and others in *Monumenta Asiae Minoris Antiqua* (Manchester, 1930–   ).

M. Gough reports on Alahan in *Anatolian Studies* 1962–72.

Side is served by A. M. Mansel, *Die Ruinen von Side* (Berlin, 1963).

Constantinople

F. W. Deichmann, *Studien zur Architektur Konstantinopels in 5. und 6. Jahrhundert* (Baden-Baden, 1956).

T. F. Matthews, *The early Churches of Constantinople* (London, 1971).

A. Van Millingen, *Byzantine Churches in Constantinople* (London, 1912).

The literature on S. Sophia is considerable. The work of E. H. Swift, *Hagia Sophia* (New York, 1940), must be related to A. M. Schneider, *Die Sophienkirche in Konstantinopel*, (Berlin, 1939), and H. Kaehler, *Hagia Sophia* (Berlin and New York, 1967).

W. Müller-Wiener, *Bildlexikon zur Topographie Istambuls* (Tübingen, 1979) offers a detailed description of every building, with ground-plans of the churches.

Egypt

A. Badawy, *Coptic Art and Archaeology* (Cambridge, Mass., 1978).

J. Beckwith, *Coptic Sculpture* (London, 1963).

Somers Clarke, *Christian Antiquities in the Nile Valley* (Oxford, 1912).

J. Clédat, *Le monastère et la necropole de Baouit* (Cairo, 1916).

U. Monneret de Villard, *Les couvents de Sohag* (Milan, 1925).

A. Wace, A. H. S. Megaw and others, *Hermopolis Magna* (Alexandria, 1959).

K. Wessel, *Koptische Kunst* (Recklinghausen, 1963). English translation: *Coptic Art* (London, 1965).

The excavations at Abu Mina are treated fully in *Mitteilungen des Deutschen Archäologischen Instituts*, particularly by Müller-Wiener (XX, 1965) and P. Grossman (XXVI, 1970).

The recently revived interest in Nubia is represented by *Kunst und Geschichte Nubiens in christlichen Zeit*, ed. E. Dinkler (Recklinghausen, 1971), and *Faras*, a topographical study by K. Michalowski (Warsaw, 1972).

North Africa

N. Duval, *Les églises africaines à deux absides* (Paris, 1973).

W. H. C. Frend, 'The Early Christian Church in Carthage', in *Excavations at Carthage 1976*, vol. 3 (University of Michigan, Ann Arbor, 1977).

R. Goodchild, *Kyrene and Apollonia* (Zurich, 1971).

C. Gsell, *Monuments antiques de l'Algérie* (Algiers, 1911).

L. Leschi, *Djemila: antique Cuicul* and *Tipasa de Mauretanie* (both Algiers, 1954).

J. B. Ward-Perkins and R. Goodchild, 'The Christian Antiquities of Tripolitania', in *Archaeologia* 95 (1953).

Greece and the Balkans

Studies of Greek churches by G. A. Sotiriou and A. K. Orlandos (mostly in Greek) include Sotiriou, *Basilikai* (Athens, 1931) and Orlandos, *Basilike* (Athens, 1952), both wide-ranging, general works, and a detailed examination by G. A. and M. Sotiriou of *St Demetrius, Salonica* (Athens, 1952).

H. F. Hoddinot, *Early Byzantine Churches in Macedonia and Southern Serbia* (London, 1963).

P. Lemerle, *Philippes et la Macédoine orientale* (Paris, 1945).

H. H. Jewel and F. W. Hasluck, *Our Lady of the Hundred Gates on Paros* (London, 1920). A full study, now rather out of date; see G. Orlandos in *Studi* 26 (1965).

For Stobi, see E. Kitzinger in *DOP* III (1946).

Spain

P. de Palol, *Arqueologia Cristiana de la España Romana* (Madrid, 1967).

Mount Sinai

G. H. Forsyth and K. Weitzmann, *The monastery of St Catherine on Mount Sinai* (Ann Arbor, Michigan, 1965–71).

Ravenna

G. Bovini, *Storia e architettura degli edifici paleocristiani di culto di Ravenna* (Ravenna, 1964).

F. W. Deichmann, *Ravenna, Hauptstadt des spätantiken Abendlandes* (Wiesbaden, 1976). For magisterial treatment of each church this work is essential.

C. O. Nordström, *Ravennastudien* (Uppsala, 1953).

Fonts and Baptisteries

There is apparently no general study of this subject, apart from articles in the reference books. A. Khatchatrian, *Les Baptistères paléochrétiens* (Paris, 1967) gives nearly four hundred plans, with an alphabetical list and bibliographical details. Full reference to notes in periodicals respecting individual baptisteries, classified geographically, is given in *RLAC*.

Mosaics

L. Budde, *Antike Mosaiken in Kilikien* (Recklinghausen, 1969), and 'Die frühchristlichen Mosaiken von Misis-Mopsuestia', in *Pantheon* XVIII (1960).

C. Cechelli, *I mosaici della basilica di S. Maria Maggiore* (Rome, 1967).

K. Dunbabin, *The Mosaics of Roman North Africa* (Oxford, 1978).

D. Levi, *Antioch Mosaic Pavements* (Princeton, 1957).

G. Matthiae, *Mosaici medioevali delle chiese di Roma* (Rome, 1967).

W. Oakeshott, *The Mosaics of Rome from the third to the fourteenth century* (London, 1967).

H. Stern, *Les mosaïques de l'église de Sainte Constance*, *DOP* XII (1958).

H. Torp, *Les mosaïques de Saint-Georges à Thessalonique* (Ninth International Congress of Byzantine Studies) (Athens, 1955).

W. F. Volbach, *Early Christian Mosaics* (London, 1945). A short essay on development and style, followed by illustrations.

T. Whittemore, *The Mosaics of Santa Sophia at Istanbul* (Oxford, 1933–52).

J. Wilpert, *Die römischen Mosaiken und Malereien der kirchlichen Bauten vom IV. bis XIII. Jahrhundert* (Freiburg, 1916).

Carved Ivories

The classic works is W. F. Volbach, *Elfenbeinarbeiten der Spätantik und des frühen Mittelaters*, third edition (Mainz, 1976). Volbach lists most of the earlier books on the subject.

J. Natanson, *Early Christian Ivories* (London, 1953) is a concise and convenient handbook.

Metalwork: Glass: Pottery: Textiles

Information about the 'minor arts' is contained in the general studies of the period as well as in the reference dictionaries. Detail may be drawn from the catalogues of the great collections or from works based on them:

E. Coche de la Ferté, *L'Antiquité chrétienne au musée du Louvre* (Paris, 1958).

O. M. Dalton, *Catalogue of the Early Christian Antiquities and Objects from the Christian East* (British Museum, London, 1901).

M. C. Ross, *Catalogue of the Byzantine and Early Medieval Antiquities in the Dumbarton Oaks Collection*: vol. 1, Metalwork; vol. 2, Jewellery (New York, 1962–65).

H. B. Walters, *Catalogue of the Silver Plate . . . in the British Museum* (London, 1921).

Special studies include:

M. G. Abbiani, *Lucerne fittili paleocristiane nell' Italia septentrionale* (Bologna, 1969). A serviceable catalogue of the lamps, with commentary on cross, dove, and other symbols.

L. Bréhier, *La Sculpture et les arts mineurs byzantins* (Paris, 1936).

A. O. Curle, *The Treasure of Traprain* (Glasgow, 1923).

A. Grabar, *Les Ampoules de Terre Sainte* (Paris, 1938).

K. S. Painter, *The Water Newton Early Christian Silver* (London, 1977).

F. Z. Roppo, *Vetri paleocristiani a figure d'oro conservati in Italia* (Bologna, 1969). A catalogue with exact description of each piece of glass.

For the silks, reference may be made to O. von Falke, *Kunstgeschichte der Seidenweberei* (Berlin, 1921).

Coins

P. Grierson, *Byzantine Coinage* (University of California, 1982).

H. Mattingly, E. A. Sydenham and others, *Roman Imperial Coinage*, 9 vols. (London, 1923–) extends so far to 395 AD.

C. H. V. Sutherland, *Roman Coins* (London, 1974).

Writings and Illustrated Books

H. Degering and A. Boeckler, *Die Quedlinburger Italafragmente* (Berlin, 1932).

H. Gerstinger, *Die griechische Buchmalerei*, vol. 1 (Vienna, 1926).

A. Muñoz, *Il codice purpureo di Rossano ed il frammento di Sinope* (Rome, 1907).

C. H. Roberts, 'The Codex', in *Proceedings of the British Academy* XL (1954).

K. Weitzmann, *Studies in Roll and Codex* (Princeton, 1947).

K. Weitzmann, *Ancient Book Illumination* (Cambridge, Mass., 1959).

E. Wellesz, *The Vienna Genesis* (London, 1960).

Index

Numbers in bold type refer to the illustrations, not to pages